SHOULDER to SHOULDER

SHOULDER to SHOULDER

Polish Americans in Rochester, New York
1890-1990

by Kathleen Urbanic

Illustrated by Frank Anders

Sponsored by the
Polonia Civic Centre, Inc.
Rochester, New York

Library of Congress Catalog Card Number:
90-90413
ISBN 0-9628578-0-7

Sponsored by the Polonia Civic Centre, Inc.
Rochester, New York

Designed by Frank Anders

Typeset by Innovative Type
Rochester, New York

Printed by Monroe Reprographics, Inc.
Rochester, New York

This project is made possible with public funds (LIFT Grant) from Monroe County and the New York State Council on the Arts. In Monroe County, the LIFT Grant Program is administered by Arts for Greater Rochester.

Additional support provided by the Polish Arts Group of Rochester, Polish People's Home, Inc., Theodore Jablonski, Jr., Mr. and Mrs. Edward Urbanic, and the Zamiara family.

In memory of my grandparents:

Jan Urbanik and Katarzyna Chomka
Jan Ziajka and Julia Glazarowska

Contents

Illustrations

Photo Credits

PREFACE

I grew up on St. Stanislaus Street in the 1950s, in the shadow of the church that graces the intersection of Hudson Avenue and Norton Street. From our home halfway down the block, my sister, brothers, and I could walk in minutes to morning Mass and to classes at St. Stanislaus School. Not far from the parish's grounds were Zamiara's meat market and Tomczak's hardware store, establishments that our parents patronized, and Andy Sykut's candy counter, where a child rich with a quarter could savor the pleasures of jaw breakers, chewing gum, ice cream, and homemade chocolate.

As we traced a route through neighborhood streets to visit our friends, we passed the homes of families whom our parents knew from church societies and from social activities at nearby clubs, and overheard conversation in Polish exchanged on front porches and across back yard fences. Most intriguing to us, since our relatives lived at a distance in Utica, was the fact that many of these families had lived in the neighborhood for three or four generations, and now formed a network of grandparents, aunts and uncles, cousins, friends, and long-standing acquaintances. The community's closeness and continuity were confirmed when we discovered that the Sisters who instructed us at St. Stanislaus School had taught grammar and arithmetic years before to many of our classmates' parents.

I took this community for granted until I left its confines to attend high school and college, surprised to learn that not all of my generation had grown up in a neighborhood where families had maintained churches, schools, and businesses for decades, where residents knew each other not only on single blocks but across a half-mile radius. I came to understand it as a distinction that, in my neighborhood, streets were named in honor of saints and heroes, children studied Polish at the public library and tumbled at the Falcon gym, and church services closed with a rising chorus of Polish hymns.

I thought often of writing about the community, and was given my first opportunity to do so in 1980 when St. Stanislaus Parish observed its 90th anniversary. The co-chairs of the celebration, Floyd Balcerak and Sister Eileen Conheady, provided me with a list of names of parishioners then in their nineties, senior members of the community like Lillian Okolowicz, Sophie Presnal, Helena Grycz, and Mr. and Mrs. Walter Nowak whose families had been among the first Polish immigrants to settle in the city. I visited those named on the list to gather information for a parish history, welcomed by persons whose memory spanned several decades and who eagerly shared experiences that evoked the rich and colorful story of Polish Americans in Rochester. From the persons whom I interviewed that year, I received a sense of Polonia's history, glimpses of the past related to my own experience that prompted me to undertake the research represented in this book.

I did so for two reasons: to record for local Polish Americans the story of their ethnic group in this area, and to share with others the contributions that Polish Americans have made to the life of Rochester. In conducting the research, I have been fortunate to have had access both to written records and to oral history. This combination of sources has allowed me to describe events and personalities in detail, and to present some pages of the community's history from the perspective of individuals whose experiences are noteworthy. Often, those whom I have profiled—whether leaders of organizations, men and women in service, or Hudson Avenue shop owners—are representative of many others. Because my intent has been to convey the hundred-year story of local Polonia as a community, I have not included detailed histories of the individual parishes and organizations, but offer instead the broader context of the community's development over a century against the backdrop of local, national, and international events.

Over the nine years in which I conducted research and prepared this history, the book has become in many ways a community project, supported and completed with the assistance and generosity of many persons. I would like to acknowledge the help provided by the staffs of several local archival collections who provided me with access to a wealth of materials: the Local History Division of the Rochester Public Library; the Rochester Diocese; the Sisters of St. Joseph of Rochester; the American Baptist Historical Society; the Association of Monroe American Baptist Churches; and the library of the Rochester Museum and Science Center. I would also like to thank two organizations for granting me permission to reprint in this book studies that I originally wrote for publication elsewhere. The profile of Franciszek Wolowski included at the end of chapter one first appeared in 1989 in the newsletter of the Friends of Mt. Hope Cemetery, and much of the text of chapter three was published in 1985 in *PNCC Studies,* the journal of the Polish National Catholic Church's Commission on History and Archives.

In the Polish community, I enjoyed full access to the records of parishes and organizations, and received a gracious welcome from scores of individuals whom I interviewed or who allowed me the use of photographs, scrapbooks, and personal collections of materials. I appreciate greatly the help of all who shared their memories and mementos. Their names are included with the illustrations in each chapter, and in the bibliographical note at the back of the book.

I would also like to acknowledge the generosity of organizations and individuals who have supported the project with contributions and grants: the New York State and Rochester Public Libraries through the National Endowment for the Humanities, which provided seed money for my initial research in 1981; Monroe County and the New York State Council on the Arts, which awarded me a LIFT Grant through Arts for Greater Rochester; the Polish Arts Group of Rochester, Polish People's Home, Inc., Mr. and Mrs. Theodore Jablonski, Jr., the Zamiara family, and my parents, Mr. and Mrs. Edward Urbanic, each of whom contributed to the book's production. In addition, I am grateful to Anthony Sulkowski's firm, Monroe Reprographics, Inc., which printed a book of fine quality at modest cost.

I owe particular thanks to the Polonia Civic Centre, Inc. (Centrala), the organization that has sponsored the book's printing and distribution. The members of Centrala received my request for assistance with enthusiasm last fall, and have taken on much of the work of publicizing the book and organizing its sale, in addition to providing a generous financial contribution that has underwritten all printing expenses. It has been my pleasure to work closely during the past few months with Centrala's Executive Officers and Book Committee: Eugene Golomb, Gabriela Jaskot, Edward Skiba, Geraldine Wilson, Helen Jasionowicz, Mary Habza, Valenteen Palis, and Walter Stek.

It would be impossible to list the names of all who, over the course of the book's preparation, offered words of encouragement. Nevertheless, I am grateful to all who did so and extend my thanks. I am especially grateful to the members of my family and to my friends who not only provided encouragement but also helped in a variety of ways, from reading drafts of the chapters to listening as I recounted details of my research. "How's the book coming?" became a familiar question put to me by family and friends many times over the years, an indication of their interest and support.

Although I cannot list by name all who offered assistance, I would like to acknowledge the help provided by a few individuals: John and Stephanie Stenclik, who took on a variety of tasks including translating materials from Polish to English, collecting and reproducing photographs, and putting me in touch with others who had information to share; Wojciech and Maria Przezdziecki, Henry and Irene Kubiak, and Mary Mazur, who assisted with Polish language translation; Walter Widlarz, who reviewed a list of all Polish terms used in the manuscript; Father Joseph Jankowiak, who translated Teofil Szadzinski's "Chronica" from Latin to English; Edward Nakas, who provided reprints of a number of fragile photographs; Joanne Stirpe, who entered the text of several chapters on computer; Albert Kusak, who provided legal advice about the book's sale and distribution; Barbara Chapman and Jeanette Rutkus of Innovative Type, who expertly prepared the typeset text; Pat Brady of Monroe Reprographics, Inc., who provided advice and liaison during the book's printing; and Bruce Litolff, who donated his time and the use of his studio to create the cover photograph.

I owe particular gratitude to five individuals whose contribution to production of the book has been extensive. Dr. Mieczyslaw Biskupski, Director of the Institute for Polish Studies at St. John Fisher College, reviewed and commented on each chapter, advised me of relevant studies in Polish American history, and offered much assistance over the course of the research. Father Robert F. McNamara, Professor Emeritus of Church History at St. Bernard's Seminary, has guided the project since I called upon him to request access to diocesan records in 1983. His encouragement and advice have been invaluable, including his review of several drafts of each chapter, the knowledge he shared about local history and American Catholic Church history, and his meticulous proofreading of the typeset text. I am proud to note that this study bears the stamp of his scholarship.

My parents, Edward and Dorothy Urbanic, have provided steady support during the years in which I have been involved in the project. Each of them has assisted in many ways, particularly my father who proofread the draft manuscript and the typeset text with his well-trained printer's eye, organized information for the map of Hudson Avenue businesses, and performed the tedious but important work of compiling the index. Their contribution, made behind the scenes, has been an important one.

Finally, I owe thanks without measure to Frank Anders, the book's illustrator, who came forward nine years ago and offered to prepare original sketches. Although his role could easily have been limited to that work, he has given of his time and ability in countless other ways to see the project through to completion. The graceful artwork and design of the book are entirely to his credit, and in addition he has shared as a full partner in the many decisions that have shaped this publication over the last decade.

In the Winter 1989 issue of *Rochester History,* City Historian Emeritus Dr. Blake McKelvey reviewed a half century of local history research, noting that the story of the Poles in Rochester has been "long neglected" and that their role in the community's life is "worthy of historical recognition." It has been my privilege to compile a study intended to compensate for that neglect. The work involved has been personally rewarding, and I will count it an additional benefit if others learn from and enjoy the history presented on these pages.

Kathleen Urbanic
January 1991

Those who are familiar with the Polish language will recognize that the English language type font that appears in this book did not provide the use of Polish accents and diacritical marks. Nevertheless, the Polish titles of organizations, publications, and documents have been included whenever appropriate, at least as an initial reference.

The use of Polish names presented a dilemma, since the local community's reliance on the language has changed greatly over the course of the past century. In chapters one through five (the period through 1918, when Polonia was made up almost exclusively of immigrant families who spoke Polish), the Polish versions of both first and last names are used. In chapters six through nine (the period from the 1920s through the present, when the community added American-born generations and has relied less heavily on Polish), English versions of names are used for persons other than new immigrants. For the sake of consistency, the Polish versions of names of persons introduced in chapters one through five are retained in chapters six through nine.

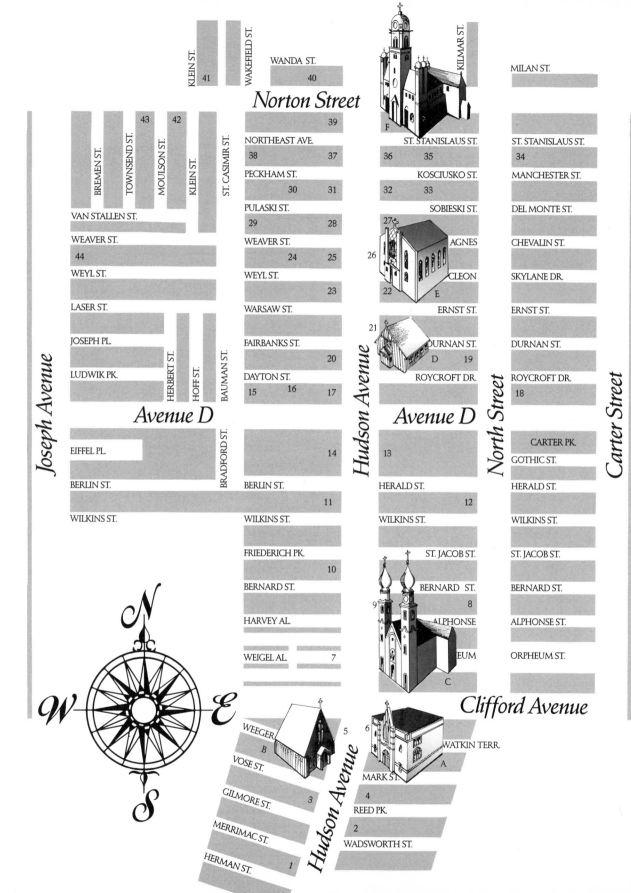

KLEIN ST.
41
WAKEFIELD ST.
WANDA ST.
40

43 42
BREMEN ST.
TOWNSEND ST.
MOULSON ST.
KLEIN ST.
ST. CASIMIR ST.

MILAN ST.

Norton Street

39

KILMAR ST.

F

ST. STANISLAUS ST.
36   35
ST. STANISLAUS ST.
34

NORTHEAST AVE.
38   37

VAN STALLEN ST.

WEAVER ST.
44

WEYL ST.

LASER ST.

JOSEPH PL.

LUDWIK PK.

PECKHAM ST.
30   31

PULASKI ST.
29   28

WEAVER ST.
24   25

WEYL ST.
23

WARSAW ST.

FAIRBANKS ST.
20

DAYTON ST.
15   16   17

HERBERT ST.
HOFF ST.
BAUMAN ST.

KOSCIUSKO ST.
32   33

SOBIESKI ST.
27
26   AGNES
22   CLEON
E

ERNST ST.

21
DURNAN ST.
D   19

ROYCROFT DR.

MANCHESTER ST.

DEL MONTE ST.

CHEVALIN ST.

SKYLANE DR.

ERNST ST.

DURNAN ST.

ROYCROFT DR.
18

Avenue D

Avenue D

Hudson Avenue

North Street

Carter Street

Joseph Avenue

EIFFEL PL.

BERLIN ST.

WILKINS ST.

BRADFORD ST.

BERLIN ST.
11

WILKINS ST.

FRIEDERICH PK.
10

BERNARD ST.

HARVEY AL.

WEIGEL AL.   7

14

13

HERALD ST.

WILKINS ST.

ST. JACOB ST.

BERNARD ST.
9   8

ALPHONSE
EUM
C

CARTER PK.

GOTHIC ST.

HERALD ST.
12

WILKINS ST.

ST. JACOB ST.

BERNARD ST.

ALPHONSE ST.

ORPHEUM ST.

Clifford Avenue

N
W   E
S

WEEGER
B
VOSE ST.

GILMORE ST.   3

MERRIMAC ST.

HERMAN ST.   1

5

6
MARK ST.
4
REED PK.
2
WADSWORTH ST.

WATKIN TERR.
A

Hudson Avenue

A Sampling of Institutions and Businesses in the Hudson Avenue Area, 1928-1938

A. St. Theresa's Church
B. St. George's Lithuanian Church
C. Holy Redeemer Church
D. Christ Polish Baptist Church
E. St. Casimir's Polish National Catholic Church
F. St. Stanislaus Kostka Church

1. Kroll's Funeral Parlor
2. Kizinski's Bakery
   Millewich & Gorski's Grocery
3. Pilznienski's Stitch Shop
4. Przysinda's Hardware Store
   Kanapickas Bakery
   A. Dynek's Market
5. Wrublewski's Shoe Store
   Figler Electric Company
   Zlotnik's Dress Shop
   Braknis Photography Studio
6. Sherman's Ladies' Apparel
7. J. Adamus, Real Estate Agent
8. Pilznienski's Grocery
9. J. Kwapich, Chiropractor
   Kudrewicz's Shoe Store
10. L. Koscianski, Physician
    S. Rozewski, Tailor
    K. Czepiel, Jeweler
11. H. Bielski, Lawyer
12. Prybycien's Market
13. Polish People's Home
    A. Smeja, Dentist
14. Kozlowski's Moving and Carting
    W. Dziekonski, Printer
    M. Kowalski, Lawyer
    Zlotnik's Service Station
15. Audycki's IGA
    A. Kusak, Real Estate Agent
16. Kosmicki's Dairy
17. Bonus Funeral Parlor
18. Konieczny's Grocery
19. Ostrowski's Market
    Nycz's Grocery
    Krochmalski's Grocery
20. A. Felerski, Lawyer
    Olszewski's Funeral Parlor
21. F. Nawrocki's Delicatessan
    T. Jablonski's Grocery
    Victoria's Dress Shop;
       S. Orzechowski, Proprietor

22. Polish Young Men's Citizen Club
    W. Nawrocki's Shoe Repair
23. Dziennik dla Wszystkich Office
    Felerski's Hudson Garage
    Janiszewski's Hardware Store
    Kazmierski's Barber Shop
24. Polish Falcon Club
25. Sable's Garage
    Karwiecki's Bowling Alley
26. Wojtczak's Bakery
    Orlowski's Market
    Mrzywka's Barber Shop
27. Osinski's Market
    Chmielecki's Bakery
    Ziminski's Ice Cream Parlor
    S. J. Nowak, Clothing
    A. Gramza, Coal Dealer
28. J. Szwiec, Tailor
    Grabowski's Bakery
29. Sobierajski's Grocery
30. Maciejewski's Dairy
31. J. Dernoga, Shoemaker
    J. Tomczak, Confectioner
32. Dziedziech's Hardware Store
    F. Kierecki, Tailor
    Brodowczynski's Market
    W. Jablonski's Grocery
33. Echo Club
34. Krajka's Market
    Bojara's Grocery
35. C. Grzywinski, Coal Dealer
36. Sykut's Candy Store
    Pawlak's Grocery
    J. W. Paprocki's Dry Goods
    J. R. Paprocki, Lawyer
37. Kaleta's Pharmacy
    Zielinski's Lumber Yard
    Rochester Rekord Office
    Franc's IGA
38. Grzeszczak's Grocery
39. Zamiara's Market
    Balcerak's Lunch Counter
40. Sewilo's Dairy
41. J. Antczak, Coal Dealer
42. H. Janowski, Plumber
43. Szyskowski's Market
44. Sulkowski's Sun Theater

Compiled from the City Directory and business advertisements. Addresses are grouped by block. Not all businesses depicted were in existence for the full decade (1928-38).

1 | *Nowe Zycie:* New Life

Hapsburg

Romanov

Hohenzollern

Their first homes in Rochester were on streets like Gilmore, Sellinger, and Weeger, in the northside neighborhood wedged between the railway tracks and the river that had been home to Irish, German, and Jewish immigrants before them. From rooms rented in this area, they could walk to factories, markets, shops, the streetcar line, and Roman Catholic churches. Although most who arrived in Rochester during the 1880s had been born in Poznania, an area of Poland under Prussian control, they did not consider themselves Prussians but professed to be Poles, offspring of a nation unrecognized in Europe for nearly a century.

Left behind were farming plots and villages that had been home to their families for hundreds of years but that now, at the end of the nineteenth century, could not sustain them all.[1] The population of Europe had doubled twice since the turn of the century, from approximately 50 million in 1800 to 200 million by 1870. One of the largest increases on the continent plagued the Polish territories, its effect exacerbated by change in a long-established way of life. During the nineteenth century, industrialization and factory production displaced the services of village craftsmen and artisans, while the spread of commercial agriculture overturned the manorial system that had dominated the countryside since feudal times. As a result, possibilities for work diminished in the villages and on the estates that had provided livelihood to artisans, farmworkers, and peasant laborers for generations.

Many Poles who sought work wandered first to developing industrial centers like Silesia, Westphalia, and the Ruhr valley, but word of other opportunities eventually led the majority to North Atlantic seaports for a journey to the west. Between the 1860s and the 1890s, more than 600,000 Poles took leave of the Prussian provinces, drawn by the promise of land and work in North America. Before 1914 they would be joined by 900,000 more from the Russian partition, and by 700,000 from Galicia or Austrian Poland. While some were

Few people are aware of the rapid growth of the Polish people in this city. . . . Before many years an important Polish settlement will be found in the vicinity of the new church. . . .

Union and Advertiser Rochester, New York April 4, 1888

political refugees or young men fleeing conscription in the armies of the Kaiser or Tsar, most were peasants and villagers torn from a centuries-old way of life.[2]

A man or woman who had saved $25 could book passage on one of the huge steamships that made the ten-day voyage from Bremen or Hamburg to American harbors like Boston and New York.[3] Single men might make the journey, or married men without their families, or single women from large families with many children to support. Those who made their way to North Atlantic ports with no hope of raising the fare might barter for passage by agreeing to work their way across the ocean, exchanging their labor in the ships' holds and boiler rooms for transport to America.

Most boarded with few possessions but carried the strong traditions of Polish life. In the countryside and villages from which they had come, a family's most valued possession was its patch of land, the acreage that provided livelihood—their *chleb* or daily bread. Although the majority of Polish immigrants would serve as factory workers, manual laborers, and miners in North America, they would retain and pass to the next generation an undiminished pride in owning land.[4] After he had saved enough from his wages to send steamship fare to family members waiting in Europe, a Pole would invariably invest in a city lot and a woodframe house, an estate regarded as highly as several acres of European soil. As the Polish arrivals clustered together, they came to consider neighborhoods their own, laying claim to city streets by choosing their names: "Sobieski, Pulaski, Kosciuszko."

The Poles' eagerness to own land was matched by their attachment to the religious faith of their homeland, a legacy of nine hundred years of Roman Catholicism intertwined with the legend, myth, and tradition of the Polish countryside.[5] The faith of these immigrants was a mixture of church doctrine, folk belief, and superstition that had been blended over centuries into the pattern of village life—the cycle of seasons matching the movement of holy days and feasts, the call to daily work in the fields announced by the Angelus bell. Significant moments of an individual's life were solemnized in the village church, while each year a succession of events brought continuity and celebration to a sometimes harsh existence: the harvest festival dedicated to Mary, elaborate processions through the village on the feast of Corpus Christi, bonfires blazing along the river in the rituals of St. John's Eve. The Poles who departed for the coal mines, foundries, and factories of North America carried with them this tradition of Roman Catholicism, and in city after city repeated a similar pattern of settlement: as houses went up, shops opened, and wives and children sailed from Europe, each Polish community would include a modest church, financed with the wages of the first immigrants to arrive.

Many of the immigrants who left the Polish territories before 1890 made their way to the farmland and thriving young cities of the American midwest. Since the majority of Poles who came in these years were artisans and farm laborers who had lived in the Prussian provinces, a good number were drawn to the German- and Jewish-owned factories, mills, and garment firms of western New York State. Here the language they had learned in Prussian schools aided them in finding jobs, places to stay, and, initially, German Catholic parishes where they could worship until they had saved enough money to build churches of their own.

The New York Central
Railway Station, where
many of the first Polish
immigrants arrived in
Rochester. (From the
Stone Negative Collection
of the Rochester Museum
and Science Center)

Opuscilismy nasza droga Ojczyzne, starozytne koscioly, i cmentarze gdzie szczatki Ojcow naszych spoczywaja, wrote one Polish immigrant who arrived in America in the 1880s: "We left our dear homeland, ancient churches, and cemeteries where the remains of our fathers rest. We came across the ocean, many hundreds of miles, seeking prosperity, and . . . we chose Rochester, New York."[6]

During the last decades of the nineteenth century, thousands of newcomers from Europe passed through Rochester on the "immigrant trains" that clattered their way northwest from New York City on Cornelius Vanderbilt's New York Central Line.[7] The Rochester station was a scheduled stop where passengers could step out briefly while railway agents checked their tickets and verified their destinations. Many of the immigrants reboarded the trains and continued on to industrial centers farther west—Buffalo, Cleveland, Detroit, Chicago—but each year others remained in the city built along the Genesee falls. The Rochester these immigrants entered ranked among the nation's 25 largest cities in the eighties, claiming 133,000 residents living on 10,000 acres of land which radiated three miles beyond the city's center at the Four Corners.[8] An area expanding in industry and commercial enterprise, Rochester would mark the fiftieth anniversary of its charter in 1884 while boasting of a young and energetic population: 68,500 persons, more than half of the city's residents, were no older than age 25 in 1890. At the same time, the foreign-born and their children (93,000 persons) accounted for approximately 70 percent of the city's population, far outnumbering the 40,000 Rochesterians who claimed descent from earlier pioneers.

The city had welcomed European immigrants since the early nineteenth century, drawing families from each new wave of settlers to its nurseries, mills, and growing industries. When the first Poles arrived in the eighties, Rochester's population represented at least a dozen ethnic or national groups.[9] Seven percent of the city's residents (10,000 persons) were first and second generation English and Welsh, supplemented by 1,800 native Scots and their children. Approximately 1,300 French Canadians had arrived in Rochester from across northern borders, and the city's Third Ward was home to 600 Blacks from the South. A few Dutch, Swiss, Scandinavians, Hungarians, Bohemians, and Chinese had also arrived by the eighties, along with approximately 500 Italians.

The ethnic groups best represented in Rochester toward the end of the century were the Germans, the Irish, and Jews from Germany and Eastern Europe. Jewish families, who had been arriving in the city since the 1840s, accounted for 4,000 Rochester residents, living predominantly in northside settlements along St. Paul Street and St. Joseph Street (later renamed Joseph Avenue). The Irish, who numbered at least 13,000 immigrants and their children, had been settling in Rochester since early in the century. Their arrival swelled the ranks of the city's Roman Catholics, and by mid-century many residents of Irish descent had risen to positions of prominence in local life. German immigrants and their children, by far the largest group, represented more than 37,000 Rochesterians. Their settlements, which had grown up in several sections of the city, included Butter Hole on the northeast side, Dutch Town and Basket Town west of the Four Corners, and a community in the area of St. Boniface Church rather inelegantly called "Swillburg." By the eighties, these German settlers, many of them skilled workers and crafts-men, had extended their influence to local banking and industry, particularly Rochester's prosperous shoe, clothing, and tool-making firms. They organized their own local press, turning out three German language dailies and a half-dozen weekly or monthly publications, and for a brief period (1872-1877) the German language was taught as part of the curriculum in city public schools.

Each group of newcomers arrived with its own heritage of religious belief, and by 1890 the spires of nearly 100 houses of worship rose on the city's skyline.[10] More than a dozen of these were Roman Catholic churches organized by Bernard J. McQuaid, first bishop of the Rochester Diocese. Each of these parishes, whether Irish, German, or French in ethnicity, supported a parochial school by the nineties, together enrolling nearly 7,000 city youngsters. All told, the city's Catholic churches held a congregation of approximately 42,000 Rochesterians in the nineties. Five Protestant denominations followed the Catholic community in number of parishes. Each Protestant group—Presbyterian, Baptist, Episcopalian, Methodist, Lutheran—had built between nine and twelve city churches by the nineties. Jewish residents supported several congregations including Beth Israel, organized by families from Poland in 1874.[11]

What drew these thousands of newcomers to Rochester during the middle and late 1800s was the prospect of finding work in a growing industrial area. Trade and travel along the Erie Canal and later on the New York Central Railway had given the city modest stature as an east-west trade route, and for many years Rochester had been known for the products of its flour mills and nurseries. Between 1875 and 1890, however, the city's character changed rapidly as the number of its industries and the value of its manufactured goods nearly tripled.[12] Shoes, men's suits, neckware, buttons, metal products from tools to safes, carriages, coaches, cigarettes, pianos, caskets, lanterns, optical goods, local brews, and patent medicine—all these were produced in Rochester in the second half of the century and distributed in many cases nationwide. The number of items produced by a local industry was often impressive: one million cigarettes rolled daily by the city's tobacco firms; 300,000 barrels of beer fermented each year in Rochester's

breweries; 3,500 dozen of one popular necktie (the "Iron Duke") sewn annually by H. C. Cohn & Company; 75,000 dozen carriage whips produced each year by Strong, Woodbury, & Company—the second largest inventory of carriage whips in the United States.

Although the production of these industries was substantial, the firms that clearly dominated Rochester enterprise in the late nineteenth century were the shoe and clothing manufacturing companies, which together provided more than one-third of the area's jobs.[13] Between 1880 and 1890, the shoe companies grouped along North Water Street doubled the number of their employees (4,600 persons in 1890) and distributed a total of $2 million in wages—the largest wage payment in the city, and the fifth largest among shoe manufacturing towns in the United States. During the same decade, Rochester's clothing industry, centered along St. Paul Street and Mill Street, grew from approximately fifteen shops to nearly 200 firms, and increased its capital investment from $2 million to $6 million. While these 200 companies employed approximately 3,000 laborers, the number of persons completing piecework in neighborhood sweatshops or in their homes raised the count of local clothing workers as high as 15,000.

For immigrants, the clothing industry in particular represented potential employment. Whether skilled or unskilled in tailoring, a newcomer to Rochester could often find work in the city's garment mills and sweatshops. In the late

Downtown Rochester at the turn of the century. (From the photo collection of the Local History Division, Rochester Public Library)

nineteenth century, immigrants and their children, including large numbers of Jews from Eastern Europe, made up 93 percent of the workers in local clothing firms. Although hours were long, wages low, and conditions often unsafe, thousands who had left Europe's ghettos and villages found their first local employment in the factories and lofts along St. Paul and Mill Streets, and made their first homes in the neighborhood north and east of the garment district—beyond Bausch & Lomb and the railway station, across the river from George Eastman's Dry Plate & Film Company. Due largely to the settlement of immigrants, the four wards on the northeast side grew more rapidly than any other part of the city during the 1880s.[14]

The first Poles who arrived in Rochester on the "immigrant trains" joined German, Irish, and Jewish settlers in the neighborhood north of Main Street and east of the river. Although Poles from the Prussian-ruled provinces had begun immigrating to America in the 1860s, most bypassed the Rochester area before 1880, traveling on to farming regions and industrial centers farther west. By the mid-eighties, however, perhaps twenty Polish families were included among the worshippers at four Roman Catholic churches on Rochester's northeast side: St. Bridget's, founded by Irish immigrants, and St. Joseph's, Holy Redeemer, and St. Michael's, founded by immigrants from Germany.[15] The three German churches were initially attractive to the families from Poznania, who spoke the German language in addition to their own. Despite their knowledge of the language, however, the Poles did not feel comfortable in the German parishes. Their homeland's history of bitter conflict with Germany, along with their attachment to Polish religious traditions, made the newcomers' assimilation into the German settlement unlikely.[16] As they sought each other out for companionship, the Poles began to discuss the possibility of founding their own parish and, in the interim, of inviting Polish priests from Buffalo to celebrate Mass and hear confessions.[17]

In their decision to organize, the Poles received encouragement and support from Father Fridolin Pascalar, pastor of St. Michael's Parish. Although involved in planning the construction of his parish's new church in 1887, Pascalar took time to help the Polish families form a fraternal society in honor of St. Casimir *(Towarzystwo Sw. Kazimierza)*, which held its first meeting at St. Michael's Parish on May 16th of that year.[18] Shortly afterward, Pascalar contacted McQuaid, requesting that the Society of St. Casimir be allowed to invite Polish priests from Buffalo to St. Michael's Parish. "I hereby grant permission," the bishop responded on June 23, 1887, "to hold services in St. Michael's for the Polish population of Rochester, and faculties for the Polish priest whom you may invite to hear their confessions."[19]

McQuaid's response indicated his support for the Poles' intention to organize an ethnic parish. Appointed first bishop of Rochester's Roman Catholics in 1868, McQuaid had been overseeing the local diocese for almost twenty years when the first Poles arrived.[20] A man of enormous energy and impressive organizational skills, his authority was so confirmed and his influence so pervasive that one popular anecdote described him as the only bishop in the United States who would still be ruling his diocese a quarter century after his death. At the same time,

McQuaid demonstrated compassion in matters concerning his people, taking particular interest in the preparation of priests and Sisters, the education of children, and charitable extensions of the diocese's work such as care of orphans, the elderly, and the sick.

In regard to work among immigrants, McQuaid maintained a less rigid stance than many of his fellow bishops. Unlike those who believed that ethnic parishes would weaken American Catholicism and who acted quickly to enforce assimilation, he believed in helping newcomers to his diocese achieve a balance between their heritage and their new loyalties.[21] The American-born son of Irish parents, Rochester's bishop consistently acknowledged immigrants' ties to their homeland while emphasizing their status as Americans. "Your sons should grow up with the love of their native country," McQuaid told the members of a local Irish organization in 1894, but he hastened to remind his listeners that their families should hold first allegiance to the United States: "While the best emotions of their souls will go out to the old land, yet it must always be second."[22] This would be his advice to every ethnic group that came under his jurisdiction.

Acting on his belief that assimilation would work itself out naturally if immigrants were encouraged to value their new citizenship, McQuaid allowed each group of European Catholics who entered his diocese to establish an ethnic parish and to be served by a priest of their own nationality. In 1890, the Rochester Diocese was home to an assortment of parishes serving primarily Irish, German, and French-Belgian congregations. The bishop entrusted the spiritual care of each parish of immigrants to a pastor who spoke the language of their homeland, and fostered assimilation among the children in parochial schools through the work of Sisters who provided instruction in both English and the immigrants' language.[23]

McQuaid's approach to the Poles followed this pattern, beginning with his decision to allow Polish-speaking priests to hold services and hear confessions for the members of St. Casimir's Society. Between 1887 and 1890, priests from Buffalo visited the Poles at St. Michael's Church, while the society began collecting money to support the organization of their own parish. In April 1888, less than a year after the society's formation, the Poles purchased two acres of land at St. Joseph Street and Weaver Street.[24] At $3,500, the cost of these lots was beyond the Polish families' means, but a loan for the full amount from the treasury of St. Michael's Parish allowed St. Casimir's Society to complete arrangements for the purchase. Two personal donations—$25 from Pascalar and $25 from McQuaid—were added to $60 contributed by the Poles in the first collection for their church building fund.

Eager to share the news of their selection of a parish site, the Society of St. Casimir sent an announcement to *Polak w Ameryce,* a Polish language newspaper published in Buffalo, early in May 1888. "We have purchased lots," the Poles informed the editors, "costing $3,500 on lovely St. Joseph Street."[25] The *Union and Advertiser,* meanwhile, sent a reporter to the northeast side to gather information about the Poles' plans for their congregation.[26] "Few people are aware," the reporter observed in an article printed that April, "of the rapid growth of the Polish people in this city. There are seventy families who have signified intention to join the new congregation. . . . Many of them have been saving money for some time, and refraining from purchasing homes until they could know the location of the

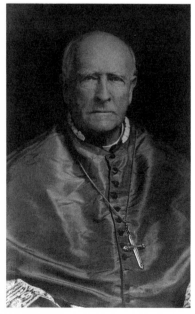

Bernard J. McQuaid
First Bishop of Rochester
1868–1909
(Courtesy of St. Stanislaus
Parish Archives)

GDYNIA •

POMERANIA

•LODZ

WARSZAWA

★

•KRAKOW

NOVOGRODEK

Rakow ○

Minsk

BYELORUSSIA

POLESIE

VOLHYNIA

•LWOW

EASTERN GALICIA

N

W E

S

church. Now that the land is bought they may be expected to buy lots and erect their homes in that section of the city."

Having determined to organize a parish, the reporter continued, the Polish families had received support from both Father Pascalar and Father Teofil Kozlowski, a priest from Buffalo who "earnestly advised them to carry out their project" and whose "zeal encouraged them to even greater efforts in this direction." Concluding his article, the writer interviewed "a German Catholic citizen" who commented frankly on the Poles' plans for a church of their own:

> The ambition of the Poles who come to this country is to secure homes for themselves. . . . [They] are naturally industrious and frugal and so readily save money out of their wages. Those in this city are artisans and laborers. They are all able to speak German, but have an aversion to the language and prefer to use their mother tongue. For this reason they prefer a church of their own, with a pastor speaking the Polish language, to attending the German churches.

The parish of St. Stanislaus Kostka, named by a vote of the Polish families for one of their homeland's saints, was incorporated according to state law on May 7, 1888—the seventh Polish Catholic congregation in New York State.[27] Father Pascalar, serving as temporary pastor and treasurer, recorded financial transactions in a ledger inscribed across its front page "In the name of the Lord and in honor of St. Stanislaus."[28] In addition to $16 paid to an attorney for incorporation fees, the parish's main expenses during its first year were the $18 stipends given to visiting Polish priests. Parish income grew each month with the Polish families' donations: $61 collected in May, $48 in June, $54 in July, $71 in August. By December 1888, the congregation had saved $621 for construction of a church.

Despite the initial excitement surrounding the Poles' purchase of land, the Church of St. Stanislaus Kostka would not be built on St. Joseph Street. While saving money to construct their church during the following months, the Polish families became dissatisfied with the location and in November 1889 convened a parish meeting to consider another site: an uncleared tract of land at the city line, extending 240 feet on Hudson Avenue and 350 feet on Norton and Salmon Streets.[29]

Town Lot 45, as the tract of land was known, claimed the city's northern boundary in 1889, more than two miles beyond the commerce and traffic of the Four Corners. A remote stretch of grass, wildflowers, and fruit trees crossed by a small stream, the area lay a half-mile north of St. Jacob Street, where the city's horse-drawn streetcar pulled to its final stop. Beyond this point, Hudson Avenue (called Hudson Street before the turn of the century) was a dirt road that cut uninterrupted through the fields until it reached Moulson's Nursery at the Norton Street line.

To the Polish families, the advantages of Town Lot 45 were considerable. Although overgrown with grass and bisected by a sluggish stream, the area contained an expanse of land on which they could build homes, a parish, and a

school—a community where their language could be spoken and their traditions maintained. The agreement drawn up by the owners of the tract, Alvin and Otto Block and Charles and August Blauw, acknowledged the Polish families' plans for a settlement.[30] In exchange for the lots on St. Joseph Street, Block and Blauw gave the Poles the parcel of land at Hudson Avenue and Norton Street, and agreed that they would sell the remaining land in Town Lot 45 exclusively to Polish Catholics for the next ten years (from Hudson Avenue east to North Street, and from Norton Street south to the street that would be named "Sobieski"). In addition, the realtors promised that they would offer these lots "at their scheduled price" for a term of one year, and for five years beyond that time would increase the price by no more than $10 per lot per year. This agreement, outlined in November 1889, guaranteed the Poles first rights to the housing plots surrounding their church, and allowed them a decade to solidify their claim.

Block and Blauw's attractive offer was brought to the Polish families for a vote at a parish meeting held in St. Michael's Hall on November 24th.[31] Nearly 100 Polish men representing St. Stanislaus' congregation took part in the decision, indicating their preference on sheets of paper designated "St. Joseph Street" and "Hudson Street." Overwhelmingly, the voters chose Town Lot 45 as the site of St. Stanislaus Parish, receiving as part of the package Otto Block's plans for the design of a wooden church.

Shortly afterward, the Society of St. Casimir organized a house-to-house collec-

The Society of St. Casimir, pictured with Father Teofil Szadzinski in front of the original Church of St. Stanislaus. (Courtesy of Rev. Alexander J. Stec)

tion among the Polish families, authorized by Father Pascalar in a letter written on St. Michael's Parish stationery.[32] A few months later, in February 1890, the society sponsored a fund-raiser at Germania Hall (later called Turner Hall), drawing a brief announcement in the *Herald:* "This evening a Polish carnival entertainment will be given at Germania Hall for the benefit of the fund for the Polish Catholic Church to be built this spring on the corner of Hudson and Norton Streets."[33] The "carnival entertainment" drew receipts of $71.05, balanced against $20.50 which St. Casimir's Society paid to organize the event. Supplementing this profit with $33.60 received in a special building fund collection, the day's activities added $84.15 to the savings of the Polish congregation.

During the same months, according to the terms of their agreement, Block and Blauw began advertising land in the settlement among Polish Catholics. In February 1890, the *Echo,* a Polish language newspaper published in Buffalo, carried a front-page description of the *nowa kolonja Polska w Rochester,* which it depicted as the most promising Polish settlement in North America.[34] An accompanying map outlined the land of Town Lot 45, with the location of the church indicated and streets already labeled "St. Stanislaus," "Kosciuszko," and "Sobieski." The article invited Buffalo Poles to investigate the area, where housing plots measuring approximately 40 feet by 150 feet were selling for $200 to $600. Those who lacked the means to pay for a lot were advised that the Rochester Poles had established a lending cooperative to help others buy land in the settlement.

The following summer, ground was broken for the Church of St. Stanislaus Kostka, and its congregation planned a day of celebration for the building's cornerstone dedication on August 3rd.[35] Led by the members of St. Casimir's Society grouped behind their handsome banner, approximately 2,500 persons (Rochester's Polish families, members of St. Michael's Church, and guests from St. Stanislaus Parish of Buffalo) walked in the blistering afternoon heat from St. Michael's Church to the site of the Polish parish. There Bernard McQuaid, attended by a dozen priests, blessed the foundation, sidebeams, cornerstone, and crucifix of the chapel under construction, then climbed to a platform at the front of the site and spoke to the persons assembled:

> I congratulate you and all the Catholics of this city on the happy beginning of this church and the formation of this congregation. We of other nationalities . . . welcome you to the bosom of the church as brothers in the religion of Christ Jesus. . . . We know what you have had to suffer at home for country and religion; what you have suffered, others have suffered before you. In coming to this new country, you will not have to undergo such persecution, and if you become good citizens all will regard you as worthy members of this great Republic. I hope before the church is completed that the young priest . . . a Pole as you are Poles, who knows what you have had to suffer and who feels for you, will be here to take charge of St. Stanislaus' congregation.

Front page of the Buffalo Echo (1890), depicting the location of Rochester's Polish settlement. (Courtesy of St. Stanislaus Parish Archives)

Following the bishop's remarks, the Poles heard a homily in their own language presented by Father Jan Pitass of St. Stanislaus Parish in Buffalo. At the close of the

MAP OF
BLOCK & BLAUW'S SUB-DIVISION OF PART OF TOWN LOT 45
T. 14 R. 7
ROCHESTER, N, Y.

GRAY & STOREY, SURVEYORS,   DEC. 1889

UNION-ADV Co ENGRAVERS Roch N Y

— — — NORTON — — — — N. LINE OF LOT 45 — — — — STREET. —

St. Stanislaus Church.

177 178 179 180 181 182 183 184 185 186 187 188 189 190 191 192 193 | 196 195 194

175 17? 174 17? 172 171 170 ?69 168 167 166 16? 164 163 162 161 160 | 159 158 157

ST. STANISLAUS   AVENUE,

128 127 126 125

129 130 131 132 133 134 135 136 137 138 139 140 141 142 143 144 145 146 147 148 149 150 151 152 | 156 155 154 153

124 123 122

121 120 119 118 117 116 115 114 113 112 111 110 109 108 107 106 105 104 10? 102 101 100 99 98 97 | 96 95 94

KOSCIUSZKO   AVENUE.

65 64 63 62 61 60

66 67 68 69 70 71 72 73 74 75 75 77 78 79 80 81 82 83 84 85 86 87 88 89 90 | 93 92 91 34 33 32

59 58 57 56 55 54 5? 52 51 50 49 48 47 ?? 45 44 4? 4? 4? 40 39 38 37 36 35

SOBIESKI   AVENUE,

3 2 1

4 5 6 7 8 9 10 11 12 13 14 15 16 17 18 19 20 21 22 23 24 25 26 27 28 | 31 30 29

30 FT. LEFT FOR NORTH STREET.

A KOLONJA POLSKA W ROCHESTER, N. Y.

175 rodzin polskich, które dotychczas były rozrzucone po całem mieście. Teraz,

ceremony, McQuaid blessed the banner of St. Casimir's Society, then all adjourned for a refreshment of beer and lemonade provided by the Polish families.[36]

When Bernard McQuaid granted the Society of St. Casimir permission to build a church, there was no Polish-speaking priest in his eight-county diocese. While the Poles were attending Mass at St. Michael's Church and contributing to their building fund, McQuaid was in communication with Florian Stablewski, archbishop of Poznan and Gniezno. Stablewski recommended as pastor for the new congregation one of his deacons, Teofil Szadzinski, a young man who was completing theological studies at the American College of the Immaculate Conception in Louvain, Belgium.[37] Since the college had been founded to train Europeans for missionary work in the United States, Szadzinski would have been anticipating an assignment in America as he neared ordination.

Teofil Szadzinski was born in Pleszew, a town on the southeastern border of Prussian Poland, in 1857.[38] He came to Rochester in August 1890 direct from his studies at Louvain, missing his church's cornerstone dedication by a few days but arriving in time to fulfill McQuaid's promise to the Poles: they would have their priest before St. Stanislaus Church was completed. Sometime after receiving Stablewski's recommendation, McQuaid had visited Szadzinski at Louvain and apparently taken charge of the remainder of the young man's preparation. Following that visit, Szadzinski corresponded with McQuaid, inquiring when he might expect to be ordained in a note written on Christmas Eve 1889:

> Right Reverend Bishop!
> By the approaching of the new year Mr. Smelsz and I cannot neglect to wish your Grace a long life, enjoyment of plenty, and prosperous government. During your sojourn at Louvain, when I had the honour to accompany your Lordship to the station, I heard, that I should be ordained priest after having finished the short course in theology. About that matter I asked now Father Rector de Neve, but received the answer, that he does not know it. Therefore I dare to take the liberty to ask your Grace, when I shall get the priesthood, resp. how many years I have to study theology. I think, it is necessary for me to know the requisite time, in order to prepare myself well and exactly for the priesthood. . . .
> Hoping your Grace will have the goodness to satisfy my wish, I remain your Lordship's most obedient and humble servant,
> T. Szadzinski[39]

Teofil Szadzinski
First Pastor of St. Stanislaus
Church
1890–1909

The Sunday after his arrival in Rochester, Szadzinski met his people and preached his first sermon to them at St. Michael's Church. That day, the congregation's collection baskets were the fullest they had been: $134.15 for the cause of the Polish church.[40] A month later, McQuaid presided at Szadzinski's ordination in St. Patrick's Cathedral on Frank Street. It was undoubtedly the first time that half the congregation in the diocesan cathedral were Poles. To mark the occasion, the parishioners of St. Stanislaus took up a special collection and presented their newly ordained pastor with a gold watch.[41]

That Szadzinski was ordained in Rochester by Bishop McQuaid indicated clearly that he was to be a priest of the Rochester Diocese who owed allegiance to the American Catholic Church. Neither Szadzinski nor the bishop nor the congregation who rejoiced at the young man's ordination in 1890 could anticipate the turmoil into which each would be drawn because of that allegiance before the Polish parish reached its twentieth anniversary.

The Church of St. Stanislaus was completed that fall, dedicated by Bishop McQuaid on November 16th, the Sunday nearest the feast of St. Stanislaus Kostka. "The Polish Catholics of Rochester now have a church edifice of their own and are rejoicing in consequence," a *Union and Advertiser* reporter wrote. "The pretty little church of St. Stanislaus . . . was tastefully festooned with evergreens and filled to overflowing with Poles who had assembled to witness the dedication of their church and listen to a sermon in their native tongue."[42] The "pretty little church" on Salmon Street (soon to be renamed St. Stanislaus Street) was designed by Otto Block and constructed by the firm of Joseph Hempel: a one-story chapel of hemlock lumber, 40 feet by 80 feet, seating approximately 400 people.[43] That Sunday, McQuaid blessed its walls inside and out, and addressed the congregation following solemn high Mass:

> I wish to say a few words to you, hoping that many of you can understand what I say and repeat it to those who cannot understand English.
>
> Here you are establishing a home for yourselves in this portion of the city, and a church for Catholics of the Polish nationality. You have left behind you much that you dearly loved, a country and a home in that Polish land, much that was most dear to your hearts.
>
> But you have brought over to this new land one home from Poland. You loved it in Poland, loved it with an undying love. And when you crossed over the ocean and put your foot down here you said, "This will be our new Poland and here we will establish our holy religion. . . ."
>
> So you have brought with you, as the Irish, German, Swiss and others did, your holy religion to this new country. This is your home before God in things spiritual. So beloved children in Christ, strangers you are, and yet not strangers before Christ. . . .
>
> True, it is only a small beginning of the work that is to be done. The Cathedral seventy years ago was not as fine as the church today. It was established by a few poor Irish people, but see where it is today. If you stand shoulder to shoulder you can be in the same position in the future. I expect St. Stanislaus to rank with the Cathedral, St. Michael's, the Holy Redeemer and St. Joseph's.
>
> And when you have a home for your priest you will want a place where your children can be educated in the principles of our holy

religion and you will build a school. When you do, I will send you as teachers Sisters who can speak both Polish and English, thus your children will make rapid progress. United and firm in their faith, religion will grow and flourish in this parish of St. Stanislaus of Rochester.[44]

Outside the small wooden church, a settlement of homes would soon transform the fields of Town Lot 45 into a neighborhood as the number of Polish immigrants continued to grow. From 27 men three years earlier, the Society of St. Casimir had expanded to include 100 members, and the 70 Polish families living in the city had doubled to 145.[45] Father Szadzinski's first tally of parishioners, taken a month before the church's dedication, accounted for 650 persons: 375 adults (communicants) and 275 children. In the next sixteen years, those numbers would swell to include 400 families and more than 2,000 persons.

Original Church of
St. Stanislaus Kostka

It was a high wind sweeping through the empty fields of Town Lot 45 that caused the roof of St. Stanislaus Kostka Church to collapse on August 21, 1890, crushing two workmen beneath the beams.[46]

The accident occurred three weeks after Bishop Bernard McQuaid blessed the church's cornerstone, as the men of Joseph C. Hempel's crew were constructing a roof for the building. A dozen workmen were lifting and securing 120 huge hemlock rafters—each 32 feet long, a foot wide, and two inches thick—to the building's collar beams when "the structure began to creak ominously" in the wind, according to a report in the *Union and Advertiser.* As the gusts increased, 80 of the heavy rafters crashed to the ground, scattering scaffolding and burying five of Hempel's men in the ruins. Two of the workers, 22-year-old Andrew Harter and 42-year-old John Bauer, were killed instantly. Three others who suffered bruises and internal injuries were carried to Schneider's Hotel on Hudson Avenue, where Dr. Charles T. Loritz "did everything possible for their relief."

Hempel, his foreman William Waterstraat, and architect Otto Block were asked to appear before Coroner Kleindienst and an impaneled jury the next day. All testified that the church's design was sound, the workmen were experienced, and procedures had been safe, that if it were not for the high wind rushing through the fields the tragedy would not have occurred. The jury concurred in its verdict delivered the same afternoon:

> We find that Andrew Harter and John Bauer came to their deaths on August 21, 1890, by being struck by falling timbers in St. Stanislaus Church, being constructed by Joseph Hempel.
>
> We also find that the collapsing of said building was due to the high wind on the day of August 21st, 1890, and from the evidence we find that all due precaution had been used and no blame is due to the contractor.

Following the inquest and the funerals of Harter and Bauer, Hempel's crew returned to Salmon Street to begin clearing debris from the site. Much of their work on the structure had to be repeated, since the accident had left only the front wall of the building standing. Despite the tragic setback, Hempel's men completed the Church of St. Stanislaus Kostka that fall, in time for its dedication in November.

At the top of a sharp rise in Section M of Mt. Hope Cemetery, in the burial ground's oldest Masonic plot, stands a tombstone inscribed on one side in English and on the other in Polish. *"Tu spoczywa Franciszek Salezy Wolowski.* . . . Here rests Franciszek Salezy Wolowski, Judge of the Supreme Court of the First Instance of the Kingdom of Poland. Born in Warsaw on January 29, 1805, he died in Rochester on July 12, 1857. . . . Please pray for him."

Wolowski's tombstone—the inscription weatherworn, a cross that once graced its top now missing—represents the intriguing story of a man who was among the first Poles known to have resided in Rochester.[47] He arrived in the city in the 1850s, three decades before a group of immigrants from his homeland founded St. Stanislaus Kostka Parish and established Rochester's Polish settlement. In many ways, he was unlike the artisans, laborers, and peasants who left Poland in search of livelihood at the end of the century. A wealthy landowner who held judicial office, Wolowski was an insurgent who plotted against Tsarist rule of his homeland and was forced to flee the country, settling eventually in Rochester where he taught languages to children and became a Master Mason of Yonnondio Lodge.

A relatively small number of Poles left their homeland in the initial half of the nineteenth century, before the first large wave of Polish immigration brought more than two million laborers and peasants to America. Most of these early emigres were educated members of the gentry, and many were political refugees who had planned or participated in uprisings against foreign rule of Poland, controlled since 1795 by Prussia, Russia, and Austria-Hungary. Some were also Masons, upholders of a tradition of Polish Freemasonry that began early in the eighteenth century and took on nationalistic fervor during the decades of Poland's partition.

The few details known of Wolowski's life are drawn from his tombstone inscription, unusual in its length, and from two articles that appeared in the *Union and Advertiser* in July 1857. "We are pained to announce," a reporter wrote on July 11th, "that Mr. F. S. Wolowski, the well known teacher of French and German languages, was struck down by apoplexy last evening. . . . He has resided here several years and is very highly esteemed by all who have made his personal acquaintance." Two days later, the newspaper followed its brief announcement of Wolowski's illness with a notice of his death that presented an outline of the emigre's life.

Born in Warsaw in 1805, Wolowski had been a "proprietor of large landed estates" which provided him "a princely income," and had served in the judicial court in Kalisz. In the forties, he became active in a nationalistic organization dedicated to opposing Russian rule. When Wolowski's membership in this group became known to authorities, he left the country clandestinely and was able to earn "a scanty living" in exile by teaching French.

He settled in Rochester in the fifties, where he and his wife, an English woman, opened a foreign language school at the corner of East Avenue and William Street. While a resident of Rochester, Wolowski gained admittance to Yonnondio Lodge, then one of four Masonic bodies in the city. His death in July 1857 drew the notice of the local press, which described the Pole as a man of "native goodness of heart" who had earned "eminent attainments in both literature and law [but] was destined to die in poverty—a stranger in a strange land." In addition to his widow, whom he had met after fleeing Poland, Wolowski left relatives in Europe: several children from a previous marriage and their uncles.

His funeral took place from Christ Church on East Avenue, and a brief announcement beneath his obituary in the *Union and Advertiser* requested all members of Yonnondio Lodge to attend "to pay proper respect to the remains of their deceased brother." Wolowski was buried in Mt. Hope Cemetery, and his tombstone was erected "as a token of gratitude" by a son in Poland. "Please pray for him," the inscription requests, "for he had a great heart and distinguished himself with honorable deeds in his own country and in America. . . . For your prayers, you will have the gratitude of his son, Zygmunt Wolowski."

2 | On Streets Named Pulaski and Sobieski

The first children born to the city's Polish immigrants grew up in the community that their parents formed near Hudson Avenue and Norton Street, in the settlement that local reporters dubbed "Little Poland" and "Polish Town." Immediately following the construction of St. Stanislaus Church, the Polish families' houses, gardens, shops, and meeting halls began to displace the wildflowers and fruit trees that had previously claimed Town Lot 45. Recording the community's growth in his parish register, Father Szadzinski noted the arrival of additional families and the birth of every child: 675 parishioners in 1891; 760 in 1892; 1,040 in 1893.[1]

To outsiders, the area seemed a place apart, a remote outpost of city life. "Most of the readers of the *Post Express* probably know more about distant Warsaw than of the Polish settlement on northern Hudson street,"

remarked one reporter who visited the settlement in 1893.[2] "The houses are separated from the city proper by a third of a mile of open fields and one must walk a mile after leaving the cars to reach Sobieski avenue." Two years later, a reporter from the *Union and Advertiser* also ventured down Hudson Avenue and described the area's rugged character: "A little nor' by nor'east, as the mariner calculates, is a section . . . situated in the midst of what might be termed a slightly rolling prairie. A few small trees and some straggling, snaky fences are all that interrupt the boisterous wind when it comes bustling in from the icy waters of the lake. In winter the air is frigid, and in summer the atmosphere is torrid. Despite these extremes the residents of that quarter of the city live, eat and sleep, and seem to be happy the year around."[3]

To the families buying housing

On entering "Little Poland" these facts become too apparent to escape notice: the houses are neat and roomy, the sidewalks are tidy and the general air of the settlement is one of comfort. . . . Buildings have spread rapidly and bid fair to cover the open fields stretching for half a mile to the east and west. The settlement is a credit to the city.

Post Express
Rochester, New York
April 24, 1893

22

Szczepan Zielinski, and an early advertisement for his contracting firm. (Courtesy of St. Stanislaus Parish Archives)

Opposite: A group of St. Stanislaus parishioners posed for this photo while on a picnic. (Courtesy of Mr. and Mrs. Leon Lustyk)

plots within view of St. Stanislaus Church, the inconveniences of living at the city's northern edge were more than offset by the significance of forming a community of their own, a "Polonia" where they could speak their homeland's language, maintain its traditions, and educate their children in Polish history and religion.[4] As reporters observed, Rochester's Polish settlement quickly became a close-knit unit of homes, shops, and societies centered around the church, a neighborhood that was removed from city services like the streetcar but that nevertheless offered its residents the comfort of familiar routines. "We live together here," one Pole told the visitor from the *Post Express,* "to do just as we used to in the old country."

Scores of houses went up in the settlement's first years, set on roads cut through the fields east and west of Hudson Avenue. The immigrants named these streets "Kosciuszko," "Sobieski," and "Pulaski" in honor of their homeland's heroes, and celebrated construction of the dwellings that represented additional families' investment in Town Lot 45.[5] Often, new property owners threw a housewarming when only the foundation and roof of their home had been built, inviting their neighbors to dance to a fiddler's lively music on the freshly laid floors.

The majority of the homes built earliest in the Polish section were constructed by the firm of Szczepan Zielinski, an immigrant contractor rated "the richest man in the settlement" in 1893, when he was 22 years old.[6] Born in Poznania in 1871, Zielinski immigrated to Rochester with his parents in 1882. After attending a local public school, the young man received an apprenticeship with the construction firm of Muller and Smith, and undertook his first independent contracting job in 1888. Following formation of St. Stanislaus Parish, Zielinski invested heavily in the land near the church and established a building firm that provided employment to other immigrants. The first wooden sidewalks on north Hudson Avenue were laid by Zielinski's crew, who are credited with construction of more than 500 homes on the northeast side between 1890 and 1910. In 1908, the contractor's assets, including his firm and a stock of lumber, hardware, paint, glass, masonry, and bricks, were said to total $40,000.

In addition to Zielinski's lumber company, the settlement included four groceries, two butcher shops, and three or four saloons at the turn of the century.[7] Three of the groceries were operated by Wojciech Kaczmarek, Walenty Nowacki, and

Antoni Nowacki; Wojciech Skromak and Tomasz Brodowczynski were proprietors of the butcher shops. Wojciech Maciejewski, Wawrzyniec Zwolinski, and a Pole from Buffalo named Gostomski operated three of the taverns which served as meeting halls, dance halls, and locations for social gatherings. By 1908, other Polish-owned businesses dotted Hudson Avenue: Stanislaw Prymuszewski's barber shop, groceries run by Jozef Borycza and Stanislaw Marcinkowski, Stanislaw Dukat's bakery, and saloons operated by Wojciech Sniechowiak and Piotr Drzewicki. Polish families readily patronized these businesses, and purchased goods not available in their settlement at the public market, in stores on Front Street, and in Jewish-owned shops on the northeast side where proprietors spoke Polish or German.

As the community grew in the 1890s, immigrants from Austrian Poland joined those who had come to the city a decade earlier from Poznania. "In Rochester, there are 250 families from Poznania and from Galicia," members of St. Stanislaus Parish wrote to the editors of *Polak w Ameryce* in 1898. "They live together at the farthest edge [of the city]."[8] After the turn of the century, Poles from the Russian partition also arrived, including several families from the village of Rakow. Some of the heads of the Polish households had been skilled workers such as leather craftsmen in Europe, and were able to secure related work in Rochester firms.[9] Others entered the local work force in jobs for which

strong shoulders were qualification enough, logging long hours each week as cement masons, construction workers, laborers on Irondequoit farms, and tenders of the glass furnaces at Bausch & Lomb. Those who had worked as tailors in Europe, carrying the tools of their trade from village to village, found employment in the city's sweatshops and clothing firms.

According to reporters, the homes of the Polish families were small and neat, plain but comfortable, maintained by housewives whose daily work was as strenuous as that of their husbands. To obtain water for cooking, cleaning, and bathing, the women hiked through tall grass and mud to wells in the fields that surrounded their homes. Oblivious of Rochester's winters, they boiled laundry in large tubs in their kitchens and hung the wash outside to dry even in bitter December. They supervised households of seven or ten or thirteen children— each born at home with the assistance of a midwife—as well as backyards populated with chickens, ducks, geese, pigs, and an occasional cow or goat. They baked bread and mended endlessly, hurried to neighborhood markets in all kinds of weather, and tended gardens which yielded many bushels of vegetables each season. On top of all this, many took jobs to supplement their husbands' income, scrubbing laundry for families in other neighborhoods or sewing piecework for garment firms in their spare hours at home.

In the Polish section, one reporter observed, "children, dogs, ducks and doves predominate. The dogs are irascible and mangy and currish, but the children are good to look upon. Fat, rosy-cheeked, with laughing eyes, they appear to be the embodiment of perfect health. They don't wear mittens on their hands, and the girls throw their shawls over their heads to protect them from the winter wind

A wedding celebration at 15 Sobieski Street. (Courtesy of Mrs. Bernard Dynski)

and snow."[10] In the homes of the Polish settlement, each of these robust-looking children was assigned a share of the household chores. The oldest daughter might supervise a crew of younger sisters and brothers scrubbing their home's wooden floors, while another sibling walked the family's cow up Bauman Hill (now Bauman Street) to graze. A young boy might tend his mother's kitchen stove, feed the pigs and chickens, or cart home piecework from a tailor shop on St. Paul Street.

The limited hours of leisure time were shared in many Polish homes, where a father might read to his children in the evening and his wife might teach them songs while finishing her sewing and mending. Sundays brought hikes to Seneca Park, exuberant picnics at Schuetzen Park, and excursions on the streetcar north to Sea Breeze. Dances sponsored by the church societies generated considerable excitement, often held at neighborhood taverns like Maciejewski Hall which boasted of "a carefully laid dancing floor."[11]

More colorful than dances and picnics, the wedding celebrations of Polish couples outdid other social events.[12] It was a precarious walk to church along wooden sidewalks for a girl in her wedding gown, but after the service a band of fiddlers led wife and husband back to her parents' house where front doors, fences, and even hen coops would be decorated with ribbon. In good weather, a family's yard would be overflowing with guests and the best of their livestock would be used to prepare meals of chicken, sausage, and *czarnina*. If the food and home-brewed beer lasted and the band endured, friends and neighbors would return several days that week to prolong *poprawiny*.

The attention that local newspapers afforded the Polish neighborhood reflected a mix of honest interest, curiosity, amusement, and, in some cases, bias against the newcomers. Some reports were complimentary, like the 1893 article in the *Post Express* that noted the neat look of the settlement and appraised Polonia as "a credit to the city."[13] Others found the community's lifestyle quaint and poked fun at the immigrants: their names, their efforts to use English, their willingness to work outside in winter weather.[14]

Other reports blatantly vilified the Poles. When three teenage boys were accused of vandalizing a vacant house on Sobieski Street in 1896, the *Post Express* reporter who covered their arraignment in police court claimed that young men of the Polish section indulged in behavior "of total depravity" and lived a "semi-barbaric existence."[15] Describing the boys' appearance before Judge Ernst, the reporter relayed the difficulty that the court interpreter had in pronouncing their names: "These poor little fellows [are] encumbered for life with unmanageable designations. . . . The interpreter had to give names to the judge in installments." When Ernst dismissed the young men with a fine and a lecture, the reporter suggested that the judge had taken pity on them because "[his] feelings had been touched deeply" by the length of their "ponderous" names.

Reporters wrote frequently about saloons in the Polish section, and some contended that the number of establishments was excessive.[16] "Four saloons exist in the settlement within a few hundred feet of each other," the *Union and Advertiser* told readers in 1896. "They are patronized almost entirely by Poles, whose families, in many instances, suffer because their earnings are spent for liquor. . . . Numerous assaults have been committed, many of them of a very serious nature, and fights without number have occurred." Some reports detailed grim incidents, such as a fight between Poles and Germans at Maciejewski Hall that ended in the death of a German patron. Others made sweeping statements about the immigrants: "The Pole is very fond of [beer]. He must have it at all hours of the day. . . . The most familiar sight is a man, woman, or child going to and from a saloon. . . ." In a city that was home to a strong temperance movement, stories of tavern brawls and domestic quarrels linked to drinking promoted an unfavorable impression of the immigrants' community among Rochesterians who had never traveled north of Avenue D.

In some cases, the press reminded readers that perceptions that outsiders held about the immigrants' community could be inaccurate. "For some reason or another," a *Union and Advertiser* reporter commented in 1895, "people have strange fancies and ideas concerning the Polish people and their methods of habitation. Such settlements are usually associated with poverty and all of its attendant evils . . . . It may in many cases be near the truth in Chicago or New York, but it is absolutely false as far as Rochester is concerned."[17] He was, he confessed, startled that the first young man he met at the edge of the Polish section spoke clear, correct English and carried a novel by George Eliot under his arm.

Equally surprising to the reporter was the testimony of a librarian at the Central Branch, who confirmed that the Poles were library patrons and readers of "the best standard works." The superintendent of postal delivery could testify on his part that the immigrants were "assiduous readers" of newspapers: "They subscribe to many, both English and Polish, although more frequently to those in the latter language, and the papers come from Buffalo, Cleveland, Chicago or New York."[18] Although not all of the immigrants had enjoyed the opportunity of education in their homeland, Polonia's sophistication was sufficient to sponsor a centennial celebration of poet Adam Mickiewicz's birth in 1898.[19]

Other community events caught the interest of the press, such as the Poles' celebration of Christmas, described for readers of the *Herald* in 1903.[20] "They will observe the day with many of the same old country ways as their brothers and sisters across the sea," a reporter noted. "The Polish Christmas customs are most picturesque and interesting." The celebration would extend across three days, and would include family gatherings, feasting, rejoicing, and daily visits to church:

> The Polish people are great churchgoers, and the church will be crowded [on Christmas Eve]. There will be special music with the singing of many Polish hymns. . . . With much music and song, the lights in all the Polish homes of the city will be kept burning until long after midnight.
>
> Christmas Day will be given up entirely to rest and to having a second fine dinner. . . . These pleasures in many cases will last over into Sunday . . . a third day for those who have drunk and danced and made merry at all the feasting to take a much needed rest in preparation for the inexorable cares and duties of work day life.

Much of the energy and activity of Polonia's first years was directed to development of St. Stanislaus Parish. Following the dedication of the church, the congregation's weekly collections supported the purchase of goods such as vestments, candles, altar cloths, Stations of the Cross, and a pump organ.[21] The acquisition of some items called for special benediction: Bishop McQuaid returned in April 1891 to consecrate a steeple bell (christened "Leo" in honor of a parishioner who had donated towards its purchase), and again in November to bless a statue of the parish's patron saint.

Several societies that formed during these years supported the work of the parish.[22] Even before the church on Salmon Street was completed, the congregation had organized two groups for men in addition to St. Casimir's Society: the Society of St. Stanislaus and the *Ulani* (Knights) of St. Michael. Four other groups were established by 1896: the societies of St. Joseph, St. Thaddeus, and St. Adalbert for men, and the Holy Rosary Society for women. Often, these groups offered benefits to the immigrants. St. Casimir's Society, for instance, invested a member's $8 initiation fee and monthly dues of 50 cents in its insurance fund. A member in good standing received payment from the fund when illness prevented him from working, and in case of his death his widow received a stipend to help cover the cost of his funeral.

Construction of a rectory and a school for the parish followed within seven years of the dedication of St. Stanislaus Church. Needed as soon as possible were living quarters for Father Szadzinski, who for ten months had to make his way from the bishop's residence on Frank Street (now North Plymouth Avenue near Platt Street), a few miles southwest and on the opposite side of the Genesee River. A rectory was completed in June 1891, built with the help of a $2,000 loan from St. Bernard's Seminary.[23] From this residence, a woodframe house next door to the church, Szadzinski took on the duties of an immigrant pastor, serving as spiritual and secular leader, translator, counselor, parish treasurer, and host of community celebrations. Justifiably proud of each step in St. Stanislaus' growth, he kept a diary of events in the parish's life: 137 young people confirmed by Bishop McQuaid in 1892; 24 children in the First Communion class of 1893; purchase of statues imported from Europe for the church interior; three days of celebration to mark the parish's tenth anniversary at the turn of the century.[24]

The most significant event of the parish's first years was the opening of St. Stanislaus School. Although there were two public elementary schools within walking distance of the Polish settlement, the immigrants preferred to establish a program of their own. From their point of view, it was less important that their children's education provide advancement in American society, more important that it transmit Polish language, religion, and traditions.[25] While parishioners saved money to finance construction of a schoolhouse, their children studied at Holy Redeemer, St. Michael's, and St. Bridget's schools or received instruction in Polish from Walenty Nowacki, a Hudson Avenue grocer and the parish's organist.[26] Under Nowacki's tutelage, neighborhood children began classes in November 1891, studying reading, writing, arithmetic, and history at benches set up in the schoolmaster's house.

In their decision to establish a parochial school, Szadzinski and his parishioners enjoyed the full backing of Bishop McQuaid, who from his installation had been a vigorous supporter of diocesan schools.[27] McQuaid championed the cause of

parochial school education tirelessly: in a series of lectures given before largely Protestant audiences in cities across the state, and in newspaper interviews and articles printed in secular publications. At the same time, he encouraged the formation of a school in each parish in his diocese and invited the congregation of St. Joseph Sisters to establish a teaching community in Rochester. Determined that academic standards in the Catholic schools would equal those of public school instruction, McQuaid required diocesan students to take examinations developed by the state's Board of Regents beginning in 1874. In 1890, the year St. Stanislaus Church was built, McQuaid's diocese ranked third in the nation, behind only the Archdiocese of Philadelphia and the Diocese of Newark, New Jersey, in the proportion of parishes that maintained their own schools.[28]

From the time when the Polish congregation was organized, McQuaid planned that St. Stanislaus Parish would also open a school. Before ground for the church was broken, he asked Teofil Szadzinski, then a deacon studying in Louvain, to write to Poland and inquire about Sisters who might serve as teachers.[29] Two years later, the bishop dispatched Father Pascalar of St. Michael's Parish to Europe to seek out Polish and German girls for the local congregation of St. Joseph Sisters.[30]

Pascalar returned from Hamburg in July 1891, along with 21 young women who had volunteered to serve as Sisters in Rochester parishes. Only one of the group was Polish: Paulina Urbanska, who had traveled alone to Hamburg from a town in Prussian Poland. One of seven children, Paulina was 18 years old when she departed Europe to enter the congregation of St. Joseph as Sister M. Adalbert (Wojcieszka). For the next six years, until St. Stanislaus School opened, she lived and studied at Nazareth Convent on Jay Street, working during the same years with orphaned and delinquent boys at St. Mary's Home on West Main Street.

Szadzinski authorized construction of a combination schoolhouse and convent

at Hudson Avenue and Norton Street in August 1896, awarding the building contract to Szczepan Zielinski for $11,625.[31] After its foundation was laid, McQuaid came to bless the cornerstone into which the Poles had sealed his picture and copies of five newspapers: the diocese's *Catholic Journal,* the *Democrat and Chronicle,* and three Polish language publications (*Gazeta Katolicka* of Chicago; *Wiara i Ojczyzna,* the journal of the Polish Roman Catholic Union; and Buffalo's *Polak w Ameryce*).

The new structure would not only serve as a schoolhouse but would also provide a location for meetings and celebrations. The first event held in the school's basement hall was an elaborate commemoration of the Polish Insurrection of 1830, organized on its 66th anniversary in November 1896.[32] The Poles "assembled in large numbers," the *Democrat and Chronicle* reported, "to honor the memory of their patriotic ancestors, whose unsuccesful but gallant attempt to throw off the tyranny of Czar Nicholas caused their imprisonment, banishment or execution during and after the insurrection." The ceremony opened in St. Stanislaus Church with Requiem Mass celebrated in honor of the fallen heroes, then continued in the hall where Father Szadzinski recounted the history of the uprising, Nowacki's pupils performed patriotic songs, and members of the congregation delivered addresses punctuated by fireworks exploded outside of the building.

Opening the school hall also made possible a community project that had been planned for some time. Since May 1893, when a collection was taken up at a commemoration of Poland's Constitution Day, money had been set aside for a library of Polish books.[33] With $17 from this fund, Szadzinski was able to order 58 selections in Polish literature, religion, and history from Buffalo bookstores in March 1897, including among his purchases Henryk Sienkiewicz's *Trilogy* and the novels of Jozef Kraszewski. The books, stored in the new parish hall, were made available to parishioners: each title could be borrowed for a deposit of five cents a week, and readers could keep their selections for fourteen days. A committee was formed to monitor the library's holdings, consisting of Walenty Paprocki, Jan Szczepanski, Jozef Tomczak, Jan Zientara, and Wincenty Wagner who served as librarian.

The parish schoolhouse officially opened the following May, and McQuaid presided at the dedication ceremonies attended by 2,000 parishioners and

These 66 children were enrolled in the second grade at St. Stanislaus School in 1912. (Courtesy of Rev. Alexander J. Stec)

guests.[34] The next day, classes began in the School of St. Stanislaus after morning Mass celebrated for the intention of its pupils. One hundred sixty children enrolled during the first week: 68 of the youngest in Class 1, 48 in Class 2, and 44 older brothers and sisters in Class 3. Three Sisters of St. Joseph, including Wojcieszka, walked daily up Hudson Avenue from Jay Street to teach the immigrants' children, as McQuaid had promised, in English and in Polish. Sixty-eight in a classroom under one Sister's eye was undeniably a challenge, but lessons began in reading, writing, spelling, arithmetic, history, and religion. In September, when their living quarters were prepared, the Sisters moved to the upper floor of the school where they handled daily chores like cooking, cleaning, and mending along with teaching duties, stepping outside to pump water from a well in the yard.

The opening of the schoolhouse represented one of several accomplishments that the immigrant community could claim as it completed its first decade. In the space of ten years, the newcomers had established a church, homes for their families, a rectory for their priest, several societies, a cluster of markets and shops, and a school for their children's education. In 1900, Szadzinski recorded the count of an expanding congregation: 212 families, or nearly 1,200 persons.[35]

To outward appearances, Polonia seemed unified and directed to common purpose. Despite those appearances, however, the immigrants' settlement had little claim to unity and peacefulness as the century turned. Soon, newspaper headlines about the community would herald instead a conflict whose bitterness would linger for decades on the streets named for Polish heroes.

"FOR THE HONOR AND GLORY OF GOD"

Sister M. Adalbert (Wojcieszka)

At age eighteen, Paulina Urbanska departed from her family and the town where she had been born to travel to a convent in the United States.[36] Her decision led her to a career of nearly six decades as a teacher of children in Polish American schools: 34 years at St. Stanislaus School in Rochester, and an additional 23 years at St. Casimir's School in Elmira.

Born in 1872 in Prussian Poland, Paulina was one in a family of seven children whose father served as foreman on the estate of a German landowner. Although she and her brothers and sisters studied German in school, they spoke Polish with their parents at home and felt the influence of Polish Catholicism in their upbringing. As a child, Paulina attended Mass each morning with her mother, slipping off the estate through an opening in the fence to avoid the notice of her father's Protestant employer. In the evenings, the family recited the Rosary and litanies together at home, and twice a week the Urbanski children received religious instruction taught in Polish.

In 1891, the pastor of the Urbanskis' church received a letter advising him that Fridolin Pascalar, a priest from America, was in Europe seeking girls to enter a congregation of teaching Sisters. Engaged to be married but unhappy with the arrangement, Paulina determined to join Pascalar in Hamburg, the port from which he would return to the United States. Her mother encouraged her to go but her father initially forbade her to leave, reluctantly granting permission only after much persuasion.

Paulina traveled on her own to Hamburg, where she found Pascalar and twenty

German girls who had decided to enter the Sisters of St. Joseph. The group arrived in Rochester in July 1891, and the girls began their training for membership in the congregation at Nazareth Convent on Jay Street. "Now, I began to feel the happiness of serving God in peace and contentment of the life of a religious," Paulina later recalled. "Learning the English became very hard at times, but the Dear Lord and kind Patron St. Joseph helped me right along, and I met with success."

As the first Polish girl to join the order, Paulina was trained specifically to help open the school planned for St. Stanislaus Parish. In 1897, after she received her habit and took the name "Wojcieszka," she became one of the first three Sisters assigned to educate children of Rochester's Polish immigrants. Wojcieszka taught at the school on Hudson Avenue for the next 34 years and served for a time as principal, providing instruction through the 1920s to hundreds of youngsters. In 1931, she was appointed principal of St. Casimir's School in Elmira. "I taught there twenty-two and a half years . . . for the 'Honor and Glory of God'," she wrote in her memoirs, "[then] it was God's Holy Will for me to retire because of my health."

Before Wojcieszka left Rochester, Father Stanislaus Wysoczynski wrote to Poland to ask that the government award her its *Polonia Restituta*. She received the honor in recognition of her work among immigrant children and the role she played in organizing a school for Rochester's first Polish parish. Wojcieszka died in 1961, seventy years after she arrived in Rochester to become a teacher. Of her work at St. Stanislaus School, she wrote: "I taught [there] 34 years, among hardships and difficulties at its beginning, but with God's help and blessing, success was attained."

During a visit to Auburn, New York, in October 1901, Teofil Szadzinski was called away suddenly from Forty Hours devotions at St. Alphonsus, the German Catholic parish where he routinely conducted services for Polish immigrants.[37] An urgent message from J. Warren Mead, warden of Auburn Prison, summoned the priest to a cell in the "chamber of the condemned" for a meeting with the man found guilty of assassinating President William McKinley.

Leon Czolgosz, 28 years old and the son of Polish immigrants, was awaiting execution following the trial in which he was convicted of murdering the president a month earlier in Buffalo. Czolgosz had been born in Detroit in 1873 shortly after his parents' arrival from Russian Poland. After a bleak childhood spent in several cities where his father moved the family of eight children in search of work, Czolgosz became intensely interested in anarchism, a movement that opposed all forms of government and political rule.

Although he had denounced religion bitterly during his trial and days in prison, Czolgosz consented to see a priest a week before his execution. Szadzinski, who had stopped during other visits to Auburn to see Polish-speaking inmates, was contacted immediately at St. Alphonsus and arrived at the prison the same afternoon, accompanied by two altar boys. According to reports in Rochester newspapers, the priest talked intently with the prisoner for two hours. Czolgosz evidently did not ask to return to Catholicism as a result of the discussion, but Szadzinski left religious literature printed in Polish with him and offered to come again. As the priest returned from Czolgosz's cell, one of the altar boys waiting for him asked eagerly about the conversation. "Patrick," Szadzinski replied, "priests don't talk about such things."

Back in Rochester that evening, Szadzinski found a reporter from the *Democrat and Chronicle* stationed near his rectory. The pastor gave the reporter no more information about his visit with Czolgosz than he had given the altar boy. As the reporter followed him down St. Stanislaus Street persisting with questions, Szadzinski remarked that he felt the press would do more harm than good if it continued to advertise Czolgosz's deed. Others, he feared, might mistake the man's notoriety for fame and attempt to follow his example.

Czolgosz remained disillusioned with religion as he awaited execution, countering speculation in the press that he would renounce anarchy and embrace Christianity before his death. He did not ask to see Szadzinski again, nor did he respond to a visit later in the week from Father Jacek Fudzinski of Buffalo. The man convicted of McKinley's murder died in the electric chair at Auburn Prison on October 30th, and was buried in an unmarked grave in the prison cemetery.

3 | The Conflict of Convictions

Toward the end of the speech he gave at the dedication of St. Stanislaus Church in 1890, Bernard McQuaid added a cautionary note that seemed out of keeping at the joyful ceremonies.[1] For all of his tenure as bishop, he told the crowd, there had been no dissension between priests and people in the Rochester Diocese. All Roman Catholic congregations had lived in "peace, unity, and harmony." Although he had been warned, McQuaid said openly, that Polish immigrants would bring trouble to the diocese, he encouraged the members of St. Stanislaus Parish to prove such vilification false. "Stand by your priest," he charged the group, "in whom I have every confidence."

None could have known it on that brisk autumn day, but McQuaid's words to the Poles would prove prophetic, for before St. Stanislaus Parish reached its tenth anniversary the immigrants, their pastor, and the bishop would be drawn into a bitter dispute which would eventually lead 150 families—25 percent of the parish—to leave the local diocese and extend their loyalty to the Polish National Catholic Church. As was the case in Polish immigrant settlements throughout the eastern and midwestern states, two main issues formed the roots of Rochester's religious schism: the immigrants' sense of ownership for the parish they had founded, and their intense identification with national heritage. Ultimately, those who believed that affiliation with the local diocese posed a threat to their rights and their national allegiance chose their identity as Poles over Roman Catholicism, abandoning St. Stanislaus Church to form the Polish National Catholic Parish of St. Casimir.

During the events that preceded their departure, the families who later chose National Catholicism would face off against Bishop McQuaid, Father Szadzinski, and the immigrants

I have been bishop nigh upon 23 years. . . . In all that time in the city of Rochester, there has been peace, unity, and harmony. There has been no discussion, no quarreling between priests and people. . . . I have been told that the Poles would be the first to give me trouble. I deny it, and I want you to show the people of Rochester that such a statement is a calumny upon the Polish race.

Bernard McQuaid
November 16, 1890

36

who elected to remain loyal to St. Stanislaus Parish. Those on this side of the dispute, particularly McQuaid and Szadzinski, held equally strong convictions regarding the authority of the Roman Catholic Church, the obedience required of its members, and the responsibility of immigrants to form new loyalties to their adopted homeland. The stage was thus set, even as McQuaid spoke at St. Stanislaus Church's dedication in 1890, for a conflict of convictions that would change the life of Rochester's Polonia.

The formation of St. Casimir's Polish National Catholic Parish is part of a larger history, one scene in a conflict that touched virtually every settlement of Polish immigrants in the United States.[2] At issue was the immigrants' loyalty, their affiliation on the one hand with Roman Catholicism and their dedication to Polish identity on the other. In the United States, these two aspects of the Poles' heritage—each an intense, deeply held allegiance—became for a time competing forces, their rivalry causing dissension in the immigrants' communities and dictating for many Poles a difficult choice between religion and nationalism.

In Poland, a staunch Roman Catholic monarchy for hundreds of years, the forces of faith and fatherland had traditionally been joined. Throughout the century of partition, the Church remained a stronghold of national identity, a reminder of and link to significant moments in Poland's history: the baptism of Mieszko I in 966, when the Duchy of Polonia embraced Christianity; the defeat of the Swedes at the shrine of the Black Madonna in 1655, a turn of events that helped ensure the return of the exiled Polish king; the victory of Jan Sobieski, "defender of Christendom," who battled the Turks in Vienna at the plea of the pope in 1683. In symbolic and tangible ways, Catholicism was a factor in Polish identity, its influence extending from the halls of monarchy to the humblest village cottages.

In North America, the relationship between faith and fatherland suffered strain in immigrant communities at the end of the nineteenth century. Some Poles, including those who had participated in the unsuccessful 1863 insurrection and were then dispersed across Europe and to the United States, believed that it was critical to keep the spirit of nationalism alive in Polish settlements abroad, and to continue to work on behalf of Poland's restoration. Their conviction that Poland would regain nationhood was nurtured by the writings of romanticists like Adam Mickiewicz, who wove an allegory of Poland as the Christ among nations, destined to suffer the pains of partition until the day when it would rise to new life. Efforts to promote nationalism among immigrants in America drew support from Poles who formed a government in exile in Europe, establishing a center of activity in Rapperswil, Switzerland.

While the nationalists held that patriotism was of primary importance, other Poles felt that the immigrants' first loyalty should be to the development of their new settlements. This camp included many members of the Polish clergy in America, administrators of the immigrants' parishes and schools who were interested in promoting the United States as a permanent home. Although they did not deny the importance of heritage, those who supported this point of view believed that restoration of Poland was remote if not unattainable, a noble ideal that should not overshadow the work of building homes, churches, schools, organizations, and a base of influence in the United States. Some members of the clergy also maintained a narrow perspective in regard to patriotism, insisting that Polish nationalism could only be Roman Catholic in character.

The rivalry between nationalism and Catholicism plagued immigrant leaders' efforts to establish a nationwide union of Poles in America.[3] An initial attempt, the organization of the Polish Roman Catholic Union (*Zjednoczenie Polskie Rzymsko-Katolickie w Ameryce,* or PRCU) in 1873, failed to win support among nationalists when, at its founding meeting, the group focused its objectives on the practical development of immigrant communities and limited membership to Roman Catholics. Later, the formation of the Polish National Alliance (*Zwiazek Narodowy Polski,* or PNA) drew the anger of members of the clergy and their supporters. Although the PNA's leaders avowed respect for Catholicism, they pointedly refused to be influenced by priests in secular matters and opened membership in the organization to non-Catholic Poles, including Jews, socialists, and atheists. The estrangement of the two camps became so severe that, in some communities, priests refused to bless the marriages of PNA members and to baptize their children. For many Roman Catholic Poles, membership in the PNA carried the risk of opposition from their priest and, in some cases, expulsion from their parish.

Although the Poles' dispute over faith and fatherland was essentially an internal conflict, it was played out in the context of the American Catholic Church, within whose jurisdiction the Poles had established parishes.[4] According to the Church's organization and rulings, parish property was legally held by bishops and priests worked under their supervision, an arrangement that added to nationalists' fears that Poles in America would lose their identity. Disturbed that the churches and schools that they had built with their savings did not belong to them, and that bishops who were not Polish retained authority in parish matters, groups of Poles often challenged a bishop's decisions—in cases, for instance, when a non-Polish priest was assigned to a Polish parish. Anger also flared in parishes in which, in the view of those who supported nationalism, priests appeared subservient to diocesan directives. Beneath the charges that they often leveled against a priest's character, loyalty, and abilities ran the larger issues of national identity and parish control.

From the point of view of American bishops, the Poles' internal bickering raised issues that had troubled their Church for most of the nineteenth century. Conscious that theirs was a minority congregation in a country largely Protestant, the bishops were divided on the question of assimilation.[5] Some, like Rochester's McQuaid, stressed immigrants' pride in both country of origin and American citizenship, while others, like Cardinal James Gibbons of Baltimore, disapproved of ethnic parishes. The Catholic Church could never hope to gain respect and exert influence in the United States, Gibbons and others insisted, if its members clung to European identities. Gibbons' argument carried particular force at the end of the century as millions of European Catholics immigrated to the United States, their arrival in overwhelming numbers each decade reawakening anti-Catholic feelings in parts of the country.[6]

In addition, since the start of the century, the bishops had faced the challenge of "trusteeism," a movement on the part of laymen to gain greater authority in the management of parishes.[7] Trusteeists, who in some cases seized control of a parish in defiance, demanded privileges that they regarded as laymen's rights, such as legal ownership of parish property and the selection of priests—demands supported by early state laws formed in the tradition of Protestant churches. The movement, which caused furor in parishes throughout the eastern states beginning in the 1780s, was largely subdued a century later as a result of changes in states' laws and decrees by American bishops. To the bishops' frustration, however, demands for greater lay authority in parishes were raised again soon afterward by immigrant groups including Poles, Slovaks, Lithuanians, and Ukrainians.

In one sense, Polish immigrant priests were caught in the middle of this trouble, between the expectations of the bishops and those of parishioners who espoused national identity. On the one hand, they were expected by the hierarchy to support American Church rulings, such as the 1884 decree by the Third Plenary Council of Baltimore that all parish property must be legally held by bishops. At the same time, each was faced with the expectations of his congregation, whose members might accuse him of betraying his heritage if he appeared loyal to a non-Polish bishop. Each pastor had to choose his way, deciding whether to extend his allegiance to the bishops, challenge their hierarchy, or abandon the American Church.[8]

Clergy who chose the third alternative found support among Poles in many communities. Toward the end of the century, priests like Franciszek Kolaszewski in Cleveland, Dominik Kolasinski in Detroit, Antoni Kozlowski in Chicago, and Antoni Klawiter in Buffalo organized Polish immigrants into new parishes which they insisted were separate from local diocesan control.[9] The move to establish independent Polish churches gained momentum when Franciszek Hodur, a young priest determined to defend the immigrants' rights, took charge of a parish that broke with the Diocese of Scranton, Pennsylvania, in 1897.[10] Drawn by his powerful preaching and his support of their grievances, approximately 20,000 Polish immigrants defied excommunication under Hodur's leadership in the next ten years, abandoning Roman Catholicism to form the Polish National Catholic Church. The secession spread quickly in Polish communities from the eastern seaboard to the midwest, its followers united by belief in their right to administer parishes and a determination to maintain their identity as Poles.

For American Polonia, establishment of the independent churches was a painful passage, an outgrowth of the rivalry between faith and fatherland that divided families, estranged friends, and changed neighborhoods. Rarely was formation of an independent church not associated with feuding, street fighting, brawls, and arrests. Inevitably, newspapers reported with interest whatever disruption occurred: conflict with a pastor, disrespect shown a bishop, police called to the Polish section. As troubles subsided so did the curiosity of the press, but down Pulaski and Sobieski Streets events were less quickly forgotten. If outsiders scarcely knew the difference between a Roman Catholic Pole and a National Catholic Pole, in Polish neighborhoods the distinction was sharply drawn and the memory spanned generations.

On the surface, Rochester's Polish settlement, founded in the combined good will of the immigrants, Bishop McQuaid, and Father Szadzinski, seemed beyond the reach of the tensions troubling other Polish communities. This harmony was deceptive, however, and merely masked a discontent which would give way to open dissension among parishioners within a few years of St. Stanislaus Parish's formation.

The spark that fired the Rochester community's troubles was the organization of a local lodge of the Polish National Alliance in 1893. Group 216, called "the Sons of the Polish Crown," was established that July with approximately fourteen members.[11] In keeping with the educational and patriotic aims of their parent group, the Sons of the Polish Crown organized a library as one of their initial projects, each member contributing whatever books he owned to the cause of community education.

Despite the peaceful appearances associated with organization of a neighborhood library, Group 216 immediately drew the disapproval of Father Szadzinski, who was aware of the controversy surrounding the PNA. Whatever the intentions of the Sons of the Polish Crown, the pastor determined to discourage the growth of the lodge, the first organization in the local settlement formed outside of St. Stanislaus Parish. With the formal backing of the church societies and part of the congregation, Szadzinski proclaimed that membership in St. Stanislaus Parish would be denied to anyone who chose to belong to the PNA.[12] The announcement proved controversial, and both the pastor's opponents and supporters hurried across town to state their opinions to the bishop. Szadzinski, hearing after the fact that his parishioners had called on McQuaid, drafted a letter explaining his position.

The Polish National Alliance, he wrote to McQuaid, existed outside of the

Father Szadzinski and the young men of a First Communion class. (Courtesy of Mr. and Mrs. Leo Hoock)

Catholic Church and had no requirements for membership as did parish societies.[13] As a result, the PNA attracted "the worst class of the people." "In parishes where such societies are existing there are always troubles," Szadzinski pointed out, citing examples of disquiet in Polish parishes in other cities. He planned, however, to follow the example of Father Jan Pitass of Buffalo, who had excluded PNA members from his church and now had "a quiet parish."

McQuaid did not interfere with the directive against Group 216, and the Sons of the Polish Crown withdrew temporarily from St. Stanislaus Parish.[14] Despite the pastor's action, however, the matter of PNA membership was not resolved and the issue surfaced again two years later. In December 1895, the Society of St. Casimir expelled from its brotherhood a man who had been a member since St. Stanislaus Church was built, on the grounds that he belonged to the PNA.[15] The man, who did not deny membership in the PNA, countered with a lawsuit against the society, charging that he was expelled without warning, and demanded $100 in damages to cover "his initiation fee, dues, and the injury done to his outraged feelings."

A few weeks after this incident was reported in the press, violent dispute erupted between those supporting and those opposing the PNA. A New Year's Eve ball at Zwolinski Hall (on the corner of Hudson Avenue and Sobieski Street) ended in a midnight fist fight following discussion of Szadzinski's Christmas sermon, in which the pastor had again rebuked the PNA.[16] Szadzinski's position, reported in the *Union and Advertiser,* was "that the Alliance is a secret, revolutionary and un-American organization, which is responsible for much of the Polish troubles in this country." The PNA now counted one hundred members, Szadzinski told the reporter, in his parish of one thousand persons.

Within the next four years, two additional local lodges of the PNA would form: Group 396, an organization of mechanics and artisans, in 1897, and Group 512, called "St. Izydor's Society," in 1900. In keeping with diocesan policy and maintaining his own position, Szadzinski forbade the display of Group 396's banner in St. Stanislaus Church, an exclusion which signified "serious humiliation to its members."[17]

Additional challenges to Father Szadzinski's authority followed the dispute over Group 216. His stand against the PNA weakened the pastor's credibility among some parishioners, and during the next four years their charges against his personality and leadership intensified while the priest's determination not to concede to their criticisms grew. The clash of wills continued to build until August 1905, when a disturbance on parish grounds brought police to St. Stanislaus and matters to a head.

Problems had surfaced in 1899, after Szadzinski received permission to visit his family in Poland. "I feel here very well, using much fresh air," he wrote to McQuaid from Poznania that June.[18] He planned pilgrimages with his brother to Rome and Czestochowa, and asked the bishop if he might remain in Europe several weeks longer.

Szadzinski's holiday was cut short, however, and he was called back to Rochester at the end of June because of difficulties at St. Stanislaus.[19] In August 1899, a committee from the congregation formally filed general charges with the bishop against their pastor's "character" and "performance of duties," charges that were carried to McQuaid a second time in December.[20] A third appeal followed in March 1900, this time containing a specific accusation: that the pastor had used the church mortgage to obtain a financial loan for the parish, and that he had failed to inform parish trustees about this transaction.[21] "We would like to know if he possesses any such right without, at least, notifying the trustees," committee members wrote to McQuaid. "This last act of the pastor has angered the congregation and they respectfully insist that he should be removed and another priest placed in charge of the church. . . . We respectfully urge that you will act promptly in this matter as this is the last time that we intend to write to you. If you do not act, the congregation will have to take such steps as they may deem necessary. . . . We feel that whatever may happen after this, we ought not to be blamed."

Although he may have reprimanded the priest for his part in the parish's troubles, McQuaid did not remove Szadzinski from St. Stanislaus.[22] Parishioners' tempers flared again when the pastor appointed as one of two parish trustees a man whom some considered his personal ally, despite the fact that a group of parishioners had asked him to choose from among several candidates whom they preferred.[23] In retaliation for this and other actions which they considered slights, members of parish societies began removing from St. Stanislaus Church the banners and candlesticks that had been their gifts.[24] In a particularly bold move, some members of the Society of St. Casimir confiscated the impressive banner bearing the likeness of the group's patron saint. Determined that this symbol of St. Stanislaus Church's formation not be taken from the parish, Szadzinski informed city police that the banner had been stolen. After considering accusations from both sides, the exasperated officers stored the banner at precinct headquarters for several days, causing Szadzinski's opponents to declare that the police had arrested St. Casimir and thrown him in jail.

In July 1905, convinced that their demands to remove their pastor were justified but that they would receive no support from McQuaid, dissatisfied parishioners sent a delegation to Cardinal James Gibbons of Baltimore.[25] Gibbons, who had no jurisdiction over the Rochester Diocese, refused to meet with them. Undeterred, the Poles tried twice to meet with Father Jacek Fudzinski, head of the Polish Conventual Franciscans of Buffalo, with the hope of persuading the Franciscans to organize a second Polish church in Rochester.[26] Aware that they had come without the approval of McQuaid, Fudzinski declined to receive the delegation.

Toward the end of August, Father Szadzinski announced the formation of a new parish society, to be called "Our Lady of Perpetual Help," and at Masses on August 20th invited "all the good people" of the parish to attend an organizational meeting that afternoon.[27] Believing that the priest meant to admit to the society only his staunchest supporters, a group of his opponents gathered at the school hall and tried to enter the meeting. Insults were exchanged, fighting broke out, and a call was put in to the Fourth Precinct police, who charged four members of the parish with riot and hustled them off in paddy wagons.

Officers patrolled the Polish section that evening, dispersing groups of people who gathered on streetcorners to share accounts of the afternoon's events. The unsettling day ended with a fifth arrest at the corner of Hudson Avenue and

Kosciusko Street: a Polish resident was led off to the stationhouse, charged with obstructing the sidewalk, after he refused to comply with an officer's order to move along. The police had interfered with the Poles enough for one day, the man declared, then stated defiantly that he intended to stay where he was.[28]

"At midnight," the *Democrat and Chronicle* reported, "the streets in the Polish section were quiet."

Bishop Franciszek Hodur (center) and Father Walenty Gawrychowski (left) with a First Communion class at St. Casimir's Parish, 1911. (Courtesy of Mary Hurysz)

The following week, the Polish community was headlined daily in the local press. "Bunch of Warrants Out for Combative Poles," and "Church Factions in Another Row," the *Democrat and Chronicle* announced. "Polish Catholic Church Row Breaks Out Again," declared the *Herald.* "Police Called in to Quell Disturbance."

From the diocesan chancery, Bernard McQuaid issued his response, in a letter that was to be read at all Masses at St. Stanislaus Church on the following Sunday.[29] He would "no longer be patient," the bishop thundered, "with the misguided parishioners of St. Stanislaus, who by their lawless and barbarous conduct of the past four months have become . . . a cause of blushing shame to every true Catholic in Rochester and in the whole country." McQuaid reiterated his support for Szadzinski, calling the charges against him "calumnious" and "greatly exaggerated." He reminded the Poles that, as their pastor, Szadzinski held the office of parish treasurer according to state law, and affirmed that the priest's financial report "showed correctness and fullness of statement as to receipt and expenditures. The church money was used economically and in accordance with the laws of the diocese. . . ." Regarding the consequences of disorder, the bishop was unequivocal: "Toward all who continue by their turbulent conduct to disturb religious discipline and worship, I will see that the necessary spiritual penalties of excommunication and interdict are applied. Those who do not like the pastor can go elsewhere to church." Concluding the letter, McQuaid expressed exasperation with the Poles' quarreling: "My experience in church affairs goes back to the days when immigrants began to come in large numbers, yet there never was anything to compare with these Polish rows and conflicts."

Before Szadzinski's opponents heard the bishop's words, however, they had taken decisive action of their own. On Wednesday following the school yard arrests, approximately 300 male members of the parish, representing six church societies and the three local lodges of the PNA, met at Zwolinski Hall and voted to establish a parish of their own—within the Roman Catholic church or, if that effort failed, independent of its authority.[30] They also agreed to raise money for the legal defense of those charged with riot and unlawful assemblage in the school yard. Two days later, approximately 250 female parishioners convened at Zwolinski Hall to endorse the action taken by their husbands, fathers, and brothers.

In a final attempt to remain within the Church of Rome, a delegation traveled to Washington, D.C., in March 1906 to appeal to Archbishop Diomede Falconio, apostolic delegate to the United States.[31] Falconio received the group and listened to their argument, but advised them that it would be best to accept the decision of their bishop. In subsequent correspondence with McQuaid, Falconio suggested that it might be "prudent" to give the beleaguered Szadzinski another assignment. Meanwhile, troubles continued at St. Stanislaus, where the refusal of some parishioners to pay pew rent ended in scuffles at the church door.[32]

The long conflict reached its climax in fall 1907, when a delegation of Rochester Poles traveled to Scanton, Pennsylvania, where they were welcomed by Bishop Franciszek Hodur of the Polish National Catholic Church.[33] At the delegates' request, Hodur and Father Walenty Gawrychowski made the journey to Rochester to address a group at Zwolinski Hall on October 15th. Following an emotional meeting during which Hodur spoke of the hardships facing immigrants in America and, according to one eyewitness, "embraced us to his heart as a father his prodigal son," those present swore allegiance to the Polish National Catholic Church. Approximately 150 of the 550 families then registered at St. Stanislaus transferred their loyalty to the new congregation of St. Casimir.[34] Some who had voted in August to form a separate parish stopped short of abandoning Roman Catholicism and remained at St. Stanislaus, frightened of the consequences of excommunication.

Those more determined to follow through with their decision began gathering donations to buy land and build a church. Before the return of Father Gawrychowski, whom Hodur had promised to send as their pastor, St. Casimir's founders collected $3,000 and purchased ten lots at Ernst Street and Hudson Avenue—five blocks south of the site of St. Stanislaus Parish.[35] Additional donations amounting to $1,225 paid for three acres of land north of the city line, to be used as a cemetery.

Szczepan Zielinski's crew began work on the Ernst Street church in spring 1908, completing a two-story brick chapel as well as a rectory the following fall.

New Church of St. Stanislaus under construction, 1909. (Courtesy of the Rochester Diocese)

Ironically, another spire was rising within sight on Hudson Avenue: the 102-foot tower of the new Church of St. Stanislaus. Having outgrown the original wooden structure, Szadzinski and the parish's 2,000 members had contracted with the firm of Gordon and Madden in August 1907, on the eve of the formal departure of those who joined the Polish National Catholic Church.[36]

Inaugural ceremonies for the two churches nearly coincided the following summer. On July 5th, Bishop Thomas F. Hickey, presiding in the absence of an ailing Bernard McQuaid, led a procession north on Hudson Avenue from Holy Redeemer Hall past the site of the Polish National Catholic parish, ending near Norton Street where he blessed St. Stanislaus Church's cornerstone.[37] Hickey's remarks traced the lineage of the Church of Rome to Christ and his Apostles. "I want to tell you, my dear Polish people," he concluded, "that there is only one Catholic Church. . . . And let me remind you that anyone who joins or helps in building up any opposition church becomes thereby excommunicated and will be deprived of Christian burial."

A few weeks later, on August 16th, several hundred members of St. Casimir's Parish gathered at Hudson Avenue and Merrimac Street to follow Bishop Franciszek Hodur in procession to the site of their church.[38] It was a charming scene, the *Herald* reported, as little girls in white carrying flowers and adults in traditional Polish dress marched to Ernst Street, where Hodur blessed the church's cornerstone. The day "brought forth a pageant of bright uniforms and waving banners, and almost all the houses within a radius of seven blocks were decked with the national banners of Poland and America."

Also on hand for the procession were members of the Fourth Precinct police: several bluecoats, four officers on horseback, and one on motorcycle. "This was made necessary," the *Herald* noted, "on account of the factional feeling which exists in this locality. The Polish people are not united in the matter of religion . . . and a demonstration of antagonism which exists between the two bodies of Polish Christians was feared. It did not materialize, but there were many evidences of ill feeling."

The troubles at St. Stanislaus Parish, resolved with the formation of St. Casimir's Church, locked bishop, priest, and people in a conflict of convictions and a battle of wills. For Bernard McQuaid, the overriding issues were the structures of the Roman Catholic Church and the immigrants' obligations to their adopted home. In his work with immigrants, the bishop consistently emphasized his belief that European nationalism should not overshadow their responsibilities as new Americans. As his letter to St. Stanislaus' parishioners demonstrated, he would not condone disobedience to religious or civil authority, and expected members of his diocese to show respect for both.

For Teofil Szadzinski, both his personal reputation and his beliefs about the parish's role in community life were at stake. As his correspondence with McQuaid suggests, he was a conservative man with a conventional view of Church authority, a pastor who took his role as community leader seriously and who distrusted any influence which he considered unorthodox—whether it were a Polish fraternal society outside of his jurisdiction, or the boldness of some

---

parishioners who sought a share in parish management beyond that allowed by Church law.

Ironically, Szadzinski also seems to have been genuinely concerned with the welfare of his parish and, to his credit, continued to carry out his duties at St. Stanislaus despite the type of turmoil that caused Polish priests elsewhere to abandon their posts in desperation. To the families who opposed him, however, Szadzinski's decisions violated their sense of national identity and their understanding of parishioners' rights. In their eyes, his rejection of the Polish National Alliance was a sign of disloyalty, and following that quarrel the pastor drew their mounting anger with each decision that favored the authority of the Church or disregarded their efforts to gain greater lay responsibility at St. Stanislaus.

As was true in other communities, the resolution of Rochester's troubles concluded years of disruption but carried elements of tragedy. For Bernard McQuaid, who died at age 86 six months after the dedication of St. Casimir's Church, his difficulties with the Poles remained the most bitter episode of his forty-year tenure and, as a local historian has written, "the saddest chapter in the history of the Diocese."[39] For Teofil Szadzinski, the secession of one-fourth of his parishioners was a personal blow, an unhappy ending to the long conflict which left him dispirited and in failing health. He became seriously ill a few months after the opening of St. Casimir's Church, and remained in poor health for much of the following year.[40] Szadzinski died within a few weeks of the dedication of his parish's new church in 1909, bedridden at the rectory during the last days of his life and unable to take part in the celebration.

For the immigrant community, the formation of St. Casimir's Parish brought relief from the bitter dispute and a new allegiance for those who had become disillusioned with American Catholicism. In the next decades, Polish families would continue to build a neighborhood on the northeast side, expanding in number and variety their organizations, businesses, and affiliations. At the same time, memories of the quarrel that caused turmoil in the community would remain with members of St. Stanislaus and St. Casimir's parishes, lingering for many years in Polish Town.

Teofil Szadzinski's nephew, Stanislaw Szadzinski, at his uncle's grave, 1909. (Stanislaw, a seminarian at St. Bernard's, was ordained in 1910. Courtesy of Mr. and Mrs. Leo Hoock.)

45

IN COURT:

The Aftermath of the School Yard Brawl

The fate of the Poles arrested as a result of the brawl in St. Stanislaus Parish's school yard held the interest of the Rochester press for several weeks in 1905.[41] In all, a dozen parishioners were arrested on charges of riot, assault, unlawful assemblage, and interfering with police officers: four at the scene of the disturbance on August 20th, one later that evening on Hudson Avenue, and several others during the following days on warrants sworn out by Father Szadzinski.

Press coverage was colorful, tinged with sensationalism and sarcasm as reporters from the local dailies alternately poked fun at the names of Polish witnesses and reminded readers of the particulars of the disturbance. "The warring brethren of St. Stanislaus Polish Catholic Church had a skirmish in Police Court yesterday," one reporter quipped in describing twelve Poles' arraignments on September 8th. "Poles in Court: St. Stanislaus' Church Matters Aired in Public," announced another in a headline above a story that recalled "the now historical occurrences" and "the exciting time of Sunday, August 20."

Reporters covered one trial in detail: the case of the man accused of swearing at and striking Father Szadzinski outside the school hall. Both the prosecution and the defense called a series of witnesses to the stand, some of whose testimony was delivered in Polish and translated by the court interpreter. Witnesses for the prosecution, including five police officers, testified that the defendant had grabbed the pastor by the coat collar, shouted at him, and called on others to beat the priest with a stick. Witnesses for the defense countered that the accused man had been an innocent bystander who had never approached the pastor during the ruckus. The most emotional version of the afternoon's events was offered by a young woman who testified that, when Szadzinski was assailed, she ran forward and put herself between the priest and his attackers.

One question critical to the proceedings was whether or not the defendant was fluent in English. Although police officers maintained that they had heard him shout an English obscenity at Szadzinski, the defense attorney contended that the accused was not well versed in English and could not have uttered the phrase. Rather, the lawyer submitted, his client had been observing the scuffle, standing on the sidelines with his hands in his pockets when he inquired, *Co to ma byc?* ("What's going on here?") Certainly, the defense appealed to the jury, the officers might have mistaken the Polish phrase for the similar-sounding English epithet "son of a bitch."

The jury found the defendant not guilty and the trial, considered the crux of the charges against the Poles, set a precedent for subsequent verdicts. A week later, charges were dropped against ten others accused of unlawful assemblage, and the next month the Grand Jury declined to return indictments for twelve parishioners charged with riot. Only one man was determined to be guilty: the Pole charged with obstructing the sidewalk on the evening after the brawl was convicted and punished with a $5 fine.

4 | Fraternity and Diversity

H. Hylas Wheaton, Rochester secretary of the North American Civic League for Immigrants, visited the city's Polish section in 1911 to observe the Poles' lifestyle and living conditions.[1] According to his calculations, 8,000 Poles lived on the northeast side in an area marked by Norton Street on the north, Central Avenue on the south, North Street on the east, and Clinton Avenue on the west. Approximately one-third of that number (2,400 people) clustered in the north end of the area, in a settlement north of Avenue D that Wheaton termed "exclusively Polish."

The Poles' community demonstrated a "practical unity," Wheaton reported, that allowed its residents to be virtually independent from the rest of the city. He was impressed with the number of Polish organizations, and pleased to find that most of the groups offered families assistance in time of illness, injury, and death. Wheaton also commented upon the line of Polish-owned businesses on Hudson Avenue, counting six groceries, five meat markets, two bakeries, a hardware store, two barber shops, a shoe store, a shoe repair shop, two drug stores, two dance halls, six saloons, a lumberyard, a photographer's studio, and a steamship ticket agency. The neighborhood's services were so comprehensive that one Polish woman who had lived eight years in Rochester admitted to Wheaton that she had visited Main Street only twice since she arrived.

The cohesiveness that Wheaton

This community, sociologically speaking, is autonomous . . . Business is principally transacted in Polish and almost entirely with Polish people, which taken in connection with the fact that the settlement has its own churches, schools and organizations, makes evident the practical unity of the community. Even the real estate is owned almost entirely by residents of the section. It is indeed, from every point of view, a town in itself.

The Common Good of Civic and Social Rochester August 1912

observed in the Polish section reflected the importance that the immigrants attached to maintaining their own neighborhood. Despite the angry words and blows that they had exchanged in the matter of religion, the Poles chose to live together in a settlement structured by their families, parishes, businesses, and societies. This community—a self-enclosed area, comfortable in its routines—weathered the troubles that had shaken it for several years, and exhibited greater evidence of diversity after the formation of St. Casimir's Parish.

One sign of the settlement's expansion and broadening of view was the array of organizations, societies, and fraternals that the immigrants supported after the turn of the century.[2] The determination of PNA Group 216 to organize independently of St. Stanislaus Church had marked the community's growth beyond the

confines of a single parish, the development of a Polonia whose members represented a variety of interests and affiliations. At the time that Wheaton visited, the Polish families' affiliations ranged from Roman Catholicism to socialism, from cultural clubs to athletic teams, from mutual aid associations to alliances formed in the interests of Polish nationalism.

A good number of the community's early organizations were associated with its churches, including approximately a half dozen formed at each of the two Polish parishes before 1910.[3] St. Stanislaus offered the societies of St. Joseph, St. Thaddeus, St. Adalbert, St. Lawrence, St. Stanislaus, Our Lady of Perpetual Help, and Holy Rosary, along with the colorful *Ulani* (Knights) of St. Michael whose members marched in plumed helmets in holy day processions. St. Casimir's Parish provided membership in its own *Ulani,* and in the societies of St. Joseph, St. John the Baptist, and Tadeusz Kosciuszko. The two congregations engaged in a brief tug-of-war for ownership of the Society of St. Casimir, the community's founding organization that held significance for both parishes. The matter appears to have been resolved when a group of charter members who pledged loyalty to National Catholicism transferred the society to St. Casimir's Parish shortly after the congregation was organized.[4]

The Ulani of St. Casimir's Parish. (Courtesy of St. Casimir's Parish Archives)

Other parish groups would form in the next years: choirs for men and women, organizations for children, sodalities for young adults, adoration societies. In general, these organizations were similar in orientation and purpose, intended to stimulate support for the work of the parish, provide opportunities for socializing, and extend sick benefits and life insurance to members. Rules for membership, outlined in a group's charter, were often rigid—limited, for instance, to registered parishioners of Polish descent who were in good health and determined to be living moral lives.[5] In the case of the Society of St. Stanislaus, those admitted to membership were expected to abide by specified standards of behavior: the man who failed to pay his pew rent, neglected to receive the sacraments, or joined an organization that opposed Roman Catholicism would be expelled.

The society's code of behavior extended to its monthly meetings, at which a member could speak if recognized by the president, but was expected to stand respectfully and to make his point in less than ten minutes. Members whose behavior fell below standards paid a fine for the offense: 25 cents for smoking during a meeting; 25 cents for leaving before the closing prayer; 50 cents for failing to attend at least one meeting a year; one dollar for neglecting to take part in the funeral service of a member. Particular recognition was afforded men who served as officers, and the society provided ample opportunity for this distinction. Its constitution outlined responsibilities for a president, a vice president, two secretaries, three financial officers, two marshals, a standard bearer, an alternate to the standard bearer, a sick and vigil committee, and a committee in charge of funeral arrangements.[6]

All members in good standing were entitled to benefit from the group's insurance fund. A man's initiation fee and his monthly dues contributed toward sick pay and, in case of his death, toward payment of his funeral expenses. A member who was out of work because of sickness or injury received a stipend for up to twelve months, provided his illness was not the result of drinking, fighting, or promiscuity. Upon the death of a member, the society presented his widow or heir with a sum to help cover funeral costs, and the members of his fraternity promised to attend the Requiem Mass and march as a unit in the procession. When a member left orphaned children, the organization pledged material support: the society would find the children a place to live, ensure their enrollment at St. Stanislaus School, and provide for each child financially until age 18.

A second natural affiliation, beyond that offered by the parishes, was the immigrants' identification with their native regions in Poland. Families who emigrated to Rochester from Rakow in Russian Poland formed a fraternity for Rakowians in 1915.[7] The group, which included the Anuszkiewicz, Bogdanowicz, Borzdzynski, Lukasiewicz, Okoniewicz, Stec, and Stupkiewicz families, began as a mutual aid society, organized when one of the men from Rakow became ill and was unable to work. His friends convened to take up a collection for his benefit, then agreed to continue meeting as an insurance association and social club. The group elected their first slate of officers in November: Stanislaw Stupkiewicz, president; Julian Anuszkiewicz, vice president; Boleslaw Borzdzynski and Tomasz Bogdanowicz, secretaries; Wincenty Anuszkiewicz, treasurer. Later, men from the district of Chraboly in Russian Poland organized a group, the Chrabolan Society, that included members of the Adamski, Daszkiewicz, Dziengielewski, Kamienski,

Krawiec, Laskowski, and Skuza families.

By the second decade of the century, the factions represented nationally in the Polish National Alliance and the Polish Roman Catholic Union were able to resolve their differences, achieving after years of bitterness a balance between faith and fatherland that opened the way to wider membership in the PNA among Roman Catholic Poles. In Rochester, this balance was affirmed in the organization of a fourth PNA lodge, Group 1020, in 1909.[8] Under the leadership of their president, Wawrzyniec Paluczynski, members chose St. Stanislaus Hall as their meeting place and convened there to organize an insurance program and social activities. The following year, an additional lodge, Group 1145, formed at Markowski Hall (Hudson Avenue and Gilmore Street), its members outlining three objectives in their constitution: promotion of Poland's independence, attainment of American citizenship, and patronage of Polish-owned businesses. The PNA movement expanded to a sixth local lodge in 1910, when a number of women joined to establish Group 1200 (*Cory Polskie,* or Daughters of Poland), and elected Wladyslawa Sosnowska their first president.

Rochester Poles affiliated themselves with a second national fraternal in 1905 when Nest 52 of the Polish Falcons of America (*Sokolstwo Polskie w Ameryce*) held its first meeting at the home of Szczepan Kwiatkowski.[9] Approximately a dozen men gathered for the organizational session: Jan Chrzanowski, Franciszek Chudinski, Wincenty Franc, Stanislaw Klodzinski, Julian Koszalka, Franciszek Kwiatkowski, Jan Naja, Wincenty Okoniewski, Jozef Polacki, Jakub and Michal Rogowski, Jozef Swoszowski, and Wladyslaw Ziebro. The group elected Szczepan Kwiatkowski their first president and, as a signal that they would not set their interest in Polish nationalism against Roman Catholicism, received Father Szadzinski's blessing on their undertaking at a Mass celebrated at St. Stanislaus Church.

Like its parent organization, Nest 52 promoted an attitude of readiness, providing training to young men and women of Polish descent in order to prepare them to serve their homeland.[10] In the physical and moral strength of the individual, the Falcons believed, lay the strength of the Polish nation. Adopting the motto *w zdrowym ciele, zdrowy duch* (a healthy spirit in a healthy body), the Falcons intended to organize a core of patriots who would be ready whenever the war for Poland's liberation began. The group's philosophy of nationalism and personal improvement won a wide following among immigrants, relayed in the activities of nests

Members of Nest 52 of the Polish Falcons exercised at locations like Schuetzen Park. (Courtesy of Mr. and Mrs. Bernard Mysliwiec)

formed in Polish communities throughout the United States and Canada.

Rochester's nest began offering drill instruction for young men shortly after its formation, convening for meetings at Maciejewski Hall and holding exercises at outdoor locations like Schuetzen Park.[11] In 1911, the group added a women's auxiliary and began to plan in earnest to build a *sokolnia,* a gymnasium in which to conduct exercises and drills. None of the settlement's meeting spots, housed for the most part in saloons, offered suitable accommodations, particularly since Nest 52 had decided to extend athletic training to children.

In 1914, after three years of fund-raising, the Falcons purchased two lots on Weyl Street near Hudson Avenue and their women's auxiliary contributed a third. The firm of Marian Wojnowski constructed the clubhouse after Falcon members prepared its foundation, working in teams to excavate the site with shovels and picks. The new hall was dedicated in the presence of distinguished guests: Teofil A. Starzynski, national Falcon president; Jozef Krysztawkiewicz, president of the third Falcon district; George Bingham Draper, a local attorney and former member of the National Guard; and William T. Noonan, an accomplished Rochester athlete.

The Falcon clubhouse became a popular meeting place for the community's young people, who responded enthusiastically to the challenge to ready themselves for service to Poland. Rumors of impending hostilities in Europe heightened interest in the activities of Nest 52, and soon Falcon members were practicing drills in formation, outfitted in the uniforms of the national organization. In 1913, when many residents of Rochester had given little thought to a European war, a band of Falcons had already pledged in writing that they would enter service whenever events summoned them to their homeland's defense.

Concurrent with the formation of Nest 52, a group whose origin could be traced to European political events organized on the southern end of the Polish neighborhood. Members of the Rochester Alliance of Polish Socialists were drawn together in 1905 under Franciszek Kryszewski's leadership.[12] Concerned with restoration of a Polish nation and the welfare of the immigrant community,

Members of Nest 52 in front of their new clubhouse, 1914. (Courtesy of Mr. and Mrs. Bernard Mysliwiec)

the group espoused a doctrine of socialism embraced beginning late in the nineteenth century by Polish nationalists in Europe.

The movement took root among Poles who formed a short-lived workers' organization called *Proletariat* in the Russian-dominated provinces in the 1880s, and a Polish Socialist Party (*Polska Partia Socjalistyczna,* or PPS) based in Warsaw in the next decade.[13] Within a few years, the PPS developed a strongly nationalistic outlook, one that brought its members into disagreement with German and Russian socialists. While the movement in those countries taught that socialism's goal was an international workers' alliance, a brotherhood that would erase political boundaries, the PPS emphasized instead their homeland's future: not world socialism, but the rebirth of Poland as a nation ruled by its people.

Polish People's Library, 1918. (From the Stone Negative Collection of the Rochester Museum and Science Center)

Interest in socialism surfaced among Polish immigrants in North America in the eighties, formalized in the organization of the Polish Socialist Alliance (*Zwiazek Socjalistow Polskich,* or ZSP).[14] The ZSP, affiliated with the PPS, promoted Polish nationalism and workers' rights through the publication of its newspaper *Robotnik Polski* (Polish Worker). Although the ZSP drew the disfavor of Roman Catholic clergy in America because of its opposition to organized religion, the Polish National Catholic Church sought for a time to build kinship with the group, hoping to forge an alliance on behalf of immigrant laborers.[15] Father Walenty Gawrychowski, who would serve as pastor of St. Casimir's Parish beginning in 1908, was among the members of the Polish National Catholic clergy who became active in socialist circles early in the century, speaking at rallies at which he urged immigrants to join the movement for workers' rights.

Rochester's affiliate of the ZSP, formed at the height of the dispute at St. Stanislaus Parish, did not become involved in matters of religion but chose to focus its energies on education.[16] One of the group's first activities was the organization of a small library (*Polska Ludowa Czytelnia,* or Polish People's Library): approximately 200 books and a scattering of periodicals and socialist bulletins, housed in an empty tailor shop on Bernard Street. In October 1911, responding to the popularity of their collection of literature, members purchased a house at 818 Hudson Avenue (south of Avenue D), abandoning the rented shop for their own meeting place and library facilities.[17] Shortly afterward, the organization opened a cooperative grocery and dry goods store, and invested in neighborhood development by establishing a corporation that constructed a score of homes in the vicinity of Weyl Street. The group also sponsored an insurance fraternal (the Polish Workers Sick and Mutual Aid Association) beginning in 1910, and organized a choral group (*Chor Ludowy,* or People's Choir) in 1913.

Chor Ludowy was one of a number of choral groups formed in the Polish settlement early in the century.[18] Beginning in 1909, St. Stanislaus Parish enjoyed the performances of *Gwiazda* (the Star Singing Society), a young girls' choir organized by church organist Franciszek Piorczynski. St. Casimir's Parish initiated a chorus for men in 1912, *Kolo Spiewu Moniuszki* (the Moniuszko Singing Circle), whose first officers included Michal Klosowski, Ludwik Koscielny, Franciszek Drzewiecki, and Maksymilian Szczepanski. Named for the composer of the opera "Halka," the group specialized in performance of traditional Polish hymns, folk songs, and anthems.

An additional chorus, a group that would become one of the most enduring in the community's history, organized modestly in February 1909 when nine men interested in choral lessons gathered at the home of Franciszek Piorczynski.[19] After they had practiced together several times, the group consisting of Jan Chlebowski, Michal Dobosz, Jozef Kuzminski, Michal Lorenc, Ignacy and Kazimierz Pilznienski, Edmund Podgorski, Franciszek Saganski, and Marian Szatkowski presented a

The Star Singing Society with their director, Franciszek Piorczynski. (Courtesy of Mr. and Mrs. Leon Lustyk)

performance at Pulaski Hall under Piorczynski's direction. Pleased with the response, the men agreed to organize formally as a singing society named *Towarzystwo Spiewackie Echo,* elected Kuzminski their first president, and adopted the traditional greeting *Gora Piesn* as their slogan. By the end of the year, the group approved a constitution, admitted eight new members, performed twice more publicly, and reported profits of $27 in their treasury.[20]

In addition to presenting their own concerts, the men of the Echo choir were soon invited to perform at gatherings and celebrations organized by other community groups. In 1910, members sang in a program that the local PNA lodges arranged to commemorate Poland's 1866 uprising. In 1911, the choir began a tradition that would continue for the next six decades when the men performed

The Echo Singing Association, 1917. (Courtesy of Mr. and Mrs. Edward Skiba and the Echo Singing Association)

at Midnight Mass on Christmas Eve at St. Stanislaus Church. Within a few years, the group's popularity spread beyond the neighborhood and its members received invitations to represent Polonia at civic events, such as the 1916 Shakespearean festival hosted by the Chamber of Commerce.

The Echo choir often combined musical performances with theatrical presentations, for the most part Polish language plays which drew an audience from the neighborhood. Although one early dramatic performance resulted in a net loss of $1.75, the club soon realized a profit from the shows, presented beginning in 1915 on the stage at Falcon Hall. Over time, the society accumulated a library of sheet music and Polish language scripts, along with a wardrobe of costumes designed and fashioned by members' wives.

Soon functioning as a social club as well as a choral group, the Echo society organized events such as an annual ball open to others in the community, and sponsored a variety of gatherings for members' families: picnics at Schuetzen Park and May Walks to the rifle range, *oplatki* during the Christmas season, yearly clam bakes. In 1912, members affirmed the ties of their fraternity when they approved a motion committing the chorus to sing in church at all weddings and funerals of Echo members. The men had their first opportunity to act upon this decision in 1915, when member Jozef Kowalski married Katarzyna Kuliberda in services at St. Stanislaus Church.

While the majority of the community's organizations emphasized interest in Poland's traditions, at least one presented an American point of view. Among the most colorful of the neighborhood's groups, a baseball nine named the Hudson Stars assembled in 1902 to compete against teams from other parts of the city. The Stars took their place in neighborhood lore in 1903, the year when they won 35 of their 36 games and defeated an East Rochester team 35 to 0, spurred on by Charles Budny who "batted with such superlative zeal that the ball disappeared completely and was never found thereafter."[21] Franciszek Paprocki, captain of the team that winning season, went on to pitch for the Baltimore Orioles in the International League in 1912, returning to Rochester after he injured his arm to join the Premiers of the City League.

In the second decade of the century, another religion established a following in the Polish neighborhood, providing additional testimony to the diversity of the immigrants' settlement. Christ Polish Baptist Church began as a missionary movement in the Polish section in 1910, within a few years of the turmoil that preceded formation of St. Casimir's Parish.[22] The effort to bring the creed of the Baptists to local Polish families was headed by the Reverend Ludwik Adamus, a native of Galicia who was completing studies in the German Department of the Rochester Theological Seminary. The parish that he founded in Rochester would become one of only fourteen Polish Baptist congregations in America, and his small group of converts would be numbered among approximately 1,400 Polish immigrants of the Baptist faith.

Wedding portrait of Jozef Kowalski and Katarzyna Kuliberda, 1915. (Courtesy of Teresa Kierecki)

Baptist missionaries worked diligently to spread their faith in the United States during the nineteenth and early twentieth centuries, led by their conviction that the nation's vitality was directly linked with Protestant Christianity.[23] Emissaries of Baptism carried their beliefs to western pioneers, Native Americans, and southern Blacks, and initiated outreach work among Welsh immigrants beginning in the 1830s. Later in the century, after enjoying success among Protestant German and Scandinavian immigrants, the Baptist Home Mission Society took on the challenge of evangelizing among Catholic immigrants from Eastern Europe.

The German Department of the Rochester Theological Seminary, where Adamus studied, was the most important training center for German Baptist ministers in North America. Founded by Augustus Rauschenbusch in 1858, the program had prepared 500 men to serve as Baptist preachers by 1924.[24] All but 31 of the 224 ministers assigned to German Baptist churches in the United States and Canada that year had received their theological training at the Rochester seminary.

Equally as important as the number of ministers that the school prepared was its decision to encourage them to preach the gospel to German immigrants in their own tongue. Although some English-speaking Baptists disapproved of the practice, use of the immigrants' language enabled the German Baptist Conference to organize 284 churches serving almost 32,000 members by the early twenties. "We do not so much wish to perpetuate the German tongue in America as we wish to perpetuate American ideas by means of the German tongue," Professor Herman Schaeffer of the Rochester seminary assured the Home Mission Society in 1882. Assimilation into American life, Schaeffer and other German Baptist leaders maintained, would follow as immigrants embraced the teachings of the Baptist faith.

The Rochester seminary's emphasis on native language preaching set the pattern for Baptist missionary work among other immigrant groups. Often, it was a German minister who first carried Baptist teachings into a settlement of Swedes, Hungarians, Bohemians, or Poles, working with a group of converts until a minister of their own nationality was ordained. These efforts resulted in a following among Swedes, Norwegians, and Danes, but the task was much harder and the number of converts much smaller among immigrants from Eastern Europe. Approximately 32,000 Germans, 31,000 Swedes, and 4,000 Norwegians were included among American Baptists in the twenties, overshadowing 1,800 Bohemians, 1,600 Hungarians, 1,400 Poles, and 500 Rumanians.[25]

The Baptists extended their first outreach to Poles among immigrants in Detroit in 1888, and followed this with missionary work in Buffalo in 1891. Aware of the religious quarrel that troubled Polish settlements, the Home Mission Society expected that its work among Poles would prove fruitful, that a large number of those who renounced Roman Catholicism would join the Baptist Church. The pull of nationalism, however, proved stronger than the message of Baptism: by the twenties, Franciszek Hodur's National Catholic Church had won the loyalty of twenty times as many Polish immigrants as had the Home Mission Society.[26]

Interior of Christ Polish Baptist Church. (From the Stone Negative Collection of the Rochester Museum and Science Center)

The hope of bringing the Baptist faith to disenchanted Roman Catholic Poles may have inspired Ludwik Adamus to begin preaching in Rochester's Polish neighborhood. In the wake of the dispute that led to the formation of St. Casimir's Parish, Adamus organized Baptist services in a home on Weddale Way and took up residence on Durnan Street with Antoni Maslanka, one of his followers.[27] Encouraged by reports of his work, the Monroe Baptist Association helped Adamus purchase a corner lot at Hudson Avenue and Weddale Way, and constructed a small building to house the Polish Baptist Mission in 1911. Two years later, the thirty members of the Polish mission were recognized as a congregation, and in 1916 the group was admitted to the Monroe Baptist Association:

> Our church is the only Protestant church among 12,000 Polish inhabitants living in the northern part of the city. Its attendants are almost all Catholic converts. In 1910, when Pastor Adamus began work, there were no members. The church was organized with thirty members October 5, 1913, and duly recognized by a Council as a Baptist church. The membership is gradually growing; now it is forty. Services are well attended, strangers are interested. Outlook is encouraging. We apply for admission into this Association.[28]

Under the leadership of Adamus, the small mission continued its work of bringing the Baptist faith to Rochester's Poles. Church services were conducted in

Polish and English, and a Sunday Bible School was opened for all interested neighborhood children. Young people who had studied the faith and chose to enter the congregation were baptized by full immersion in a huge font constructed on the altar at the front of the church.[29] Plain in design compared to the neighborhood's two other churches, the building on Weddale Way featured white walls, an oak-beamed ceiling, and windows tinged in amber, green, and blue. A single cross marked the altar at the church's front, rimmed with potted palms in wicker baskets. A choir loft extended over the baptismal font, which could be concealed behind sliding doors when it was not in use.

After the church was completed, parishioners prepared a residence for their pastor, constructed and furnished with the financial assistance of the Monroe Baptist Association. Members of the congregation contributed as they could toward the parish's programs and the maintenance of its property. "We [have] paid all current and mission expenses (amounting to $246.85) except the pastor's salary," Adamus reported to the association in 1917. "Have a large and difficult field to work, and are trying to do our best."[30]

Beyond extending its financial support, the association took an active interest in the spiritual work of the Polish mission. Leading members of the association often visited the church for Sunday assemblies, and the Poles were invited to attend weekly services at the Baptist Temple. Members of the Lake Avenue Baptist Church established a close relationship with the Polish mission, sending lay workers to Weddale Way to help organize youth groups, Bible classes, and church societies, and including the Poles in functions held at their parish west of the river.

Adamus served as pastor of Christ Polish Baptist Church until 1918, when he left Rochester to become an instructor at the National Slavic Training School in Chicago.[31] He was succeeded by Ryszard S. Lesik, a native of Warsaw and a graduate of the Slavic Training School who emphasized evangelical work among the neighborhood's young residents. "[We] have concentrated efforts on adolescent boys and girls," Lesik indicated in one annual report in which he observed that attendance in the Sunday School had grown larger than membership in the church.[32] "Our services are fairly well attended," he noted in another year. "We are conscious of our part among the Polish people here, and trust that God will bless us with the fruits of our work."

Christ Polish Baptist Church

"One fact is worthy of note," H. Hylas Wheaton wrote in 1912 after his visit to the Polish neighborhood.[33] "No mention of any Polish organization or society is made in the city directory, notwithstanding the fact that other nationalities are well represented therein. This, of course, only further reflects the ignorance on the part of Americans specially of the existence of the Polish section and of its life and activities."

Wheaton's observations about the

Polish community were presented in two installments of *The Common Good of Civic and Social Rochester,* a monthly publication devoted to discussion of social issues such as labor, poverty, health, and child welfare.[34] Organized by a group of social workers, teachers, and ministers interested in civic reform, *Common Good* focused its articles on problems that beset urban areas early in the century: exploitation of factory laborers, including women and children; health and sanitation in overcrowded tenements and slums; diseases such as smallpox and tuberculosis. Because these problems often affected the country's immigrants, *Common Good* took particular interest in Rochester's immigrant communities and frequently published articles describing the conditions under which they worked and ways of life in their settlements. In doing so, its publishers intended to build understanding and respect for newcomers, counter prejudice against them, and arouse public sympathy for difficulties that they faced.

In his study of the Polish section, H. Hylas Wheaton admired the enterprise that the immigrants had shown in organizing a settlement that he described as "self-sustaining . . . a town in itself," complete with churches, homes, businesses, a school, and organizations.[35] He credited the Poles with providing aid to each other through the work of societies "which enable them to care for members in case of illness, death, injury, or distress." He praised a recently formed Polish businessmen's association that, in his opinion, promised "to become a most valuable asset to the community. . . . Having the most prominent Polish business men and citizens as members, it will be able to wield an influence for local betterment."

These compliments aside, the local secretary of the North American Civic League for Immigrants was sharply critical of the Poles and maintained that their remoteness from the city proper deterred their assimilation. In Wheaton's view, four qualities impeded the Poles' entry into the mainstream of local life. "In the first place," he wrote, "practically all of them have an abnormally developed sense of nationality. Their greatest hope is some day to possess a Poland." The second difficulty, Wheaton believed, was the Poles' reliance on their own language. "To reach the Pole, you must speak his language, and he only learns yours when compelled by necessity." The third deterrent was "the attitude of suspicion" with which Wheaton claimed the Poles viewed persons from outside their community. "They carry the air of expecting to be exploited by every stranger who approaches." Finally, the civic league secretary charged that the Poles had a "tendency . . . to commit crimes against property, such as larceny, thievery, etc. . . . Any criminal trait, of course, being opposed to law and order, is an obstacle in the way of declaring allegiance to a government."

Among his observations, Wheaton criticized the immigrants from Austrian and Russian Poland, stating that the German Poles were "the most desirable and possess the most readily assimilative elements." He expressed dismay at "the presence of so many saloons" in the settlement: "Of these, there are no less than six within two short blocks. . . . All of these places sell a low grade of beer and liquor." Houses were overcrowded, he felt, inhabited by large families and sometimes subdivided into more than one household.

The women who cared for these households lacked knowledge "of many important facts," Wheaton stated after conducting a survey of fifteen Polish housewives. Only ten of the fifteen could tell him the location of the nearest public school, seven could provide directions to the courthouse, five could describe the route to city hall, and two knew how to contact the commissioner of charities. Two women refused to answer Wheaton's questions entirely, and none in the group could tell him the name of Rochester's mayor—a "most remarkable thing," the civic league secretary commented.

Wheaton's unflattering portrayal of the immigrants' community was vehemently protested by Ludwik Adamus. In a letter to the editor of *Common Good*, the pastor of the Polish Baptist Church refuted the civic league secretary's view of Austrian and Russian Poles, denied that the settlement's houses were overcrowded, and stated that the immigrants desired to learn English, often paying tutors to help them acquire the language.[36] "They are very cordial towards strangers," he countered, "and . . . have no greater tendency towards crime than other nationalities." Stating that the Polish newcomers wanted to be considered part of Rochester, Adamus challenged the civic league to help the immigrants "by co-operation rather than criticism."

Wheaton's view of the Poles was also called into question by the Reverend Edwin Rumball, minister at the First Unitarian Church and editor of *Common Good*. In a discussion of Rochester's ethnic communities published near the time of Wheaton's study, Rumball reminded readers that the Poles had "carried for many decades the tragedy of a lost land. . . . We count the Irish a nation equally with the English, but we do not count the Poles equally with the Germans or the Russians.

A view of Hudson Avenue, looking north from Sobieski Street, 1913. (From the photo collection of the Local History Division, Rochester Public Library)

. . . It is one of the pities that America should emphasize in any way their loss."[37] Regarding the Poles' character, the minister wrote:

> They work on our roads and in our factories like other immigrants and judging from the Rochester men and women of this race that we know and from the sight of the streets and houses where they live, they form one of the most desirable of the newcomers that we have. In cities like Buffalo where they have long been residential, they have made a valuable place for themselves in the community and their members hold places in all the professions and positions of esteem in the city. This is undoubtedly what Rochester can expect from the few thousand who have come to us to help us realize in America a land of freedom and light.

Other Rochesterians' opinions did little to disturb the way of life in the Polish section, home by 1912 to several thousand immigrants and their children. In the years after Wheaton's visit, the Polish families' view would turn more intensely inward as Polonia's preoccupation with events in Europe increased. The battle of powers that loomed on the continent signaled an opportunity for Poles, a moment when they could act upon what Wheaton had recognized as their greatest hope.

The Hudson Stars, the first baseball team in the Polish settlement.

The mutual aid that the immigrants received from their organizations did not mitigate the type of disaster that struck the Polish settlement on May 2, 1913.[38] One of the largest fires in the city's history blazed for more than twelve hours at Szczepan Zielinski's lumberyard, destroying $200,000 worth of the contractor's property along with six Peckham Street homes.

The blaze began in the planing mill on Zielinski's fifteen-acre lumberyard, which spanned a city block at Hudson Avenue near Peckham Street. Sparks from an overheated motor used to drive machinery in the mill ignited the fire at 2:00 p.m., and flames spread quickly to the garage where Zielinski stored his automobile and a supply of gasoline. The explosion that followed scattered sparks to a shaving shed, lumber sheds, carpenter shop, tin shop, and stables. By the time firefighters arrived, summoned by alarms rung frantically from every firebox in the neighborhood, the blaze had jumped to the homes on Peckham Street.

While firefighters pumped water on the flames and smoke billowing upward for 200 feet, women who resided in the threatened homes led their children across the street to safety, then ran back to salvage what they could of their belongings. Boys poured water on the burning homes with garden hoses, an initiative that firefighters later acknowledged kept the blaze from spreading to south Peckham Street. So much smoke and flame clouded the air that residents feared St. Stanislaus Church was also ablaze, but to parishioners' relief the church and its property escaped undamaged. As the first flames crossed the lumberyard, several men had climbed into the tower and, stationed there, diligently doused any sparks that fell on the steeple.

When fire crews finally calmed the blaze in the early hours of the morning, Zielinski's property lay in ruins. The man reputed to be the wealthiest in the Polish section had lost his sheds, mill, garage, stables, shaving bin, thirty wagons, and an estimated fifty million feet of lumber. No lives were lost, but five firefighters suffered injuries and six families from Peckham Street were left homeless.

Zielinski's insurance covered $35,000 of the $200,000 in damages that his firm sustained, and he was able to rebuild his company in the next years. The families who had lived on Peckham Street were less fortunate. Only the week before the fire, two of them had tried to buy homeowner's insurance but were unable to pay the high rates quoted for houses near the lumberyard. Ironically, the *Herald* ran a notice regarding insurance on May 3rd, beneath an article and photographs that depicted the fire: "Dutton's insurance office in the Wilder Building cheerfully advises with insurers as to the best manner of arranging their fines; any insurance placed with this office is a guarantee of absolute protection and prompt, satisfactory settlement in case of loss."

5 | Under the Ancient Polish Flag

1831

1863

1917

A full year before an assassination sparked the outbreak of World War I, young Polish men were training for battle outside Rochester's city limits.[1] Dressed in surplus army fatigues and toting heavy rifles, the recruits drilled and practiced maneuvers on suburban land owned by Polish farmers. As war threatened in Europe, the field drills continued, not only in Rochester but in Falcon units across the United States, and a charge went out to all nests from the national headquarters: "Wait, be on guard, and train."

For Poles in Rochester, as for Polish immigrants throughout America, the First World War would be fought not only to "end all wars," but also to end—forever, Poles believed—their homeland's subjugation to foreign regimes. Although Poland had been wiped from the map of Europe, divided among neighboring powers at the end of the eighteenth century, the dream of her liberation survived throughout the decades of partition.[2] Poland would rise to new life, new stature among nations, nineteenth-century writers like Adam Mickie-

wicz foretold, at the close of a great war that would draw many countries of the world into battle. Other poets and novelists echoed Mickiewicz's theme of their homeland's rebirth, while in the partitioned provinces bands of patriots staged several ill-fated insurrections (1830, 1848, 1863). These unsuccessful attempts to spark revolution scattered Polish nationalists across Europe and to the United States where, armed with Mickiewicz's prophecies, many continued to plan for the day when they would rally again beneath the standard of the Polish White Eagle.

To nationalists and patriots-in-exile, Poles who had immigrated to North America represented a force that would be of great service at the hour of their homeland's rebirth.[3] As the number of Poles in the United States increased, messages from Europe were published in America's Polish language newspapers, urging those who had emigrated not to forget their *ojczyzna,* the land from which they had come. *"Jeszcze Polska nie zginela poki my zyjemy* ... Poland shall not perish while we live to love

The Poles of Rochester were not found wanting when the "Knight Among the Nations" called upon her children, scattered to the four corners of the globe, to help re-establish the nationality of the motherland, restore the ancient glories of the land of Thaddeus Kosciusko and the Great Yagellons, and resume her traditional duty of defending Christendom from the barbarians from the East.

Post Express
Rochester, New York
July 9, 1920

her," immigrants sang in response in churches and meeting halls where they gathered to commemorate the unsuccessful insurrections. Their organizations embraced and amplified the theme: the Polish National Alliance, formed to preserve the immigrants' ties with their heritage; the Polish Falcons, whose drilling and gymnastics thinly disguised paramilitary purposes; choral societies, which often ended their performances with a round of anthems and marches. Although the spirit of nationalism grew so intense that it bred division in immigrant neighborhoods at the close of the nineteenth century, by 1914 the factions represented by the Polish National Alliance and the Polish Roman Catholic Union had achieved cordial relations, both acting to support Poland's cause when the Great War began.[4]

Preparations for the war to free Poland were underway among Poles in the United States shortly after the turn of the century. As early as 1907, three Polish immigrant organizations sponsored paramilitary training for young men: the Polish Army *(Wojsko Polskie)*, the Union of Polish Youth *(Zwiazek Mlodziezy Polskiej)*, and the Polish Falcons.[5] The maneuvers and campaigns which these groups staged were so exuberant that, in at least two skirmishes, participants were wounded and required medical treatment. Beginning in 1912, the Falcons introduced more extensive training for the drill instructors of local nests. That year, 45 young Falcons participated in the organization's first military training program at St. John's College in Philadelphia: a four-week session covering military theory and practice, Polish history, and first aid. Two years later, the Falcons expanded their military program to include an eight-month officer training course held at Polish National Alliance College in Cambridge Springs, Pennsylvania. This session, which emphasized scouting, military science, and physical training, culminated in a 38-mile march from Cambridge Springs to Erie. Proud of the prowess shown by his troops, Teofil Starzynski, national Falcon president, contacted the War Department to suggest that the Falcons might be of service in America's border dispute with Mexico. The War Department politely refused Starzynski's offer, indicating that the country would rely on the National Guard.

Fund-raising to support Polish forces in the event of an insurrection also began several years before the start of the war.[6] The outbreak of the Balkan Wars in 1912, which threatened general war in Europe, accelerated activity among nationalists like Jozef Pilsudski, who organized paramilitary units based in Galicia and initiated formation of a Polish War Treasury. In the United States, the Falcons responded to the treasury's appeal for support by calling a meeting of all Polish American organizations in December. The Committee for National Defense (*Komitet Obrony Narodowej,* or KON) was organized at this meeting to oversee a network of local fund-raising groups. Although the KON suffered from internal bickering—chiefly between Roman Catholics and socialists—it represented the first nationwide attempt to channel contributions from American Polonia to Poland.

No matter how crucial the fate of Poland seemed to the Poles, their homeland figured little in the events that led to the outbreak of the war. In the first weeks of August 1914, world attention focused on the movements made by Europe's major powers: Austria, Germany, Russia, Britain, France. All but lost in the turmoil as the huge armies mobilized was the appearance of a Polish brigade, 180 men who advanced into the Russian-ruled area of Poland under Pilsudski's leadership on August 6th.[7] This offensive on the part of Pilsudski's recruits marked the first step in military action that Poles believed would return their homeland to prominence in Europe.

Although Pilsudski had been bold enough to move against Russia, Polish nationalists disagreed among themselves regarding the course of action they should take. The Great War had pitted two of Poland's conquerors—Austria and Germany—against the third. Various committees and councils-in-exile declared themselves the voice of the new Poland, and cast their lots with either the Central Powers or the Western Allies.[8] For their part, each of Poland's ruling powers quickly conscripted Poles within their borders, and attempted to win the nationalists' loyalties with promises of independence. "Poles!" Russia's Grand Duke Nicholas proclaimed publicly two weeks into the war. "The hour has struck in which the sacred dream of your fathers and forefathers will be realized . . . May the Poles in Russia unite themselves under the sceptre of the Russian Tsar! Under this sceptre Poland shall be re-born, free in faith, in language, in self-government. . . . With friendly feelings and cordially-outstretched hands, the Great Russian Empire steps forward to meet you."[9] In Germany, General Ludendorff planned a similar strategy: "My eye turns again to the Poles. . . . The Pole is a good soldier. Let us create a Grand Duchy of Poland and immediately after a Polish Army under German command."[10]

The dilemma of which side to choose was particularly disturbing for American Poles, who for the most part were split politically into two camps: those who believed in alliance with Austria, and those who favored support for Russia and the Western Allies. In 1914, however, the United States government had no intention of becoming involved in European politics. Although Americans followed the course of the war with interest in the press, there was no movement initially to commit United States forces to the conflict, and certainly no rallying around the cause of Polish independence. Frustrated, the Falcons watched a few of their members break rank to join the Polish forces being organized in Europe: Pilsudski's Austrian-based legion, other Polish contingents in the armies of the Central Powers, or the "Pulawy Legion" fighting for the Russian Tsar. As the war continued and the United States retained its neutrality, the Falcons began clandestine negotiations with the Canadian Army, hoping to form a legion of immigrant Poles beyond the United States border.[11] The Canadian government agreed to undertake the training of Polish officers, and in January 1917 American Falcons began to cross the border to begin their military preparation on the University of Toronto campus.

Although the United States' neutrality curtailed mobilization of the American Falcons, it did not dampen fund-raising for the Polish cause. Shortly after fighting began in Europe, American Polonia made a second attempt to join the energies of all its organizations, forming a Polish Central Relief Committee in America (*Polski Centralny Komitet Ratunkowy w Ameryce,* or PCKR) in competition with the pro-Austrian KON.[12] The Central Committee allied itself with two organizations based in Europe: initially, with the General Assistance Committee (founded in

Switzerland by novelist Henryk Sienkiewicz and pianist Ignacy Paderewski), and later with the National Committee (headed in Paris by Roman Dmowski, a leading nationalist who favored cooperation with Russia and the Western Allies). As a unifying force in Polonia, the Central Committee proved immensely successful. From 1914 through the end of the war, it garnered the support of the major Polish American organizations, and expanded its focus beyond raising money for war relief. In 1916, the Central Committee created a National Department (*Wydzial Narodowy,* or WN) which undertook additional activities to further the cause of Poland's independence: chiefly, a press campaign to spread information about the homeland to both Polish and English language newspapers; lobbying in government circles to gain American support for the Polish cause; and, when the United States finally entered the war, coordination of immigrant recruitment for the Polish Army in France.

In 1915, the Central Committee received support from an international figure who arrived from Europe to stir American sympathy for the Polish cause. Paderewski, the renowned concert pianist, launched a one-man campaign that in three years took him across the country and to every state several times, championing Poland's case for independence while raising money for relief of the areas torn by warfare on the eastern front.[13] In speeches delivered before thousands of Americans, the man who had written a symphony commemorating the 1863 uprising outlined his position in simple language: "I am a Pole, a faithful son of the fatherland. The thought of a strong and great Poland, free and independent, was and is the theme of my existence; its realization was and is the one goal of my life." His emotional appeals, which included an overview of Polish history, closed with reference to the bond between Poland and the United States:

> If I have succeeded, pray speak about Poland to your kind, good friends. Tell them that far away from your prosperous, opulent, happy country there are great people in great poverty, in great need, suffering beyond the limit of human endurance. Tell them that these very people in the days of your need sent you Kosciuszko, offered you Pulaski, and not for the pleasure of fighting the English, but for the noble joy of contributing to the glorious conquest of human liberty.[14]

Paderewski's campaign extended its influence to the White House beginning in 1916, when the musician developed a friendship with Colonel Edward House, President Woodrow Wilson's close personal advisor.[15] Wilson had already demonstrated public sympathy for Poland, proclaiming New Year's Day 1916 "Polish Day" in the United States and encouraging donations to Paderewski's relief fund. With Colonel House on his side, Paderewski increased his access to the president and, in January 1917, House asked Paderewski to draft a memorandum on Poland for Wilson, who was preparing an address for delivery to the Senate.[16] In that address, in which he discussed the war and outlined acceptable terms for peace, Wilson also spoke directly on behalf of Polish independence: "I take it for granted . . . that statesmen everywhere are agreed that there should be a united, independent, and autonomous Poland. . . ." Three months later, when Congress adopted

Wilson's resolution of war against Germany, Paderewski was in Pennsylvania at the Polish Falcons' national convention, calling for the organization of an "army of Kosciuszko" to fight alongside the American and Allied forces. The Falcons, who had waited since the first signs of war to mobilize, overwhelmingly adopted the motion and, after winning approval from the War Department in October 1917, officially began recruitment for an army of Polish American volunteers under the direction of the Polish Military Commission.[17]

At stations set up in the country's Polish American communities, the Falcons enlisted 24,000 American Poles for service in General Jozef Haller's "Blue Army," a force being organized in France with the intention of leading Poland's liberation.[18] Poles from America, who trained at camps in eastern Canada and Fort Niagara, New York, comprised one-fourth of Haller's force of 100,000 men. At the same time, Polish Americans responded to Woodrow Wilson's call for volunteers to the United States forces. Although they made up only 3.2 percent of the country's population in 1917, Poles accounted for 40,000 of the first 100,000 volunteers for American service.[19] From the largest immigrant settlements to the smallest, the fervor to serve was the same. In Illinois, at least 8,000 of 12,000 men who registered with the Chicago Commons draft board were of Polish descent, while in South Bend, Indiana, 94 of the first 100 men who volunteered for service were Poles.

Paramilitary training for Rochester's Polish men began as early as 1913, under sponsorship of the local nest of the Polish Falcons.[20] Nest 52's troops engaged in field maneuvers on suburban farmland, brandishing ponderous carbines left over from the Spanish-American War. Although no shots were fired, those taking part in the training sessions learned the rudiments of loading, unloading, and cleaning their weapons. That the field exercises were not idle amusements was verified in a written agreement signed by 24 of the Falcons: they would be ready to serve, the young men pledged, whenever the call to battle would come.

Fund-raising for Poland's defense, like the Falcons' preliminary military training, also began in Rochester before the start of the war. Rochester Poles organized a local chapter of the KON after the convention that launched the national group in 1912.[21] Like chapters in settlements across the country, the Rochester committee planned to coordinate collection of funds in anticipation of the next insurrection. After war broke out in 1914, however, bringing Germany and Russia to battle in the Polish provinces, the focus of local fund-raising shifted from Poland's defense to humanitarian relief for Poles left homeless or injured in the wake of the conflict. One campaign for donations, launched in June 1915, extended beyond Polish Town when an appeal to the larger Rochester community was printed in the *Union and Advertiser:*

> We, the Poles of Rochester, appeal to you for help for the follow-
> ing cause:
> The terrible predicament into which Poland has been thrown
> through the war now raging in Europe only begins to be known in
> America. Only recently, through the efforts of such men as

On pages 68 and 69: Nest 52 of the Polish Falcons of America, 1912. (Courtesy of Mr. and Mrs. John B. Stenclik)

H. Sienkiewicz and I. J. Paderewski, as well as of several Americans that visited Poland, the world has become acquainted with unspeakable suffering to which peaceful Poland has been thrown. The civilian population has been deprived of shelter and of all means of subsistence.

The people of Poland are dying from hunger and cold through no fault of their own. Help—and quick help—is an absolute necessity. Therefore we, the Polish Central Committee of National Defense, appeal to you, fellow citizens, to help us, the Americans of Polish descent, to feed and clothe our unfortunate brethren in Poland.

All contributions may be sent to Mrs. S. Karger, 273 Weyl Street, Rochester, N.Y. The money received will be deposited in the Union Trust Company and later forwarded to the general committee in Chicago, to use with all other money collected for such purposes.[22]

By 1916, the work of the local KON had been transferred to a Rochester chapter of the Polish Central Relief Committee, the group affiliated with Paderewski's campaign for Polish relief.[23] The relief committee took charge of fund-raising in Rochester's Polonia and had accumulated donations totaling approximately $1,000 by November 1916, the month Paderewski was scheduled to appear in concert at Convention Hall.[24] Delighted at the opportunity to present Rochester's donations to the pianist personally, the committee sent a delegation backstage on the day of the recital. This reception committee, which included Stanislaw Dukat, Adam Felerski, Stanislaw K. Kowalski, Ludwik Kubiak, Adam Norwich, and Maksymilian Sosnowski, handed Paderewski "a substantial purse" as he left the stage after performing selections from Bach, Beethoven, Chopin, and Liszt. The pianist thanked the group for their gift "very profusely, saying that it made him very happy to see that the local committee were doing what they could for their war-stricken brethren in Poland." A concert review printed the next day in the *Post Express* praised both Paderewski's performance and his work on behalf of his homeland: "Paderewski's patriotism is as sincere as his art, and he is a fine type of his nation which has never lacked plenty of genius and courage amid its years of political subserviency."

Poland needs the help of her sons, Captain Jan Zebrowski told the young men. General Haller will lead us from France in the fight for Poland's liberation.[25]

Zebrowski, a Polish Army officer assigned to the recruiting station in Buffalo, delivered a stirring address to the Falcons of Nest 52. It was spring 1917, and the United States had entered the war against Germany, paving the way, Polish patriots believed, for the immediate mobilization of American Poles. The fact that the United States War Department had not yet recognized their battalions did not deter Zebrowski and other recruiters, who made the rounds of Polish Falcon nests seeking volunteers for the "army of Kosciuszko."

After his talk, Zebrowski mingled with the young men in the hall, drawing a few of them aside for private conversation. There is no need to wait; we are enlisting men now, he told Jan (John) Pospula and Wladyslaw Czaban, urging the two to depart with him that evening. They would be trained as officers at Polish National Alliance College in Pennsylvania, then travel north to join other Polish soldiers in Canada. They would need to leave immediately, he cautioned, without a word to family or friends.

Pospula and Czaban were stirred by the captain's message and, although they declined his offer to depart immediately, promised that they would enlist in their homeland's service soon. Pospula, then 23 years old, had come to America six years earlier, arriving in Rochester to join his brother who had settled on Bernard Street. John was one of six children whose widowed mother owned less than an acre of land in Galicia, where prospects for the young man's future had been bleak. In America you can find work, his brother wrote from Rochester, encouraging John to make the voyage despite his initial misgivings. The most vivid impressions Pospula had of the United States were drawn from his reading of *Uncle Tom's Cabin,* given to him in Polish translation by his parish priest. He was horrified by the story of Eliza, a young woman who fled desperately across a frozen river from those who held her family in slavery. With some trepidation, John said goodbye to his mother and made his way to Hamburg, carrying a small suitcase and a *pierzyna* (down-filled comforter). From Hamburg, he sailed in steerage along with men and women from Hungary and Czechoslovakia, and like many others became deathly seasick a few days into the voyage. When the ship finally docked in New York harbor, John had lost track of his suitcase and his shoes, and walked onto Ellis Island in slippers with his *pierzyna* tucked under one arm.

On Ellis Island, Pospula was able to buy a new pair of shoes before immigration officials completed his review and directed him to a train headed north. After passing through several other cities he arrived in Rochester, on a May afternoon in 1911 which he would long recall for its glorious weather. He boarded with his brother and sister-in-law on Bernard Street, looking for work and, in his spare time, studying English by learning to read neighborhood signs. John was hired before long in a clothing firm owned by a Jewish tailor who spoke Polish, and at his brother's urging joined the local nest of the Polish Falcons. That was a turning point for Pospula, for whom the Falcons provided camaraderie, kinship, and the opportunity to meet other young Polish people.

His involvement in the activities of Nest 52 also provided him with patriotic expression, and John listened intently to Captain Zebrowski's call for recruits in spring 1917. That June, four months before the United States government recognized General Haller's "Blue Army," Pospula and his friend Wladyslaw Czaban became two of the first five local Polish men to depart for military training in Cambridge Springs. They joined Tadeusz Gedgowd, who had enlisted in March, and two others: Wincenty Bancer and Wladyslaw Stugiewicz.[26]

In Cambridge Springs, on the campus

Members of Nest 52 engaged in field maneuvers.

of Alliance College, Pospula and Czaban studied with other young men from Polish American settlements. Toting heavy rifles as they had during their excursions with the Falcons in Rochester, the two began training in the cadet corps under the command of Poles who had served in the Austrian Army. Discipline was strict, and lessons focused primarily on military theory and officer conduct. Toward the end of the session, the recruits completed a written examination, after which those who had passed were told they had three days to put their affairs in order at home. On the fourth day, they would cross the border to continue their preparation in Canada.

Pospula and Czaban were stationed briefly in Toronto then transferred to Camp Borden, where they pitched their tents among other Polish Army recruits. The Canadian officers who supervised their training showed patience with the volunteers, many of whom had poor command of the English language. Their routine included lessons in English, along with military theory and maneuvers. Dressed in uniforms worn years before by Canadian soldiers, the officer probationers studied the use of rifles and grenades—weapons which they did not fire because all available ammunition was needed by the Polish battalions in Europe.

Pospula and Czaban trained in Canada into the fall and winter of 1917, visited occasionally by relatives and friends. After several months of study, they completed a written examination along with other officer candidates. The probationers who passed this test qualified as officers in the Polish Army, and began to help instruct the thousands of recruits who were now arriving. On one cold but memorable day, the new officers lined up for inspection by Paderewski, who had taken a break from public appearances to visit the "army of Kosciuszko."

In March 1918, after nearly a year of training, Pospula, Czaban, and other recruits traveled from Canada to New York City, boarded a Russian vessel, and sailed at last for Europe. Upon arriving in France, they joined General Haller's battalions at Camp de Ruchard, where they donned the "horizon blue" Polish uniform, began additional training, and existed along with other soldiers on a diet consisting for the most part of potatoes and bread. In place of textbook lessons in officer conduct and military tactics, the men now took up the grimmer study of trench warfare and poison gas. A few weeks later, Pospula's battalion was ordered into battle, passing as they moved eastward trains which were returning wounded men from the front. That sight, Pospula would recall years later, taught him more in a moment about the Great War than his months of preparation had.

A "Recruiting Unit of the American Contingent, Polish Army in France," opened at Rochester's Polish Falcon Hall in October 1917, four months after Pospula and Czaban departed for Cambridge Springs. "Men Going From This City to Join Polish Recruits," local newspapers announced. "Will Aid Allies in France," "To Fight for Free Poland," "Will Start To-Night for Training Ground."[27] Within a few days of the station's official opening, two dozen young men from Polish Town had pledged their services to the army of Poles being organized in France. On October 15th, after an emotional observance in honor of the hundredth anniversary of Kosciuszko's death, the first round of recruits marched from Falcon Hall to the New York Central Railway Station, accompanied by a cheering crowd and sere-

World War I panorama: (1) Jozef Pilsudski and Edward Rydz-Smigly, two leaders of the Polish armed forces; (2) Anna Badura, Grey Samaritan from Rochester; (3) Jozef Haller with Polish troops in France; (4) members of the Polish cavalry; (5) John Pospula, Polish Army officer from Rochester; (6) Semyon Budyenny and members of the Red Army cavalry.

naded by Nest 52's military band. The volunteers would "be doing a great thing toward restoring Poland and reestablishing her national independence," Stanislaw K. Kowalski, supervisor of the local recruiting station, informed newspaper reporters. Rochester's recruits, he added proudly, would soon be marching "under the ancient Polish flag."

During the height of enlistment for the Polish Army in the last months of 1917, the recruiting station at Falcon Hall remained open fourteen hours a day—from 7:00 a.m. until 9:00 p.m.[28] Men between the ages of 18 and 45 who were not eligible for the American service were recruited as volunteers, pending examination by a medical officer. The *Herald,* covering a farewell reception given at Falcon Hall for 22 new recruits, noted that a number of men who could not have served in the United States Army had volunteered for the Polish forces:

> In the number enlisted with the Polish Army were none that were cheating the draft of Uncle Sam. Many of them were older and some were younger than those called for the National Army, but even those within the draft age were not eligible for service with the American forces, most of them being of German or Austrian nationality. Some of the men who went away last night left not only wives behind but also children.[29]

Before the recruiting station closed in February 1919, 258 local men had joined the American contingent of the Polish Army.[30] Beyond these enlistments, at least 700 Poles from the Rochester area entered the war in the service of the United States forces.

At first, as the men marched off from Falcon Hall, Polish women could do little other than organize homefront support. Approximately eighty wives and sisters of soldiers contented themselves with joining the local chapter of the Polish Red Cross, a group whose members stitched bandages and knitted gloves for Polish troops in Europe.[31] Within a short time, the women had completed 200 pairs of mittens which they offered to Captain Zebrowski for shipment to Polish recruits.

Early in 1918, a visitor who had fled her home in Poland appealed to local women for a greater act of service. Laura de Gozdawa Turczynowicz, the American wife of a Polish count, spoke at Convention Hall that January at the invitation of the Rochester Red Cross and the local Women's Society for the Polish Army Relief.[32] Four years of war had devastated Poland, the countess told a capacity crowd, moving many in the audience to tears with her descriptions of looted villages and children left homeless. She called upon the daughters of Poland for assistance, proposing that a nursing corps of Polish American volunteers set out for Europe to aid in their homeland's restoration.

Following the countess' visit, ten local girls registered for a "probationers' course" in first aid sponsored by the local YWCA.[33] Anna Badura, Stella Czemerowska, Tekla Dernoga, Elzbieta and Constance Figlerowicz, Antonetta Friebe, Marta Graczyk, Leokadya Muszynska, Maria Nita, and Zofia Zagata volunteered to complete the training which they hoped would lead to their selection as

Opposite: John Pospula, recipient of the Virtuti Militari, posed for this portrait in the 1960s.

Below: Anna Badura of the Grey Samaritans. (Courtesy of Mr. and Mrs. Leon Lustyk)

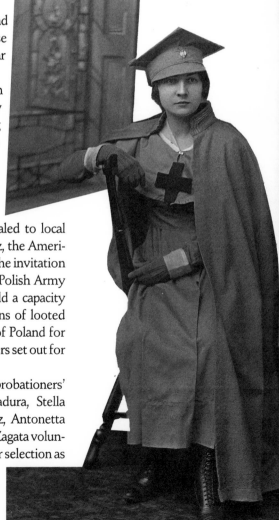

members of the Polish Grey Samaritans. "Never had brighter girls in my life," declared Dr. Marcena S. Ricker, who provided the prospective Samaritans with three weeks of first aid training, then supervised their nursing internship at the Homeopathic Hospital.[34] "They are eager to learn," Dr. Ricker informed a local newspaper reporter, and entered their training "with a zest most gratifying . . . in order to work in stricken Poland." Before beginning their studies, a three-month course designed to give them "rapid and varied experience" in nursing, the girls were treated by the YWCA to a weeklong outing at the Sea Breeze Vacation House.

The training which Rochester's volunteers received was similar to that completed by approximately 300 Polish American girls in other cities: Cleveland, Chicago, Trenton, Milwaukee, Detroit, Buffalo, Pittsburgh.[35] Ninety of these girls, including five from Rochester (Badura, Friebe, Graczyk, Muszynska, and Nita) were selected to continue in the program and, in January 1919, traveled to New York City for six months of additional study supplemented by work in orphanages, kindergartens, and hospitals.[36] The corps of prospective Samaritans was trimmed again to the thirty most hardy, and in July 1919 four of Rochester's recruits (Badura, Friebe, Graczyk, and Muszynska) sailed for Europe wearing the uniforms of Countess Turczynowicz's nurses.[37]

In cooperation with the American Relief Administration, the girls began service in Polish refugee camps and villages, where they supervised the distribution of food and clothing and tended to children suffering from malnutrition, typhus, cholera, smallpox, and dysentery.[38] As the Polish-Soviet War intensified in the summer of 1920, the "Greys" extended their ministry to wounded soldiers evacuated from the battle front. The work was taxing and often gruesome, as Marta Graczyk wrote to her family that August: "I am telling you, people, why life lately is just full of shocks, disappointments, and surprises . . . What is happening to poor Poland at the present is beyond a human being's imagination. . . . I thought lately that I would be 'quits' with everything, but when one thinks of the nursery left behind we just cannot refuse to go on."[39]

The Grey Samaritans remained in Poland for three years, most of the group refusing the opportunity to return home during the worst months of the Polish-Soviet War.[40] All told, the small unit of women distributed tons of food and clothing to hundreds of thousands of Polish children. Their work in their homeland was, according to an ARA official, "one of the most interesting phases of the child relief. . . . We all feel that their devotion and service, given under the most trying conditions, forms a record which has no equal in American relief work in all the countries of Europe since the Armistice."[41]

Rochester's Grey Samaritan volunteers during their nursing internship at the Homeopathic Hospital. (Courtesy of Mr. and Mrs. Leon Lustyk)

"Remember," Maksymilian Nowak enjoined 2,000 persons gathered at Convention Hall in January 1918, "that as American citizens you have a two-fold duty:

your duty as Americans, and your duty to avenge your people. Besides what you have already done, remember that over there—way over there in the eastern part of Germany—your fathers, your children, your relatives are lying massacred under the sod.... Remember that, at the present time, your people are working in the German trenches, in the Prussian mines, laboring under the lash of autocracy. Poles, can you remain quietly here? Can you sit idly by . . . ?"[42]

The call to support for Poland was sounded in Rochester during the war at assemblies such as that at which Nowak, chairman of Buffalo's Polish Mobilization Committee, delivered his emotional appeal. Two local organizations took the initiative in sponsoring these rallies: the Polish Army Mobilization Committee *(Komitet Rekrutacyjny),* concerned with recruiting men for service, and the Polish Citizens Committee *(Komitet Obywatelski),* responsible for fund-raising for Polish relief. Both committees were formed under the leadership of Ludwik (Louis) Kubiak, who had emigrated from Poznania in 1903, settling in Rochester where he married, raised seven children, and played an active role in community life.[43] As a longtime Falcon member, Kubiak was a prominent figure in Rochester's Polonia, and through his position as a superintendent with New York State Railways had also established contacts beyond the settlement. Under his direction, the Mobilization Committee and the Citizens Committee brought an array of speakers to

Grey Samaritans during their training in New York City. (Courtesy of Mr. and Mrs. Leon Lustyk)

Rochester for rallies, patriotic gatherings, and assemblies. In addition to Nowak, the list of guests included Leon Olszewski, editor of Buffalo's *Polak w Ameryce;* Jan F. Smulski, a Chicago banker and chairman of the Polish National Department; Honorable Jan Wedda, the United States government's representative to France on Polish matters; Countess Laura de Gozdawa Turczynowicz, founder of the Grey Samaritans; and Polish Army officers from Camp Kosciuszko at Niagara-on-the-Lake. One event featured thirty musicians known as the Polish Military Band, along with eight ballet dancers from Warsaw's Royal Opera House in performance at Convention Hall.[44]

For the most part, the events sponsored by the Polish Army Mobilization Committee and the Polish Citizens Committee were held either at the Falcon clubhouse or, when a larger audience seemed likely, at Convention Hall. Often, the day's program opened with introductory remarks by Kubiak and an invocation by Father Ignacy Klejna, pastor of St. Stanislaus Parish. Before the appearance of the day's main speaker, the Falcon orchestra might accompany the Echo chorus in Polish and American patriotic airs. At the end of the assembly, the chorus typically returned to lead all present in several verses of the hymn *Boze Cos Polske.*

While the activities of both groups received attention in the local press, it was the Citizens Committee that represented Poland's cause outside of the immigrant settlement through its affiliation with Rochester's War Chest, the organization responsible for coordinating local fund-raising for war relief. In addition to Kubiak, the Polish Citizens Committee included among its active members Kazimierz Damsz, Stanislaw Dukat, Adam Felerski, Adam Norwich, Jan Owczarczak, Dr. Alojzy Smeja, and Franciszek Zborowski.[45] Soon after its formation in 1918, the group approached the War Chest's Executive Board (including City Comptroller Henry D. Quinby; University of Rochester President Rush Rhees; and industrialists George Eastman, Elmer Fairchild, and Joseph T. Alling) with a suggestion for the opening of its relief campaign: the Citizens Committee would bring Paderewski to the Chamber of Commerce to speak about the Polish cause. Attorney Adam Felerski traveled to New York City to deliver the committee's invitation personally, and arrangements were made for the pianist to address the Chamber of Commerce on June 12, 1918.

"Many Eager to Hear Talk by Paderewski" the *Democrat and Chronicle* reported the day before the address.[46] During the previous weeks, requests for tickets had been "constantly received" at the Chamber of Commerce, made "by letter, telephone and personal call." As reservations were filled, the press engaged in lively speculation about Paderewski's arrival. "Information has been received," one newspaper confided, "that Paderewski will come to Rochester in his special car, accompanied by Major Kozlowski of his staff." On hand to greet the pianist would be six officers from the Polish Army training camp at Niagara-on-the-Lake, as well as a contingent from the Polish Citizens Committee.

The crowd that filled the Chamber of Commerce the following day exceeded expectations. The banquet hall

Antonetta Friebe of the Grey Samaritans. (Courtesy of Mr. and Mrs. Leon Lustyk)

was "stormed," newspapers reported, by "persons not only from this city but from many surrounding towns who filled the main floor and the balcony of the hall to overflowing." A squad of police officers monitored the crowd pushing into the foyer and, despite an effort to fit additional guests in the galleries, hundreds who waited in hopes of being seated were turned away disappointed.

Paderewski's remarks outlined Poland's history beginning with the First Partition, emphasizing his country's repeated sufferings at the hands of other nations. Flanked by an honor guard of Polish Army officers, Paderewski also praised the dual patriotism that American Poles demonstrated during the war. In supporting government fund drives and enlisting in both Polish and American forces, "the Poles are doing twice their duty," Paderewski declared. "They are not 100 percent Americans, but 200 percent Americans." In closing, the pianist appealed to those assembled to "stand behind your great President. . . . The eyes of suffering mankind are looking at you as the last hope of civilization, right and justice. . . . While protecting yourselves you will free many other nations that now suffer the worst sort of oppression."

Their cause advanced by Paderewski's address and the excitement that it stirred, the Citizens Committee began negotiations for a donation from the War Chest.[47] Early in 1919, on behalf of the people of Rochester, the War Chest's Budget Committee allocated $100,000 of

its funds directly to the Polish National Department in Washington, D.C., an amount transferred in five checks of $20,000 apiece from the "Rochester Patriotic and Community Fund, Inc." Supplementing this generous gift was an additional $14,000, forwarded to the National Department by the Citizens Committee from the Polish families of Rochester.

The news that the Great War had ended came to Rochester early on November 11, 1918, "in the hour just between darkness and daylight when the city slumbered."[48] Newspapermen working the night shift were the first to hear that the Armistice had been signed, and rushed to city hall to ring the building's huge tower bell at 3:00 a.m. By 4:00 a.m. the bell had been joined by a chorus of factory whistles, and by 5:00 a.m. citizens eager to celebrate were filling downtown streets. By mid-morning Main Street, "overflowing with men, women and children," was closed to streetcars and automobiles as at least 150,000 Rochester residents descended on the center of town, waving flags, clanging all manner of noisemakers, and throwing confetti in "a delirium of delight."

City officials quickly planned a victory parade for the afternoon, inviting local military and fraternal organizations to take part in the triumphal march. Although they convened in short order, these groups were not the first to display their

The Polish Citizens Committee, with chairman Ludwik Kubiak (center). (Courtesy of Mr. and Mrs. Leo Hoock)

Opposite: A parade on Hudson Avenue near Roycroft Drive, led by soldiers of the Polish Army and Grey Samaritan nurses. (Courtesy of Mr. and Mrs. Leo Hoock)

Ignacy Paderewski while in Rochester, June 1918. (From the Stone Negative Collection of the Rochester Museum and Science Center)

colors to the crowd. As the Civil War veterans, State Guardsmen, Home Defense League, and Loyal Order of Moose gathered to launch the parade at East Avenue and Culver Road, those waiting downtown witnessed a smaller, impromptu display. Arriving before the official delegations was a jubilant line of residents from the Polish section, who "sounded their joy with a spectacular parade . . . drawing cheers everywhere."

Like others across America, Rochester Poles rejoiced heartily at news of the Armistice. For them, the end of the war brought not only the triumph of the United States and her allies, but also the restoration of their homeland—the great moment prophesied by Mickiewicz and ardently awaited through the years of partition. The day before the Western Allies and the Central Powers formally signed the Armistice, Jozef Pilsudski, leader of Poland's military forces in the homeland, had arrived unchallenged in Warsaw, symbolically accomplishing the nation's liberation after 120 years of foreign domination. Paderewski, meanwhile, retained his favored position with Edward House and Woodrow Wilson, and it only remained for the Western Allies, convening at the Paris Peace Conference, to draw up boundaries for the resurrected Polish nation.[49]

As Polish nationalists had foretold half a century before, the millions of Poles in America had come to play a significant role in their homeland's rebirth. Polish American families had sent 24,000 of their sons to fight under the standard of the White Eagle, making up one-fourth of the soldiers in General Haller's Army.[50] In addition, approximately 300,000 Polish Americans had entered the United States forces; the war closed with many of their names on the country's casualty lists. Although Poles represented less than 4 percent of the United States' population in 1918, it has been estimated that 12 percent of the American soldiers who lost their lives were of Polish descent.

As Polish Americans were generous in sending their sons to military service, they proved their dedication in supporting efforts

for Poland's relief.[51] Across the country, Polish parishes and fraternal societies participated vigorously in the fund-raising drives designed to aid Poland economically. Before 1921, the Polish National Fund—the largest of the relief campaigns—channelled more than $5 million of Polish immigrants' savings to their homeland: a donation of at least one dollar for every American man, woman, and child of Polish descent. Beyond this, Polish immigrants subscribed to American loan drives and Red Cross campaigns, a participation which Paderewski cited with pride during public appearances:

> No other nationality here in the United States has taken so active a part in the Red Cross campaigns as the Poles. In proportion to their number they have been the largest contributors to this worthy cause. In some American city of 300,000 population, $3,750,000 has been collected for the American Red Cross, which represents $12.50 per capita, which included a number of American millionaires. The Polish population of the same city—7,000 people, almost exclusively belonging to the laboring class—contributed to the fund $160,000, which makes $23 a head.[52]

The immigrants' monetary contributions continued to flow after the Armistice. Jan Smulski, chairman of the Polish National Department, estimated that, during the war and the years immediately following, American Poles contributed $200 million to their homeland in the form of money sent to relatives, purchase of Polish government bonds, donations to relief drives, and investments in Polish firms—in addition to $67 million which they invested in Liberty Loans. The enormity of the contribution made by American Poles and the extent of their loyalty were acknowledged by Paderewski when he returned to his homeland in December 1918: "I would never have been in Poland," he wrote, "and Poland would never have been free, except for the generous-hearted people of the United States."[53]

Marta Graczyk and Tadeusz Gedgowd. (Courtesy of Mr. and Mrs. Leon Lustyk)

Perhaps unexpectedly, the immigrants' participation in the "war for Poland" also advanced their participation in American life. In the decades since their arrival, residents of the isolated immigrant settlements had never used to such effect the advantages of American citizenship: from establishing important contacts in the political structures of their communities, to drawing upon the power of coverage in the American press. Polonia's drive to aid the homeland took place within, not separately from, the United States' part in the war. Most significantly, Poles who had spent a generation in the shelter of their own neighborhoods sent hundreds of thousands of their sons into American service and supported beyond expectations the country's relief campaigns, displaying for the first time a dual patriotism that would continue to characterize their communities in coming years.[54]

In Rochester's Polish community, residents had reason to be proud of the contributions of 258 young men who had served in the Polish Army and several hundred others who had joined America's armed forces. Of the Rochester Poles who marched in Europe with General Haller's regiments, two returned home decorated for bravery in battle. Antoni Nogaj was awarded the *Croix de Guerre* from the government of France, and John Pospula received the *Virtuti Militari,* the

Armia Polska. 1^{szy} Putk Strzelców Pieszych.
d. 13/11 1918 Cytacja Pułku № 109.

TADEUSZ GEDGOWD SIERŻANT.

PODOFICER INTELIGENTNY, DYSCYPLINARNY, I STARANNY, WYPEŁNIAŁ PARE RAZY Z ENERGJĄ, FUNKCJĘ SZEFA SEKCJI JAKO OCHOTNIK NA PATROLE, DAWAŁ PRZEZ SWĄ ŚMIAŁOŚĆ CHĘĆ I OCHOTĘ SWEM KOLEGOM.

W ARMJI DNIA 8^{go} LUTEGO 1919
Dowódca 1^{go} Pułku
P. PUŁKOWNIK

Polish government's highest military decoration, along with an honorary commission of captain following his regiment's stand against Budyenny's Cavalry during the Polish-Soviet War (1919-20).[55]

Two others from Rochester who volunteered for the Polish Army lost their lives in action and are buried in France: Julian Brzezinski, an immigrant from Prussian Poland, and Ludwik Koscielny, the oldest son in a family of sixteen children.[56] Koscielny, who entered the Polish Army after being refused by the United States forces because of "poor eyesight," was assigned to the 5th Machine Gun Company, 1st Regiment, of the Polish Army and sailed for Europe early in 1918. When he was killed in battle the following July, the soldiers who recovered his body found a tiny American flag that had been a gift from his sisters sewn on Koscielny's horizon-blue uniform.

Approximately 25 of the local Polish men who entered the American forces also gave their lives in service during the war.[57] One family, the Talaskas of Weddale Way, lost two sons within three months in 1918. Jan, serving with the 20th Company, 5th Regiment, of the U.S. Marines, was killed at the Battle of Belleau Woods in June. His brother Wladyslaw, who enlisted in the Naval Aviation Service after graduation from Holy Cross College, died near Bay Shore, Long Island, the following September when an airplane in which he was flying fell into Great South Bay.

Supplementing this record of military service were the local community's charitable contributions to Poland's relief. Rochester's Polish families forwarded at least $15,000 of their savings to drives for the aid of their homeland, in addition to donations which have never been tallied sent directly to relatives in Europe. Beyond this, the Polish Citizens Committee helped channel the generous sum of $100,000 from Rochester's War Chest fund to the Polish National Department, along with an additional gift of $35,000 sent to the Hoover Relief Commission after the war.[58] Polish Town's residents could also point with pride to their contributions to Poland's reconstruction. A number of local Polish Army recruits, as well as the community's Grey Samaritans, continued to serve in Europe

Tadeusz Gedgowd's Certificate for Service in the Polish Army. (Courtesy of Mr. and Mrs. Leon Lustyk)

following the war, taking part in the rebuilding and charitable work organized by the new Polish government.

In a gesture that brought honor to all of Rochester's Polonia, the new Polish government selected seven local citizens to receive its Cross of Merit after the war: Stanislaw K. Kowalski, president of Polish Falcon Nest 52, who had energetically recruited young men for Haller's Army; Ludwik Kubiak, chairman of the Polish Mobilization and Citizens Committees, which together had initiated impressive homefront activities; Adam Felerski, the attorney who helped coordinate the work of the Citizens Committee; Fathers Ignacy Klejna, Stanislaw Szupa, and Stanislaw Wysoczynski of St. Stanislaus Parish, who had actively supported fund-raising efforts; and Marta Graczyk, the Grey Samaritan who had been imprisoned briefly during her stay in Europe.[59] Two local men not of Polish descent were also decorated by the new government, an honor acknowledged with pride among Rochester's Polish residents. Dr. Rush Rhees and George Eastman, both of whom had served on the War Chest's Executive Board, were awarded the *Polonia Restituta* for their interest in Poland and for generous personal contributions.

While a number of Rochester's Polish immigrants, along with Poles from other settlements, returned to rebuild their lives in Europe following the war, the proportion of Poles who re-emigrated remained small: as low as one percent of America's Polish population.[60] For Polish immigrants, the patriot's dream of a restored homeland was now weighed against the draw of the parishes, communities, and homes they had built in the United States. The large majority elected to stay, and in the decades following the war acknowledged with greater confidence their identity as Polish Americans.

In Rochester's Polonia, the coming years would be a time of enterprise and new ventures, a time to invest in community projects including a Polish language newspaper and a clothing factory. New businesses, shops, and a fourth Polish parish would extend the neighborhood south and west, while more than 700 children would crowd St. Stanislaus School. Their debt to the homeland in one sense repaid, the growth of Polish Town would dominate the lives of neighborhood families following World War I.

S. K. Kowalski and Father Ignacy Klejna, two of Rochester's recipients of the Cross of Merit.

RECRUITER FOR THE POLISH ARMY

S. K. Kowalski

The man who recruited one-fourth of Rochester's volunteers to the Polish Army was born in Pilzno, Poland, in 1862.[61] Stanislaw K. Kowalski immigrated to the United States in 1884 at age 22, settling initially in South Brooklyn where he joined the Polish National Alliance. Convinced of the value of community organization, Kowalski soon initiated the formation of two other groups: a company of Polish riflemen, and a fraternity of Polish craftsmen which enrolled more than 100 members at its first meeting.

In 1889, Kowalski married Antonia Osielska, a native of Jodlowy, Poland, and moved with his bride to Paterson, New Jersey, where he helped organize a chapter of the Polish National Alliance. Two years later, the Kowalskis relocated to Schenectady, New York, and joined a group of forty Polish families who had banded together to form a Polish parish. In the months before that goal was realized, Kowalski arranged for a Polish priest to visit the settlement from Newark, New Jersey, generously helping to cover the priest's expenses from his personal savings.

Kowalski learned the trades of electrician and draftsman while working for General Electric Company in Schenectady, and at the outbreak of the Spanish-American War volunteered for the United States Engineer and Signal Corps. In 1907, Kowalski received a job with the Electric Motor Company in Rochester. Once settled in the Polish neighborhood, he joined Polish Falcon Nest 52 and was elected to its presidency in 1912. In the years before World War I, he entered energetically into the life of the community, helping organize an insurance fraternal and a Falcon scout troop. On October 9, 1917, Kowalski was given command of the recruiting unit located at Falcon Hall, and five days later registered his first seventeen volunteers. Although his own request to join the Polish Army was not approved because of his age, he campaigned vigorously for new recruits, not only in the Rochester area but also in Dunkirk and Niagara Falls. By 1919, when Rochester's recruiting station closed, Kowalski had personally signed up more than sixty of the local community's 258 recruits.

Kowalski continued his involvement in Rochester's Polonia until his death at age 79 in 1941. Among the honors he received for his contributions to the community were the Polish Government's Cross of Merit, the Polish Falcons' Legion of Honor Cross, the Polish National Alliance's Cross of Honor, and the Sword of Honor presented by veterans of the Polish Army.

MARGUERITE AND THE POLISH COUNT

As Laura de Gozdawa Turczynowicz traveled across America organizing Grey Samaritan volunteers, a woman from Rochester whose life in some ways mirrored that of the countess was also using her talents on behalf of wartorn Poland.[62] Marguerite Melville Liszniewska, American-born wife of a Polish nobleman and an accomplished pianist, performed extensively in the United States during the first three years of the war, donating proceeds from her concerts to Polish relief.

Marguerite Melville was born in New York City to Scottish and Irish parents, and lived during her childhood in Rochester where the family had many relatives. Marguerite showed musical ability at an early age, and her parents sent her to Berlin to study piano with Dr. Ernst Jedliszska. Later, as recipient of a Steinway scholarship, she continued her training in Vienna, where she met and married Count Karol Liszniewski, a Polish nobleman serving as ambassador to the Austrian court. Countess Liszniewska won acclaim as a concert pianist during her years abroad, appearing in Scandinavia, Germany, Austria, Switzerland, Great Britain, and Holland.

Marguerite and Karol left Europe shortly before the war began, resettling in the United States where the countess performed on behalf of her husband's homeland. Following the war, Count Liszniewski donated his family's European land to the Polish government, which opened a hospital on the once elegant estate. In return, the count received a ring engraved with a simple inscription: "I have given all for my country."

Count and Countess Liszniewski moved eventually to Ohio, where Marguerite joined the Master Faculty of the Cincinnati Conservatory of Music. The couple's story was remembered in Rochester, not only in Marguerite's family but also among members of the Polish community. Many years after the war, Gertrude Hughes Furlong, one of Marguerite's cousins, stopped at St. Stanislaus Convent with her daughter, Sylvia Furlong Baglin. One of the Sisters greeted the visitors with delight when she learned of their ties to Marguerite Melville, wife of the count who had "given all" for his homeland.

IN SERVICE TO POLAND

Marta Graczyk of the Grey Samaritans

Her story is one of courage, service, adventure, and romance, of experiences not anticipated for a young girl growing up in Rochester's Polish neighborhood in the early 1900s.

Marta Graczyk, one of eleven children of Marcin and Marianna Graczyk, volunteered for work with the Polish Grey Samaritans in January 1918, after Countess Turczynowicz's address at Convention Hall.[63] Her fiance, Tadeusz Gedgowd, had already enlisted for service with the Polish Army, and had left Rochester for training at Polish National Alliance College early in March 1917. "My fiance was the first one in our city to respond to the call of the Polish Army," Marta wrote in her memoirs, "long before the time that he was to be called to the ranks of the American Army." Three of Marta's close friends would also volunteer for service: Wladyslaw Czaban and Jan Pospula, who joined General Haller's "Blue Army," and Anna Badura, who along with Marta entered the Grey Samaritans.

After completing the course in first aid offered at Rochester's Homeopathic Hospital, Marta traveled to New York City where she lived for six months, studying health and hygiene along with other young women who had responded to Countess Turczynowicz's appeal. Taking leave of her father, sisters, and brothers was "heartaching," Marta later recalled, but before long she developed a camaraderie with the other Grey Samaritan trainees, whom she described as "young girls full of life . . . of one nation's descent," who shared a commitment to serving their homeland.

The girls' schedule in New York was full: courses in welfare work, health, and hygiene at the School of Philanthropy and at Columbia University's Teachers College; field work sponsored by United Charities in hospitals, kindergartens, and orphanages; visits to institutions for handicapped and crippled children; evening study in the Polish and English languages. There was also time for talking, laughing, and playing pranks on each other in the dormitory where the girls lived during their stay in New York. "Those were school days, young days, never to be forgotten," Marta wrote.

In July 1919, after an anxious wait during which the girls were not sure when they would leave for Poland, Marta and nineteen of the "Greys" with whom she had trained sailed for Europe. She served with the nursing corps for the next three years, moving from city to city in Poland on assignments relayed to her by telegram from headquarters in Warsaw. Initially, she assisted in an orphanage near Warsaw, caring for children of refugees fleeing the conflict with the Bolsheviks on Poland's eastern border. Later, on assignment to the American Relief Administration, she supervised the distribution of food and clothing to children and elderly left impoverished by the war. Along with other Grey Samaritans, Marta also instructed Polish women in health care, training girls in each village to continue relief work after the Grey Samaritans departed.

During her duty with the Grey Samaritans, Marta experienced the hardships of life in Poland after World War I: food shortages, rides in horse-drawn carts over rough country roads, nights spent in drafty village inns. Despite the often unpleasant conditions, she responded with enthusiasm to her work and found satisfaction in aiding her parents' homeland. Marta's memoirs also relate many joyful experiences: singing Christmas carols with Polish soldiers returning from the front; seeing her fiance in Warsaw after a separation of two years; meeting her mother's sister for the first time in a Polish village, finding in her aunt's features the image of her mother who had died when Marta was a child.

Marta also endured a frightening experience in November 1920, while she was serving near the border of Poland and Lithuania. After crossing into Lithuanian territory, she was arrested by government officials and accused of being a Polish spy, apparently because she had been corresponding with Poles who lived in the area. Upon return to the United States, Marta described the incident with composure to a Rochester reporter:

> At the time of my arrest I had left Wilno, Poland, for [a nearby town], where I had been previously engaged in the work of distributing food to the children and aged people . . . Almost immediately upon my arrival in this town I was arrested by representatives of the Lithuanian government on a charge of being a spy. . . . The fact that I spoke the Polish language and was found within the Lithuanian boundary seemed to be sufficient to warrant my arrest. . . .
>
> I was kept under guard for about three days, after which I was given the freedom of the city. However, that freedom consisted

90

chiefly of being constantly shadowed by someone . . . prepared to
prevent any attempt of escape. . . . My freedom was finally procured
by one of the assistants of the commissioner of Riga and a representative of the American ambassador in Warsaw.

After her duty with the Grey Samaritans, Marta returned to Rochester where
she married Tadeusz Gedgowd. Both were decorated for their service to Poland,
and Marta applied her experience abroad to a profession in America, working in
social welfare for the rest of her life. She also recorded the experiences of her years
as a Grey Samaritan. "In Poland," she later recalled, "there would be no end to
mention of happenings there. . . . It seemed that . . . similar tales would be only
stories in books."

6 | New Ventures

Six months after Poland was restored as a nation in the Treaty of Versailles, the new republic sent its United States envoy to Rochester "to see at first hand the methods employed by Rochester manufacturers, whose fame has extended to all parts of the world."[1] During his three-day visit as the guest of the Chamber of Commerce and the city's Polish societies, Prince Kazimierz Lubomirski toured Kodak Park, Bausch & Lomb, the Hickey-Freeman clothing firm, Taylor Instrument Company, and the plant of Todd Protectograph. At Kodak Park the prince admired "the dining room and other provisions for the welfare of the employees." At Hickey-Freeman he addressed an impromptu assembly of the firm's Polish employees, and at Bausch & Lomb a committee of Polish workmen presented him with two handsome pairs of binoculars: one for himself and one for his wife, Princess Teresa.

Lubomirski's tour of local firms also took him to three Polish-owned and operated businesses on the northeast side: Adam Norwich's Polish Clothing Manufacturing Company at 850 Hudson Avenue; Rochester Auto and Tool, an automobile supply house at 17 Andrews Street; and Branch No. 5 of the Polish Mechanics Corporation of the United States, a stock organization founded to purchase American machinery for factories in Poland.[2] As Lubomirski entered their headquarters at 538 Hudson Avenue, the officers of the Mechanics Corporation welcomed him with the traditional greeting of bread and salt, and the prince returned their hospitality by investing $100 in the company's stock.

That evening, Lubomirski addressed 2,000 members of the local Polish community at Convention Hall. "The Prince spoke in Polish," the *Herald* noted, "much to the delight of his audience, and his dramatic delivery caused frequent outbursts of wildly enthusiastic applause."[3] Flanked by an honor guard of Poles who had served with the American forces, Lubomirski praised the wartime contributions of Polish immigrants, and asked those

Water power, manufacturers, wonderful streets: ah, yes! Rochester is a wonderful city.
General Jozef Haller
November 29, 1923

gathered to continue to aid their homeland. He also acknowledged that, as Rochesterians of Polish descent, their first loyalty must be to America "and after that to their beloved Poland." This plea for "full-fledged Americanism," a local reporter wrote, was answered by the audience's "hearty response."

As Lubomirski's visit illustrated, local citizens of Polish descent began to move confidently into the life of the city after World War I. Participation in the war effort had brought Rochester's Polonia important benefits: increased visibility, greater local respect, a heightened sense of community pride. Bolstered by their wartime experience, the sons and daughters of the first Polish settlers entered the twenties with optimism, better prepared than their parents had been to explore the opportunities available in Rochester's civic, commercial, and cultural life.

Polonia's sense of optimism after the war reflected Rochester's outlook as its young men returned from service.[4] When the decade began, local industrial leaders predicted that the twenties would herald a period of renewed productivity and prosperity. The birth rate was rising, life expectancy was lengthening, and the city's population had remained remarkably stable despite the war's disruption: all signs that Rochester could be expected to hold its place as the 21st largest among American cities.[5] Anticipating a strong economy, politicians and industrialists turned their attention to civic reform through the work of three organizations: the Chamber of Commerce, the Planning Bureau, and the Bureau of Municipal Research. Rochesterians would see a number of practical improvements following the war, from new efficiencies in street lighting, street repair, and refuse collection to general expansion of health services and hospital facilities. At the same time, city officials would take pride in the growth of Rochester's university, the creation of its Museum of Arts and Sciences, and the gala opening of George Eastman's impressive theater.

For Rochester's foreign-born, who represented approximately 70,000 of the city's 300,000 residents in the twenties, the post-war years brought increased recognition and acceptance.[6] Some immigrant groups, such as the Irish and Germans, had shared in the city's life for nearly a century, and had produced many

Walenty Strojny's construction company built many homes and businesses on the northeast side, including this home on North Street in 1925. (Courtesy of Cecelia Whalen)

citizens of leadership and distinction. Others, like the Poles, Ukrainians, and Italians, were entering their second generation in local neighborhoods and had proven their worth as hard-working members of the city's labor force and professions.

Early in 1920, the city officially acknowledged the contributions of its foreign-born at the Homelands Exhibition, an elaborate, ten-day festival held at Exposition Park.[7] Billed as "one of the most unusual events of its kind in the history of the United States," and "the greatest civic endeavor . . . ever undertaken in this city," the exhibition attracted thousands of Rochesterians to Exposition Park, where representatives of fourteen immigrant groups displayed folk art, demonstrated handicrafts, and performed traditional dances. A full-page advertisement in the *Times-Union* on the festival's opening day explained the city's interest in hosting the event: "Because we have not fully appreciated the contributions of art, music and industry streaming into this country and enriching it, Rochester has asked its sons and daughters of foreign birth to show to the Rochester public . . . these contributions. . . . Come to Exposition Park and see the fascinating entertainments typical of the lands from which our adopted brothers and sisters have come."[8]

The city's Polish community participated enthusiastically in the Homelands event, under the leadership of Adam Felerski, Ludwik Kubiak, Dr. Leon S. Kurek, Jozef Kuzminski, and Jan Owczarczak. The Poles' entertainment included performances by three choirs, folk dances by adults and children, and piano and violin solos by a number of neighborhood musicians.[9] The display of Polish folk art attracted great attention, most notably for the pottery fashioned by Stanislaw Okoniewicz. Working at a wheel built especially for the exhibition, Okoniewicz caught the eye of many visitors, including one local reporter who described the immigrant's craft in a feature article: "He speaks very little English, but his hands speak a beautiful language that finds its expression through the medium of the meaningless mass of clay which he fashions with consummate skill and accuracy, without the aid of molds, dies or tools of any sort. His fingers are all that he employs, unless one includes the wealth of imagination that lies behind his engaging smile."[10]

Members of Rochester's Polish community at the Homelands Exhibition, 1920. (Courtesy of Mr. and Mrs. William Pospula)

In the twenties, Hudson Avenue was a thoroughfare lined with the shops of Polish merchants and the offices of Polish tradesmen. The run of small Polish-owned businesses began a few blocks south of Clifford Avenue, and extended in an almost unbroken row north to Norton Street. Other establishments owned and operated by Poles were located on North Street, and occasionally a storefront boasting a Polish name stood tucked away on a sidestreet to the east or west. Some of these commercial ventures would prove to be short-lived, while others would remain neighborhood landmarks for decades: establishments like Kaleta's pharmacy, Bonus' and Kroll's funeral homes, Ostrowski's meat market, Kanty's paper box company, Figlerowicz's electric appliance shop, Przysinda's hardware store, Antczak's fuel company, Mrzywka's barber shop, Sykut's candy store.

In number and variety, these shops confirmed a healthy sense of commercial enterprise as more members of Polonia joined the ranks of the city's self-employed businessmen. Bakers, grocers, butchers, hardware merchants, dairymen, tobacconists, clothiers: following World War I, the City Directory listed an increasing number of Poles as independent shopkeepers, supplementing those cast in the immigrants' traditional roles of foundry worker, factory worker, laborer.[11] During the same years, a growing number earned their living as tradesmen and craftsmen—shoemakers, tailors, carpenters, painters, plumbers, barbers, and automobile mechanics who, like the shopkeepers, maintained storefront headquarters on Hudson Avenue. The Polish neighborhood also offered consumers a few uncommon services, notably the natural remedies prescribed by herb specialist Jacob Trzeciak, and the bonesetting and muscle massage offered by Joseph Kwapich.[12] Kwapich, who later opened a chiropractic office on Oxford Street, produced an exclusive liniment reputed to ease all aches and pains, sold to many a weary housekeeper and laborer at Kaleta's pharmacy.

Their interest in commercial enterprise led several Polish businessmen to invest in two ambitious projects during the twenties. The first of these, the Polish

Frank and Stella Nawrocki's ice cream and candy store at 952 Hudson Avenue, 1920s. (Courtesy of Mr. and Mrs. Thaddeus Nawrocki)

Clothing Manufacturing Company, seemed an idea with promise in a city where approximately 1,000 Poles worked in clothing factories and garment firms.[13] The Polish Clothing Manufacturing Company (Norwich Clothes) was incorporated in 1919 under the leadership of Adam Norwich, Adam Felerski, and Stanislaw Dukat. Five thousand dollars in preferred capital stock was made available to the community, and many families invested their savings in the venture at $100 a share. Each stock certificate outlined the company's ambitious goals, stating that the firm intended to carry out business "throughout the State of New York and the United States, especially in and throughout Poland and elsewhere."[14] In 1920, Norwich constructed a spacious factory at 850 Hudson Avenue (on the corner of Avenue D) at a cost of $120,000. Scarcely a year later, however, the company ended its operations, unable to survive a recession which forced the closing of many small local businesses.[15]

Shortly after the closing of Norwich Clothes, Felerski joined his brother John, James B. Kaleta, Casimir Mrzywka, and John Grycz in organizing a Polish language newspaper, the *Rochester Rekord*.[16] The group invited John Lelesh, an experienced linotype operator, to relocate from Buffalo and produce the weekly publication under Francis Openchowski's management.[17] In 1924, after only a year of publication, the newspaper's sponsors sold the *Rekord* to Joseph Zlotnik, a night watchman at one of the city's public schools who had moved with his family to Rochester after mining coal in Pennsylvania for several years. Zlotnik bought the business for his four sons—Leonard, Anthony, Henry, and Al—who turned out weekly issues for the next five years from a small office at 1119 Hudson Avenue. The brothers translated news from local English language dailies into Polish, set the copy by hand and by linotype, then carried the proof sheets home for their mother to examine and correct if necessary. These news items were supplemented by a weekly editorial written by Stanislaw K. Kowalski. The *Rekord* enjoyed a healthy circulation of approximately 3,000 issues weekly, delivered by mail and sold at several Hudson Avenue shops.

Because they owned a Polish type font, the Zlotnik brothers took in a steady flow of business from neighborhood merchants, parishes, and families: posters, flyers, letterhead stationery, business cards, tickets to dances, invitations to weddings and neighborhood gatherings. During the fall, their services were sought by local politicians who hoped to carry campaign messages to the city's Polish-speaking voters. As business increased, the Zlotniks hired an Italian printer to assist them, and as a sideline helped him produce an Italian language newspaper at the shop.

In 1929, fire broke out at the *Rochester Rekord's* office, fueled quickly by the benzine used to wash the newspaper's leaden type. Although firefighters arrived to put out the blaze, the company suffered $8,000 in damages, principally to its linotype and printing press. The *Rekord* was forced out of business, but the experience provided Anthony and Leonard Zlotnik with the skills to find employment at English language publications. Anthony Zlotnik would later become a leading figure in local printing, elected president of the Rochester branch of the International Typographical Union.[18]

The Zlotnik brothers' print shop received many requests for service from Polish organizations which, like neighborhood businesses and shops, grew in number following World War I. During these years several new societies, most of them promoting a civic or cultural focus, joined the array of organizations that had been formed previously.

Young men returning from service in the Polish and American forces organized two associations for veterans: Pulaski Post No. 782 of the American Legion, and Post No. 27 of the Polish Army Veterans Association of America (*Stowarzyszenie Weteranow Armii Polskiej w Ameryce*). Pulaski Post, a union of Polish American veterans of the American forces, was formed in December 1919 on the initiative of Max Szczepanski, Michael Klosowski, and Louis Matuszewski.[19] The group was

The Polish National Cubs, 1924. (Courtesy of St. Casimir's Parish Archives)

granted a charter by the American Legion in 1920, and held its first meetings under the leadership of Commander Louis Nowak. The following summer, Franciszek Mularz was elected president of Post No. 27, an association for local men who had served in General Haller's Polish Army.[20] The post's first slate of officers also included Jozef Nawrocki, Wladyslaw Jarus, Jozef Mazur, and Stanislaw Wroblewski.

At St. Casimir's Parish, an additional organization for young men promoted the responsibilities of citizenship.[21] The Polish Young Men's Citizen Club, established under the guidance of Father John Wroblewski in 1920, opened a cooperative food store (the White Eagle Grocery) in a small building at 972 Hudson Avenue as one of its first ventures. Gradually, the group turned its interest to social activities and civic affairs, recruiting members primarily from among naturalized Polish American men, and converted the *stary budynek* (old building) from a grocery store into the club's headquarters.

Other groups with more directly political aims were also formed among Polish Americans during and after the war. The Polish Citizens Social Republican Club, the first neighborhood organization aligned with an American political party, held its opening session in 1914 with Andrew Grzeszczak as president.[22] Men who joined were encouraged to apply for citizenship, and the group directed its energies to lobbying for municipal improvements in the Polish section. After several years, however, the club de-emphasized its affiliation with a single party, opening the way for formation of the Polonia Republican League. Organized for men in 1926 and expanded three years later with a women's auxiliary (the Polish Women's Republican Club), the league included John Felerski, Frank Zientara, Leo Adamski, Chester Bialynski, and James B. Kaleta among its founding members.[23] Shortly after its formation, the group successfully backed John Felerski's candidacy for city deputy sheriff, a post which he would hold for nine years.

In 1931, a group of neighborhood Democrats led by John J. Kaleta expressed their party affiliation with the formation of the Polish Democratic Union.[24] The union, representing a second attempt to organize neighborhood Democrats, continued the work of a club initiated under the leadership of John Leszczynski and Stanislaw K. Kowalski before the war. During the thirties, Kaleta served as the city's deputy welfare commissioner, and built ties for the neighborhood with the local Democratic Party in his role as ward district leader for the Polish Democratic Union.[25]

Although the community's participation in American politics was increasing, two organizations formed earlier in the interests of Polish nationalism remained among Polonia's most popular and active groups. Nest 52 of the Polish Falcons, elevated to new stature through impressive wartime activities, remodeled its Weyl Street clubhouse in 1922 in order to accommodate a growing membership.[26] The same year, Polish People's Home, Inc., a membership corporation that had formed in 1918, opened a community meeting hall at 818 Hudson Avenue, behind the Polish People's Library.[27] The new facility was available for use by all Polish organizations that purchased bonds in support of its operation. Built under sponsorship of a corporation of shareholders, *Dom Ludowy* opened as the meeting place of the local chapters of the Polish National Alliance, the Rakowian Society, the "New Life" insurance fraternal, the Polish Workers Sick and Mutual Aid Association, and the Polish local of the Amalgamated Clothing Workers union. Other groups would join in the coming years as Polish People's Home widened the scope of its activities to include dances, concerts, amateur theater, adult and youth choirs, and a folk dance group.

The Polish Socialist Alliance, whose members supported the organization of *Dom Ludowy,* retained a following among local Poles after the war. In 1921, the group welcomed delegates from across the country to the annual convention of their parent organization, the ZSP.[28] During the three-day conference, timed to coincide with the Labor Day weekend, delegates discussed the platforms of American socialism and the socialist party in Poland, and endorsed a new constitution which allied their work with the activities of both. The group also emphasized their fellowship with the American labor movement by inviting John Fitzpatrick, president of the Chicago Federation of Labor, to share with them his views regarding workers' rights.

One of the groups that met regularly at Polish People's Home had particular interest in the workers' movement. Local 206 of the Amalgamated Clothing

98

Workers of America, organized to represent Poles employed in the city's garment firms, was one of only four Polish branches of the ACWA in the country.[29] Local 206 drew its members from among the hundreds of Rochester Poles who worked in clothing manufacture, many of whom had taken part in the struggle to bring unionization to Rochester's tailoring industry beginning in 1913.[30] By 1920, the ACWA had formed seven locals in Rochester, including branches for coat makers, cutters and trimmers, pants and vest makers, women, Italian coat makers, Lithuanian coat makers, and Polish workers. In 1924, the Poles of Local 206 joined other clothing workers for a May Day observance during which thousands of ACWA members paraded to Convention Hall in a show of solidarity.[31] In

acknowledgment of the large number of those present who were immigrants, organizers of the rally scheduled speeches in Polish, Russian, and Italian to follow the keynote address in English.

Additional organizations representing citizens' interests formed in Polish Town during the twenties, including an affiliation of neighborhood shop owners called the Polish Business Men's Association.[32] Like the Polish Clothing Workers' Local, the group met initially at Polish People's Home, under the leadership of Stephen Milosz, Felix Wrublewski, Albert Kusak, Walter Kurowski, and John Szwajkos beginning in 1927. Members concerned themselves with problems shared by independent businessmen, and took an interest in the welfare of the neighborhood.

Cultural heritage also remained a focus of neighborhood organization after the war. The men of the Echo society continued their eminent choral performances, specializing as they had since the group's formation in the musical traditions of Poland.[33] In the twenties, Echo members leased a small building on Sobieski Street from Max Kierecki and later purchased land on the block, constructing a clubhouse for $15,000 in 1934. In addition to the Echo chorus, both St. Stanislaus and St.

A group of Polish businessmen, 1920s. (Courtesy of Mr. and Mrs. Thaddeus Nawrocki)

Casimir's Parishes featured choral societies, most notably the St. Cecilia Choir of St. Stanislaus Church, and the Moniuszko Singing Circle and Kalina Circle of St. Casimir's Parish.

A number of cultural societies were formed specifically for young people, the children growing up in families of six, ten, or more who made up a large proportion of Polish Town's population. At St. Stanislaus Parish, assistant pastor Stanislaus Wysoczynski organized the "Filarets" (*Towarzystwo Filaretow i Filaretek*), a social and educational sodality for high school students.[34] The group, whose activities emphasized Christian values and Polish heritage, was overseen by Father Wysoczynski, a slate of student officers, and a board of directors which included neighborhood businessmen. In 1926, the Filarets commemorated the tenth anniversary of Sienkiewicz's death, beginning with a memorial service in church and concluding with speeches, musical performances, and recitations from the novelist's writings presented before a capacity crowd at Falcon Hall.

At the Polish Baptist Church, young people met in the Educational Society of Enlightenment (*Towarzystwo Naukowe Promien*), a discussion group whose activities were carried out in Polish but often featured an American theme.[35] In their meeting rooms, the stockholders of Polish People's Home offered Saturday morning classes in Polish language, history, and traditions beginning in 1932.[36] This *Fakultet Szkolki Polskiej* proved popular and soon expanded its activities to include a troop of *Harcerstwo* (Polish Scouts), sponsored at *Dom Ludowy* by Lodge 512 of the Polish National Alliance. To the north on Weyl Street, the Falcons continued to emphasize physical fitness in gymnastic classes for children, who could begin their training as *sokoly* at an early age.

Sports in the American tradition rounded out activities for the neighborhood's young people. Societies and businessmen sponsored baseball, football, and basketball squads including the Polish Nationals, a baseball team hailing from the Polish Young Men's Citizen Club; the Cadet Football Club, underwritten by pharmacy owner James B. Kaleta; the Roycrofts, a baseball team wearing uniforms purchased by baker Walter Wojtczak; and boys' and girls' basketball teams sponsored by the Filarets.

Young people growing up in Polish Town during the twenties enjoyed one distinct advantage related to the location of their neighborhood.[37] Until Benjamin Franklin High School opened in 1930, the city hosted traveling circuses and carnivals on the expanse of land just beyond St. Stanislaus Parish, at the northeast corner of Hudson Avenue and Norton Street. Each year, children eagerly lined Hudson

The Filaret men's basketball team, 1927–28.

Avenue to see jugglers, acrobats, and exotic animals in horse-drawn cages parade toward the circus grounds from the New York Central Railway Station. Those bold enough to venture closer would follow to the open field, hoping for a better view of an elephant or a chance to watch the huge tents rise.

As neighborhood businesses and societies began to reflect a growing interest in American ways, the community along Hudson Avenue also maintained a strong interest in events in Poland. Following Prince Lubomirski's visit in January 1920, local Poles responded to a nationwide sale of Polish government bonds. Advertisements appeared in local newspapers under Lubomirski's name, urging immigrant families to invest in the future of their homeland: "You sons and grandsons and great-grandsons of Poland will not desert the Motherland in her hour of need. . . . To whom can she appeal, if not to you—you who have peace and plenty? She asks you to invest your savings that your kindred over the sea may have tools with which to work, seed to sow, and that their industries may be revived. Answer, you sons of Poland, so that all the world may know—Poland shall live!"[38]

The ads were placed in local newspapers, and in newspapers across the country, by the National Campaign Committee for the Republic of Poland Loan, whose goal was to raise $50 million for the reconstruction and industrial development of Poland. Rochester families contributed approximately $110,000 toward the drive, pledging $10,000 of that amount at an outdoor rally held near the intersection of Hudson Avenue and Norton Street in July 1920.[39] These donations fell considerably short of the local quota, however, and the drive ended as a disappointing failure in Rochester and across the country. Because of division in the Polish community nationwide and problems in organizing the loan with American banks, only a fraction of the $50 million goal was subscribed.

Three years later, another prominent member of the new Polish Republic visited Rochester

Rochester's Harcerstwo, 1930s. (Courtesy of Mr. and Mrs. Karol Anders)

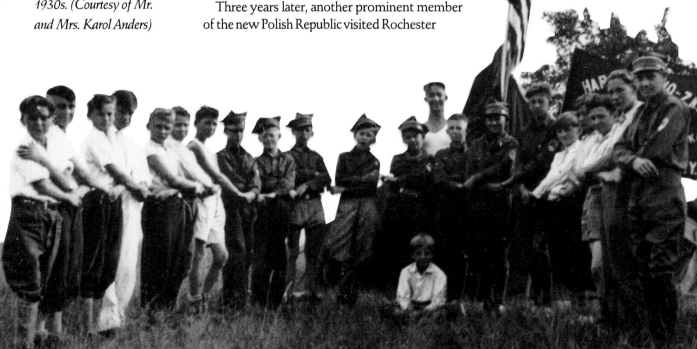

while on a tour of the United States. General Jozef Haller, who had led Polish troops based in France during World War I, arrived in 1923, stopping for the most part in cities with large Polish settlements. Unlike Lubomirski's visit, the general's stay in Rochester was complicated by European politics, and troubled by a heated exchange between the city's Poles and their Jewish, Lithuanian, and Ukrainian neighbors.

Animosity had festered between local Poles and local Jews, Lithuanians, and Ukrainians since the end of World War I, a reflection of wider controversy over the determination of Poland's borders.[40] The Treaty of Versailles, signed in June 1919, had established only a portion of Poland's boundaries, pointedly neglecting to define the new nation's eastern frontier.[41] Discussion regarding Poland's territories was complicated and charged with emotion, since any attempt to draw boundaries for the new Polish state brought sizable ethnic minority groups under Polish rule—notably Ukrainians, Lithuanians, and Jews—and left large numbers of Poles outside the national territory. The delegates' decision to leave Poland's frontiers ill-defined, and to call for plebiscites in a number of disputed regions, set the stage for a series of border wars and skirmishes between Poland and its neighbors. The designation of Poland's eastern border was not resolved until after the Poles defeated the Soviet Russians in the war of 1919–20. The resulting frontier was officially recognized by the United States in 1923.

The dispute over Poland's boundaries evoked a number of bitter, longstanding rivalries, including the Poles' and Lithuanians' tug-of-war for the city of Wilno, and the Poles' and Ukrainians' alternate attempts to gain Eastern Galicia. In the case of each conflict, accusations of brutality and atrocities surfaced on both sides and were reported in the international press. During the same period, a series of articles printed in the London *Times* accused the new Polish government of carrying out brutal pogroms against its Jewish citizens.[42] Ignacy Paderewski, now premier of the Polish Republic, denied the reports of persecution of Polish Jews and asked Woodrow Wilson to form a commission of Americans to investigate the charges.[43]

Against this backdrop of accusation and invective, General Haller launched his good-will tour of the United States. Three days before his arrival in Rochester in November 1923, approximately 1,000 Lithuanian, Ukrainian, and Jewish residents met at St. Josaphat's Ukrainian Church and approved a written protest which delegates carried to city hall the next day.[44] The document, which called Haller "a European propagandist of militant imperialism, nationalistic hatred and religious intolerance," "leader of the anti-Semitic movement in Poland," and "perpetrator of military outrages in Lithuania and the Ukraine," recited claims of Polish atrocities and urged Mayor Clarence D. Van Zandt not to extend the city's welcome to the general. Haller, then in Buffalo, vigorously denied the charges and offered to meet while in Rochester with "representatives of all nationalities who wish to confer with him on any subject pertaining to the Polish government."[45] Van Zandt, caught in the middle of this unpleasantness, declared to the press: "Our City Hall is no place for threshing out the merits of European disputes. I have given my word to contribute to the reception of General Haller and shall keep my word."[46] Never-

St. Stanislaus school-children welcoming General Jozef Haller to Rochester, 1923. (Courtesy of Rev. Alexander J. Stec)

theless, Van Zandt left for a vacation in Atlantic City the evening before Haller's arrival, and Alderman Abram DePotter greeted the general at city hall.

No further protests marred the general's stay in Rochester, on a whirlwind day which included services at St. Stanislaus Church, a motorcade through the Polish neighborhood, a luncheon at the Chamber of Commerce, a visit with George Eastman, and an evening reception at Falcon Hall. Along Hudson Avenue, at least, Haller received a rousing welcome: "The street was thronged on both sides with cheering crowds as the party drove through the Polish section of the city and thousands were turned away from the door of the hall, within which every available space was filled by the enthusiastic audience which stood on its feet during the two hours of the program, so closely packed that persons could scarcely raise their hands to clap. The hall echoed time and again with enthusiastic cheers."[47] The general appeared to enjoy his view of Rochester, proclaiming the city "wonderful," according to the *Democrat and Chronicle,* and "departing, as he arrived, to the cheers of Rochester members of the Polish legionnaires in their uniforms of bleu d'horizon."

The city's citizens of Polish descent cheered heartily again four years later, when the government of Poland confirmed its highest civilian honor on one of Rochester's most famous sons. In a ceremony held at the Chamber of Commerce on December 10, 1927, George Eastman received the *Polonia Restituta* for his philanthropic work on behalf of Poland.[48] Dr. Stefan Roscicki, secretary of the Polish legation in Washington, D.C., conferred the award on Eastman and spoke on behalf of the government of Poland and its citizens. Roscicki recounted the hardships which his country had faced after the war, when Poland lay "prostrate and bleeding, utterly despoiled by the various invaders . . . those times were very dark for the people of Poland." In response to the country's appeals for assistance, forwarded to the Rochester War Chest by the city's Polish citizens, Eastman allocated funds for Poland's relief in his role as War Chest president: $100,000 in

General Jozef Haller was greeted by Polish Army veterans during his visit to Rochester in 1923.

1919, $25,000 in 1920, $10,000 in 1921. Acknowledging these generous contributions and the industrialist's "many activities for the uplifting of those less fortunate," Roscicki extended his government's gratitude to Eastman and assured him that "the records of my country will perpetuate your name forever."

Eastman accepted the award with a brief speech in which he recalled the inspirational address delivered by Paderewski at the Chamber of Commerce in 1918. Of his own contributions, Eastman Kodak Company's founder commented modestly: "That [Poland] should select me as one to honor for my unpretentious part during the war is more than I deserve, but as a token of good will from my Polish friends and fellow citizens, I accept it with profound gratitude and sincere appreciation."

During the dinner, guests including Chamber of Commerce members and prominent Polish American citizens were treated to a performance by the Echo chorus and the St. Cecilia Choir. Colonel Francis Fronczak, health commissioner of the city of Buffalo and nationally prominent leader of Polonia, delivered the evening's keynote address, declaring that "few names are known throughout the world as is that of George Eastman. . . . In Warsaw, I was told by many persons that Mr. Eastman is the only man well known from this part of our country, not only because of the product which bears his name but also because of his humanitarian views and broad outlook on life." In conclusion, Fronczak wished Eastman well on his upcoming expedition to Africa: "In a few days, Mr. Eastman, you are leaving for a distant land. You may be sure that millions in Poland will pray for you and ask that all blessings fall upon you. Thousands have been saved through your encouragement and help and they will not be lacking in gratitude. . . . My prayers and the prayers of Polish children will follow you in your travels."[49]

From the point of view of the Sisters at St. Stanislaus School, there was no disputing the growth of the Polish community following the war. Enrollment at the parish school had climbed steadily since the turn of the century, when five Sisters welcomed 365 children to daily lessons.[50] In 1916, when the school's classrooms could hold no additional pupils, the Sisters moved from their living quarters on the building's second floor to a convent on Norton Street, leaving space that was quickly filled with rows of desks and additional students. By the mid-twenties, however, even these new classrooms were filled to capacity as the number of youngsters registered at St. Stanislaus topped 500.[51] Undaunted, the Sisters laid claim to space in the church sacristy where they opened an additional classroom temporarily.

In 1926, as the school's enrollment showed no signs of dropping, Father Stanislaus Szupa purchased three portable buildings containing two classrooms each. These awkward structures lined parish grounds for the next five years, heated during the winter months by stoves which the Sisters stoked between history and grammar lessons. Before long, even the portables were packed with students and, at the urging of Bishop John Francis O'Hern, Szupa launched a drive to raise funds for a new school building.[52] The lawyers, merchants, tradesmen, and shopkeepers whose businesses lined Hudson Avenue donated to the drive, and each of the school's 600 children was asked to collect enough pennies to cover the cost of a single brick.

Penny by penny, the building fund grew and, in 1929, the parish called upon architect George Lorenz to prepare a design for the new school. Lorenz's plans outlined a two-story brick building which would contain ten classrooms, a large auditorium with a stage and basketball court, and a basement meeting hall with four bowling alleys. Bishop O'Hern blessed the school's cornerstone in June 1930 and work proceeded on the huge structure for the next fifteen months, the project accumulating costs of $180,000 for the parish.[53] The building was ready in September 1931, the year that 750 children from the Polish neighborhood pushed St. Stanislaus' enrollment to third highest in the diocese.

As St. Stanislaus School's enrollment rose, the population of the Polish neighborhood spilled beyond Clifford Avenue to the south and North Street to the east. Weeger Street, Baron Street, Remington Street, and Reed Park were now dotted with the homes of Polish families, many of whom had arrived in Rochester following the war. Some walked a half-mile or more to attend services at St. Stanislaus on Sundays; others joined the congregation of German Catholics at Holy Redeemer Church. Those who wanted their children to study the Polish language sent their youngsters off each morning to St. Stanislaus School, a trek which the children completed four times a day—once in the morning, then home for lunch, back to school for afternoon lessons, home again at the end of the day.

Feeling themselves too far removed from St. Stanislaus Parish, a group of families who lived at the southern end of the Polish neighborhood approached Father Szupa in 1927 and asked for his help in forming a second Roman Catholic parish for Poles.[54] Szupa supported the plan, and agreed to help the group arrange a

Graduating class of 1927, St. Stanislaus School. (Courtesy of Rev. Alexander J. Stec)

meeting with Bishop Thomas F. Hickey. The bishop received the delegation and, as an initial step, asked them to canvass their neighborhood and collect the signatures of potential parishioners. Among those who expressed early support for the new parish were Joseph Kaminski, Walter Markowski, Stephen Milosz, John Polanowski, Ignatius Sapikowski, Andrew Sykut, Leon and Stanley Szarlacki, and Felix Wrublewski.[55] Bishop Hickey, for his part, contacted the Franciscan Fathers, Order of Minor Conventuals, to offer them stewardship of the Polish congregation. After Father Justin Figas, the Franciscans' provincial, accepted Hickey's offer, the bishop announced the formation of the Parish of St. Theresa of the Child Jesus in September 1927.[56] The boundaries of the new parish would

extend from the Genesee River on the west to Carter Street on the east, and from Wilkins Street on the north to the edge of the Polish neighborhood on the south.

Fifteen days later, the new congregation of approximately 200 families held its first services in Concordia Hall, on the grounds of Holy Redeemer Parish.[57] Father Szupa was given the honor of celebrating Mass, and Monsignor John Francis O'Hern, as apostolic administrator, conveyed the congratulations of the Rochester Diocese to St. Theresa's parishioners. Those assembled also had an opportunity to meet Father Michael Drzewucki, the young Franciscan who would serve as St. Theresa's founding pastor.

For the next year, the members of St. Theresa's congregation held services in Concordia Hall and Drzewucki boarded in a home on Trust Street while the Polish families raised money for the purchase of property.[58] Parishioners donated approximately $60 at services each Sunday, an amount which was supplemented

New School of St. Stanislaus, 1931. (Courtesy of Rev. Alexander J. Stec)

by collections taken door to door in the Polish neighborhood. In September's house collection, the families of St. Theresa's contributed $846 to the parish treasury, and their neighbors at St. Stanislaus raised $1,100. By October 30th, the new congregation had collected $2,500, more than enough to cover their first month's expenses which included $100 for the rental of Concordia Hall, a stipend of $125 for Father Drzewucki, $240 for furnishings used at Sunday services, $25 for altar wine, $35 for coal, and $4 for gas and electricity.

During the next months, parishioners continued to contribute toward the building fund, and received donations from neighbors and friends such as the Polish Falcons of Nest 52, who sent $38 in November. Gradually, the congregation acquired items and supplies for the parish, many purchased from Polish merchants: lumber with which to build kneelers for the chapel in Concordia Hall from Szczepan Zielinski, coal to heat their rented facilities from John Antczak, kitchen utensils from Przysinda's hardware store, and silverware from Czepiel's jewelry shop. In February 1928, their savings bolstered by a loan of $24,000 from Lincoln Alliance Bank, the parish trustees agreed to purchase property on Mark Street: two lots and adjoining land which would extend the parish's grounds to Hudson Avenue on the west and to Watkin Terrace on the north.[59]

Shortly after the deed of purchase was signed, Father Drzewucki and the parish trustees called upon architect George Lorenz to develop plans for a combination church and schoolhouse. A construction crew cleared the Mark Street property of old houses and a barn, and began digging the building's foundation in spring 1928. On July 4th, Hickey officiated at the blessing of the church's cornerstone, an event which drew the attendance of Mayor Joseph C. Wilson, Public Safety Commissioner George J. Nier, the pastors of the neighboring churches of Holy Redeemer and St. George, and at least 1,000 parishioners from St. Theresa's and St. Stanislaus.[60] Following the ceremony, Drzewucki described the building's design to the press: the Gothic structure, of red brick and white stone trim, would extend

Church of St. Theresa of the Child Jesus. (Courtesy of Mr. and Mrs. Joseph Zablotski)

62 feet on Mark Street and 118 feet toward Clifford Avenue, and would contain a first-floor chapel, a basement auditorium, and six classrooms and office space on the second floor. In order to eliminate the use of pillars in the chapel, the building would be supported by "six of the longest single-span steel girders in the city."

While their church was being constructed, parishioners purchased two homes: one which would serve as a rectory and the other, at 19 Watkin Terrace, which would become a convent for the school's Franciscan Sisters of St. Joseph.[61] Repairs and remodeling began on the houses in the spring, carried out by neighborhood tradesmen including plumber Henry Janowski, carpenter John Ryszkowski, and builder Victor Czerkas. The purchase of 23 varieties of trees and shrubs—among them high bush cranberry, honeysuckle, lilac, mountain ash, Japanese barberry, forsythia, and snowberry—completed plans for the beautification of parish grounds.

Parishioners crowded in front of the Church of St. Theresa on December 9, 1928, carrying American flags and the banners of religious societies as Hickey, now a titular archbishop, presided over the building's dedication.[62] A month later, 106 children began their education in the second-floor school, which included six classrooms, a teachers' room, janitor's room, supply room, clinic, and library. The parish of 200 families counted approximately 1,100 persons: the majority of Polish descent, including many new immigrants. It had taken St. Theresa's families only a year to organize their parish, build a church and school, and prepare homes for their priest and Sisters. In the early months of 1929, their satisfaction at this accomplishment overshadowed concern for the size of the parish's debt, which now totaled $165,000 in loans from the Lincoln Alliance Bank.

At the close of the twenties, St. Theresa's Parish stood as a sign of the Polish

A group of St. Theresa's parishioners, posed in front of their church on Mark Street. (Courtesy of the Palis Family)

*First graduates of St.
Theresa's School, 1930.
(Courtesy of John Hoholuk)*

neighborhood's growth and its residents' confidence in the future, the fourth parish formed to serve an expanding community which held 10,000 persons.[63] Polish Americans now represented the fourth-largest ethnic group in the city, distinguished by their claim on the homes, organizations, and businesses spread east and west of Hudson Avenue. Until the last months of 1929, few in Polonia had reason to doubt that the coming decade would extend their prosperity.

*Father Michael Drzewucki
First Pastor of St. Theresa's
Parish*

On the north aisle of St. Stanislaus Church, at the end of a row of vivid stained glass saints, is a window that depicts St. Cecilia, patroness of musicians. The face of the saint has graced St. Stanislaus Church for more than sixty years, but few who see the window realize that it holds the story of Emily Dukat, a girl from the Polish neighborhood.[64]

Emily was one of six children of Stanislaw and Aleksandra Dukat, owners of a successful Hudson Avenue bakery in the early 1900s. A promising violinist, Emily performed with the Rochester Symphony Orchestra at age 16 and was invited to appear in concert at the Genesee Valley Club. She performed often at events in the Polish community, and in January 1920 was given the honor of playing before Prince Kazimierz and Princess Teresa Lubomirski during the couple's appearance at Convention Hall. Emily's rendition of Wieniawski's "Kujawiak" so delighted the envoy and his wife that they paid a visit to the young violinist later at her home.

A few days after Lubomirski's visit, Emily contracted influenza and the virus quickly developed into pneumonia. She died on January 28, 1920, less than a week after her triumphant appearance at Convention Hall. An obituary in the *Democrat and Chronicle* observed:

The character and musical ability of Miss Dukat were a matter of pride with a large proportion of the Americans of Polish descent living in Rochester. She was looked upon by hundreds of her people as a sort of representative of them, and in all she was and all she did she realized their ideal of what they wished Rochester as a whole to esteem in them.

Emily was buried from St. Stanislaus Church in the gown that she wore for her performance before the Lubomirskis. The envoy, who after leaving Rochester had continued on his tour of the United States, sent a bouquet of flowers to Emily's wake when he learned of her death.

In Emily's memory, Stanislaw and Aleksandra Dukat gave Father Ignacy Klejna money to purchase a stained glass window for St. Stanislaus Church, requesting that the memorial be designed in honor of St. Cecilia and that the window's artist work from their daughter's photograph. The St. Cecilia window, more meticulously detailed than other windows in St. Stanislaus Church, depicts the patron saint of musicians posed before an organ, looking out across the aisle with the pensive smile of Emily Dukat.

Adam Felerski

He was one of the first children born to Polish immigrants in Rochester, as noted in the records of St. Michael's Parish several months before the opening of St. Stanislaus Church: Adam Felerski, born May 19, 1890, to Franciszek Felerski and Jozefa Wozniak.[65] Fifty-five years later, at the time of his death, Felerski's name was among the most familiar Polish names in Rochester, and a local newspaper acknowledged him as a "moving force" in the development of the city's Polonia.

Felerski attended St. Bridget's parochial school and East High School, where he compiled an academic record that won him entry to the University of Buffalo law school. Adam would be the only one of the six Felerski children to attend college, and when he graduated as president of his class he would become one of the first members of the local Polish community to hold a university degree.

A few years after he completed law school and returned to Rochester, Felerski became a central figure in his community's campaign to support Poland during World War I. As a member of the Polish Citizens Committee, he worked closely with George Eastman, Rush Rhees, and other members of the War Chest's Executive Board to raise funds for Poland's defense and reconstruction. An articulate young attorney, he traveled to New York City to speak with Ignacy Paderewski, a meeting which resulted in the pianist's 1918 address at the Chamber of Commerce. The same year, tragedy touched Felerski's life when he and his wife Martha suffered the loss of their two infant sons during the great influenza epidemic.

Following the war, Felerski increased his visibility in Polonia and in Rochester's political circles, emerging repeatedly as an organizer of community gatherings and

112

a spokesman for citizens of Polish descent. Felerski's name would be associated with virtually every event in the immigrant community during the next 25 years, from the 1920 Homelands Exhibition to the 1942 Polonia Civic Centre's Charity Ball. An active Republican, Felerski took an interest in local politics and participated in the work of the Polonia Republican League, one of the first partisan political groups in the Polish neighborhood. The impression he made on Kazimierz Lubomirski during the envoy's 1920 visit to Rochester led to Felerski's appointment as the first consular representative to the new Polish government in the United States. Later, he served as a representative of the Polish Council located in Buffalo, a post in which he supervised legal transactions between Poles in western New York State and their relatives in Europe. After helping to organize the Pulaski State Republican League, Felerski rose to prominence in state politics and worked extensively on Governor Dewey's election campaigns.

A quiet entrepreneur, Felerski invested in a number of projects launched in Polish Town, most notably the Polish Clothing Manufacturing Company and the Polish newspaper, *Rochester Rekord*. His interest was piqued by any promising idea in which Poles were involved, and he did not hesitate to underwrite the patent application for an electric ladies' shaver when its designers, a group of local men including some of Polish descent, described the invention's merits and requested his support.

For years, Felerski maintained two offices, one downtown in the Ellwanger and Barry building, the other in his home on Hudson Avenue. As one of the first lawyers of Polish descent in the city, he paid particular attention to requests for his services from neighbors, and often accepted payment in the form of backyard produce from immigrants who did not have the money to pay his fee. His home was always open to those who had an affiliation with Poland, whether the guest was an immigrant who needed help with resettlement, or an international figure such as actress Pola Negri.

Adam and Martha raised two daughters, Arlene and Celeste, and remained parishioners of St. Stanislaus Parish throughout their thirty-year marriage. Although he talked often of visiting Poland and applied for his passport, Felerski found it difficult to clear his busy schedule and postponed the trip to his parents' homeland a number of times. He died suddenly of heart failure in 1946 at age 55, after a routine day spent in his downtown office. "He was interested in every local Polish affair and project," the *Democrat and Chronicle* noted in Felerski's obituary, "and although he never held official posts in the local organizations, he was recognized as the moving force in each of them."

Wojtczak's Bakery

When they opened their first bakery in 1915, Walter Wojtczak's work day began at midnight and his wife Madeline's began at 4:00 a.m. Walter mixed and kneaded dough for bread, rolls, and pastry through the early morning hours, and before sunrise Madeline loaded a pushcart with the fresh *babka* and *placek* that she sold door to door in the neighborhood. Although their hours on the job would change little, during the next forty years the Wojtczaks built their modest shop into a bakery renowned throughout the city for fine pastries, sold in the forties at more than 100 outlets in the Rochester area.

Walter (Waclaw) Wojtczak and Madeline (Magdalena) Ladra met in Rochester after emigrating from their homes in Poland.[66] Walter had completed his apprenticeship in baking in Europe and, following their marriage in 1914, the couple opened a shop in a building south of Brodowczynski's meat market. The bread and pastries that Madeline peddled door to door and delivered to grocery stores sold well, enabling the Wojtczaks to buy Stanislaw Dukat's spacious bakery at 990 Hudson Avenue in 1921. *Pierwszorzedna Polska piekarnia,* they announced in advertisements. "First-class Polish bakery: freshest, most wholesome pastries of the old country and America. We also carry fresh meat and provisions."

At that time, the store featured bread, kuchen, and cakes, and stocked a few groceries that housewives might add to their purchase when they stopped for baked goods. Walter started his yeast doughs at midnight six days a week, and worked until noon with a crew of three or four bakers. Madeline opened the doors to customers at 5:00 a.m. and supervised sales until the store closed: at 6:00 p.m. Mondays through Fridays, at 9:00 p.m. on Saturdays.

Ten years later the store sold baked goods exclusively, on the strength of the reputation the Wojtczaks had earned for Walter's specialty, fine European pastries: Danishes, seven-layer torte, Sahara torte, melange, rum soak, *paczki,* butter cookies, and butter kuchen with thick fruit filling. As his success in pastries grew, Walter traveled to baking centers in the United States and Europe to collect additional recipes and to seek out master bakers and pastry chefs for his staff. Increasingly, the Wojtczaks' shop filled requests for pastries for weddings, banquets, and teas, noting in a 1938 advertisement: "We welcome orders for all occasions."

While her husband supervised the pastry kitchen, Madeline took charge of sales at the counter, arranged displays, and managed the store's finances. A crew of girls from the neighborhood helped her wait on customers, dressed in the white aprons that Mrs. Wojtczak insisted be freshly pressed when the girls came on duty. She also insisted that display cases and windows be kept spotless, and would polish the glass herself if her clerks were busy filling orders.

During the thirties, the Wojtczaks expanded their trade to a network of other stores, delivering bread and pastries to approximately 150 groceries within a

The Wojtczak family with employees of their store. (Courtesy of Mr. and Mrs. Joseph Zablotski)

five-mile radius of Hudson Avenue. By the forties, they had purchased seven trucks to carry deliveries to additional outlets beyond city limits. The Bond Baking Company sold Walter's rye bread on consignment, two westside food stores featured his baked goods, and the Manhattan Restaurant on East Avenue included his tortes and teacakes on its dessert menu. At the close of the Second World War, when the Wojtczaks' son Carl became a partner in the business, the company employed a crew of 36 (including 10 full-time bakers, clerks, truck drivers, and an accountant), delivered baked goods to stores and homes along seven routes, and earned a quarter million dollars in sales annually.

As owners of a successful business, the Wojtczaks played prominent roles in Polish community activities during the thirties and forties. Walter, a member of the Polish Falcons and the Echo Singing Association, served on steering committees for a number of events including General Jozef Haller's visit to Rochester in 1934. Madeline, active in Centrala, organized a troupe of dancers who performed traditional mazurkas, poloniases, and obereks at community gatherings in the thirties. She served on the organizing committee for several of Centrala's Charity Balls, and for many years was a member of Zonta, the local league of businesswomen.

The couple also gave generously, often anonymously, to local charities, and regularly donated their excess baked goods to convents and orphanages. Over the years, they contributed substantially to St. Stanislaus Parish, support acknowledged in 1931 when Walter became one of five local laymen honored by papal designation as Knights of St. Gregory.

In 1955, the family sold their business to new owners who kept the Hudson Avenue store open under the Wojtczaks' name and continued to prepare many of their recipes. A few years later, Walter and Madeline grew restless with retirement and convinced Carl to start a new "Wojtczak's" on Titus Avenue. The Irondequoit store was a family enterprise in which three generations—Walter, Carl and his wife Elva, and their son Dean—collaborated in preparing traditional Wojtczak's pastries. Although that store closed in 1972, the Hudson Avenue store remains open under other management, still drawing customers from throughout the area for the *babka,* kuchen, and *paczki* that won Wojtczak's bakery a wide following early in the century.

7 | Unity, Guidance, Commonweal

Helen Eurack, oldest daughter in a family of five children, scrubbed floors and washed clothing six days a week in a wealthier family's residence. Katarzyna Sojka, a widow, raised four daughters and met mortgage payments by sewing garments, paid by the piece, at her Sobieski Street home. Michal Wojciechowski, a father of five, sold his overcoat and used the profit to buy groceries for his family when he was out of work. These stories echo the experience of thousands of others who weathered the Great Depression in Rochester's Polish community, during lean years when children went barefoot in the summer to save shoe leather, when a schoolgirl might own two dresses (one to wear while the other

was being laundered), and when young men paid for 25 cent haircuts in installments of a nickel a week.[1] In the 1930s, the sustenance of the family became the primary goal and all had a responsibility in that effort, from the child who walked to the bakery to purchase day-old bread to grandparents who stitched piecework at home.

Beyond the energy needed to sustain its families, the community faced the task of maintaining four parishes, two schools, an avenue of businesses and shops, an array of meeting halls and organizations—the neighborhood built at considerable sacrifice over the previous four decades. If opportunities for work were sporadic and savings all but depleted, the Polish families could draw upon reserves of self-sufficiency and a sense

These people, living in our midst for the past fifty years or more, have proved in myriad ways their loyalty to American ideals and to the best traditions of Rochester. . . . This community has determinedly set about to prove to the city that its members, as acknowledged Poles, intend to shoulder a just portion of civic responsibility, and intend to make the greatest possible contribution to the city.

**Norman T. Lyon
"50 Years of the Polish Community in Rochester"
October 8, 1933**

of neighborhood alliance. Self-sufficiency, a value passed on from the first immigrants, would help innumerable families through the worst of the hard times, while community cohesiveness would be best expressed in the work of "Centrala," the civic society that came to prominence during a decade of instability.

Life in Rochester was not immediately disturbed by the stock market crash of October 1929.[2] Local industries and banks had been prosperous for too long for city residents to feel threatened by a financial crisis that appeared to be centered elsewhere. Nevertheless, Rochester would maintain its complacency for only a few months, until the winter of 1929–30 when the Great Depression began to take its toll on the local economy, affecting even staunch employers like Eastman Kodak, Bausch & Lomb, and the clothing firms.

Local unemployment rates, which had been increasing ominously since 1928, swelled in the weeks following the crash: at least 10,000 Rochesterians out of work in January 1930, as many as 15,000 laid off from their jobs in March.[3] That month, as several thousand without work marched on Washington Square, city leaders established a Civic Committee on Unemployment, made up of representatives of the Chamber of Commerce, the Council of Social Agencies, the Federation of Churches, Catholic Charities, the Central Trades Council, and the Bureau of Municipal Research. Despite the efforts of seven subcommittees organized to combat the problem, the count of unemployed citizens continued to rise and reached an estimated 19,000 persons in November.

"Gentlemen," City Manager Stephen B. Story wrote to City Council on November 1st, "the situation facing the City of Rochester is today more serious than it has been for a long period of years. We believed circumstances to be bad a year ago. This fall we find them to be considerably worse. It is sufficient to point out that there are more persons than ever before walking the streets out of work and seeking jobs."[4] Noting that local appropriations for public welfare and charity had increased by 44 percent during 1930 and that state revenue would provide little support in the coming year, Story proposed in his budget for 1931 an Emergency Work Fund, designed to create jobs for several hundred local workers. He included a list of projects to which the workers could be assigned, consisting for the most part of municipal improvements such as removing dead trees from Durand-Eastman Park, cleaning city property near the Charlotte Blast Furnace, planting and seeding at Maplewood Park, and laying a water line to the Polo Field at Cobbs Hill. "Surely," the City Manager appealed to council members, "we could by this self-respecting means enable many a deserving family to avoid starvation and help partially to eliminate the ill effects of a dole system." Council approved Story's plan at its next meeting, and within days the first contingent of workers set off to clean, beautify, and repair city property.

Although the Emergency Work Fund provided jobs for several thousand citizens, the local economy deteriorated further in 1931 and the number of unemployed Rochesterians increased. Hoping, at least, to forestall financial disaster for individual families, City Council poured more than $5 million into charity and work relief in 1932.[5] Acting on their own initiative, meanwhile, fourteen local corporations organized voluntary programs of unemployment insurance, offering workers who had been laid off 60 percent of their salaries beginning in January 1933. The Civic Committee on Unemployment, which had coaxed $6 million for work relief from private citizens in 1931, put aside $16,000 for "subsistence gardens" in 1932. Two thousand families lined up for allocations of free vegetable seeds, and planted a total 250 acres of backyard crops that spring. Despite such efforts to counteract the grim economy, city leaders could do little to raise the morale of hard-pressed citizens, who celebrated the opening of the new Veterans Memorial Bridge by organizing a lottery: the winner needed only to guess the day and hour of the first suicide from the bridge.

By the end of 1932, it was clear that local initiative and resources would not be strong enough to restore the city's vitality. Many Rochesterians placed their hopes that fall in the presidential campaign of Franklin Delano Roosevelt and, like residents of cities throughout the country, welcomed federally-sponsored projects which carried the promise of jobs for local citizens: Civilian Conservation Corps, National Recovery Act, Works Progress Administration, Civil Works Administration. The effects of federal aid were felt almost immediately: in Rochester, more than 2,000 young men found work with the CCC between May 1933 and January 1934, while 16,000 local laborers re-entered the work force through projects funded by the CWA in winter 1933–34.[6]

Confident that the worst was over, Rochester staged one of the most impressive parades in its history in support of the National Recovery Act on September 26, 1933.[7] As many as 80,000 citizens joined in the six-hour march, cheered by 175,000 others who crowded the sidewalks along East Avenue and East Main Street. Military bands, high school bands, Boy Scouts, Girl Scouts, and color guards filed through downtown followed by workers from the city's commercial and industrial firms. Eastman Kodak Company, the Lincoln Alliance Bank, the *Times-Union,* Neisner Brothers' Stores, IGA, A & P, Gleason Works, Taylor Instrument, Shuron Optical—the list of companies in the line of march was extensive. Representatives of many of the city's immigrant groups also turned out to show their alliance with the president's recovery plan, among them a unit of Polish Americans from the northeast side. All cheered the message of imminent prosperity delivered by Mayor Percival Oviatt: "We stand on the threshold of what seems to be a better day. Let everyone join in the general rejoicing over the word which has been received, that the prodigal which we call prosperity is soon to return. Let everyone join in the celebration of the good news and its promise that life is to be a little more worth living."

Despite all hopes to the contrary, Oviatt and the others were wrong about the timing of prosperity's return: the Great Depression would drag on in Rochester and across the country for the next six years. Some disillusioned citizens disregarded the mayor's call to general rejoicing in 1933, staging instead a May Day parade to protest the plight of the American worker.[8] On May 1st, members of the Proletarian Party and "militants of the working class" converged on Washington Square in four columns from the four corners of the city. Those who formed the column from the north gathered at 818 Hudson Avenue to begin their march, in front of *Dom Ludowy,* Polish People's Home.

The wage earners of Polish Town were hard hit by the Depression. Factory workers and laborers felt the effects of the ailing economy first, many dismissed from their jobs on the city's assembly lines and in its industrial shops. Although the hundreds of Poles who were clothing workers fared slightly better, avoiding indefinite layoff under the guardianship of the ACWA, most faced two or three months at a stretch without income as the garment firms rotated available work among their employees.[9] While laborers sat idle, trade dwindled in neighborhood shops. Grocers, bakers, butchers, and dairymen offered their wares to regular customers on credit, a practice initiated before the Depression as a convenience but now extended to many households of necessity.

For the better part of the thirties, frugality and economy replaced the spirit of enterprise and investment promoted during the previous decade. For the majority of the city's 10,000 Polish residents, maintaining their families in food, clothing, and housing was now challenge enough.[10] During the Depression, the Poles' traditionally large households became a liability from one point of view and an advantage from another: having a family of seven children meant a dinner table set for nine, but also represented a number of possibilities for work. The wife of a laborer who had been laid off could serve as a chambermaid at a downtown hotel. A teenage daughter could be pulled from school and sent to a wealthier household to clean, cook, and launder. Children as young as age five could spend several weeks in the summer harvesting fruit on the farms north of Polish Town, earning for their work in the fields a handful of change a day. In many cases, income from these domestic, part-time, and seasonal jobs kept a family financially solvent while the head of the house was out of work.

With income uncertain or meagre, frugality became a virtue and economy a daily practice. Some weeks, half a loaf of bread from Wojtczak's bakery was as much as a family could afford, and black bread sprinkled with sugar was the sweetest dessert children could expect. New shoes were often a luxury, and parents became adept at cutting patches and fitting soles for worn shoes from strops of leather. Backyard gardens provided many families with a winter's supply of vegetables and fruit, after mother and daughters spent hours in a steaming kitchen canning the harvest of tomatoes, cucumbers, beets, pears, peaches, and cherries.

For some in the Polish neighborhood, as elsewhere, the burdens of the Depression—unemployment, collapse of a small business, loss of the family

Father Joseph Kula with altar boys of St. Casimir's Parish, 1933. (Courtesy of Mr. and Mrs. Thaddeus Nawrocki)

120

home—were debilitating and culminated in personal tragedy: bankruptcy, alcoholism, shattered family life, suicide. Many others found they could help offset troubles by drawing upon the support of extended families, fraternal societies, and parishes.[11] During the thirties, it was not unusual for a newlywed couple to board with one set of parents for several years, or for a widow and her children to stay with an in-law, sister, or cousin temporarily. A man who belonged to one of the Polish societies could depend upon a stipend of a few dollars a week while he was out of work, particularly if he were recovering from an illness or injury. A member of St. Casimir's Parish who had few financial resources could offer his children a summer vacation, thanks to Father Joseph Kula who persuaded a friend to turn open land on Conesus Lake into a campsite. Parents paid no more than fifty cents a child for the excursion, and many Polish merchants donated food and supplies to the campers.

Reliance on relatives, friends, and colleagues in a community organization was acceptable and, for many families, an alternative to public assistance. Although those hardest hit by troubles might stand in line at city hall for a handout of canned goods, few would register for the welfare available at relief agencies.[12] Hard work and self-help had long been promoted in the neighborhood and public assistance, in contrast, became a mark of individual failure and a matter of community shame. From the point of view of the majority of immigrants and their children, it was better to impose on relatives, borrow from friends, or ask help of a parish priest than to apply for and receive the city's charity. Because work relief projects carried less stigma, many from Polish Town sought help at the Public Employment Center, in the hope of being matched with even a menial job.[13]

The aid provided by societies and parishes was a form of community assistance, dependent upon Polonia's continued support for these institutions. During the thirties, the residents of Polish Town maintained their parishes and schools, but not without difficulty. At St. Theresa's Parish, organized just two years before the stock market crash, 250 families shouldered a debt of $165,000—the accumulated cost of purchasing land and establishing a church, school, rectory, and convent.[14] "This financial burden carried by the parishioners of St. Theresa Church, at times, seemed to be unbearable," the author of a parish history recalled forty years later. "Under all these circumstances, there were parishioners who, not with idle words but with deeds, helped the pastor carry the burden of church expenses."

At St. Casimir's Parish, approximately 200 families continued to underwrite pastor's salary, mortgage payments, and building repairs, and did not hesitate to organize lavish ceremonies to celebrate the parish's 25th anniversary in 1933.[15] Particular excitement surrounded the arrival of Bishop Franciszek Hodur, who traveled from the Polish National Catholic Church's cathedral in Scranton to take

Camp Kula, 1930s.
(Courtesy of Mr. and Mrs.
Thaddeus Nawrocki)

122

part in the jubilee. In acknowledgment of those who had given steady financial support through the years, the members of the Silver Jubilee Committee noted: "We unite with the believers, priests of the past, both living and dead, and the Rev. Bishop Hodur, First Bishop of the Polish National Catholic Church of America, in a prayer of thanks for all that has been accomplished. We also unite with the secular organizers, business men, friends and all those of good will for their frequent gifts and aid toward our betterment, and in their observing of our Silver Jubilee."

A few blocks north on Hudson Avenue, the parishioners of St. Stanislaus faced a massive debt incurred with the construction of their new school. In poor health and despondent over the parish's financial circumstances—$400,000 in debt with overdue payments on the church mortgage, outstanding promissory notes, and accumulated bills—Father Szupa resigned from the pastorate in December 1933.[16] He was succeeded by a man whom the *Democrat and Chronicle* described as "a jovial, friendly priest of great aplomb, yet businesslike and efficient with always a merry twinkle in his eye."[17] Joseph Balcerak, a graduate of St. Stanislaus School, returned from an assignment in Elmira to take charge of the parish of 1,100 families. With the help of Archbishop Edward Mooney, who persuaded local banks to reduce St. Stanislaus' interest rate from 5 percent to 3 percent, Balcerak set to work to reduce the parish's huge deficit, a task that would require his attention for the next fifteen years.

Smallest but not without support, the Polish Baptist Church maintained its membership of approximately 55 persons and met the portion of its expenses requested by the Baptist Union of Rochester and Monroe County.[18] Although this donation was minimal, it represented a sacrifice since, as the Reverend John Czajkowski pointed out in his 1932 report, his parishioners faced difficult times, "some of them losing their homes and nearly all of them being out of employment." Still, Czajkowski noted optimistically, this circumstance offered "an excellent opportunity for the preaching of the gospel."

Although the uncertain economy forced some of the neighborhood's businessmen to close their shops, others saw self-employment as their best or only option and attempted private enterprise in the thirties. Ludwik Skalny, a weaver of willow born in Poland, began making baskets in his home to sell to local florists when he lost his job before the stock market crash. Kazimierz Zamiara, a sausage maker who had sold his meats in towns west of Rochester, moved his family of seven children to the city in 1931 and opened a new market near St. Stanislaus Church. Teofil Jablonski held his job as a foreman at Fashion Park and added to his family's income with sales of canned goods and fresh produce at a Hudson Avenue grocery. Victor Anuszkiewicz, who was in high school when the Depression hit,

First Communion class of St. Theresa's Parish, 1938. (Courtesy of John Hoholuk)

used his savings to lease a small restaurant in Sea Breeze, the city's summer park on the lake, in 1934. During the years when retail sales were slow and the purchase of goods minimal, dozens of Polish-owned establishments carried on as they had in the past or opened for business: Sewilo's and Maciejewski's dairies, Chmielecki's and Grabowski's bakeries, Janowski's plumbing, Kozlowski's moving and carting, Grzeszczak's and Sobierajski's groceries, Zlotnik's dress shop, Czepiel's jewelry store, Smorol's dental supply company, Kujawa's farm market, and a litany of others.[19]

One recent immigrant was among those who succeeded in new enterprise during the Depression. Stanislaw Jezowski arrived in Rochester in 1932 to offer the neighborhood a service it had not enjoyed for some time: publication of news in Polish.[20] With a one-man operation headquartered on Hudson Avenue, Jezowski gathered and recorded information about events in Rochester's Polonia, then forwarded his reports to Buffalo for inclusion in *Dziennik dla Wszystkich,* a daily that claimed distinction as "America's largest Polish newspaper."

Jezowski was born in 1903 in Sietesz in Malopolska, youngest in a family of eight children. As a young man, he was keenly interested in Poland's development as a nation, and kept informed of political events and social movements by subscribing to newspapers and periodicals published in Poland and abroad. His home soon housed a substantial library of information, and served as a meeting center for others who would stop by to discuss the new Polish Republic, struggling to rebuild national identity and economy after the war.

In 1929, when the editors of one of the Polish American newspapers to which he subscribed suggested that they had a position for him, Jezowski decided to emigrate, hoping to build a stable life for his family in the United States. He left his wife Wladyslawa and three children (Zosia, Stasia, and Jozef) in Sietesz, expecting to sponsor their immigration after he had established a place for himself with the newspaper. To his disappointment, the position did not materialize and, as the American economy faltered, Jezowski joined his brother in Utica, New York, where he found a job at a steel mill. The young man's fortunes took a grim turn in the first years of the Depression when a huge steel girder fell on his foot, crushing bones and disabling him for a full year.

Unable to get another industrial job, Jezowski trained as a barber, planning to open a shop until he learned that the editors of *Dziennik dla Wszystkich* were interested in establishing a branch of their newspaper in Rochester. He relocated from Utica in 1932 as *Dziennik's* Rochester representative, and organized for work in a building in which he set up both an office where he could write and a barber's chair. At 969 Hudson Avenue, Jezowski collected information about activities in Polonia, developing a network of personal contacts that ensured him notice of events, activities, and human interest items from the local community. He dispatched his accounts regularly to the main office, where they were included on the page reserved for Rochester news. Issues of *Dziennik,* delivered daily by express train from Buffalo, were distributed to local families by a crew of neighborhood boys and girls who filled canvas sacks with copies at Jezowski's office, then dashed off to deposit the papers on doorsteps before 6:00 p.m.

Dziennik enjoyed a healthy circulation in Rochester's Polonia and in other Polish communities, shared in living rooms and on front porches by families eager to

Barbara Anuszkiewicz Stira delivering Dziennik dla Wszystkich on Warsaw Street.

read the United States news of the day, learn of developments in Poland, and find descriptions of activities sponsored by their parishes and organizations. The newspaper provided important service in the thirties to communities where many still relied upon the Polish language. Balancing pride in heritage with helpful advice on integrating into American culture, the publication offered a point of view unavailable in the English language press and served as a unifying force in the Polish neighborhoods in which it was circulated.

In Rochester, *Dziennik* increased its following with the opening of a local office, and soon Jezowski added photographs provided by the Braknis Studio to his stories. He also arranged for advertisements from local retailers to accompany the Rochester page, surrounding his articles with messages to Polish consumers from

Stanislaw Jezowski, and the Rochester office of Dziennik dla Wszystkich. (Photo courtesy of Mr. and Mrs. Joseph Zablotski)

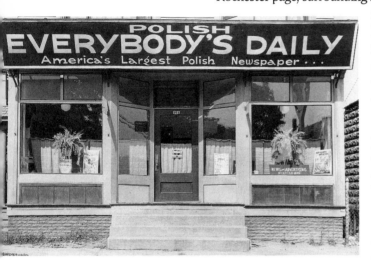

neighborhood tradesmen and department stores like Sibley's, McCurdy's, and Edward's. Within a few years, he was promoted to Rochester editor, and was sometimes asked to contribute a column published under his name on the editorial page of the national edition.

In the latter half of the thirties, when he had been a resident long enough to acquire citizenship, Jezowski sought permission for his family to immigrate to the United States, working with a sense of urgency as Germany's Third Reich expanded its influence in Europe. The family was reunited in 1938 when Wladyslawa arrived from Poland with Zosia, Stasia, and Jozef. The Jezowski children assisted their father with small tasks for the newspaper after school, walking to the office of the German *Abendpost* to fetch copy for announcements that the two papers shared, or hurrying to the Post Office to deposit envelopes for delivery to Buffalo when a deadline was tight.

The articles that families read on the Rochester page of *Dziennik* in the thirties offered news of a community that, for the most part, had turned inward, compelled by hardship to rely upon its own resources and institutions.[21] Those who had been Polonia's early settlers made the adjustment as a matter of course, falling back upon the values of hard work, self-reliance, and frugality that had characterized their experience as immigrants. For those of a younger generation, children and grandchildren of immigrants, the implications of an uncertain economy were more keenly felt. Their options and mobility limited, most in this group found that their first obligation was to contribute to the welfare of their families—usually, by securing a job in a reliable trade immediately after high school; sometimes, by leaving school before graduation to become a wage earner full-time. In the context of the need for job stability and family security, few of the community's young people aspired to the luxury of college education or departed the close-knit neighborhood that now looked to their support.

For young and old, the decade was of necessity a time of hard work and simple pleasures, of long hours on the job when a job could be found and of amusements that cost little money: dances at neighborhood clubs, parish picnics, field days hosted by the Falcons and PNA, concerts by the Echo chorus, amateur theater

presented by the Polish Dramatic Club, folk dance performances by young people in elegant costume.[22] Girls rode the streetcar or walked downtown to window-shop, and met their friends for ice cream sundaes at the Green Mill Parlor or at Andy's. Boys competed on athletic teams sponsored by the parishes, organizations, and businesses, and treated their dates to films and newsreels at the Dixie Theater and Sulkowski's Sun Theater. Families might go swimming at Sunset Point on the edge of Durand-Eastman Park, lingering afterward around a bonfire, or gather at home for card games spiced with a refreshment of homemade wine.

One neighborhood athletic team organized during the Depression grew from a diversion for young people into a local sensation, its accomplishments eventually earning the squad a feature story in *Life* magazine. The Filarets girls' basketball team, organized as part of the youth sodality at St. Stanislaus Parish, were energetic competitors who became the ranking female team in the city in 1932–33, the season when they won 25 of their 26 games.[23] Coached by Roy Van Graflan, an American League umpire, beginning in 1933–34, the Filarets played according to men's rules and advanced to competition against teams from out of state, strengthening their roster with players from Buffalo, Cleveland, and Chicago. The girls packed Falcon Hall for their home games and often played on double bills with the Rochester Seagrams, the men's team who later became the NBA's Rochester Royals. In 1940, when the Filarets' cumulative record was 338 wins, 12 losses, the team logged their 100th consecutive victory in a game whose final score was 100 to 16. Four years later, the girls broke the national record for consecutive victories held by a men's team when they won their 160th straight game, a distinction that propelled them to coverage in *Life* and gave them an eleven-year total of 523 wins, 12 losses.

As the number and variety of neighborhood societies attested, Polonia was capable of promoting a confusing collection of organizations whose interests sometimes coincided, but at other times conflicted. If groups with similar focus, like the Echo chorus and the St. Cecilia Choir, might find opportunities to work together, there were others that seemed unlikely candidates for affiliation. In some cases, tradition and deeply rooted rivalries prevented the members of

Polish dance group of St. Casimir's Parish, 1932. (Courtesy of Mr. and Mrs. John T. Skalny)

similar organizations from associating formally with others. History dictated, for instance, that the religious societies of St. Stanislaus Parish would not ally with corresponding groups at St. Casimir's Church.

Internal quarrels and grudges notwithstanding, neighborhood societies proved that they would rally behind a common cause during World War I, when groups including the Polish Falcons, Polish National Alliance, Polish Socialist Alliance, Echo chorus, and church societies joined in efforts to support Poland's independence. For several years after the war, the Polish Citizens Committee attempted to maintain this spirit of alliance by serving as the representative of Polish organizations in civic affairs, and by organizing activities on behalf of local Polonia.[24] In 1924, the group's objectives were transferred to the Polish American Citizens' Central Committee (referred to as "Centrala," and later renamed the Polonia Civic Centre, Inc.).[25] John Grycz, who had been active in a number of community ventures including the publication of the *Rochester Rekord,* was elected the committee's first president. During the next few years, under the leadership of Grycz and then attorney Henry E. Bielski, Centrala lobbied successfully with city government for a number of neighborhood improvements including a playground at the intersection of Carter and Norton Streets, expanded police services for the northeast side, and streetlights along Hudson Avenue.

Baseball team of Polish Falcon Nest 52, 1934–35. (Courtesy of Mr. and Mrs. Henry Kubiak)

During the Depression, Centrala increased its stature in Polonia and the larger Rochester community under the chairmanship of Edmund Lorentz. A native of Russian Poland who served as a translator in city court, Lorentz recognized the importance of consolidating the energies represented in Polonia's assortment of religious, fraternal, and partisan societies.[26] If the community were to expand its visibility and influence in Rochester, one group would need to speak for Polish Americans on matters that touched their interests and concerned their neighborhood. Lorentz and those who assisted him envisioned Centrala as the committee that would promote shared interests and represent Polonia in the city's civic and cultural circles.

More than thirty organizations affiliated themselves with Centrala and collaborated in activities directed to its goals of "unity, guidance, and commonweal."[27] The committee drew together representatives of parish societies, choirs, cultural groups, and veterans' posts; the local lodges of the Polish National Alliance, Polish Roman Catholic Union, and Polish Falcons; women's groups, young adults' organizations, the regional affiliations of Chraboly and Rakow; Democrats and Republicans. Some projects focused on the welfare of the neighborhood, such as the annual Charity Ball organized to benefit needy families. Although the fund-raiser was initially of interest only to Polonia, its prestige grew and, by the mid-thirties, the event received lavish coverage on the society pages of the Rochester press.[28] Dozens of patrons, including many civic dignitaries, supported the Charity Ball, called Polonia's "outstanding social event of the year."

Other projects emphasized heritage and citizenship, such as the Polish community's participation in Rochester's 1934 centennial celebration. The centennial, planned by local officials since 1929, was an elaborate festival intended to boost sagging morale by cheering the city's century of progress. Polish Day, held on August 19th, drew 10,000 spectators to Edgerton Park for musical performances by the Falcon band, Echo chorus, and Moniuszko choir, and folk dances presented by young people in native costume.[29] "I am very gratified to know," Roman Kwiecien, consul general of Poland in New York, wrote to city officials on the occasion, "that . . . the numerous citizens of Polish extraction residing in Rochester, by their industrial labors and untiring efforts, have added their share to the material and spiritual welfare of your city."

As the city celebrated its century of progress, the neighborhood built by Polish immigrants marked its fiftieth anniversary on the northeast side.[30] In recognition, Centrala hosted a testimonial banquet in honor of early settlers and organized a full day of exercises at Benjamin Franklin High School: speeches, folk dances, a band concert, an athletic competition, and a parade that traced the borders of the Polish neighborhood. During the ceremonies, Centrala presented the community with the *History of the Polish People in Rochester,* a study of Polonia's half-century in the city which the organization had commissioned Norman T. Lyon to prepare.

In its efforts to reinforce the good name of Polonia, Centrala also joined with its member organizations in 1934 to organize a civic welcome for General Jozef Haller, who returned to Rochester that May to appeal for support for disabled Polish veterans. Hoping to offset the unpleasantness that had marked the general's visit eleven years earlier, 38 Polish organizations asked City Council to adopt a resolution in acknowledgment of Haller's return.[31] The resolution, which the council accepted unanimously a month before the general's arrival, encouraged city officials and private citizens to display the Polish flag on public buildings and residences during the two days of Haller's stay. The council also appointed 250 persons to the "General Jozef Haller Reception Committee," an assortment of civic officials, industrialists, religious leaders, and representatives of the Polish community who were asked to arrange a program for the general's visit on council's behalf.

Members of the Polonia Civic Centre, with President Edmund Lorentz (center, with ledger). (Courtesy of St. Stanislaus Parish Archives)

Newspapers heralded Haller as a "remarkably courageous and venturesome" military leader when his motorcade pulled into Rochester on May 11th.[32] Reporters described him as "a general out of a picture book," "Poland's idol and messenger of peace," resplendent in his uniform decorated with medals for valorous service. During his stay, Haller attended a series of events organized by the reception committee: dinner with local officials at the Genesee Valley Club, a gathering of Polish Americans at Benjamin Franklin High School, a parade past Hudson Avenue shops, services at St. Stanislaus Church, a meeting with the members of Pulaski Post and *Harcerstwo* at Falcon Hall, a memorial service at which he placed a wreath beneath a plaque honoring Rochester's war dead. Despite the intentions of the reception committee, Haller's visit drew one protest—a resolution that local Ukrainian Americans passed at a meeting at St. Josaphat's Hall.[33] "General Haller . . . was instrumental in invading and destroying the independent state of Western Ukrainian Republic," those gathered at the meeting maintained, reiterating feelings that they had raised a decade before.

Centrala's promotion of community ideals found its best expression in the observance of Pulaski Day, a holiday that Polonia celebrated with a flourish in October. The tradition of exuberant parades, patriotic speeches, and solemn ceremonies in honor of Polish American war dead began on the eve of the stock market crash and gained momentum during the next decade, an annual demonstration of community spirit during difficult times.

The first Pulaski Day was a national observance designated by President Herbert Hoover in 1929 to acknowledge the country's citizens of Polish descent. The president's gesture, won after persistent lobbying by Polish American organizations, cleared the way for local ceremonies in honor of Kazimierz Pulaski, the brigadier general who had died in the colonies' cause during the Revolutionary War.

Centrala began preparing for the first Pulaski Day eighteen months before the occasion. Having agreed that the holiday should be marked by appropriate ceremony, members dispatched two representatives, Henry E. Bielski and Stanislaw K. Kowalski, to a meeting with Congressman Meyer Jacobstein in May 1928.[34] The following October, the two men told Jacobstein, Centrala wanted to organize a

Members of PNA Lodge 1200, Daughters of Poland, 1930. (Courtesy of Mr. and Mrs. J. G. Sass)

celebration that would include the full Rochester community, not only citizens of Polish descent. With Jacobstein's support, Centrala then carried its proposal to City Council, which proclaimed October 19, 1929, a municipal holiday and named 100 prominent citizens to an honorary committee which would assist in coordinating the day's events.

The program in honor of Pulaski spanned a full day, opening with Mass celebrated by Bishop O'Hern at St. Stanislaus Church.[35] A dozen priests assisted the bishop and processed through the church, followed by representatives of parish societies and children carrying Polish and American flags. Local dignitaries and neighborhood residents filled the pews to capacity, kneeling beneath bunting of Poland's red and white and the United States' red, white, and blue.

After the service, 2,000 marchers assembled at the corner of Pulaski Street, the starting point of a parade that carried the day's ceremonies from the Polish neighborhood to Convention Hall. Five bands, the National Guard infantry, the 121st Cavalry, Polish American veterans, and children in Polish folk costume proceeded south on Hudson Avenue, greeted as they turned on Main Street with a shower of confetti. "Crowds lined the curbs all along the line of march," wrote one reporter, as they waited to catch a glimpse of the celebration which seemed to have drawn "the entire Polish population of Rochester" to the center of town.

At Convention Hall, an audience heard addresses on the theme of patriotism delivered by four speakers, including Waclaw Sieroszewski, personal representative of Jozef Pilsudski. "The figure of Kazimierz Pulaski, the valorous crusader of

The young ladies of a Polish folk dance group, 1930s.

liberty, links the Poles with the Americans," Sieroszewski declared in his remarks, greeted by vigorous applause. A simple service completed the day's activities at Washington Square Park, where Kowalski and veterans of the Polish Army laid a wreath at the base of the Soldiers and Sailors Monument. The day "impressively demonstrated . . . the keen patriotism of the Polish people," concluded a reporter.

The economic hardships that dominated city life in 1930 did not dampen Polonia's enthusiasm for honoring Pulaski. A few months after the celebration, City Council received two petitions in quick succession, each requesting that members change the name of Carter Street Park (at the intersection of Carter and Gothic Streets) to General Kazimierz Pulaski Park.[36] The change of names was slow in coming, however, and the idea of a memorial surfaced again a year later when ground was broken for a public library branch at Hudson Avenue and Norton Street. The building would be the city's fourteenth library branch and only the second housed in a new facility. "Gentlemen," the members of the Polonia Republican League wrote to City Council after funds were appropriated for the branch, "the news . . . was received by the taxpayers, voters and residents of this section of our great City with much enthusiasm, hope and satisfaction. . . . This organization, as one of the largest units representing this part of the City, hereby expresses its sincere thanks to the City Council for starting such a great event."[37]

In March 1931, two weeks after construction began, the members of Centrala met in special session to endorse a proposal regarding the name of the library.[38] Ninety-four representatives of 31 organizations signed the petition which requested that City Council dedicate the building in honor of Kazimierz Pulaski, "whose illustrious service in the war for American Independence is well known to all who are familiar with our history." Citing Pulaski's contribution to "our present liberty, happiness and freedom" and acknowledging that the library would meet "a long-felt need" in the Polish neighborhood, the delegates asked permission to install a bust of the general in the building which they hoped to name the "Pulaski Memorial Branch Library."

City Council forwarded the petition to the Library Board of Trustees, who discussed its merits in July. Naming the building in honor of Pulaski would set an unwelcome precedent, the trustees agreed, citing their policy that each branch be assigned a name that would suggest its location.[39] Nevertheless, the trustees were willing to negotiate Centrala's proposal, and sent Board President Charles Wiltsie to a meeting at Falcon Hall. After Wiltsie clarified the board's position on the naming of branches, Centrala countered with its second suggestion: that a bust or tablet commemorating Pulaski be placed prominently in the library. Both sides agreed to this compromise, and a committee was formed to manage the project which would be financed by Centrala.

The Pulaski Tablet Committee began meeting the following October to consider the memorial's design, an appropriate inscription, and a suitable location in the library.[40] Centrala delegates and city representatives agreed that City Historian Edward R. Foreman should write the plaque's inscription, and awarded the commission to Alphonse Kolb, a German immigrant whose specialty was metal sculpture. Kolb created a sixteen square foot bronze tablet on which he rendered Pulaski's portrait framed in laurel wreaths and flanked by insignia of the United

Handbill announcing the 1933 Pulaski Day celebration. (Courtesy of Mr. and Mrs. J. G. Sass)

Oddajmy Cześć Naszym Bohaterom!

PUŁASKIEMU I KOŚCIUSZCE
w Środę 11-go Października, 1933

Spłaćmy im dług chociaż częściowo, za ich poświęcenie i ofiarę dla nas.

UDEKORUJMY DOMY NASZE w SZTANDARY
i Kolory Amerykańskie i Polskie,

dla okazania czci nigdy niewygasłej w naszej pamięci.
Świętym obowiązkiem każdego jest, wziąść UDZIAŁ w PARADZIE;
Starsi, Młodzież i Dziatwa, płci obojga powinni z obowiązku
poczucia narodowego, tak Polskiego jak i Amerykańskiego,
poświęcić chwilę czasu naszym Wielkim Bohaterom,
którzy za wolność waszą i naszą, krew przelali.

PROGRAM

1. Solenne Nabożeństwo we wszystkich Polskich Kościołach o **godzinie 9-ej rano.**
2. Początek parady z przed Sokolni o godzinie 1-ej
3. Obchód w Auditorium Św. Stanisława, o godz. 2:30 po południu.
4. Dedykacja Tablicy pamiątkowej Pułaskiego w Bibliotece miejskiej przy Hudson i Norton Ulicy, o godz. 3:30 po poł.
5. Defilada Polonji Rochesterskiej, przed Tablicą Pułaskiego.
6. Bankiet w Rochester Chamber of Commerce, o **godz. 7-ej.**
7. Mowy będą wygłoszone przez Radio, Stacji **WHEC:** przez Majora miasta, **PERCIVAL D. OVIAT,** Konsula E. **KALEŃSKIEGO** i Pułkownika O. **SOLBERT'A.**

∴ NA TEM KOŃCZY SIĘ UROCZYSTOŚĆ. ∴

Niechaj Duch nieśmiertelny Pułaskiego i Kościuszki, pobudzi
serca nasze do wzięcia udziału w całej Ceremonji,
i wzmocni nas w jedności.

Wierni w służbie dla Was,

Centrala Polskich Towarzystw.

Drukiem W. Dziekońskiego - 809 Hudson Ave. Rochester, N. Y.

States and Poland. Beneath the portrait, he cast Foreman's inscription: "Patriot, warrior, hero of two continents, a great soul who gave his life . . . for the people of America in the cause of freedom." At Centrala's request, Kolb also welded a small bronze box to the back of the plaque. When the memorial was hung on the library wall, the box would serve as a time capsule in which Centrala could store documents descriptive of Polonia's history.

Centrala presented its gift to the Hudson Library on behalf of Polonia in October 1933, the year that the building opened, and planned a celebration calculated to overshadow other local news of the day.[41] Mayor Oviatt opened the observance with a proclamation issued on October 10th, recognizing Pulaski as "the friend of freedom everywhere" and urging Rochesterians to fly the American

flag on the following day. In the Polish neighborhood, citizens took the message to heart and decorated buildings with banners along the route of the Pulaski Day parade. Thousands turned out for the march, which wound through neighborhood streets and ended at St. Stanislaus Hall where Polish Vice Consul Edmund Kalenski, State Assemblyman George Kelly, and Councilman Edward Miller spoke of patriotism. Following these addresses, the crowd crossed Hudson Avenue to the building which a local reporter acknowledged was "commonly known in that neighborhood as the Pulaski Library." There, Stanislaw K. Kowalski presented the Pulaski memorial, now dominating the wall behind the circulation desk, to the city on behalf of its Polish American citizens, and Mayor Oviatt turned stewardship of the gift over to Library Director John Adams Lowe. The *Democrat and Chronicle* reported that "the library proved entirely inadequate to shelter all who desired to witness the ceremony, and thousands waited long outside and filed through the library long after the ceremony had been completed just to get a glimpse of the plaque."

That evening, Kalenski was honored at a reception at Falcon Hall, and WHEC radio broadcast a program of speeches and Polish music. All in all, the day was "impressive," the *Democrat and Chronicle* observed. "Glorious!" John Lowe enthused in his report to the Library Board.

The 1933 Pulaski Day observance set a precedent for annual celebration in the general's honor. In subsequent years, members of Centrala and veterans of Pulaski

In parade on Hudson Avenue. (Courtesy of Mr. and Mrs. J. G. Sass)

Post organized elaborate ceremonies patterned closely on the successful program: memorial services in the Polish churches, patriotic addresses, radio broadcasts of classical Polish music.[42] Often, a special activity marked the celebration, such as presentation of the *Polonia Restituta* to University of Rochester President Rush Rhees in 1934, and the sale of tiny lapel buttons bearing Pulaski's likeness in 1936. Each year, the highlight of the day was a parade which featured scores of marchers: Polish Army veterans and the members of Pulaski Post, Veterans of Foreign Wars, members of the Monroe County American Legion, Boy Scouts, Gold Star Mothers, Daughters of the American Revolution, and assorted drum and bugle corps. Consistently, the line of march led to the Hudson Branch Library, where Polonia would salute Pulaski at the base of the memorial plaque.

Prosperity remained out of Rochester's reach as the thirties drew to a close. Certainly, life had improved since the bleak years of 1931 and 1932, but at the end of the decade the city could not claim full economic recovery. Although Rochester ranked high in a national study of standards of living in urban centers, thousands of residents continued to receive welfare payments in 1938 and 1939.[43] "Preparation of the 1939 budget has presented a number of problems difficult of solution," City Manager Harold Baker reported to City Council in October 1938.[44] "Many requests . . . to provide worthwhile service to the citizens of Rochester have had to be denied. . . ." In 1939, the city set aside $4 million for public welfare, an increase of more than $1 million over the allocation for the previous year, and rolled over $1,300,000 to support WPA projects. Public relief seemed an unending cycle as, month by month, the number of names added to the welfare list remained approximately the same as the number of persons who found work.[45] Perhaps most disturbing for a city that had long prided itself on the strength of its industry, the hardships of the decade had disrupted the area's stability: only 57.6 percent of those who were Rochester residents in 1930 were named in the City Directory in 1935, a statistic that reflected the greatest local transiency since the 1860s.[46]

The Polish section resisted transiency, and remained among the city's most stable neighborhoods during the Depression. If families moved, most often they shifted residence within Polish Town, where relatives, friends, and societies could be relied upon for support. One survey demonstrates that 81 percent of the families on nine neighborhood streets remained in the Polish section between 1926 and 1933.[47] Individual streets suggested higher rates of stability: 90 percent of the residents of Pulaski Street and 100 percent of the residents of Peckham Street moved only within Polish Town, if at all, between 1926 and 1933.

To the credit of its residents, Polish Town retained its character through the thirties: neat rows of homes, a thoroughfare of shops, four parishes, and an assortment of organizations now allied centrally. Hard work, thrift, and self-reliance had proven their utility during lean years, and an emphasis on heritage had fostered unity. During a decade when small accomplishments held significance, Polonia could cite the cohesion of its families, the proportion of neighborhood residents who retained their homes, the upkeep of its parishes, and the civic spirit of its organizations as evidence of the quality of life in Polish Town.

Adam Felerski presenting Ignacy Paderewski with a copy of the History of the Polish People in Rochester, 1939.

The thirties closed for Polonia with a ceremony that recalled an earlier decade and honored the end of a legendary Pole's career. In May 1939, Ignacy Paderewski returned to the Eastman Theater to perform in concert during a tour of the United States.[48] The pianist and former premier of Poland was nearly eighty years old, "an old friend—a great pianist, a great patriot, a great man" to the thousands of Rochesterians who filled the concert hall. He had first performed in Rochester in 1892 and returned several times during the next forty years but, certainly, this appearance would be his last on the local stage. The audience watched as members of the American Legion entered the theater carrying the flags of Poland and America, then all rose in "reverent tribute" as Paderewski walked slowly from behind the curtain. "Time and worldly sorrows have taken their toll of the man," wrote one music critic, but he "still is able by his supreme musicianship to go through with an exacting program, and to rouse his audience by the inspiration of his playing. . . . Last night's experience is one that never will be forgotten by those present. There never will be another Paderewski."

After the concert, which drew two encores, members of Polonia met Paderewski backstage "in a brief ceremony so touching that tears came to the eyes of several onlookers."[49] Adam Felerski, Walter Wojtczak, Wladyslaw Jarus, John Stenclik, Frank Dabrowski, William C. Brodie, and Edmund Lorentz greeted the pianist on behalf of the local community and presented him with a copy of the *History of the Polish People in Rochester.* Paderewski shook hands with the delegates and thanked them in Polish, then departed for the New York Central yards and a train ride to his next performance, at Madison Square Garden.

That performance never took place, and Rochester "won a sad and significant" distinction as the last city in which Paderewski played publicly.[50] The pianist collapsed minutes before his concert at Madison Square Garden and cancelled the remainder of his American schedule. From New York, he departed for his home in Switzerland, and the 1939 tour which was cut short after Rochester became Paderewski's final series of recitals.

Ironically, the pianist returned to New York within a year to take up, despite his age and failing health, the patriot's role which he had assumed during the First World War. The armies of Germany's Third Reich crossed into Poland in September 1939, igniting the Second World War and destroying the Polish Republic, reborn only two decades earlier after a century of partition. Along Hudson Avenue in Rochester, veterans spoke of raising an army to fight under the Polish colors as Polonia had 25 years before.

A VISION OF UNITY

Edmund F. Lorentz

In city court, Edmund Lorentz was a translator, proficient in several languages, and a statistician who brought order to the court's reports. In the Polish community, Lorentz was president of Centrala, an organizer who encouraged more than thirty groups to work together on behalf of neighborhood and heritage.

Lorentz was born in Russian Poland in 1895, and as a young man served in a branch of the Imperial Court of the Tsar.[51] He left Europe in 1913 and immigrated with his brother to Camden, New Jersey, where he held a series of jobs while attending night school: grocery clerk, insurance salesman, bookkeeper, confectioner, real estate agent, delicatessen owner. Lorentz learned English quickly and began teaching the language to other immigrants, then enrolled at Temple University where he completed a year of course work.

In 1920, Lorentz relocated to Rochester with his wife Marie, and accepted a position in the office of a clothing firm. A few years later, armed with his knowledge of languages (Polish, English, Russian, Ukrainian, German, Czech, Swedish, Norwegian, Serbo-Croatian), he completed the Civil Service examination for court interpreter, although he confessed that he "didn't have the faintest hope of getting the job." He scored 100 percent, an accomplishment that caught the attention of local officials and won the young man placement as a translator in city court.

For the next two decades, Lorentz served as a representative of the foreign-born in matters before the court. His linguistic skill proved valuable to local judges, and his diplomacy allowed him to mediate many incidents out of court. His co-workers once estimated that four of five disputes involving immigrants never reached city court because of Lorentz's ability to coax opposing parties into a settlement. In addition to his daily contact with foreign-born residents, Lorentz translated approximately 200 letters a year, many sent to the police chief by European families hoping for information about missing relatives.

Shortly after he began work, Lorentz was placed in charge of the court's reports to the state. The record books had not been touched for a year, and Lorentz devised his own system to organize the information. His analysis allowed the district attorney's office to prepare a report of its proceedings which earned praise from the Department of Corrections in Albany. Lorentz was called to the capital to confer with officials, who recommended his system to all lower courts in the state.

During his years with city court, Lorentz resided in the Polish neighborhood with his wife and three children (Leopold, George, and Marie). His interest in strengthening Polonia's influence in civic affairs led to his election as president of Centrala in 1933. Under Lorentz's leadership, approximately 35 neighborhood organizations worked in concert as representatives of Rochester's Polish American residents. The activities that Centrala initiated during Lorentz's presidency emphasized neighborhood unity, charity, education, Polish heritage, and American citizenship. After his tenure with Centrala, Lorentz headed the Rochester Council of Polish National Alliance lodges, participated in the work of the Polonia Republican League, and served on the national committee of Americans of Polish Descent during World War II.

Lorentz and his wife opened their home to immigrants from Poland and to those who sought advice about legal matters. "It was a rare evening in our home when no one came for help," their daughter Marie has recalled. "There was almost always someone waiting to see father when he came home from work." The family were active members of St. Casimir's Church and participated in many functions at the parish. In addition, Lorentz found time to open an insurance firm with his friend John T. Skalny. The Skalny-Lorentz Agency maintained offices downtown and in the Polish neighborhood, offering workman's compensation, automobile coverage, and protection in the event of fire, theft, and flood.

In 1948, Lorentz received an appointment as interpreter with the United States Department of Justice. He and his wife moved to Washington, D.C., where he resumed his college education in the evenings at Georgetown University. He planned to complete his undergraduate degree and, upon retirement, study for ministry in the Polish National Catholic Church. Those plans were never realized, however; Lorentz suffered a heart attack in June 1959 and died three weeks later. He was buried from St. Casimir's Church in Rochester, in the city where he had worked vigorously as a representative of Polonia.

FRESH SAUSAGE SIX DAYS A WEEK

Zamiara's Meat Market

Each day of the week except Sunday, Kazimierz Zamiara prepared one variety of homemade sausage in the basement of his Hudson Avenue butcher shop. Using cuts of pork, veal, and beef that he selected personally at local packing houses, Zamiara ground and mixed the blends of meat and spices which his wife, Teofila, sold in their store.[52] *Krakowska, kiszka, kielbasa,* ham sausage, ring baloney, steamers—each week the aroma of Zamiara's fresh sausages filled the store which, over four decades, established a following of customers throughout Monroe County.

Zamiara left Goslinowo, Poland, in 1909 at age 17, and joined an uncle living in Michigan. After a short stay in the midwest, he resettled in Buffalo where he learned the trade of sausage maker at the Szelagowski meat company. In Buffalo, he also met and married Teofila Lewandowska, and with her raised a family which eventually included seven children: William, Casimir, Rose, Stanley, Anthony, Steven, and Frank. After their marriage, Zamiara went into business for himself and moved his family a number of times, opening sausage shops in upstate towns like Medina and Middleport.

In 1931, Zamiara moved his family again, this time to Rochester where he opened a shop at 1110 Hudson Avenue, in the block between St. Stanislaus and Kosciusko Streets. Despite competition from well-established markets like Brodowczynski's, Orlowski's, and Ostrowski's, Zamiara's drew a portion of neighborhood trade during the Depression, and three years later the couple relocated their store to a larger building across the street from St. Stanislaus Church. The new site, at 1129 Hudson Avenue, included a ground floor store, an adjacent smokehouse, a large basement kitchen, and an apartment for the family on the second floor.

Zamiara's routine began early on Mondays, when he buttoned on his white butcher's coat and made the rounds of local meat packing firms. By the end of the morning, he had selected his cuts of meat for the week and had tagged each item himself, a precaution that ensured no mistakes would be made in delivery. Back in his kitchen for the afternoon, Zamiara began preparing batches of sausage, one variety each day through Saturday. A crew of a half-dozen workers joined him at stainless steel tables to grind meat, add spices measured from 100-pound bags, and stuff blends of meat and spices into casing. Hundreds of rings and links were prepared each week and piled into coolers, hung in the smokehouse, or carried upstairs for sale across the counter.

Teofila managed the ground floor shop, open six days a week: from 7:00 a.m. until 6:00 p.m. Mondays through Thursdays, until 8:30 p.m. on Fridays and Saturdays. She supervised a crew of employees, filled display cases with meat, stocked shelves with bread, pickles, and condiments, rang up sales, and tallied expenditures and receipts. Her help included her children, each of whom worked the front counter or assisted in the kitchen after school and on Saturdays.

Within a few years, the store had earned a wide following and was particularly busy at Christmas and Easter, when customers came from around the county to place orders for their holiday meals. At Christmas, they stood in line for Polish sausage, fresh ham, and the pressed cheese used to fill *pierogi*. At Easter, they returned to buy *kiszka, kielbasa,* and *baranki* (butter molded in the shape of a lamb). Some customers appeared regularly each year to place their orders, after a drive of 25 miles or more from outlying towns.

The Zamiaras' routine varied little over the years. Kazimierz worked from his original recipes, refusing to adopt procedures that would save time but alter the flavor of his meat. He advised Teofila never to accept credit in the shop, and would sooner give groceries away to a family who was short of cash. Both insisted on cleanliness, and required employees to wash the front windows twice a week, scrub counters and cases with ammonia daily, and change the sawdust on the floor before the store closed for the evening.

The experience in meat preparation and retail sale that the Zamiaras' children gained in the store led to a series of additional ventures in food service. Bill, the oldest son, opened a second butcher shop on Hudson Avenue in the thirties, catering to customers who lived at the south end of the Polish neighborhood. After World War II, when Casimir and his wife Angela assumed management of the original store, Anthony and brother-in-law Chester Waver opened a restaurant on West Ridge Road, and Bill joined with Stanley to open a sausage company in Elmira. When this new outlet for Zamiara meats proved profitable, Anthony Zamiara and Chester Waver moved to Elmira to help expand the business into Maplecrest Foods, Inc., a retail meat supplier that manufactured and marketed sausage wholesale to grocery chains. Frank, the youngest brother, joined the firm a few years later when Maplecrest relocated its headquarters to Rochester.

During the sixties, Maplecrest Foods became one of the largest meat suppliers in western New York State. Based in a small building on West Ridge Road, the Zamiara brothers' firm filled orders from every supermarket chain in Rochester, Syracuse, and Buffalo, and marketed $10 million of meat products annually. In Monroe County, the supermarkets of Star, Loblaws, and Wegmans featured the Maplecrest brand of meat, which included varieties like "Krakow Smoked

Sausage" and "Krakow Kielbasa."

Casimir and Angela closed the Hudson Avenue store in 1968, and Maplecrest Foods ended its operations in 1985. By that time, members of the Zamiara family had expanded their interest in food service to the management of five restaurants in the Rochester area: two locations of Rick's Prime Rib Restaurant, the Plantation Party House, the East Rochester Country House, and Wavers' Nortic Village. Anthony Zamiara, who had served as president of Maplecrest Foods, later opened a meat supply house that now operates on a smaller scale. For most of the year, his Holiday Meat Products company sells ham and beef to stores and distributors. Twice a year, at Christmas and Easter, Zamiara maintains a longstanding tradition when he prepares Polish sausage and sells the links directly to families who, in many cases, have ordered Zamiara meats since the days when Kazimierz made *krakowska* in the Hudson Avenue store.

A TRADITION OF LAND DEVELOPMENT

Jablonski Homes, Incorporated

The neighborhood between Browncroft Boulevard and Blossom Road beyond the eastern expressway is a quiet tract of elegant homes, stylish ranches of wood, stone, and brick secluded among shade trees. Many in Rochester know that this area, the Browncroft Extension, was originally owned by Charles J. Brown, a prominent nurseryman, realtor, and landscape architect. Few realize that the distinctive homes were built by Teofil Jablonski, a Polish immigrant who invested his savings in Brown's undeveloped land after World War II.[53]

For Jablonski, homebuilding was originally an avocation, a trade to which he aspired while employed as a tailor in local clothing firms. The oldest son in a family of six children, Teofil found work at the Hickey-Freeman Company soon after his arrival in Rochester in 1910. Although he would work in tailoring for the next forty years, he drew an interest in construction from his father, Michal, a cabinetmaker who built his family's home on Dayton Street.

Fourteen years old when he arrived from Europe, Teofil took a full-time job immediately. His earnings contributed to the support of his family and were set aside to help underwrite his younger brothers' college tuition. After completing his own education at Polish National Alliance College, Teofil married Charlotte Kaleta at St. Stanislaus Church and settled into a job as foreman at Fashion Park in the twenties. Although he enjoyed a comfortable status at the clothing company and took an additional job teaching tailoring in the evening, Jablonski hoped to build a second career in land development. Working in his spare time from an office which he named the Northeast Realty Company, Teofil sold farmland and other property around Monroe County, and collaborated with carpenter Victor Czerkas in the construction of homes on Gothic Street.

When the hardships of the Great Depression slowed his company's sales, Jablonski tried his hand at another commercial venture. During the thirties, he operated a shop on Hudson Avenue, advertised as a *pierwszorzedna Polska grosernia*—first-class Polish grocery. The Jablonskis and their two children, Theodore and Dorothy, moved into rooms above the store, and Teofil stocked the shelves with fresh meat, fruit, and vegetables which he purchased each morning at the Public Market. Charlotte managed the store after her husband left for a full day's work at Fashion Park.

Jablonski sold the grocery store at the end of the decade and, as the outlook for land development brightened, returned to selling real estate part-time. In 1938, he invested in his first subdivision: a block of property behind Benjamin Franklin High School's athletic field, identified on city maps as Radetski Park. Supported by a bank loan, Teofil hired a small crew of carpenters to build a row of single-family homes between Hudson Avenue and Kilmar Street. Three generations of Jablonskis contributed to the project: Ted was enlisted to chip cement from bricks and Michal, a frequent visitor to each construction site, salvaged bent nails that he hammered into shape for a second use. Houses sold for $4,500 apiece on the street that Charlotte christened Shady Lane Drive.

Although the development on Shady Lane Drive was a success, Teofil's plans to expand in homebuilding were interrupted again by World War II. It was not until 1948, when the market for new homes reopened, that Jablonski was able to develop his next subdivision. This time, Teofil invited Ted, now a Navy veteran and Hobart College graduate, to join him in incorporating as a partnership, "Jablonski and Son." The two men assembled a crew of carpenters, painters, and an electrician (friends like Victor Anuszkiewicz, Chester Balcerak, Edward Dobner, Henry Kucinski, and Raymond Piendel) to assist them in developing several streets on the Rogers Estates in West Irondequoit, and a stretch of houses west of the river on Winchester Street.

In 1949 Teofil's lawyer, Leo Sawyko, suggested that the builder consider acquiring property in the Browncroft Extension, 200 acres of land formerly owned by Charles J. Brown. The property adjoined an exclusive neighborhood that Brown had built during World War I on his nursery east of Winton Road, a showcase of Georgian and Colonial homes set along parkways lined with spruce, elm, maple, lilac, magnolia, and wisteria. Brown planned to replicate the architecture and landscaping of Browncroft in his extension between Newcastle and Landing Roads, but his hopes for the project ended abruptly. When he died in 1933 his firm was bankrupt, overextended during the worst years of the Depression.

Fifteen years later, when the Monroe County Tax Foreclosure Department offered the lots to land developers, many considered the property an investment risk. Restrictions in the area were high, calling for construction of large homes, and the extension lacked residential conveniences like public transit. The tract, sporting only pavement and landscaping, had become best known as a network of streets where drivers in training could practice their turns undisturbed by traffic.

Encouraged by Sawyko, Teofil bid successfully on 170 lots in the extension, committing $100,000 to construction of homes in the area. Because he had neither sufficient capital nor collateral, Jablonski agreed to pay the county in installments as he built and sold houses on Corwin Road, Coniston Drive, Fieldston Terrace, and Blossom Circle. The gamble proved successful and the homes sold steadily for $13,000 to $45,000 each, quickly realizing the Jablonskis' original investment.

The success of the Browncroft development enabled father and son to undertake other projects in two expanding suburbs, Penfield and Perinton. As Ted assumed more responsibility in the business during the next two decades, Jablonski Homes developed White Village, Ellison Hills Drive, Huntington Meadow, and Panorama Trail, residential tracts where individual homes have sold for $35,000 to $150,000 apiece. After Teofil's retirement, Ted expanded the company's interest in commercial property with the development of Browncroft Corners Plaza and other land in Penfield. In the seventies, Ted's son Peter opened Jablonski Development Corporation, a companion company to Jablonski Homes that carries on the family tradition begun in the Northeast Realty Company.

8 | The Ties of Blood

On September 3, 1939, two days after the armies of the Third Reich crossed Poland's western border, Victor Dastyk of Avenue D sat vigilantly at his radio, listening through the night for news from Europe.[1] Intermittently, the air waves brought word of the Wehrmacht's push toward Warsaw and speculation as to whether Britain and France would honor their alliance with the Poles. The next morning, the 65-year-old carpenter wept openly as he spoke with a local reporter, devastated by news of fighting in his homeland but relieved to learn that the Allied powers had declared war against Germany in Poland's defense.

In the first days of the Second World War, thousands of local Polish Americans waited as Dastyk did for word from Europe. Other Rochesterians were able to set aside reports of warfare half a world away as they packed cars, boarded trains, and headed for county parks at the start of the summer's last holiday: "Marching men and exploding bombs in Europe apparently meant little to Rochesterians today as they flocked toward a carefree Labor Day weekend," the *Times-Union* noted on September 2nd. "By train, plane, bus, auto, boat, the throngs of pleasure seeking Rochester people began their march last night, and were keeping it up through most of today."[2] In the Polish neighborhood, in contrast, word of the war overshadowed holiday plans as families spoke with concern of relatives in cities and villages near the battle front, and veterans of the previous war shared rumors of the formation of a Polish American legion. Within a day of the German invasion, the officers of the local Polish National Defense Fund Committee, organized the previous spring to raise funds for the Polish Army, issued a call to Rochester residents of Polish descent. All were urged to attend a rally at Falcon Hall on September 6th to protest German aggression, and to begin a

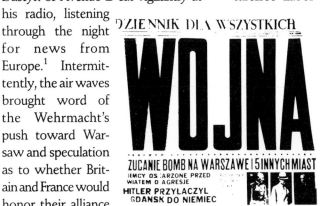

First of all, Polish-Americans have the interests of the United States at heart. After that, and everyone can understand why, we are bound by the ties of blood to do what we can for the homeland.

**Marian Wojnowski
Rochester Chairman
Polish National Defense
Fund Committee
September 3, 1939**

campaign for the support of their ancestral homeland.[3]

Members of Polonia had followed events in Europe intently since the previous spring, when Nazi troops marched into Czechoslovakia. Shortly after the annexation of the Czech territories, Britain and Poland signed a reciprocal defense agreement, an action that prompted Rochester's Centrala to send a cablegram of support to Ignacy Moscicki, president of the Polish Republic: "We commend Poland for the prompt and courageous defense of its independence and territorial integrity. We are confident that Poland's fearless stand will halt the Reich's violent and vicious invasion of world peace."[4] At the same time, the community organized a chapter of the Polish National Defense Fund Committee to raise money to help Poland prepare for the protection of its borders.[5] By the end of April 1939, the committee had collected $3,500 in cash donations and had sold an additional $1,500 worth of Polish bonds. "We started raising this money when Hitler got fresh with Czechoslovakia," spokesman Stanley Orzechowski told a reporter. "Poland has been preparing for this move by Hitler for more than a year. Poland isn't getting ready to fight Hitler; Poland *is* ready."

Faith in Poland's ability to defend its borders characterized opinion in the Polish section the week before the invasion.[6] "Every one interviewed, from 16 to 70 years old, asserted Poland would defend her independence to the last drop of blood and the last gun," a *Times-Union* reporter wrote in summary after speaking with a dozen Polish Americans. "Poland will stand firmly. . . . Poland will fight. . . . If there's a war, Poland will pull through," ran the opinion shared by those whom the reporter met on Hudson Avenue. "Poland won't give even one inch," Stanislaw Jezowski, correspondent for *Dziennik dla Wszystkich* insisted. "The Polish love independence; they have nothing to lose but life." Adam Felerski, interviewed by a *Democrat and Chronicle* reporter the same week, reiterated Jezowski's sentiments: "Yes, Poland will fight rather than yield so much as a button off a soldier's uniform."

Optimism like that expressed staunchly at the end of August was crushed during the next month as Poland, unaided by its allies, fought a desperate campaign against Nazi forces on the west and Soviet armies on the east.[7] As the fighting began, members of the Polish National Defense Fund Committee made plans to intensify their efforts to send financial support to the Polish government. Within a few days of the war's outbreak, however, the group had confirmed the implications of the United States' Neutrality Acts, which prohibited American citizens from aiding belligerents in the event of hostilities in Europe. At a "grim rally" at Falcon Hall on September 6th, 1,000 Polish Americans listened as John Pospula, veteran of the Polish Army in World War I, explained the limits of their response to the war: "I know your hearts are crying just as mine is. I know you look for some guidance from this committee, but in view of the neutrality of our adopted land we are at a loss on what to do except to collect funds for the relief of the war victims."[8]

Before the close of the rally, the Defense Fund Committee ceded authority to a new group, the Polish War Victims Relief Committee, designated to collect funds to purchase food, clothing, and medical supplies for Polish civilians.[9] Those in attendance left $1,000 in donations with John Stenclik, elected chairman of the Relief Committee that night, and 72 committee members representing 49 local

Polish institutions agreed to meet every Monday "as long as the war lasts." The next evening, a subcommittee of 60 women led by Aniela Antczak set to work knitting sweaters and rolling bandages to send to Polish soldiers.

Two weeks passed before committee members had assurance that their contributions could be forwarded to Poland.[10] On September 18th, the day after Russian troops crossed the eastern Polish border, Stenclik received confirmation that the State Department would allow the Red Cross to channel funds and supplies donated by American citizens to Polish civilians. Committee members cheered the news, and prepared to send the Red Cross $3,000 and a supply of clothing collected since the first days of the war.

In the fall of 1939, newspaper publisher Frank Gannett spoke for many in Rochester when he insisted that the United States should remain removed from European politics and powerplay.[11] At the time of the invasion of Poland, Europe had been in crisis for more than a year and a series of other territories—the Sudetenland, Bohemia, Moravia, Slovakia—had already fallen to the Third Reich's domination. Although the Reich's move into Poland and the Western Allies' subsequent declarations of war against Germany were dramatic and unsettling events, popular opinion in Rochester, as elsewhere in the country, favored the stance taken by Joseph Kennedy, America's ambassador to Britain: "As you love America, don't let anything that comes out of any country in the world make you believe you can make the situation one whit better by getting into the war. There is no place in this fight for us."[12]

Americans' resolve not to become involved in other nations' troubles stemmed largely from lingering disillusion with the effects of the First World War, the loss of thousands of American lives on behalf of struggles in Europe.[13] During the thirties, as the countries the United States had assisted failed to repay their war debts, hardships at home convinced many that America's first responsibility was to safeguard its vitality. Speaking from widely different points of view, liberal pacifists and conservative critics of Franklin Roosevelt's New Deal agreed that the United States must never again waste its youth and resources in foreign wars. Sentiment for isolationism ran so strongly that, following the German invasion of Poland, 67 percent of Americans polled by Roper indicated that they wanted no part in the war and, furthermore, felt that their country should favor neither side in selling supplies and armaments.

In Rochester, the editorial pages of the Gannett press repeatedly presented the case for isolationism through the summer and fall of 1939.[14] At the end of August, while decrying Hitler's "terror-reign" and lauding the Western Allies' "quiet determination" to negotiate on behalf of peace, the *Democrat and Chronicle* reiterated the wisdom of the Neutrality Acts and advised that the American people must not be drawn into Europe's internal conflicts. Calling on the government to maintain its perspective on the consequences of the First World War, the editors reasoned that "the present climax is not a crisis of this year . . . it in reality is a crisis of a generation. . . . Nothing the United States might have done in recent months would have affected the course of events."

On September 3rd, the day Britain and France issued their declarations of war, the newspaper outlined with urgency its position on continued neutrality.[15] The previous war represented "colossal and tragic futility," a conflict in which thousands of Americans lost their lives for objectives never attained, a senseless adventure in which even the peace settlement was tainted by the spirit of revenge. This time, the United States would serve world interests far better by remaining outside of the fight: "Our moral position will be stronger; the acceptability of our suggestions for saner economic and political adjustments more probable; if we preserve our position from the warping and blinding influences of war-participation. Only if the western democracies faced actual extinction—and their superior resources make such a contingency improbable—should we consider any act that would impair our neutral position."

Local citizens' letters to the editor during the same weeks represented various points of view in regard to the troubles in Europe. Some who wrote spoke out on behalf of a tough stance against Nazism, but most stopped short of advocating direct American involvement in European problems.[16] Others expressed agreement with the editors' views on neutrality.[17] One reader spoke on behalf of pacifism on September 7th, urging fellow citizens to "share with the populations of afflicted Europe our bread and food supplies but not our machines of destruction. . . . Let us keep our wonderful country at peace . . . and trust in God for the future of all humanity." More poignantly, a disabled veteran of World War I wrote to remind others of the consequences of war: "To those now thinking of helping out the foreign countries, it would be well to take an hour's ride from Rochester and visit the veterans hospital at Canandaigua, Bath or Batavia, and see the suffering men there, and realize the terrible cost of the past war, and who is paying for it."

Against the backdrop of editorial and public opinion, much of it favoring neutrality, Rochesterians with ties to Europe reacted to the outbreak of the war.[18] Like Polish Americans, veterans of the British and French armed forces gathered early in September to organize assistance to their respective homelands, working within the restrictions imposed by the Neutrality Acts. Rochester's Jewish community continued work it had begun several years earlier, aiding in the resettlement of refugees from Austria and Germany, and lobbying on behalf of American support for a Jewish state in Palestine. German Americans, caught in a difficult position as they had been twenty years earlier, publicly pledged loyalty to the United States through the member societies of the German Club.

As the war extended to other nations through 1939 and into 1940, corresponding groups in Rochester mobilized in the form of public protests and relief campaigns. Residents of Finnish descent took action in December, those of Danish, Norwegian, Dutch, and Belgian descent the following spring.[19] Religious leaders urged their congregations to pray for peace, and civic leaders indicated their increasing concern by forming two committees (Stop Hitler Now, and Defend America by Aiding the Allies) for the purpose of assisting in the Allied countries' defense.

Although activities such as these indicated that organized local response was widening, Rochesterians' involvement in the war remained limited until the last weeks of 1941. For area residents, the chief effects of the first two years of the war were a substantial increase in local employment and heightened interest in civil defense. The federal government's decision to strengthen the country's supply of armaments brought lucrative contracts in 1940 to dozens of Rochester firms, including Bausch & Lomb, Stromberg-Carlson, Taylor Instrument, Eastman Kodak, Symington-Gould, and Rochester Products.[20] During the next year, orders for telescopic sights, telephone switchboards, medical equipment, military fatigues, electrical parts, tank armor, and high-explosive shells added $75 million in revenue to local industry and created thousands of new jobs. The increase in opportunities for work was so dramatic that, by 1941, the city faced an acute labor shortage—welcome change from the dole lines in which many had stood a few years before.

While debate on the merits of American neutrality continued, city officials took steps to ensure that Rochester would be prepared in the event of attack.[21] As early as spring 1938, Mayor Lester Rapp had contacted federal authorities to request an anti-aircraft unit for the city, and the Red Cross had distributed a list of local air raid shelters. After the war began, the Red Cross increased its first aid training while the city's newly formed Defense Council outlined action to be taken if the area came under attack, including the mobilization of a bomb demolition squad. Until Japan's attack on Pearl Harbor brought the battle to their country's borders, however, these activities did little to disturb the aloofness with which most Rochesterians regarded the war.

Polish Americans "are ready to rise again and bear arms to protect the freedom, not only of the United States but of the whole world!" Teofil Starzynski's resolve rang through Rochester's Falcon Hall on July 6, 1940, where delegates from Falcon nests from across the United States and Canada had assembled for the organization's national convention and *zlot* (athletic competition).[22] The Falcons lent their full support to Franklin Roosevelt's defense program, Starzynski told the crowd, and waited to answer the president's call "to any duty that this great country of ours will require in these grave and humanity-shocking days." Punctuating Starzynski's message, 3,000 young Falcons gathered at Franklin High School's athletic field to perform a drill in unison to the strains of Polish hymns and marches. As representatives of the Polish, Czech, and Dutch governments-in-exile watched, the athletes rose from their knees and lifted their arms: "From the smoke and ashes and our brothers' blood, Poland arise. . . . Poland is not yet lost."

Starzynski's words and the Falcons' dramatic drill testified to the sense of immediacy that local Polonia felt in regard to the European war. Unlike those who viewed the conflict with detached interest, many Polish Americans followed news reports closely, concerned for the welfare of relatives in areas torn by battle. Even those who had no contact with family in Poland understood Starzynski's reference to the Falcons' service in the First World War, and knew by upbringing that their loyalty was to include both Poland and the United States. As twenty years earlier, most felt that Poland's situation required their response and, in that spirit, supported activities organized locally to aid Poland and draw attention to its loss of independence.

As its members had promised in September, the Polish Relief Committee met regularly to collect and relay donations to the American Red Cross, while its women's auxiliary packed blankets, sweaters, and bandages for shipment to Polish soldiers.[23] Hoping to build public sympathy for Poland's position, the group also sponsored presentations by speakers who had witnessed the German invasion. Joseph Winnicki, a Buffalo priest who had been in Warsaw during the first week of September, shared his experiences with a crowd at St. Stanislaus Hall on November 6th.[24] Declaring that Poland would not accept subjugation, Winnicki described the advance of German forces that had indiscriminately attacked both military and civilian locations. A week later, Julien Bryan, a freelance photographer who had remained in Warsaw through September 21st, corroborated Winnicki's report that hospitals, homes, and churches had been hit by German artillery.[25] On November 12th, while an organization called the Fellowship of Reconciliation campaigned for peace on Main Street, Bryan spoke at the Columbus Civic Center and displayed his photographs, "filmed evidence" of the destruction in Warsaw.

During the last months of 1939, other organizations joined the Relief Committee in raising funds to aid Polish citizens. Early in October, Group 1145 of the Polish National Alliance hosted a dance and bazaar at St. Theresa's Hall, the first of sixteen benefits planned between October and the first of the year by Polish societies.[26] In January, Centrala President William C. Brodie announced that proceeds from the organization's annual Charity Ball would also be forwarded to Poland to help war sufferers and refugees.[27] Mayor Samuel Dicker and other city officials joined Centrala members in the ball's grand march, which opened the event at St. Stanislaus Hall to 2,000 guests.

In spring 1940, the Relief Committee expanded its work with a drive to raise $12,000 among Rochesterians of Polish descent, its quota in a $3 million campaign led by the National Council of Relief Organizations for Poland in America.[28] If every adult would give at least one dollar, the committee appealed in advertisements, Rochester could approach its goal in a house-to-house canvass of Polish Americans. Additional speakers brought the community news of Poland that year, including two representatives of the Polish government: Jozef Haller, the crusty World War I general, and Antoni Wawrzykowicz, a member of the last Polish parliament.[29] Haller railed against the German Army, whom he branded "a uniformed gang of murderers and thieves" intent on the destruction of Polish culture and nationhood. Wawrzykowicz addressed an assembly following a church service at which 500 local Polonians mourned Polish soldiers and civilians who had died since the start of the war.

Such sobering reminders of conditions in Poland reached Rochester as local families tried without success to forward private contributions to relatives in Europe.[30] The Post Office could give no assurance that letters and packages to occupied countries would reach their destination, and many banks, as a matter of policy, discouraged customers from drawing money orders for persons in Eastern Europe. "The country that once was Poland [is], temporarily at least . . . a lost country, as inaccessible as the legendary villages in Tibet," the *Times-Union* noted in March 1940.

That summer, officials of the Polish Falcons of America met in Rochester and announced their organization's pledge to increase aid to Poles fighting against Germany with the British.[31] Endorsement of their platform calling for assistance to Poland culminated the Falcons' national convention, the weeklong gathering hosted by Nest 52 in July. Pointedly, the opening march of 3,000 uniformed Falcons from Nest 52's clubhouse to Franklin High School's athletic field featured a Red Cross ambulance, one of 25 purchased with contributions from Polish Americans and sent to Polish Army units serving in England and France. During the next four days, while athletes competed in track, field, and swimming events, Nest 52's women's auxiliary sold handiwork for the benefit of the relief fund, and Starzynski arrived at the Hotel Seneca to offer the services of his organization's members to the United States government, "for whatever purpose Uncle Sam needs us." Later, at their business meeting, 300 delegates unanimously approved a resolution of support for Roosevelt's defense program, pledged continued aid to victims of the war in Poland, offered assistance "compatible with the laws of the

United States" to the Polish Army in England, and urged each Falcon member in the United States and Canada to contribute ten cents a month to the Polish Red Cross.

By the fall of 1940, the Third Reich had seized control of most of Eastern Europe, Scandinavia, and the Low Countries, and had forced the French to sign a humiliating armistice after German troops reached Paris in June.[32] Although the United States still stood by the tenets of the Neutrality Acts, Americans' concern for events in Europe increased through the fall and winter as the Luftwaffe launched attacks against Britain. In Rochester, Polish Americans found that their homeland's resistance to Nazism, carried out by the Polish government-in-exile and the underground Home Army *(Armia Krajowa),* commanded wider public attention than at the war's outset.

That October, an American citizen who had fled Poland a year earlier related his experiences to local audiences and spoke in an interview on WHAM radio.[33] Paul Super, general director of the YMCA in Poland at the time of the war's outbreak, visited Rochester at the invitation of Centrala and the local YMCA during a nationwide tour to raise money to aid Polish refugees and soldiers in exile. In speeches at the University Club, the University of Rochester, the metropolitan YMCA, and St. Stanislaus Hall, Super painted a grim picture of Poland under Nazi

Members of Nest 52 of the Polish Falcons, 1940. (Courtesy of Mr. and Mrs. John B. Stenclik)

> The American press is publishing much less than the truth about atrocities in Poland. The terrible things happening in Poland are simply unheard of. There are personal, cultural and economic atrocities. People have been murdered by the tens of thousands, and that is only the beginning of the story.
>
> A minimum of a thousand persons a day will die in Poland when the cold weather sets in, and more likely the figure will be 5,000. And there is no way to feed these people.

A week after Super's visit, 2,000 residents of the northeast side assembled for Pulaski Day ceremonies at which a small city park was officially renamed in honor of the Polish-born Revolutionary War general.[34] Mayor Dicker, City Council members, and American Legion veterans gathered with Polish Army veterans and members of Pulaski Post on a low hill at Carter Street and Gothic Street to raise the colors of Poland along with the Stars and Stripes. The observance held double meaning for Polish Americans, the *Times-Union* reported. "They paid tribute to the exile who was mortally wounded . . . in the American Revolution. And they sorrowed for their homeland, which has lost its freedom and entered dark days."

In February 1941, Dicker followed Governor Herbert Lehman's lead in proclaiming a day to honor Poland.[35] Polish American organizations coordinated local activities, which included a joint session of the Polish, British, and Dutch war relief committees at Falcon Hall, and services at several city churches. In a radio address the same day, attorney Norman Lyon sketched Poland's turbulent history of invasion and defense of its borders, and declared that "weapons of hatred" would not break the spirit of the Poles. Appealing to the ideals of democracy, Lyon recalled Mickiewicz's vision of Poland's struggle for independence, the romantic theme that had mobilized a generation of Polonians in the previous war:

> Again there goes on the strange attempt to stifle the deep, abiding faith of the Polish people . . . [but] the roots of the spirit of freedom are far beneath the storm, too wide, too deep to be wrenched loose. . . . And no nation can know better than Poland the fearful price which history exacts in the long, bitter fight for freedom.
>
> To Poland we speak, across the world, a message of good cheer for tomorrow, a message of the gratitude of free men for the battle she is waging, a message of strong faith in a new, free Polish nation.

Lyon's address played to public sentiment that, by 1941, had changed considerably since the opening days of the war.[36] The extent and intensity of conflict in Europe and, increasingly, in the Far East led many to fear for America's security and to applaud Roosevelt's stance on defense, expressed in heavy appropriations for armaments, a lend-lease program that channeled American supplies to the Western Allies and, for the first time in its history, a draft enacted when the nation was not at war. Support for isolationism was quickly receding, replaced by the president's call for "Four Freedoms" as the country's moral foundation: freedom of speech and expression, freedom of worship, freedom from want, freedom from fear—the assurance "that no nation anywhere will be in a position to commit an act of physical aggression against any neighbor." Rochesterians, like others across the country, felt the significance of the war more acutely, although few anticipated that men and women from the city would be stationed at battle fronts within the next year.

From his station aboard the USS *Castor,* Peter Anuszkiewicz saw the warplanes marked with red Rising Suns head across the bay to the northeast shore of Ford Island, where the battleships of the American Pacific Fleet were moored.[37] Through the smoke and flames that filled the harbor, the crew of the *Castor* glimpsed the turrets of the *Nevada, West Virginia,* and *Arizona,* and heard the explosion of bombs and torpedoes that sank the three with hundreds of sailors aboard. The *Castor's* crew turned their ship's guns on the planes passing overhead and were credited with taking one down, but suffered little damage in return from the Japanese fighters intent on the battleships. Had the pilots known that the *Castor* was loaded with explosives for Pacific Fleet submarines, they might have counted the supply ship among their targets in the attack on Pearl Harbor.

Peter Anuszkiewicz was one of approximately 5,000 Rochesterians in the armed services in December 1941, and among the few local men at Pearl Harbor on the day the United States entered the war.[38] One of five children of immigrants Julian and Maria Anuszkiewicz, he had entered the Naval Reserve with two friends when the war began in Europe, prompted by an interest that the three shared in sailing.[39] Anuszkiewicz was called to active duty early in 1941, and boarded the *Castor* in New York harbor when the ship was commissioned for service that March. Because of his civilian experience as an employee of Timely Clothes, he was assigned as the ship's tailor in a unit of services for the crew of 400 that also included machinists, carpenters, armorers, cobblers, barbers, cooks, bakers, and a ship storekeeper.

Beginning in May, the *Castor* made a series of cargo voyages between the west coast and Pearl Harbor, carrying equipment and explosives for Pacific Fleet warships and submarines. In October, the ship dropped Marine reinforcements at Wake Island—most of whom would be taken prisoner or killed when war reached the island in the next weeks. After a return voyage to San Francisco to load more explosives, the *Castor* docked at Pearl on December 4th, three days before the Japanese attack. As the harbor filled with flames at dawn on December 7th, Anuszkiewicz was called to his station as a gun loader, assigned to pass ammunition from the lower decks to the ship's gunners for the battle's duration. Only when he was released from his station after the fighting was over did he feel the stinging in his palms, and find that they were covered with welts and bruises gained during his first battle experience.

At their home on Warsaw Street, the Anuszkiewiczes were among the families who waited anxiously for news of a son's safety following the harbor bombing. In the days that passed before Washington released official lists of the dead and wounded, local newspapers scrambled to compile a count of area men stationed in Hawaii and the Pacific islands, while city and county governments set previously outlined defense plans in motion.[40] The Rochester police placed a heavy guard around the lake port, airport, and reservoir, and increased their patrol of plants that produced military supplies. "Enemy aliens" were detained for questioning, residents participated in a citywide "blackout," and local Veterans of Foreign Wars and the Spanish American War wired Washington to offer their services to the government. "It is war, all out war, war for every one of us," Frank Gannett wrote in a statement carried on the front page of both his newspapers on December 8th.[41] "The day has now passed when we can argue whether we want war or not. It is upon us and the die is cast."

Enlistments ran high at local recruiting stations through the end of December and into the first months of 1942.[42] Nearly 400 young men volunteered for service in the Army, Navy, Marine Corps, and Coast Guard in the first three weeks after the United States entered the war, joined by an additional 800 by the end of March. At the close of 1942, more than 4,000 Rochester men had enlisted for service and several thousand others had been drafted under the Selective Service Act, bringing the count of local men stationed in the Pacific Islands, Australia, China, North Africa, and Europe to more than 18,000. Before the end of the war, a total of 40,000 men and 2,000 women would leave Rochester and its surrounding towns in the country's service.

Represented in those numbers were nearly 1,000 men from the Polish community, a roster of names distinguishable from the lists for other parts of the city: Adamski, Ambrozewicz, Andruszkiewicz, Antczak . . . Daszkiewicz, Dziengielewski, Dzierzanowski. . . Jablonski, Jankowski . . . Nawrocki, Nowak . . . Szymula, Szczepanski. . . Wajda, Woloszyn. . . Zielinski, Zientara, Zolnierowski.[43] The families of St. Stanislaus Parish sent 700 of their sons to the United States Army, Air Corps, Navy, Marine Corps, and Merchant Marines—nearly 20 percent of the parish's members, and more than three-fifths of its men over age eighteen. One hundred twenty of St. Casimir's 1,000 parishioners entered the service, along with 130 from St. Theresa's Parish and a representative number from the Polish Baptist Church. Many families saw more than one son don a uniform and leave for duty, like the Anuszkiewiczes whose front porch window displayed five stars for four brothers and a brother-in-law stationed overseas.

A number of women were included among those from the Polish neighborhood who volunteered to serve, representing the families of the northeast side in the WACS, WAVES, and military nursing corps. Wanda Pietrzak, one of a dozen girls from St. Stanislaus Parish who entered service, was among the first 100 Rochester women who answered a call for army nurses in summer 1942.[44] Sent to France after completing training at Camp Livingston, Louisiana, Wanda cared for wounded soldiers through the end of the war—living with other nurses in tents pitched close to battle lines, and trudging through mud to a hospital where she routinely worked fifteen-hour days.

At home, those active in the campaign for Polish relief encouraged enlistments, viewing the participation of the community's young people in the Allied effort both as an expression of American patriotism and as support for Poland. Appeals for enlistment began before the United States entered the war, delivered at gatherings such as the memorial ceremony in honor of Poland's war dead held at St. Stanislaus Church in September 1940.[45] Citizens of Polish descent should honor

Al Okoniewicz, visiting his mother while on leave. (Courtesy of Mr. and Mrs. Joseph Stira)

their heritage by volunteering for the American forces, Antoni Wawrzykowicz told a crowd of 500: "Emulate Pulaski who fought in the name of democracy." Calls to service took on a new imperative after the United States' declaration of war. Polish Americans should not wait to be drafted, Stanley A. Nowak, Michigan state senator, urged the audience at a victory rally at Polish People's Home in January 1942, but should register for either the armed forces or for civil defense.[46]

As the community had done in the First World War, the Polish Relief Committee promoted service in Poland's armed forces as an alternative for the neighborhood's young men, and opened a recruitment program before the United States entered the war. In September 1941, committee members collaborated with local Falcons and World War I Polish Army veterans to organize a Rochester unit of

Friends of the Polish Soldier in Canada *(Kolo Przyjaciol Zolnierza Polskiego),* a national group formed to draw American recruits to the Polish Army's induction center in Windsor, Ontario.[47] Opened that July under command of Major General Bronislaw Duch, the center was intended to bolster the strength of the exiled government's armed forces by pulling volunteers from Polish American communities. Appealing to "those whose ancestry goes back to a mutual homeland" and to others "who seek adventure as they see it in war," Duch and his staff offered military training at Kosciuszko Camp near Owen Sound, and an opportunity to join the fight against the Third Reich while the United States maintained its neutrality.

Rochester's unit was headed by John Pospula, who had distinguished himself in service with Haller's "Blue Army" in the First World War. The group had no authority to enlist soldiers, but could circulate information on behalf of the Polish Army and solicit volunteers. To general surprise, the first young man to commit to enlistment was a Madison High School graduate without a trace of Polish ancestry.[48] Maurice Mercer, nineteen years old, took a bus across town from his home on Danforth Street to attend one of the first meetings of the unit. Although he was a few inches too short for the American Air Corps, his ambition was to serve as a flyer, Mercer told the group. "I've always admired the Polish people. If they're training an army in Canada for action overseas, I'd like to go along." Taken off guard by his offer but delighted to count their first volunteer, members of the Rochester unit arranged the details of Mercer's departure for Windsor, and feted him the evening before he left with a dinner at Falcon Hall.

The second volunteer to come forward was, like Mercer, not of Polish descent.[49] Frank Yawman, a 38-year-old sheet metal worker and Navy veteran, left Rochester a few days after Mercer to join a Polish Army tank unit in training at Owen Sound. Yawman traveled to Canada with another Rochesterian, Leopold (Lee) Lorentz, who had tried to enlist in both the American and Polish forces but had been turned down each time because of poor eyesight. Once in Windsor, Lorentz intended to offer the Poles his services as a writer, and held out the hope that he might persuade the recruiters to admit him to active duty.

Leopold was the oldest of three children of Edmund Lorentz and his wife

Brothers Peter and Karol Anuszkiewicz met in Noumea, New Caledonia, while they were in service. (Courtesy of Mr. and Mrs. Karol Anders)

Marie.[50] In 1941 he was 23 years old, a high-spirited and determined young man who his mother conceded was "so full of energy that you think every minute he will fold up and collapse." At sixteen, Lorentz had hitch-hiked to Texas and back with his friend Karol Anuszkiewicz, wearing the uniform of the Polish *Harcerstwo* and working for farmers along the way to earn spending money. A few summers later, he made his way by bus and train to a dozen cities in the northeastern states, a self-appointed "good will ambassador" looking for information about Polish American organizations and publications. An aspiring writer, Lee recorded his impressions on the trip through New York, New Jersey, and Pennsylvania, then forwarded the articles to Polish American newspapers. At his parents' urging, he settled into a job as an insurance agent but maintained his interest in journalism by writing news reports and scripts for the radio program that his father hosted once a week on WSAY.

In October 1941 Lorentz left Rochester again, this time with Frank Yawman to join the Polish Army in Canada. Yawman had passed the preliminary physical given in Rochester but Lee had not, a ruling that he decided would not alter his plans to enlist. The morning after his arrival in Windsor, Lorentz convinced a captain at headquarters that he could be of use writing and editing publicity materials. "I am in the HQ of Polish Army in Windsor," he wrote home on October 6th, "translating some stuff from Polish to English from *Ameryka Echo* about General Duch. . . . Boy, they sure do need English writers. . . . I like it immensely. The captain builds me up to all who come into the office, and he is saying things about keeping me here."

For the next three weeks, Lee wrote and edited copy for news articles, radio broadcasts, and publicity releases, building a case for his enlistment through his work. By the end of October, he had overcome the restrictions placed on poor eyesight and was admitted as a recruit to a Polish tank unit. Elated, he wrote to his family: "In the morn after chow, I fill out application, and all the fellows I have known [while] in civies are curious and glad. . . . I am fitted out and when I come upstairs again all decked out, everybody simply tries to shake my hand off. . . . With the very heavy overcoat and all the strange, heavy warm clothes, I run to HQ . . . and for the first time come to attention. . . . All staff congratulates me left and right, and I am feeling just perfect." The next day, after participating in his first drill, Lee reported to his office assignment and was told he would be given a month to close out his business at home. Working at his desk that afternoon, he had difficulty concentrating: "Keep thinking how the path of my entire life is hence-forth changed. No more insurance, radio, etc. What awaits me in Europe, Poland? Can't stop thinking about it every once in a while."

Between November 1941 and July 1942, Lorentz completed his preliminary training and continued to write for the information office—scripts for radio interviews with Polish Army officers; descriptions of the Poles' role in the Allied defense in Europe; notices and announcements designed to encourage Americans to enlist in the Polish forces. "If you want a chance to learn another language," ran the text of one announcement, "a chance to help rebuild the damage in Europe after this war, a chance to serve America and at the same time noble Poland—the first nation to say 'no' to Hitler—then you will join the Polish forces in Canada." As part of his work, Lee began writing articles about his experiences at camp,

Leopold Lorentz

publishing these under the title "With the Polish Armed Forces in Canada" in *Zgoda, Dziennik Polski, Sokol Polski,* and other newspapers.

In November, headquarters dispatched Lorentz on publicity tours in the northeastern states, part of an effort to increase the disappointing number of Polish American recruits. During that winter, he visited high schools, Falcon clubs, Polish neighborhood centers, church halls, libraries, and radio stations to describe the Polish armed forces' participation in the Allied war effort and to distribute information about enlistment.[51] Lee's travels took him more than once to Rochester, where he spoke in uniform at Franklin High School, St. Stanislaus School, and St. Theresa's School, visited members of parish societies at St. Casimir's Hall, spoke on radio, and led a parade from Falcon Hall to St. Stanislaus Church.

In July 1942, Lee received orders for transfer to Scotland where the troops of the First Polish Armoured Division were stationed. Before he sailed, he prepared a column for the newspapers that had carried his articles on life at camp, this one headlined "A Polish Soldier's Farewell":

> I've been waiting here quite some few months for this day, and now that it is here, I don't know just exactly how I feel. . . . I must admit that I am a little bit afraid. Yet, at the same time, so terribly glad that I am to be permitted to take part in this battle for the justice and rights of mankind, and especially for the land of the White Eagle. Yet, I am a little afraid about it all, for I am only a young man like all your brothers, boy friends, etc., who has ambitions, desires, and wants to live. And I think now for the first time really—tenderly of my dad and mom . . . the kid sister, brother, all. And I think I am not the only one of the boys sailing who wonder if we shall ever see things so dear to us again. . . .
>
> 'Nuff said. . . . Remember, some day I expect to be back working among the Poles in America—and I'll want to meet you all then, and shake your hands. *Do widzenia—i pamietajcie—Polska zyje.*

"It was a patriotic assemblage," the *Democrat and Chronicle* reported in January 1943, "that attended the annual Polish Relief Ball in St. Stanislaus auditorium last night."[52] Adhering to the ban on pleasure driving recently announced by Governor Thomas Dewey, most of the 1,500 guests left their automobiles at home, and rode buses or trudged in the cold to the benefit. Many of the women dispensed with long gowns in the interests of practicality, preferring to hike up Hudson Avenue in shorter dresses. Once at the hall, ticket holders greeted the guests of honor, WAC recruits Louise Smorol and Irene Chlebowski, viewed a "Spirit of Victory" pageant put on by Red Cross volunteers, and registered to give blood to launch a weeklong campaign for donations from the Polish community.

While the large majority of the neighborhood's young men were at war, family members at home participated in a steady series of fund-raisers, assemblies, and ceremonies organized by the Polish Relief Committee, Centrala, veterans' posts, and the Polish churches. These activities, which dominated Polonia's fraternal and social life through the end of the war, punctuated years characterized on the homefront by defense work, food and fuel rationing, victory garden harvests, and the salvage of all manner of goods—paper, burlap, rubber, nylon, iron, copper, tin. Most events emphasized the community's dual interest in the outcome of the war, and heavily promoted Poland's case for post-war independence.

Financial contributions to the war effort alternated between United States defense and assistance to Poland. In various capacities—as parishioners, members of societies, veterans, relatives of servicemen and women, individuals—Polish Americans purchased war bonds and underwrote the work of the Polish Relief Committee, whose receipts surpassed $14,000 in 1941.[53] At St. Stanislaus Church, parishioners supported a second Sunday collection which went toward the purchase of war bonds three weeks a month and to the Relief Committee on the fourth week.[54] Donations ranged from $40 to $110 a Sunday, providing for

purchase of 32 defense bonds of $100 apiece in 1942, and a year-end donation of $544 to the Relief Committee. The Echo Singing Association, unable to host its annual concert in 1941 because so many men from its chorus were in service, purchased $35,000 worth of government bonds between 1939 and 1945, donated an additional $1,000 to the Polish Relief Committee and Polish Red Cross, and remembered its members in service at Christmas with gifts of $10 each.[55] In 1942, Echo members on the homefront also agreed to attend as a group Centrala's Charity Ball, half of whose proceeds were used to purchase defense bonds.

In addition to financial contributions, community members donated goods and volunteered time to aid Polish civilians and both Poles and Americans in service. Women's groups were particularly generous in this regard, folding blankets, rolling bandages, recruiting blood donors, and packing cartons of sweaters for those overseas. Women's societies associated with the Polish churches and Polish clubs also sewed coats and jackets for war orphans, and collected goods such as shoes, soap, and cans of food for shipment to Poland.

The most successful relief collection, sponsored by Centrala early in 1945, gathered 100 tons of clothing and 40,000 bars of soap for Polish citizens in a one-day, citywide drive.[56] In collaboration with the local Salvage Department and the State Guard, Centrala's 250 volunteers tossed bundles left at curbs throughout the city onto trucks, and prepared packages for shipment at the Salvation Army

Members of the Polish War Victims Relief Committee, 1942, with Chairman John Stenclik (third from right). (Courtesy of Mr. and Mrs. Joseph Zablotski)

warehouse. Downtown merchants and Polish businessmen contributed to the campaign, and children in city public and parochial schools collected the bulk of the soap.

Fund-raising and collections for Polish relief took place against a backdrop of speeches and ceremony that emphasized Poland's status as an occupied nation and the suffering that her people endured because of the war.[57] In July 1942, Centrala called on Polonia to observe a moment of silence one day at noon, as tribute to Polish women who had died under Nazi occupation. Mayor Dicker issued a proclamation inviting all in the city to participate in the silent protest, and the Polish churches expanded the memorial at Sunday services. In May 1943, the community commemorated the signing of Poland's Constitution with prayers for war victims and an address by Aleksander Jachimowicz, attache at the Polish Consulate in New York, who spoke with optimism of Poland's renewal after the end of the war.

In July, shoppers and visitors to the E. W. Edwards store passed through a collection of battle flags, insignia, photographs, drawings, uniforms, and aircraft equipment—an exhibit titled "Poland Fights On" set up to display the Poles' resistance to invasion and participation in Allied campaigns. The same month, local Polish Army veterans led a procession of 500 persons along Hudson Avenue, their standards draped in black in mourning for General Wladyslaw Sikorski, premier of the Polish government-in-exile who had been killed in a plane crash off Gibraltar. "A heroic man in religion and patriotism, virtuous, faithful to God and to country," Father Joseph Balcerak said in eulogy during Mass at St. Stanislaus Church, one of three memorial services held for Sikorski at the Polish parishes.

Observances in honor of Poland's part in the war culminated in September 1943 in a weeklong "Tribute to Poland," planned locally in accordance with Governor Dewey's proclamation of Poland Week in New York State.[58] Mayor Dicker and Frank Gannett chaired a local committee of forty community leaders and Polish American representatives who organized church services and a memorial program of speeches, films, and folk song that drew a capacity crowd to Franklin High School's auditorium. The Poles had paid "a terrible price" for resisting Nazi rule, Gannett said in opening remarks. "The brave people of Poland chose death before dishonor, and tonight all the free people of the world applaud the Poles for the fight they wage for justice and freedom." A series of speeches in praise of Polish resistance followed, and the gathering concluded with a resolution endorsed by

Packing goods for shipment to Poland, 1941. (Courtesy of Mr. and Mrs. Joseph Zablotski)

Gannett's committee calling for full restoration of Poland at the end of the war.

By the early weeks of 1944, press reports predicted a close to the long conflict and an Allied victory as the Russian Army began to push German forces across Poland to the west. The news was received with uneasiness in the Polish neighborhood, where spokesmen questioned the Russians' intentions toward Poland. "Our emotions are mixed," said Edmund Lorentz. "We cannot declare our reactions until we learn Russia's aims."[59]

In the next months, as Poland's return to independence after the war became increasingly less secure, local representatives of Polonia took part in state and national activity. In May, Rochester's Polish churches and societies sent delegates to Buffalo for the first assembly of the Polish American Congress, at which 3,000

Betty Adamski, Zosia Jezowski, and Stasia Jezowski stand beside General Sikorski's portrait at the "Poland Fights On" exhibit, 1943. (Courtesy of Mr. and Mrs. Joseph Zablotski)

representatives of American Polonia lobbied for Poland's right to democratic elections and a return to her pre-war boundaries.[60] During the opening session of the three-day assembly, the delegates cheered a message sent by General Wladyslaw Anders, commander of the Second Polish Army Corps then fighting in Italy: "The Polish flag flies above Monte Cassino. . . . Over a most difficult terrain, against great fortifications and the best German units, we performed our soldierly duty, fighting unyieldingly for honor, liberty and integrity." Two months later, nine representatives of the local branch of the Pulaski Republican League traveled to Syracuse to set strategy to win Polish American votes for Governor Dewey's presidential election campaign.[61] The league contended that Roosevelt did not support Poland's right to sovereignty after the war, and on that basis planned to build a case to draw the largely Democratic Polish American vote to Dewey.

The latter part of 1944 was marred by the grim news of the Warsaw Uprising, the Polish Home Army's effort to free their capital and help the Allies drive the German Army west that ended with 200,000 Warsaw citizens dead, and the city a devastated landscape of graves and ruins.[62] During the first weeks of the two-month battle for the Polish capital, members of Rochester Polonia gathered at St. Casimir's Cemetery to pray for Warsaw's defenders and to commemorate those who had died.[63] "We Americans are pleading with Jesus to let freedom for Poland and all the down-trodden people reign again," Reverend Stephen Stryjewski said in his sermon. "Many of the ill-informed would wonder why we have gathered here and some would shrug their shoulders, others would sneer, but the men and women who left the old country to come here. . . know the answer."

Early in September, word reached the American public that, while Polish insurgents were battling German troops in Warsaw's streets and sewers, the Russian Army had halted its march on the bank of the Wisla River, refusing to

The 1940 drum and bugle corps of PNA Lodge 1020. (Courtesy of Mr. and Mrs. Eugene W. Golomb)

161

Leopold Lorentz and soldiers of the First Polish Armoured Division, passing inspection by Field Marshal Montgomery.

come to the Poles' assistance and denying landing rights to Allied planes that might have dropped ammunition and provisions. Members of local organizations drafted resolutions of protest and dispatched them quickly to the president, secretary of state, congressmen, and senators: "As Christians, we appeal to you in the name of humanity to bring utmost pressure on Russia and our Allies to send munitions and food immediately to Warsaw."[64] The Rising endured but the Poles received no assistance from the Red Army or the Allies. On September 11th, at a commemoration of the fifth anniversary of the invasion of Poland, Father Patrick J. Flynn spoke to a somber gathering of local Polish Americans, acknowledging that "today, Poland has been abandoned by the statesmen of the world and all she has left is hope in God. The betrayal . . . of the Polish Underground in Warsaw is one of the most shameful stories of the war."

Their concern for those suffering in Poland remained coupled with local families' thoughts of sons and daughters in service, stationed in 1944 at battle fronts in many parts of the world.[65] At the traditional *Wigilia* dinner hosted by St. Casimir's Parish at Christmas, friends repeatedly extended one wish as they broke and shared the *oplatek:* "I hope your son returns home safely and soon."

In the opening days of August 1944, when the streets of Warsaw had become a battlefield and its buildings were in flames, the soldiers of the First Polish Armoured Division received the order to march toward Falaise from the beaches of Normandy, joined with the Second Canadian Corps in the Allied offensive to regain France.[66] During the next eight weeks, as reports of destruction and death in the Polish capital became increasingly more grim, the First Armoured Division pushed through France and into Belgium and Holland with British and American forces, taking part in decisive and bitter battles for control of the continent: Chambois, Falaise and the Argenten Pocket, Ghent, the Mark Canal. After Warsaw had fallen, the Poles moved on through Holland, sustaining heavy losses in seven

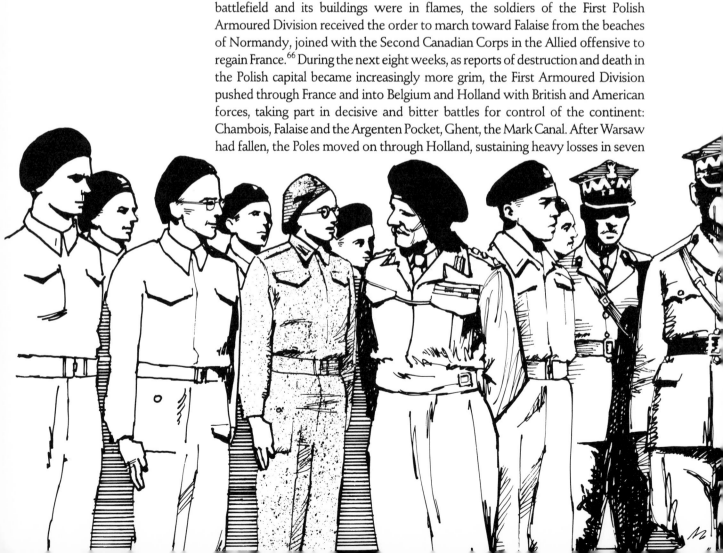

months of combat that closed in May 1945 when the Polish colors were hoisted over the German naval base at Wilhelmshaven.

Until he was wounded by German mortar fire in the battle of the Mark Canal in October, Leopold Lorentz marched with the Poles of the First Armoured Division. Stationed near Haddington, Scotland, for the previous two years, he had trained and waited for combat orders along with soldiers who had battled German forces in Poland at the war's onset. Many of the men with whom Lorentz served had been members of the Polish Army units whose survivors had crossed into Hungary, Yugoslavia, and Rumania after Poland's fall, then made their way to France to join in the defense of the Marne. Others had fought with the Allies in Norway and North Africa after fleeing Nazi-held Poland. Some had escaped German prison camps or forced labor in Siberia. Some, like Lorentz, were immigrants or men of Polish descent, recruited for service from the United States, Canada, South America, and Australia.

Enrolled in the cadet officers' school, Lorentz trained for assignment with the mechanized units.[67] "We are up at 6:30 mornings here. Morning prayer, breakfast, orders for the day, and off to this task of learning," he wrote at the start of the course. "Theory comes first—how an engine works and why. . . . At the end of the training we are to be mechanics and drivers for trucks, motorcycles and tanks." When he had learned to operate a motorcycle and repair its engine, Lorentz was assigned his own machine and sent regularly with his unit on maneuvers in the British countryside. After several days of marching or riding, sleeping in the open, and advancing against the "enemy," the troops arrived exhausted at camp, often having sustained injuries and casualties in the use of machinery, arms, and live ammunition. "Last night about 8, returned almost a walking corpse from three days of maneuvering all about England," Lee wrote to his family in summer 1943. "Hours of riding . . . rain . . . cold . . . no food . . . no sleep." Still, he acknowledged, the training was toughening him. "How am I? Very fit. . . . I never thought I had it in me. . . . [This is] damn hard work."

Like other Polish Army soldiers stationed in Scotland, Lorentz was befriended by a local family who extended their hospitality to him. In his free hours and when on leave, Lee often visited the Turbynes of nearby Dirleton, enjoying at their home a hot meal, conversation, and a good night's sleep. At Christmas and on other holidays he was included in their family circle, and invariably returned to camp with a generous bag of provisions packed by Mrs. Turbyne. "Keeps me and Frankie alive all week," he claimed after departing the Turbynes' with a "huge lunch" after one weekend stay. When Mrs. Turbyne tried to slip him money to repair his broken eyeglasses, Lee refused. "They do so much for me," he wrote to his parents. "Dad and Ma, words cannot describe how I love these people. There is no family in the world next to my own I love as much. . . . I will never forget them."

When they learned of Lee's interest in writing, the Turbynes provided him with a room at their home where he could enjoy privacy and work on his "Diary of a Polish Soldier." During his two years at Haddington, Lorentz continued to prepare articles describing his experiences with the Polish Army for Polish American journals and newspapers. These essays, subtitled "Somewhere in England," appeared regularly in publications like *Zgoda* and *Sokol Polski,* depicting his life as a cadet officer and sharing his observations on topics from European politics to the Scottish terrain.

In a number of columns he described his training and the rigors of maneuvers, and admitted to an initial recklessness that resulted in several mishaps and spills on his motorcycle. Others detailed his travels through Britain while on furlough, with stops at Inverness, Edinburgh, Liverpool, and London. Some columns resembled excerpts from a tourist's diary, like the depiction of his tour of a thirteenth century Scottish castle: "My first castle . . . well. Wish you could be with me, treading reverently mid the stone ruins of this medieval abode. A dark winding staircase . . . slits in the wall overlooking the drawbridge—can you see the archer poised there, bow drawn taut and trembling? And the deep dark cistern. . . ." Some, in contrast, stood as reminders of a world at war, like Lorentz's description of his first air raid, experienced on a visit to London, and of the first airplane crash he witnessed, one in which a pilot and a Scottish workman were killed: "Although three days have swept past, its awful vision will not leave my mind. . . . Mangled steel and mangled bodies, grotesque, scorched . . . no longer resembling men."

His most thoughtful articles shared Lorentz's impressions of the soldiers with whom he served. Readers at home learned through Lee's articles of the Poles' sometimes awkward attempts to master English and converse with Scottish girls, their boisterous camaraderie, their homesickness and melancholy singing in the camp canteen, the kindness extended to them by Scottish villagers. Lee sometimes shared glimpses of their histories: Witek, forced into service with Rommel's army in Africa, waiting for an opportunity to escape to join the Allies; Jozef, mobilized with Polish forces in July 1939, crossing the frozen Drava River into Yugoslavia at night after Poland's defeat; a group of volunteers, each no more than nineteen years old, who had been taken with their families to Siberia at the war's outbreak, later making their way through Persia and North Africa to join the Polish forces in Britain.

Lee found one figure particularly poignant: not a soldier, but a civilian who worked in the army kitchen, a Pole who had been allowed to depart a Siberian labor camp but had had to leave his family behind, looking each day for word that they were still alive. One son, the man told Lorentz, had died on the journey to Siberia: "Eight little ones. . . . Eight of them. . . . The youngest was four. He lived at the start when they took us out of our home and packed us in train wagons. . . . But he could not stand it when we were in Russia, moving along in freezing weather on horse cart. They would not let me bury him. I had to wrap him in what we had and shove his little body into the snow." "I looked at his honest, tired face—his gnarled, calloused hands," Lee wrote, "What can I say to this man. . . ? Here he is in Scotland, a sad and broken man. . . . alone with his thoughts."

During their years in Scotland, Lorentz and the other soldiers of the First Armoured Division waited restlessly for combat orders.[68] Rumors that their units would depart imminently circulated often, as early as February 1943 when Lee informed his family of the latest speculation around Haddington: "Not a Pole in Scotland by April." Anticipating their move into battle, Lee organized his personal belongings—letters, photographs, a few books, a briefcase filled with his writing—and entrusted these to the Turbynes, indicating in an accompanying note that his possessions were to be forwarded to his parents if he did not return.

Despite recurring rumors, the First Polish Armoured Division did not march from Britain until July 1944, a few weeks after D-Day, when they and other reinforcements were ordered across the channel to Normandy. After a brief wait near Caen, the Polish units under command of General Stanislaw Maczek advanced toward Falaise in concert with the Fourth Canadian Armoured Division. During their march, Lorentz managed to scribble down notes which he later transcribed into additional entries for "Diary of a Polish Soldier," now identified as written "Somewhere in France."[69]

Lee's view of combat changed quickly during his first days at the front, his initial exhilaration at being called to duty sobered by the sight and stench of death on the route to Falaise. The massing of his division in the wheat fields was "a wonderful and terrible sight," he wrote of his feelings before the Polish units' first march. "Tanks of all kinds, our Polish tanks. . . ! Armoured cars, trucks and lorries and jeeps, thousands of vehicles poised ready to leap. . . . Suddenly you felt a part of the great organization. . . ." Later, overwhelmed by weariness and horror "after a fortnight in hell," he wrote of viewing the corpses of his friends and hearing the moans of the dying, of burying a seventeen-year-old Pole "who had lived through Russian prisons and still had hopes of seeing his people. Hurriedly, we had to dig a shallow grave and carefully bury him in his coat, and mark the place with his helmet." Lying one night in a straw-strewn dugout and trying to sleep, Lee thought of life at home: "It all seems so very, very far away now—I pray I will see that life again."

Lorentz drew resolve from his status as a cadet corporal with men under his command. "When I see them watch me out of the corner of their eyes, I am able to straighten myself a bit. . . . Having responsibility gives you a little courage," he wrote in his notes at the end of August, not knowing then that he and one of the men in his command would be hit by a mortar grenade two months later at the storming of the Mark Canal. Bleeding heavily from the back and arm, Lorentz shouted at the weeping soldier to calm him as a military truck carried them from the battlefield through a hail of shrapnel. After his wounds were dressed quickly at a medical station outside the front, Lee was moved first to a British hospital at Turnhout, then to a Canadian hospital in Antwerp for surgery. The following day, he was flown to England to recuperate at the Royal Hospital in Wolverhampton, where he wrote another entry in his soldier's diary:

> Imagine how I felt when I learned that the next day, my battalion was forced back across the Mark again at great loss. . . . So there will be still more faces I will never see again.
>
> Now, I have no pain really and it is easy to forget about that even in a place like this. All you need do is look about—see men without legs and arms, hear the pitiful moans at night—to realize and again be thankful you have been spared.
>
> I get used to this life now and it makes going back all the more fearful. Yet, there—there is a satisfaction. There you are *doing* something. It has been three months of life in mud and dirt—but glorious. And my muscles are hardened from digging slit trenches two or three or ten times a day as the Polish infantry marches on.

Poland's post-war fate was set early in 1945, formalized at the February Yalta Conference at which Stalin won Allied support for Russian dominance of Eastern Europe. Learning that Poland's borders were to be redrawn and that the Allies had recognized a Communist government in Warsaw, representatives of local Polish American organizations spoke in anger to the press.[70] The "Big Three" had failed a "moral test" by dishonoring Poland's right to independence, Henry Laboski said on behalf of the Rochester Committee of Americans of Polish Descent. The United States had destroyed the faith of the world's small democracies, charged Edmund Lorentz, president of the local Council of the Polish National Alliance. Adam Felerski, vice president of the state's Pulaski Republican League, stated that

he never expected to "live to see the day when the United States would participate in such a criminal thing."

Attempting to exert political influence and gain public sympathy for Poland, neighborhood organizations endorsed statements of protest, signed petitions, and supported the lobbying of the Polish American Congress.[71] Centrala garnered support for a memorandum to President Truman in April 1945, urging that decisions made at Yalta regarding Poland be overturned at the upcoming San Francisco Security Conference. Two months later, delegates to the district PNA conference passed a resolution demanding "justice for Poland and protection against aggressors." The Rochester chapter of the Committee of Americans of Polish Descent voiced its opinion in communications sent in 1946 and 1947 to Truman, Secretary of State James Byrnes, and Congressman Kenneth Keating. In conjunction with Pulaski Day ceremonies in 1950, local PNA lodges urged Keating to work for Congressional action to restore Poland's independence.

Poland's status stirred high emotion but, as the war closed, no event drew more heartfelt response than the return of the neighborhood's young men and women: the sons, daughters, brothers, and sisters who had been away from their homes for as long as five years. The service stars that signified their absence came down from front porch windows as families on Kosciusko, Sobieski, Weaver, and

Father Joseph Balcerak (left) and Father Henry Adamski (right) at the dedication of the plaque to St. Stanislaus Parish's war dead. (Courtesy of Mr. and Mrs. Joseph Zablotski)

Warsaw Streets celebrated homecoming. Reflecting the general joy, Centrala replaced its Charity Ball with a victory dance to cheer the war's end in 1946.

Many of the neighborhood's soldiers, sailors, and flyers returned decorated for bravery in combat in the European or Pacific theaters of war. Pride in this record of service mixed with the pain of those who came home maimed and wounded, and with the sorrow of families whose sons did not return from the war. Eighteen of the 700 enlisted from St. Stanislaus Parish lost their lives while in service: Frank Balawender, Roman Gorney, Chester Jozefski, Alexander Kachuk, Joseph Katlewski, Melvin Michalski, Chester Napierala, Robert Nowak, Telesfor Okolowicz, Edward Pelc, George Petrowski, John Pietrowski, Edward Psyk, Julian Rogowicz, Edward Solowski, Bernard Stachowiak, Frank Suski, Thaddeus Wandasiewicz.[72]

Special tribute was paid to one of these, Melvin Michalski, by his colleagues in the Echo Singing Association. In April 1946, Echo members installed a bronze plaque in the front hall of their clubhouse, dedicated in honor of Michalski who was killed a few months before the end of the war in action with the 182nd Infantry Division on Cebu Island.[73] Flanked by a color guard that included Michalski's brother and two close friends, Echo president Henry Cwalina announced that the club would establish a $15,000 college scholarship fund in the staff sergeant's name, to be distributed in annual grants to children of Echo members. A crowd of 400 watched in silence as veterans of the new American Legion Post named for Michalski saluted his memory with a volley of shots that rang from Echo Hall down Sobieski Street.

One neighborhood soldier's homecoming drew press attention at the end of 1947. Second Lieutenant Leopold Lorentz, still an officer in service with the Polish Army, arrived at the New York Central Station on Christmas Eve, home to spend the holidays with his family after an absence of six years.[74] A *Times-Union* report recounted his career with the Polish forces, his receipt of the Cross of Valor, and his decision to return to England to assist in the resettlement of fellow servicemen. Lorentz remained on assignment with the Polish Army for three years after the war, in charge of repatriating volunteers who held American citizenship. He stayed until that work was complete, returning to Rochester in 1948 as the last American volunteer demobilized from the Polish forces.

Back at home with his new bride Olga, a young Polish woman whom he had met in England, Lorentz joined with William Brodie, Stanislaw Klodzinski, and others to organize a Polish Displaced Persons Committee that helped 600 Polish families uprooted by the war to resettle in Rochester.[75] Some of these refugees were members of the Polish forces, his comrades whom Lorentz called "the saddest soldiers in the world"—men who had fought at Narvik, Tobruk, Arnheim, Falaise, and Monte Cassino, cut off from their homes by a peace settlement that

Edward Stira (left) and Edward Solowski (right) in service in the Philippines. (Courtesy of John Solowski)

left Poland under Communist rule, dispersed as displaced persons at the close of a war in which they had served with the victors. Others were members of the Polish Home Army, survivors of the bitter battle to reclaim Warsaw. Some were civilians who had spent the war years in German or Soviet labor camps, removed from their homes when the Nazi and Red armies entered Poland in 1939. All had seen their lives disrupted by the war in Europe, and carried stories of the war's suffering, horror, and loss.

Men like Mieczyslaw Jopek and Leon Holowacz arrived as veterans of the Polish armed forces.[76] Jopek, 23 years old when the war began, battled Nazi troops in his homeland in September 1939, then crossed the border with the First Polish Mounted Rifles Unit to join the Allies fighting along the Maginot Line. After the fall of France, he was sent to Scotland to train recruits to the First Polish Armoured Division, and dispatched across the English Channel in July 1944 for the march from Normandy to Wilhelmshaven. Wounded three times, Jopek survived the brutal campaign but buried friends in battlefields that mark the Polish division's route to Germany. He received sixteen decorations for service in six countries, and remained with the Allied Occupation Forces for an additional two years before immigrating to the United States.

Leon Holowacz, a railway employee, was arrested by Russian soldiers in eastern Poland at the close of 1939, considered dangerous after remarking to a co-worker that life under Russian rule was worse than German occupation. He was held for a month in a crowded prison, thrown in a filthy room with dozens of others, then herded out for a forced march on which guards shot those too exhausted to continue. After he had walked for a week, Holowacz was put on a train that carried prisoners to a labor camp outside Moscow, where he remained for the next two years. Freed as a result of the 1941 Sikorski-Maisky Pact, in which the Soviets agreed to release 100,000 imprisoned Poles eligible for military service, Holowacz was evacuated to the Middle East to join the Polish Army. Assigned to the First Armoured Division, he traveled from Russia through Iran and Palestine, then around the Cape of Good Hope and up the west coast of Africa, reaching a Polish military camp in Scotland in 1942. Holowacz fought with Polish forces in France, Belgium, and Holland in 1944 and 1945, and served until 1947 with the Occupation Army in Germany. After trying a job with British Railways following the war, he immigrated to the United States at the urging of a brother who had resettled in Rochester.

Other Poles who arrived were civilians, families who had experienced separation and the hardships of life in German or Soviet labor camps. Some whose homes had been in western Poland had been forced into labor for the Third Reich, ordered to munitions factories in Germany, Austria, and Czechoslovakia. Many who had lived in Poland's eastern provinces had been routed from their homes by the Red Army in the last months of 1939, packed into cattle cars, and transported to Siberia. Jozef Grzebieniak, twelve years old, made the three-week journey to a remote collective farm with his mother and two sisters shortly after his father, a sergeant in the Polish Army, was sent to a prison near Murmansk.[77] One of few Polish families among many Russians, the Grzebieniaks were not allowed to work during their first year on the farm, forced instead to barter their belongings and scrounge odd jobs in order to survive. Later, his mother was assigned as a nurse's

The War in Poland: (1) Polish partisans with villagers; (2) partisans on the march; (3) Ignacy Moscicki reviewing Polish cavalry before the invasion; (4) General Sikorski attaching a battle ribbon to a regimental standard; (5) members of the Home Army in Warsaw.

Wlodzimierz Jablonski, during his service with the Polish Home Army.

aide in a small hospital and Jozef was put to work pushing a horse-drawn plow. Denied documents that authorized travel, the family was forbidden to leave the farm and received no information for two years about Jozef's father.

When he was released from prison in 1941 as a result of the Sikorski-Maisky Pact, Sergeant Grzebieniak searched for his wife and children, located them with the help of relatives, and secured papers that permitted them to leave the farm. After a long journey to the southern Russian border during which they were challenged a number of times by Soviet police, the Grzebieniaks crossed into British territory in the Middle East, where Jozef, too young to join the army, entered a Polish military school. His father enlisted with General Anders' Second Polish Army Corps, and fought at Monte Cassino during service with the Allies in Italy. Reunited in England after the war, Jozef and his father joined the Polish Resettlement Corps, helping Polish soldiers gain admittance to western countries before immigrating themselves to the United States.

Jan Piotrowski had determined to build a better life for his family when he returned to Poland from the United States in 1932.[78] He and his wife Zofia had emigrated in the 1920s, but the couple sailed back to Europe with their six-year-old daughter Celia when Jan lost his job during the Depression. They were able to buy two farms in eastern Poland, and prospered until Soviet soldiers confiscated their land in 1939. The family was sent to a work camp in the Siberian timberlands, where all three labored for two years in a sawmill, existing on meager rations and sleeping without blankets on boards in winter. When Poles eligible for military service were released from Russian captivity, Piotrowski, in his midforties, enlisted and took his family from the sawmill to Teheran. There they were separated, Jan entering the Polish forces while Zofia and Celia continued on to a refugee camp near Bombay.

The two lived in refugee camps for the next five years, until Celia, who had been born in the United States, boarded a ship for America a few days before her 21st birthday, arriving in time to retain the citizenship she would have lost if she had reached 21 on foreign soil. She traveled to Rochester, where the Piotrowskis had relatives, and worked for a year to arrange her parents' immigration. Jan and Zofia arrived in 1948 and, with the help of Celia's fiance Henry Iglinski, moved into a house on St. Stanislaus Street—the family's first home in the nine years since they were forced from their land in Poland.

A small group of those who came to Rochester after the war had been citizens of Warsaw and members of the Polish Home Army, men and women who had battled Nazi troops during their city's uprising. They had survived two months of siege, faced tanks and mortar fire from encampments in the ruins, crawled through sewers carrying ammunition and supplies, pulled wounded comrades from the streets, and buried dead neighbors in rough graves in the city's rubble. Among them were Wlodzimierz Jablonski, a first lieutenant who had served in the Home Army throughout the German Occupation, and his wife, Aleksandra Zieleniewska, who had been a nurse in his unit.[79] Jablonski, whose horse had been shot out from under him during fierce fighting against Nazi troops in September 1939, had escaped to Warsaw where he joined the Underground, secretively training recruits to the Home Army for the next five years. Like others who survived the Warsaw Rising, he spent the last months of the war in a German prison camp, enlisting in the Second Polish Army Corps for additional service when he was liberated in May 1945. Aleksandra, whom Jablonski had married two months before the Rising, escaped from German guards on the journey to a concentration camp, remained in hiding until the end of the war, then made her way by train and on foot through Germany and Czechoslovakia to rejoin her husband in Italy. After two years with the Polish Resettlement Corps in England, the Jablonskis left Europe and arrived in Rochester in 1951.

Olga Pulawska, also a veteran of the Rising, had seen her family's world destroyed in 1939.[80] After German tanks leveled their home in Warsaw, Olga's father, a newspaper publisher and Polish Army officer, learned that the Nazis had marked him for execution. He sent his wife and two daughters to eastern Poland to stay with his brother, a member of the Polish senate, and joined them later when he was able to escape the city. By the time the family arrived at the senator's home in Krzemieniec, a town near Lwow, the Red Army had seized eastern Poland. During the next two years, while her family lived under Russian occupation, Olga worked in a peat bog where she cut bricks for the Soviets in exchange for food. In 1941, when it became necessary for them to separate, Olga returned with her mother and sister to live with cousins in Warsaw while her father, now a member of the Home Army, remained in the eastern part of the country under an alias.

In Warsaw, Olga attended high school clandestinely, instructed by teachers in private homes in defiance of the Nazis' ban on secondary education for Poles. As a member of the Polish Scouts, she assisted the Underground in small ways, such as by distributing anti-Nazi literature, and joined the Home Army when she was eligible at age seventeen. It was 1944, and the Underground was preparing to launch an effort planned since the start of the war, a civilian uprising that Poles hoped would reclaim their capital from German rule.

The Rising began on August 1st, when the Home Army called the Warsaw population to arms against Nazi troops now being pushed west by the Red Army. Given the alias *Mysz* (Mouse), Olga was trained and assigned as a nurse, responsible to pull the wounded from the front lines and tend to their injuries. Caught in gunfire on the last day of the Rising, she was injured badly herself in the right shoulder but insisted on remaining with her unit when Nazis rounded up its members. Sent with other women to a prison camp at Oberlangen, she experienced brutal treatment at the hands of her captors before the camp was liberated by the First Polish Armoured Division in 1945.

Olga joined the British Occupation Army as a member of its Polish units, traveling eventually to England where an uncle was assigned with the Polish Army. Her mother was alive, staying with a friend outside Warsaw, but other members of her family had not survived the war. Her sister had died in a streetcar accident, her father had died while in service with the Home Army near Lublin, and the uncle with whom she had stayed in Krzemieniec had perished in Dachau. Olga took a job in London at Polish Army headquarters, where she met Leopold Lorentz while he was working to resettle members of the Polish forces. The two were married, and Lorentz brought his bride to Rochester when he returned from service. Their first child was born in 1948, and Olga assumed American citizenship in 1951. "It seems to me," she told a reporter who covered her story that year, "[this] is a country in which you can make many plans. You can hope to educate your children; you can enjoy the great standards of living; you can look forward to the future. . . ."

"[I] keep thinking how the path of my entire life is henceforth changed," Leopold Lorentz had written to his parents from Windsor in 1941, the day after he was admitted to the Polish Army. In that letter, he spoke for others of his generation, millions of young Americans whose lives would be profoundly altered by their part in the Second World War. Like Lorentz, each of the hundreds of enlisted men and women who returned to homes in the Polish community at the end of the decade carried experiences of service, camaraderie, combat, and death that would affect them for the rest of their lives.

Like its individual members, Polonia had also been marked by the experience of war, most notably in the loss borne by families whose sons had died in service, and in the unity expressed in Polonia's support for Poland. As during the First World War, this support had been charged with emotion but tangible, a steady donation of funds, clothing, and supplies that attested to the "ties of blood." Unlike three decades earlier, however, support for Poland had been tempered by the community's view of itself as Polish American, its sons committed to service in the United States forces and its energy devoted to American homefront activity as well as to Polish relief.

In another sense, Lorentz's statement spoke for the hundreds of Poles who arrived in Rochester at the close of the decade, servicemen and civilians whose lives had been torn by the worst episodes of war. From a different generation and of an experience in many ways removed from that of the first immigrants, these displaced persons represented the largest influx of newcomers to Polonia since early in the century. Their membership in the Polish parishes, and their support for established and new organizations, would bolster the strength of the community in the next decades.

There would be additional changes beginning in the fifties, results of a renewed economy and the assimilation of the community's third and fourth generations. Some of these changes would be matters of pride and accomplishment, such as the education that would be attained and the careers that would be built by children born following the war. No change would be more significant or more painful, however, than change in the neighborhood, its dissolution in the next decades as the city's Polish Town.

THE VOYAGE OF THE POLESZUK

Julian Ramotowski

In the last days of August 1939, as the threat of war rumbled along his country's western border, Julian Ramotowski was in Rochester on a mission of good will, one of a crew of Polish Sea Scouts who had just completed a journey across the Atlantic Ocean in a 45-foot sloop.[81] Their adventure had begun a year before at Gdynia and had carried them 7,000 miles—along the west European and African coasts, across the ocean to Brazil, north through the Caribbean Sea and along the east American coast to New York harbor, then up the Hudson River to the Barge Canal and the Great Lakes. It was a voyage of exploration and peace that ended a month after the small ship docked in Rochester, its crew returning quickly to Europe in the first weeks of war to join the Polish Army mobilizing in France.

Ramotowski, a 31-year-old insurance assessor, had taken part in preparations for the voyage of the *Poleszuk,* a motorboat that he and other Sea Scouts had converted into a sailing vessel for trans-Atlantic crossing. They planned a journey that would touch four continents and bring them ultimately to Chicago, where they would present the *Poleszuk* as their gift to Polish American Sea Scouts. The boat departed Gdynia in July 1938 with a crew of three young men: Captain Ludwik Walasik, Mieczyslaw Wroblewski, and Fryderyk Tomczyk. Several weeks into the voyage, they were joined by Wladyslaw Henoch and by Ramotowski, who caught up with the expedition in French Guinea after coaxing his employer into granting him a twelve-month leave.

Julian Ramotowski (far right, holding mascot Bu-Bu) and the crew of the Poleszuk. (Courtesy of Mr. and Mrs. Julian Ramotowski)

On one of their stops in West Africa, the crew of five took on a sixth passenger—a lively monkey which they christened *Bu-Bu.* Perched along the *Poleszuk's* rigging or cuddled in one of the sailor's laps, *Bu-Bu* served as their companion on the voyage, providing diversion during the long weeks in which they had no sight of land. Their crossing to the east tip of Brazil took 27 days, a month on open seas from the time the *Poleszuk* pushed out into the Atlantic from the African coast.

During the crossing, the crew were buffeted several times by heavy winds and drenched by high waves crashing over the *Poleszuk's* bow. The sailors braved much of this rough weather without protection, after discovering early in their voyage at the height of one fierce storm that their canvas safety belts had deteriorated. When the sea was calmer, they passed the time by reading, and were able to observe the habits of dolphins, whales, and sharks.

The *Poleszuk's* voyage caught public attention, and the Sea Scouts were interviewed by reporters at each port of call. They also received hundreds of letters and post cards at stops along the way, many sent to them by Polish schoolchildren. Ramotowski and the others answered each correspondence with a card of their own, responding to the children's notes with a message from *Bu-Bu:* a photograph of the monkey seated atop a lowered mast, her paw print stamped in ink on the opposite side.

After reaching Brazil, the *Poleszuk* navigated north through the Caribbean Sea and along the east American seaboard to New York harbor. From the Hudson River, the boat entered the Barge Canal and docked at Rochester's Canal Terminal on August 21, 1939—a full year after its departure from Gdynia. The voyage nearly ended there when, having survived ocean storms and shark-infested waters, the *Poleszuk* narrowly missed being crushed against the canal bank by a ponderous barge that swerved into its path. The craft escaped with minor damage—one broken stay on the starboard side—and its crew deboarded to enjoy a reception and dinner sponsored by the Polish American community at Falcon Hall. Questioned by a reporter about tensions in Europe, the sailors responded that they would return to Poland immediately to assist in its defense if the need arose.

The war in Europe began when the *Poleszuk* was moored at Cleveland. Now in the last days of their yearlong journey, the crew continued on to Chicago where, according to plan, they presented their vessel to a unit of Polish American Sea Scouts. As soon as travel to Europe could be arranged, the young men made their return voyage by steamship, under circumstances less joyful than they had expected when they left home. By the time they arrived, Poland had fallen and its soldiers were gathering in exile in France.

Ramotowski, a reserve officer, reported for duty in Paris and served in France until Polish troops were evacuated to England. Hoping to be selected for an air drop into Poland, he volunteered for training as a paratrooper with the Polish units of the RAF. Frustrated when the war dragged on without his being called for an air mission, he requested transfer to the First Polish Armoured Division where he was appointed captain of a 120-man company. After service in the Allied march through Holland, Ramotowski remained with Occupation Forces in Germany for an additional two years.

As he sorted out his life at the close of the war, the young man learned that his sister and her six children had spent two years as laborers in Siberia, and that his brother had died of typhus in Teheran after release from a Soviet prison. When his mother, still in Poland, advised him not to return, Ramotowski emigrated from Britain to the United States. He sought work in New York and Detroit, and lived briefly in Chicago where he married a Polish girl from Wilno. At the urging of Leopold Lorentz, whom the crew of the *Poleszuk* had met when they passed through upstate New York, the couple moved again to Rochester. Ramotowski found employment at Burroughs Corporation, purchased a home with his wife, and helped his sister and her family settle on a farm outside Weedsport. Among the belongings that he brought to his new home, saved through a decade of military service and transiency, were photographs of the voyage of the *Poleszuk,* the craft that departed a Poland at peace and reached its destination as Europe entered the Second World War.

IN SERVICE IN THE PACIFIC

Edward Bartles

"We would sortie early, at 3:00 a.m.," Edward Bartles recalled, "and fly eastward more than 150 miles from our carrier to Japan. Our first strike was on Honshu, attacking air bases. My view of that beautiful island, with Fuji very prominent, was shattered when anti-aircraft blossomed around us. . . ."[82]

Bartles, a Navy fighter pilot, was one of the hundreds of young men from Rochester's Polish neighborhood who served with the United States forces in World War II. His tour of duty took him thousands of miles from home, to the Pacific theater of war, where he flew an F6F Hellcat for the Third Fleet under command of Admiral William Halsey. During his months in the Pacific, Bartles participated in air strikes on Wake Island and advanced with Task Group 38.1 to Japan, flying over Honshu, Hokkaido, Shikoku, and Kyushu in the critical air campaigns that closed the Pacific war.

The youngest of five children of Stanislaw Bartles and Marianna Hubinska, Edward was born in his family's home on Dayton Street in 1921. His parents had emigrated thirteen years earlier from Poland to Rochester, where his father, a carpenter, found steady work with local building contractors. After attending St. Stanislaus School, Edward entered Edison High School and took a job as a machinist at Kodak Camera Works upon graduation.

In November 1942, at the height of American enlistment for service in the Second World War, Bartles was one of approximately 120 local men admitted to the "Genesees," a naval flight training unit organized in Rochester. After instruc-

tion in the V-5 program at Colgate College, the group practiced flying Taylor Cubs at Dansville airport, and studied mathematics and physics with Alfred State College faculty members in rooms at a Dansville hotel. The Genesees' pre-flight training, completed at the University of North Carolina, required additional work in navigation, meteorology, aircraft recognition, electronic transmission, and naval rules and regulations. As follow-up to the classroom program, Bartles was sent to Bunker Hill, Indiana, where he trained with a bi-plane called the "Yellow Peril," flying in an open cockpit in the dead of winter.

Flight training continued through 1943 and into 1944 at three stateside locations: Barin Field in Florida, called "bloody Barin" by recruits because of the number of deaths of pilots in training there; the Great Lakes, where flyers qualified to make carrier landings; and Daytona Beach, where new pilots had their first opportunity to take up the F6F Hellcat, the naval fighter prepared specifically to challenge the formidable Japanese Zero. Sent at the end of this training to Pomona Field, New Jersey, Bartles entered Air Group 94 with a high gunnery score that drew the attention of his commanding officer. He was chosen the commander's "wing man," assigned to fly off the wing of the officer's plane and provide protection during air strikes.

In 1945, Air Group 94 sailed from the west coast to Kahalui Field on Maui and was assigned to action in the Pacific, operating from the aircraft carrier *#16 Lexington.* After volunteering for a second sortie during one of their first strikes on Wake Island, his flight group leader was hit and Bartles saw the plane explode in flames thirty feet from his own. He returned from the mission shaken, troubled for the first time by the sight of death and no longer able to think of himself as invincible in the air.

The *Lexington* advanced to a station off the coast of Japan, where it joined the powerful Third Fleet of carriers, cruisers, battleships, and destroyers under Halsey's command. From this base, Bartles and other pilots flew strikes over the Japanese islands regularly, strafing air fields and military installations during exhausting six-hour missions on which the risks of death were high. As the weeks passed and the strikes continued, many of the men with whom Bartles served lost their lives on assignment—some caught by enemy fire, others unable to negotiate the difficult carrier landings in inclement weather.

"During combat you were scared," Bartles wrote years after the war, "but I don't think any fighter pilot was afraid of the enemy he could see. The forces of nature were more frightful. . . ." Many times, pilots had to navigate their Hellcats through dense ocean fog that intensified the hazards of flight and landing. Occasionally they flew through fog at night, as Bartles did while on photo assignments that required him to cruise straight and low over enemy territory. Worse than the fog were Pacific typhoons, powerful gales like one that tossed the *Lexington* as though it were a toy and ripped huge aircraft from the landing deck.

In July 1945, Bartles was assigned to a group of bombers sent to attack the Japanese naval base at Kure, a port on the Inland Sea. A tightly fortified location, the Kure base hid the remaining battleships of the Japanese Navy in naturally protected fjords along a rugged coast. In order to find their targets, the pilots were required to fly straight down into a barrage of Japanese ground fire. Bartles was the first to reach the capital ship *Ise,* dropping a bomb that hit the ship's fire control center during fierce action in which a dozen Japanese warships were sunk or damaged. At the close of the Kure attack, seen as the U. S. Navy's revenge for Pearl Harbor, Halsey sent a message to his ships: "Mark well this day the 28th of July. To the Dumbos and lifeguards, to combat air patrol and men of the surface team, to the valiant British force on the right flank: well done. For the flying fighters who fought it out over Japan to a smashing victory, I have no words that can add to the record with their courage, their blood, and their lives."

With the explosion of the atomic bomb early in August, the war in the Pacific came to a close and Bartles participated in a demonstration of American air strength, flying over Japan in a squadron of 1,000 planes launched from an armada of carriers off the coast. He completed his tour of duty at Guam, then returned home to marry, earn a college degree, and take a job in engineering with Eastman Kodak Company. For his service in the war, he received the Air Medal and was honored with the Navy Cross in recognition of heroic action in the battle at Kure.

"MAYOR OF POLISH TOWN"

William Brodie

Between 1937 and 1971, the United States elected eight presidents, New York State had five governors, and the City of Rochester saw six mayors come and go. During the same three decades, Rochester's Polonia Civic Centre had only one president: William C. Brodie, who was elected to head the union of Polish organizations more than thirty times, in consecutive terms that kept him in that office nearly half of his life.[83] During his tenure with Centrala, a stretch of time that began during the Great Depression and ended during the Vietnam War, Bill Brodie became known as "the mayor of Polish Town," recognized both in the neighborhood and in wider local circles as chairman of Polonia's organizations, spokesman for its causes, and advocate for its interests at city hall.

Brodie was christened Boleslaw Brodowczynski in 1897, one of four children born to Tomasz and Franciszka Brodowczynski. His parents were among the city's first Polish settlers and its earliest Polish proprietors, owners of a meat market opened on Hudson Avenue in 1898. Their homemade sausage and fresh meats sold well among neighborhood housewives and the shop was soon popularly known as "Brodie's Market," its title shortened to accommodate suppliers and delivery men who had given up on pronouncing the full Polish name. The store

*William C.
Brodie (right)*

was a family enterprise that remained open for seven decades, its operation passing to the Brodowczynskis' sons when the three young men were old enough to earn their own living.

Beginning in the thirties, the name of Boleslaw Brodowczynski emerged repeatedly on the rosters of Polish American organizations. A United States Army veteran of the First World War, Brodie became active in Pulaski Post after his tour of duty, and assisted with the organization of Pulaski Day celebrations early in the decade. By 1935, he had assumed leadership of three neighborhood groups, serving simultaneously as commander of Pulaski Post, president of the Polish Business Men's Association, and president of the Polonia Republican League.

In 1937, Brodie was elected president of Centrala, the local federation of Polish societies. During the next three decades, he encouraged the organization to sponsor activities that benefited the neighborhood, showcased Polish culture, assisted Polish immigrants and Poles in Europe, and afforded Polish Americans a high profile in civic affairs. His broad smile and expansive personality made him a natural spokesman, and the contacts he established as a businessman and Republican Party member allowed him access to the city's social and political circles. Direct and persistent, Brodie visited city hall often to lobby with officials on behalf of Centrala's causes, rarely bothering to call ahead and arrange an appointment.

During the Second World War, Brodie led Centrala in organizing activities intended to aid Polish citizens and draw attention to Poland's role in the war: fund-raising; collection of clothing, shoes, and other goods; ceremonies such as the citywide moment of silence observed in 1942 in honor of Polish war victims; lobbying on behalf of Poland's post-war independence. Often, these projects featured broad collaboration on the part of the Polish churches and Polish organizations, as well as on the part of city government and local agencies. For Centrala's 1945 relief drive which gathered 100 tons of clothing and 40,000 bars of soap for shipment to Poland, Brodie garnered the cooperation of more than thirty Polish societies, the Salvation Army, the New York State Guard, the Rochester Salvage Committee, the City Bureau of Employment, a carting company, downtown merchants, public and parochial schools, and dozens of individual volunteers.

Among Brodie's favorite projects was the observance of Pulaski Day each October. He relished helping to organize the colorful parades that featured scores of marchers from local veterans' posts, and for many years personally took part in the memorial ceremony at the Hudson Library's Pulaski plaque. In 1940, he was instrumental in convincing city government to name a patch of land at Carter and Gothic Streets in honor of the Polish general, a full ten years after neighborhood residents first made the request.

During his forty years of volunteer activity, Brodie also served as president of the Polish Northeast Food Merchants Organization, board member of Nest 52 of the Polish Falcons, president of the Polish Displaced Persons Organization, member of the Welfare Board of the American Legion, member of the Chamber of Commerce, Republican leader of the Fourth Ward, vice president of the New York District of the Polish American Congress, and member of the National Council of the Kosciuszko Foundation—in addition to holding a twenty-year term as president of the Polonia Republican League. Often, groups that Brodie chaired met at the home he shared on North Street with his wife Barbara Kwiatkowska Brodie, and during the war volunteers sorted and packed hundreds of boxes of clothing for Poland in the couple's garage.

After the war, Brodie expanded his interests to the cultivation of roses and joined the Rochester Rose Society, winning several trophies for the varieties he grew in the yard of his home. When he was elected the society's president in 1950, he led the group's campaign for a municipal rose garden, a project that culminated in the planting of 6,000 roses at Maplewood Park. One bed of white flowers was included as Brodie's personal donation, planted in memory of Tomasz and Franciszka Brodowczynski.

Poor health slowed Brodie's work early in the seventies, when he suffered a stroke that left him partially paralyzed and confined to a wheelchair. Before he died in 1974, he was honored many times by Polish American organizations and other groups, cited often for his contributions to Polonia and to the city's northeast neighborhood.

9 | If You Don't Have Your History . . .

The sound of angry voices spilled from Polish Falcon Hall on an early spring evening in 1949, audible the length of Weyl Street where neatly tended squares of lawn and the season's first flowers rimmed a row of sturdy homes.[1] Outside the clubhouse, people stood on the pavement and pushed toward the door, the overflow of a crowd of 1,200 neighborhood residents who had turned out for a meeting with City Council representatives and the assistant state housing commissioner. "What kind of people do you think would come here if they make only $1,800 a year?" a speaker at the microphone inside demanded while others in the hall conveyed their opinions with catcalls and shouts. "Who's going to make

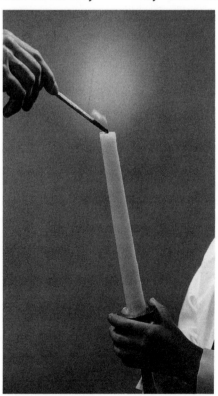

the money out of this thing?" and "Why don't they put this out in Brighton or Charlotte?" additional speakers challenged, as neighbors seated behind them registered support with cheers and applause.

At issue that evening was the City of Rochester's proposal to construct a low-rent housing project near the intersection of North and Norton Streets, approved a few days earlier by City Council and the City Planning Commission. Described in the press as the first step in a master plan to address the city's housing problem, the project provided for construction of apartment units in an area east of Benjamin Franklin High School bounded by Kilmar, Milan, Baird, and Buonomo Streets. The

Bill and Terry Thompson, along with their four children, had driven to St. Stanislaus from their home in Fairport . . . because this was [Terry's] old neighborhood, where her grandparents, immigrants from Poland, had settled. "We think it's important," Bill said, "to get the kids involved in their heritage, to see some of the Polish traditions. . . . If you don't have your history, then you don't really have anything."

**Democrat and Chronicle
Rochester, New York
February 1, 1982**

four-room apartments would rent for $40 a month, primarily to families from impoverished areas like the Baden-Ormond district that the city planned to redevelop.

Less than a week after City Manager Louis B. Cartwright announced the plan, the Polonia Civic Centre and a newly formed organization named the "Individual Home Owners, Businessmen, and Veterans Association of the Northeast District" called an open meeting at which residents could air their opinions about the project to Assistant New York State Housing Commissioner William H. Davis and City Councilmen Henry L. Schlueter and Frank Niger. The officials faced an angry crowd jammed into Falcon Hall, representing for the most part the Polish neighborhood that adjoined the tract proposed for development. The three were subjected to rounds of booing during opening remarks in which they attempted to describe the merits of the project. Davis, who earlier in the day had had to endure a group of residents shouting and shaking their fists as he led state officials on a tour of the housing site, drew the loudest hostility when he stated that the proposed apartments would be of "an attractive garden type."

Those who feared that the neighborhood would change for the worse with the addition of public housing did not disguise their feelings in remarks to Davis and the councilmen. Some charged that the housing project would deteriorate into slums, and stated that they would not welcome residents relocated from neighborhoods plagued with poverty and crime.[2] Others expressed outrage that a score of houses already built in the area would have to be razed and their owners displaced to make room for the apartments. His voice breaking, veteran Leo Rogowicz described how he had built a home for his family in the section marked for the housing project, working on his own "on Saturdays, Sundays, holidays, and any other darn time. . . . I say it's the best house in the vicinity, and if somebody thinks they're going to chase me out, they're foolish."

Before the meeting ended, Niger and Schlueter stepped to the microphone to announce that residents' vehement opposition to the plan had caused them to change their opinions. "We came down here tonight to hear the voice of the people," Niger said. "I'm satisfied. I for one will be against [the project] 100 percent." "It's the people's command," Schlueter seconded. "I will be against the project." Davis also conceded that the apartments would not be built on the northeast side. "This is the end of this housing project," he was overheard to say at the close of the meeting.

The next evening, City Council voted unanimously to shelve a resolution that would have formally launched the housing development, dropping its plans to request a $3 million loan for the project from the state.[3] The proposal had been "shoved toward the boneyard" by the opposition of homeowners on the northeast side, editors of the *Times-Union* wrote, praising the residents for "defending their rights in property as a human right" and for exposing the "hypocrisies of public housing." Others saw the matter differently and leveled charges of bigotry at the group who had assembled at Falcon Hall. "Racial or religious prejudice must not rob any minority in Rochester of decent housing," Rabbi Philip S. Bernstein declared three weeks later at the annual meeting of the Rochester branch of the NAACP. He felt obliged to speak out, Bernstein said, "against the feelings of racial prejudice which I am reliably informed provided the undertone for the protest meeting which defeated the project."[4]

The neighborhood that City Council had proposed as the location for housing development retained in 1949 the appearance that it had held for many years. Solid working-class homes, most constructed of wood and sporting front porches, faced each other in even rows along sidestreets that lined the northeast side's major thoroughfares. The oldest of these had been standing for six decades on streets like St. Stanislaus and Kosciusko, shaded by elm and chestnut trees, trimmed with a few square feet of lawn in the front, and decorated with a patch of garden in the back. At the point where the sidestreets joined Hudson Avenue, homes and shade trees gave way to private enterprise: grocery stores, meat markets, bakeries and sweet shops, lunch counters, barber shops, pharmacies, tailor shops, automotive service centers, plumbers' and electricians' offices, funeral parlors, taverns and meeting halls. Visible for blocks in each direction, the spire of St. Stanislaus Church jutted above the homes and shops, its bell reliably sounding a call at dawn, noon, and dusk.

Residents' opposition to change in this area could be characterized as a stand for homeowners' rights, the opinion offered by the *Times-Union* editors, or as prejudice, the charge raised by Rabbi Bernstein. Neither point of view, however, acknowledged the character of the Polish section, where many families had lived for three generations and now counted cousins and relatives through marriage on most neighborhood streets. Older residents had been among the area's early settlers, the group who had built homes in the section, dug the foundations of its churches, and exchanged blows in Zwolinski Hall in the dispute over religion and nationalism. Younger residents who retained membership in clubs like Echo, Falcons, Rakowian, Polish People's Home, and the Polish National Alliance marked continuity with relatives who had founded the organizations and written their

charters. Popular businesses enjoyed longstanding patronage, like Brodowczynski's market, which had served neighborhood housewives since 1898; Zielinski's construction company, its lumber stacked since the turn of the century between Northeast Avenue and Peckham Street; Wojtczak's bakery, dating to 1915 when its owners peddled bread and pastries door to door. If neighbors bickered over shared fences and gossiped about each other's problems, by and large residents knew the others on their block and felt comfortable enough to leave home for hours without locking the doors.

At the close of the Second World War, the neighborhood adjoining the tract proposed for housing development was still appropriately known as Polish Town, an enclave whose original settlers had deliberately distanced themselves from the city proper and showed interest in local civic affairs only when those affected their neighborhood. In this area, homes and businesses were passed from parent to child, parishes educated children, couples met at dances at neighborhood clubs, and fraternal organizations dispensed sick pay and insurance. In 1949, many members of the community held to those traditions, and raised angry voices to protest what they considered interference by city hall and a threatening intrusion of outsiders.

Although residents succeeded at the end of the forties in turning away the project that many believed would alter the neighborhood, Polish Town would nevertheless change significantly in the following decades as its fourth generation, easily assimilated, left the community's institutions and Rochester grew beyond traditional borders into a metropolitan area. By the seventies, Polish Town would relinquish its ethnic character and, for the first time since its beginnings in Rochester, Polonia would maintain an identity independent of the neighborhood's.

Rochester faced a welcome emergency in 1946, in the months after a jubilant crowd of 100,000 cheered on Main Street to celebrate V-J Day. Thousands of servicemen and women were returning home, creating a demand for housing so acute that the city hastily converted two former school buildings and a set of army barracks into apartments, and the Chamber of Commerce convened a full-day conference to discuss the problem.[5] In January, when barely half of the county's 42,000 veterans had come home, officials estimated a shortage of 8,000 housing units, a number expected to swell considerably by the end of the year.

Like the need to provide housing for veterans, Rochester's concerns in the first years after the war were for the most part matters of resurgence and growth. Not only were the city's young men returning, they were also marrying and starting families, providing Rochester with 3,500 more births than deaths each year during the first half of the fifties. Many of these new husbands and fathers found work in Rochester's industries, which employed 110,000 people annually in the decade after the war. Eastman Kodak Company provided jobs for 35,000 Rochesterians and doubled its net earnings twice during the forties and fifties. A number of smaller firms also increased their production significantly, including a dozen whose workforces multiplied from 500 to 1,000. In the seven years that followed the war, Rochester industry built 76 factories, constructed 99 additions to plants, and established 77 new companies.

Reflecting the vigor of a renewed economy, the average wage of local factory workers nearly doubled in the decade after the war, rising from $47 to $85 a week. The city launched municipal improvement projects that included construction of the inner and outer traffic loops, and the design of a combination auditorium and sports arena to be dedicated to Rochester's war dead. Private enterprise flourished as well, notably among local builders who had completed 24,000 new single family homes in the Rochester area by 1955.

Of particular significance was the growth demonstrated in Rochester's suburbs, which gained status as residential and commercial centers between 1950 and 1960.[6] During that decade, the population of towns and villages adjoining the city rose dramatically, achieving a combined growth of 100,000 residents while the city's population dropped by more than 16,000. The suburbs also exceeded Rochester in the percentage of growth of school-age children as many young families relocated from city neighborhoods to housing tracts in Irondequoit, Webster, Brighton, Chili, and Greece. At the same time, the percentage of city residents older than age 65 increased to 14 percent, and new groups replaced European immigrants as Rochester's minority communities. The most significant of these were Blacks, who increased in number from 7,600 in 1950 to 16,000 in 1957, and Hispanics, whose numbers surged from a handful of families in 1950 to at least 2,000 persons by mid-decade.

These population changes accompanied new home construction, commercial development, and industrial expansion in the county's villages and towns. Both RG&E and Rochester Telephone Corporation extended their services widely during the fifties to reach new residences, stores, and businesses in the suburbs. Many firms including Haloid, Bausch & Lomb, Wilmot Castle, Duffy-Mott, and the Strasenburgh Company expanded or relocated their facilities outside city limits. As early as 1950, eleven new suburban shopping centers had opened, most of these small plazas which gave way later in the decade to huge malls occupied by dozens of merchants and supplied with parking for thousands of cars. Services formerly associated with downtown and with city neighborhoods opened for business in the malls, from bank branches furnished with drive-up windows to supermarkets with extensive aisles of products.

Stores, businesses, industries, banks, motels, cinemas, schools, and churches all took up residence in suburban areas in the fifties, thriving in those locations and in many cases drawing patronage from their counterparts in the city. The Rochester community was rapidly becoming metropolitan in lifestyle, territory, and focus, a development that would increase prosperity in the county but diminish in some respects the vitality of the city proper. Chief among the aspects of city living that would undergo change was life in the old neighborhoods, sections like the one settled by Polish immigrants and still dominated by their descendants at the close of the war.

"If someone ran a contest to pick Rochester's cleanest street," a Gannett newspaper reporter observed, "the nominations would have to include Warsaw Street. . . . Almost every morning and evening, many of the residents are out with broom and dustpan. They sweep not only their steps and sidewalks, but the street in front of their homes, too."[7] Citing the pride that homeowners on the street took in their property, the reporter admired the carefully cropped lawns and colorful flower beds, and commented that no paper or other litter could be seen the length of the block. "There's no secret in how the folks here do it," Peter Lelek, a Warsaw Street homeowner for thirty years explained. "We sweep, we fertilize and water the lawns, we keep the yards clean. All the people along Warsaw Street do." That practice had been the norm, Lelek said, as long as he could recall.

For the most part, the pattern of life in the Polish American section was little different in the fifties than it had been for many years. Although the congregation of the Polish Baptist Church disbanded shortly after the war, three sizable parishes retained their status as centers of community activity.[8] The largest of these, St. Stanislaus, included 1,000 families (more than 4,000 persons) and filled its school with 750 children. St. Casimir's Church held most of its pre-war membership of 250 families (approximately 1,100 persons). St. Theresa's Parish added families with the arrival of Polish displaced persons, pushing its membership to more than 300 families (approximately 1,200 persons) and maintaining an enrollment of 200 students in its school. Each congregation marked a milestone in its history in the decade that followed the war: St. Casimir's Parish celebrated its fortieth anniversary in 1948, St. Theresa's Church reached its silver jubilee in 1952, and the parishioners of St. Stanislaus burned the mortgage on their property in conjunction with the parish's sixtieth anniversary in 1950.

Polish American organizations, many rivaling the parishes in longevity, held healthy memberships drawn for the most part from neighborhood families. Parish societies, lodges of the Polish National Alliance, veterans' posts, neighborhood Democratic and Republican leagues, cultural organizations, and long-established groups like Polish People's Home continued their affiliation with Centrala, which retained its status as Polonia's central organizing committee. Nest 52 of the Polish Falcons remained among the best supported neighborhood clubs, increasing its membership from 250 before the war to 370 in 1955, enrolling more than 100 children in its 1951 gymnastics program, and offering members nine types of insurance with provisions that included yearly dividends and weekly sick benefits.[9] The Echo society, which like the Falcons celebrated its golden jubilee in the fifties, counted 340 members in 1947 and held almost $140,000 in assets: property, savings accounts, government bonds, and scholarship funds.[10] In addition to its 52-man chorus, the organization supported a ladies auxiliary and sports league, and added an outdoorsmen's club, the "Fishmikes," in 1950. Until that year, when Echo members adopted an English language version of their constitution, all official business was conducted in Polish, and Polish remained the language used to record proceedings at meetings of the governing board.

Like activity at the parishes and clubs, commercial enterprise along Hudson Avenue was vigorous after the war, dominated by Polish-owned businesses as it had been since the turn of the century. An impressive number of the businesses in operation at the close of the war had served neighborhood customers for at least three decades, many of them family enterprises that had been founded by an immigrant and then passed to the second or third generation.[11] Wojtczak's bakery opened its doors to customers at dawn, as it had since the First World War; Kaleta's pharmacy featured Kwapich liniment as it had thirty years before; and Gajewski's White Oak Dairy, originally headquartered on St. Casimir Street, continued to provide housewives with milk, cream, and cheese produced on a farm in Gates. Many other neighborhood enterprises maintained continuity from early to mid-century, including Mrzywka's barber shop; the funeral homes of Bonus, Kroll, and Olszewski; the meat markets of Brodowczynski, Zamiara, Orlowski, and

A procession at St. Stanislaus Parish, 1950s. (Courtesy of Rev. Alexander J. Stec)

Ostrowski; Sykut's soda fountain and candy store; Czepiel's jewelry store; Sewilo's dairy; and Wanda Pilznienski's dry goods store and stitch shop.

Businesses that had a history in the neighborhood often traded on that distinction in their advertisements: Skalny Insurance, serving the community since 1938 . . . Kaleta's, Rochester's first Polish drugstore . . . Martin Przysinda and Sons, plumbing supplies and hardware since 1914. Other proprietors modernized their services and changed the bent of their advertising, like Stanislaw Rozewski whose tailor shop sold "gents and boys clothing" in the twenties, but sported ads as "Stanley's style shop for men" thirty years later. During the decade after the war, enterprises appropriate to a renewed economy also offered service to the neigh-

borhood: radio and television repair, home decorating, dry cleaning, air conditioning.

Encouraged by healthy memberships and prospects for the future represented in the number of children crowding parish schools, two of the Polish churches and three neighborhood clubs undertook programs of expansion. Scarcely a month after the smoke had settled from the burning of St. Stanislaus Parish's mortgage in 1950, Monsignor Joseph Balcerak presented the congregation with plans for construction of a new convent, one that could comfortably house the thirteen Sisters who staffed St. Stanislaus School.[12] The bulk of the $200,000 needed to underwrite the project was raised over the next seven years, and in September 1959 the Sisters moved into spacious accommodations adjoining their original convent on Norton Street.

Even before the war ended, St. Casimir's Parish had announced its intention to expand its property, opening a building campaign in 1944 in conjunction with the burning of its mortgage.[13] Five years later, the congregation unveiled plans for construction of a $100,000 community center west of the church, on Hudson Avenue between Cleon and Ernst Streets. The proposed Polish National Home would house bowling alleys, meeting rooms, a lounge, a kitchen, and a banquet room with capacity for 200 persons. Seventy thousand dollars was raised by April 1950 when Pastor Marian Czerny turned the first spadeful of earth at the site. Eighteen months later, the building was opened with ceremonies at which Wojciech Kolacki, one of the parish's founders, spoke on behalf of St. Casimir's senior members: "On the occasion of the dedication of this new building, I cannot help expressing a deep feeling of pride which I hope our younger generation will

Sherman's Ladies' Apparel, Hudson Avenue. (Courtesy of Mr. and Mrs. Ed Sherman)

also feel. Here is our Polish National Home. May all who enter in be imbued with the spirit of service. . . . May the work of the Polish people of Rochester continue to grow and prosper."[14]

Across Hudson Avenue from the Polish National Home, members of the Polish Falcons completed an expansion of their clubhouse in 1949.[15] The project represented the second time that Nest 52's *sokolnia* had been remodeled since members dug its foundation near the corner of Weyl Street in 1914. President Joseph Paprocki and other officers hosted an open house at the facility on May 1st, proudly showing a revamped gymnasium, shower rooms, bowling alleys, and meeting hall to national Falcon President Teofil Starzynski, city councilmen, and representatives from Falcon nests in other northeastern cities. The reconstruction,

which had been planned for six years, amounted to a $130,000 investment in Nest 52's headquarters.

Two other neighborhood clubs joined the Falcons in expanding their facilities after the war.[16] Pressed for space in a twenty-year-old clubhouse, members of the Echo Singing Association agreed to enlarge and modernize their Sobieski Street building in 1951, directing $52,400 to the project. Three years after the work was completed, the society purchased a house and adjoining lot on Kosciusko Street behind the clubhouse, spending an additional $8,000 to convert the space into a badly needed parking lot. A few years later, the Polish American Citizens Club redesigned its meeting hall at 1021 Hudson Avenue. The group, an outgrowth of the Polish Citizens Social Republican Club formed in 1914, met monthly at its remodeled clubhouse and hosted a variety of gatherings for members: dinners, dances, parties for children, holiday festivities.

A number of new organizations formed in the community early in the fifties, complementing the growth demonstrated in expansion on the part of well-established groups. Polish American veterans opened a new American Legion Post

named for Melvin Michalski, and immigrants who had served with the Polish armed forces in exile formed a branch of the Polish Veterans of World War II (*Stowarzyszenie Polskich Kombatantow*).[17] Affiliated with a group based in England whose aim was to unite Polish soldiers resettled around the world, local Post No. 4 quickly organized activities including an exhibit of Polish folk art at the Rochester Museum, and a petition sent to the United Nations appealing for the release of Polish church leaders imprisoned by the Communists.

A second new society, whose aim was "to foster Polish culture in America," held its organizational meeting in September 1954.[18] Among its early activities, the Polish Arts Group of Rochester (PAG) sponsored performances by artists of Polish descent and created a "Paderewski Award" to help finance the education of a Polish American student at the Eastman School of Music. In 1958, the PAG hosted the national convention of the American Council of Polish Cultural Clubs, welcoming 200 delegates from affiliate groups to the University of Rochester for a five-day session to advance appreciation of Polish art, music, and literature. The following year, the group held a reception for Artur Rubenstein during his visit to Rochester, and presented the pianist with his portrait painted in oil by Rochester artist and PAG member Stanley Gordon. During the sixties, the PAG promoted Polish culture by sponsoring musicals and art displays, celebrating the millenium of Poland's Christianity with a symphony concert, hosting a medieval harvest convivium, and presenting a sgrafitto mural of Copernicus designed by a Polish artist to St. John Fisher College.

In the decade after the war, both new and long-established organizations promoted Polish relief and demonstrated interest in Poland's status as a nation.[19] Raising funds to aid Polish citizens remained a well-supported cause, taken up in 1959 by the PAG whose members forwarded the proceeds of a dinner-dance to the school for blind children in Laski, Poland. The Polonia Civic Centre collected $2,000 to assist in the resettlement of Poles repatriated from territory given to Russia at the end of the war, and relayed the funds to the Roman Catholic Church in Poland to bypass the Communist regime. In an expression of support for the Polish government-in-exile in London, Centrala also welcomed General Wladyslaw Anders, Commander of the Second Polish Army Corps, to Rochester in 1956.[20] Centrala members and local veterans of the Second Polish Army Corps greeted Anders with the traditional offering of bread and salt, then escorted him to meetings with Mayor Peter Barry and Bishop James E. Kearney, interviews with local reporters, and an address to an audience of 800 at St. Stanislaus Hall.

While Poland's situation remained a rallying cause for Centrala and other organizations, a number of individuals from the neighborhood turned their interest to local politics and achieved status in elected or appointed office. Russell Felerski, wounded in service with American forces in Sicily, served as county commander of the American Legion in 1946, the same year that Father Leo Matuszewski was named chaplain of the county organization.[21] Members of the Polish American Citizens Club and Melvin Michalski Post celebrated with a testimonial dinner in the pair's honor, pointing out that, for the first time in 27 years, two Polish Americans held office in the Monroe County legion.

A Polish American woman who had been a captain in the Army Nursing Corps broke ground in 1949 when she was elected the first female commander of a county legion post.[22] Wanda Pietrzak, who had been among the first 100 Rochester women to volunteer for nursing service in 1942, became active in Pulaski Post after her discharge in 1946, and three years later was chosen to head the unit. While working full-time at Highland Hospital, Wanda went on to win election as the first female vice commander of the county legion and, in 1954, was one of seven local citizens named by Mayor Dicker to oversee operation of the city's new War Memorial Auditorium. "The men at City Hall are taking increasing notice of Wanda Pietrzak," *Times-Union* reporter Calvin Mayne wrote that year. "A newcomer to city government, she is the sole woman member of the Community War Memorial Commission . . . [and] has risen steadily through Legion ranks against stiff, though friendly, male competiton. . . . A staunch Legionnaire, . . . she is quick to promote the veterans' view in commission meetings." Active as well at St. Stanislaus Parish and in community groups, Wanda served the first of several terms as president of the Polish Arts Group in 1962.

In the decade after the war, Polish Americans also saw one of their own elected for the first time to citywide office. Leonard V. Tomczak won an at-large seat on City Council in 1953, running on the Republican ticket and backed among others by William Brodie and Charles Kanty, a neighborhood businessman who served as his campaign manager.[23] In background and experience, Tomczak was a favorite son: one of eight children of Polish immigrants, a graduate of St. Stanislaus School, and owner of a Hudson Avenue grocery who had begun his career modestly while in high school as a clerk in an A & P. During the war, he served as an army sergeant with an anti-aircraft battalion, took part in the invasion of Normandy, and was decorated with the Bronze Star, six battle stars, and the Bronze Arrowhead. Outgoing and personable, Tomczak was a familiar figure in organizations including Pulaski Post, the Echo club, the Polish Falcons, the Polish American Citizens Club, and Centrala.

"I feel proud to have been elected," he told a reporter, "because the people of Polish Town never had one of their own represented before. It's a real challenge, but I figure I'll make as good a councilman as the next fellow, if being honest and trying hard means anything." The symbolic importance of Tomczak's victory to Polish Americans was not lost on the Republican Party, which organized a special installation ceremony designed to highlight his election. As his wife Ann and two oldest children, seven-year-old Rosemary and five-year-old Margaret, looked on, Tomczak was sworn in by Judge John Van Voorhis at the county court house in December. Reporters were invited to attend the ceremony, as were prominent local Republicans and Polish Americans who had worked on the campaign. Less publicized but more exuberant was the testimonial dinner given the same month at Echo Hall, during which Tomczak was toasted by friends and congratulated by Monsignor Balcerak on behalf of St. Stanislaus Parish's members.

Defeated for re-election in 1957 as the Democratic Party gained influence at city hall, Tomczak was appointed to terms as Republican leader of the 17th and 22nd Wards. In 1964, County Manager Gordon Howe named him county purchasing agent, a position in which he supervised the merger of the city and county purchasing departments. Later, Tomczak became district administrator of the State Worker's Compensation Board, honored while in that post as "boss of the year" by the Genesee Valley Chapter of the Rochester Business Women's Association.

Leonard V. Tomczak

A second Polish American active in the Republican Party aspired for a seat on City Council after Tomczak's term. Charlotte A. King (Kwiatonski), a member of St. Casimir's Parish and an Ernst Street resident, ran unsuccessfully for office in 1963, her candidacy supported by credentials as president of the 22nd Ward Republican Women's Club, first vice president of the Federation of Women's Republican Clubs, vice president of the Republican Women's Forum, corresponding secretary of the Empire State Republican Council, and member of the Executive Committee for Congressman Frank Horton's election campaign.[24] Her husband Edward, a Fourth Ward Republican leader active in county and state politics, received a presidential appointment as marshal for Western New York in 1970. "[He is] the first Polish American to hold that office," a publication of the Polish National Catholic Church announced. "We extend our best wishes . . . that he perform and fulfill judiciously his duties."

For Polish Americans with party affiliations and for the community as a whole, the observance of Pulaski Day each October remained a premier celebration, unrivaled in colorfulness and visibility. The ceremonies sponsored by Pulaski Post extended across a full day and featured services in the Polish churches, a memorial gathering at the Hudson Library, a military ball, and, most prominently, a parade that wound through the streets of Polish Town.[25] The line of march typically included hundreds of people—American and Polish Army veterans, members of Polish societies, Gold Star Mothers, Boy Scouts, children in Polish costume—organized in a half-dozen divisions, each led by a drum and bugle corps. Politicians who courted the vote of northeast side residents in the following month's elections seldom passed up the opportunity to ride in the motorcade or walk with the marchers, waving as they moved along to crowds gathered outside homes decorated with Polish and American flags.

A parade on a broader scale wound down Hudson Avenue in September 1962, beginning at the thoroughfare's southern end near the New York Central Railroad bridge and extending to the city line at the grounds of Franklin High School. The "Parade of Light," organized by the Hudson Avenue Area Association of businessmen, celebrated the installation of new street lights the length of the avenue, a city project that the businessmen had endorsed heartily.[26] "This is the day the Hudson Avenue Area Association has long awaited," Secretary Clinton Wall wrote to members in announcing the event. "What better way to show our appreciation than to honor the people who now live or formerly lived here, the people who shop here or are otherwise interested in this area [than] to have a parade?"

Emphasizing the area's ethnic diversity as the theme of the day, the association invited representatives from the communities that radiated off Hudson Avenue to take part in the festivities. Fifty units of residents joined in the march, filing past the new street lights in groups that showcased many backgrounds: Boy Scouts and Girl Scouts of Holy Redeemer Parish; Ukrainian American veterans of Onufryk Post; the dance group of St. George's Lithuanian Church; the Little League team of Hanover Houses; the Baden Street Scouts; the Knights of St. John; children from Schools No. 26 and 36 who represented twenty national and racial groups.

Residents of Polish descent marched in a dozen units including those of Centrala, the Echo Singing Association, Michalski Post, the Polish Falcons, Polish Army veterans, the Polish Young Men's Citizen Club, and the Polish Women's Alliance. Mayor Henry E. Gillette reviewed the parade from the steps of St. Stanislaus Church, and remarked that he was impressed to see such a festive event in honor of street lights. "Large multi-million dollar projects may be more dramatic," he said in his speech, "but the real appreciation of people is for the improvements in their own areas."

Two summers later, the mood of the businessmen's association was grim as members received reports of the looting of stores a few blocks away on Joseph Avenue, during three days of riots that shook the city from complacency about race and poverty.[27] The weekend of violent confrontation between citizens and police began on a hot Friday in July and dissipated the following Sunday, leaving Joseph Avenue littered with broken glass and the debris of damaged storefronts. As residents learned of the anger and destruction enacted in the Seventh Ward, the Rev. Arthur L. Whitaker of Mt. Olivet Baptist Church spoke out strongly, stating that "while violence cannot be condoned, it must be understood."

The Joseph Avenue riots were the most graphic manifestation of the dilemmas that Rochester faced in the sixties, a decade during which the contrasts between urban and suburban living widened. Between 1950 and 1960, the central city had lost 16,000 residents while expanding suburban towns gained 100,000.[28] That trend intensified in the sixties, when city population dropped by 24,000 persons and the suburbs added 150,000 residents—a growth rate of 50 percent for the villages and towns. Although the economy remained strong in Monroe County as a whole, the majority of home construction during the sixties took place in the suburbs, while the city razed sections of old neighborhoods to make way for expressways and low-income apartments.

More dramatic than the shift in number of residents in city and county was an unprecedented increase in the number of Black and Hispanic Rochester residents.[29] During the fifties, the city's Black population tripled from less than 8,000 to 23,600, then doubled again to reach 50,000 in 1970. Hispanics, first counted as a group in the 1960 census, numbered 2,000 persons in that year's tally and more than doubled in 1970, when their community included 5,500 persons.

For many of these newcomers, Rochester's attraction was its reputation as a prosperous industrial area where jobs were plentiful. The gap between promise and reality, however, proved great as 10 to 25 percent of Black Rochesterians—at least 4,000 persons—were unemployed in the year of the riots, at the same time that Rochester's overall unemployment rate held at 1.8 percent. This discrepancy was caused in part by a poor match between Black residents' qualifications for work and the type of employment available: while 60 percent of the openings in Rochester called for a high school diploma and 15 percent required a college degree, 54 percent of the unemployed Blacks had less than a ninth grade education. Intensifying this difficulty were indifference and prejudice on the part of others, attitudes that relegated many Black families to overcrowded, substandard housing in the Third and Seventh Wards, the neighborhoods where 80 percent of the city's Black citizens resided. In the sixties, Rochester faced a crisis of poverty and race relations evident in employment statistics, housing conditions in Black

196

Father Alexander Stec enjoying the Swieconka blessing at St. Stanislaus Church, 1960s. (Courtesy of Rev. Alexander J. Stec and Gannett Rochester Newspapers)

neighborhoods, and de facto segregation in the public schools.

The issues that confronted the city in the sixties were complex and carried economic, social, and moral considerations. As the number of residents dropped and ethnic ratios changed, the population stability on which Rochester had long prided itself dipped to its lowest point since the Great Depression. White residents of means moved to the suburbs as poorer Blacks and Hispanics entered, contributing to a rise in the proportion of city households at poverty level: 14 percent in 1970, compared to 3 percent of households in the county. In the sixties and seventies, the reverberations of these changes would dominate city government and affect city neighborhoods.

When the sixties began, there was little indication that Polish Town would be altered by the end of the decade. The parishes remained well-supported, and both St. Theresa's and St. Stanislaus' congregations invested in the upkeep of their facilities in preparation for anniversary celebrations.[30] St. Theresa's parishioners, approaching their fortieth year, paid the debt on their property, burned the

mortgage, and raised $20,000 to renovate the church in 1966, during Father Ambrose Walas' pastorate. At St. Stanislaus, Father Alexander J. Stec and the church's members anticipated the parish's 1965 diamond jubilee by redecorating the church interior and underwriting repairs to the school, rectory, auditorium, and courtyard. Membership held steady enough to warrant six Masses on Sundays (although only two of those now featured a sermon in Polish), and the school, whose enrollment continued to spill past 700 early in the decade, graduated 91 students in the class of 1961.

The neighborhood, still close-knit, was distinguishable from other parts of the city by routines that had become traditions for many families.[31] Early in the sixties,

a housewife could purchase many of her family's provisions in a walk or drive through the neighborhood: groceries at corner stores like Mysliwiec's, Lesniak's, and Karolczak's; meat at Zamiara's, Habza's, and Osinski's; hardware at the Przysinda and Tomczak brothers' stores; clothing at Stanley's shop for men and Victoria's dress shop. If their home needed repairs, she and her husband could call on electricians like Joe Ostrowski, heating companies owned by the Antczaks, Cieslinskis, and Gramzas, painting contractors Barnash and Kuchinski, and residential fencing experts Walter and Edward Bielaski. For insurance, there were companies owned by the Skalny and Lorentz families. On Hudson Avenue, Charles Mrzywka gave haircuts, Joe Nowak repaired fenders, Frank Gorecki sold television sets, and the Palis and Bogaski service stations tended to automobiles.

Neighborhood children, many of them enrolled at St. Stanislaus and St. Theresa's schools, tumbled and drilled in formation at the Falcon Club, studied Polish on Saturdays at the Hudson Library, and saved nickels and dimes to buy triple-scoop banana splits at Andy's ice cream store. Their parents might stop for drinks and a fish fry at Zielinski's (Greenie's) tavern, join bowling leagues at the Polish National Home and St. Stanislaus Hall, and kick up their heels at Saturday night polka parties at Markowski's Tavern. Men from neighborhood households still performed classical and contemporary music in the Echo chorus, young girls vied annually for the title of "Miss Polonia," high school students applied for college scholarships offered by Polish People's Home, and those interested in heritage attended art exhibits, concerts, and recitals sponsored by the Polish Arts Group.

Despite routines that suggested continuity, Polish Town was a neighborhood in

The Echo chorus in concert. (Courtesy of Mr. and Mrs. Edward Skiba and the Echo Singing Association)

transition in the sixties, one that would lose its ethnic identity by the start of the next decade. The trends affecting the city as a whole began to be felt in the area as families seeking newer homes and a more prosperous lifestyle made the decision to move from the northeast side. Although St. Stanislaus School graduated large classes of students through most of the decade, for the first time in its history the community lost its young adults when they finished high school and left the area to pursue college education and careers. New immigrants from Poland, while drawn to the churches, were not linked by history to Polish Town and increasingly chose not to settle on neighborhood streets. Most distressing to older residents, use of the language that had long typified the neighborhood's character diminished markedly in homes, churches, organizations, and shops as a younger generation shook off ethnicity.

By the first years of the seventies, the waning of Polish Town's identity was pronounced, evident in the parishes, organizations, and businesses that had previously represented stability. St. Stanislaus Parish's membership had dropped to 3,100 persons, a loss of 25 percent since the start of the previous decade.[32] St. Theresa's Parish had lost 100 of the 360 families included in its congregation in the sixties. St. Casimir's Parish counted the smallest group, fewer than 500 members, only half of whom lived in the neighborhood and 30 percent of whom were older than age 55. Organizations cited comparable drops in membership, and included noticeably fewer young people in their numbers.

A smaller assortment of Polish-owned businesses lined Hudson Avenue, their number curtailed as longtime shop owners retired, passed away, or closed their establishments in the face of competition from supermarkets and shopping malls. "Hudson Avenue is losing its Polish accent," *Times-Union* reporter Del Ray wrote early in the decade, using the thoroughfare's shops and clubs as a measure of change:

> You can still order a drink of Zubrowka vodka from Bernie Krajka in George's Restaurant . . . you still can get homemade chocolate bears in the candy shop Andy Sykut founded 42 years ago. . . you can still have your car greased by Paul Bogaski or the dents removed by Joe Nowak . . . you can still go to parties at Polish Falcons Hall and the Polish-American Citizens Club . . . you can still have a funeral arranged by Richard Felerski or Casimir Bonus. . . .
>
> But the Polonaise Restaurant has become Club Eldorado . . . the hardware stores run by the Przysinda brothers and the Tomczak brothers are gone . . . Henry Osinski plans to close his 27-year-old meat market and grocery in a few weeks . . . Walt and Martha Zielinski have sold their Greenie's Tavern to a couple named Hancock . . . and Bernie Mysliwiec has cut back on the hours at his grocery.
>
> "This street," said Osinski sadly, "used to be Polish Town. But not now. Now it's something of everything."[33]

During the sixties and seventies, the incidence of crime in the neighborhood increased—a rise in the number of purse-snatchings, muggings, and robberies that disrupted the security of a section where it had been common not to lock front doors.[34] In response to members' uneasiness, the churches and clubs began scheduling activities during the day rather than at night, installed brighter lighting on their property, and hired security guards to patrol parking lots. Although the police department reported similar increases in crime in other parts of the city, residents of the Polish section were convinced that the extent of crime resulted directly from loss of their neighborhood's identity. "At one time, the streets were safe here," former City Councilman Leonard Tomczak commented in a 1974 newspaper article headlined "Fear Walks the Street of Polish Town." "People knew each other. . . . But there doesn't seem to be any more of that camaraderie we had years ago." "Older people just don't want to come out at night," Father Melvin Walczak, pastor of St. Casimir's Parish observed. "Many really still are living in the years gone by. They long for the time when they could walk up and down the streets and talk with their neighbors, and not worry about anything." Aware of residents' concern about safety, Governor Malcolm Wilson traded on the theme while campaigning at 1974 Pulaski Day ceremonies. Speaking at Falcon Hall, Wilson promised to work to preserve "the freedom to walk the streets without assaults or muggings, so neighborhoods will survive."

Between 1972 and 1975, the neighborhood suffered three blows in succession as three of its institutions announced plans to close or leave the area. In June 1972, St. Theresa's Parish graduated its last class of students and shut the school that it had operated for 44 years.[35] Enrollment, which had topped 200 after the school opened in 1928, had fallen to scarcely more than 100 students spread across eight grades, the largest proportion of loss having occurred since the sixties when the school enrolled 185 children. Citing the declining number of students, a shortage of teaching Sisters, and the expense of operating the program, Father Ferdinand Cisek confirmed in the spring that the school on Mark Street would not reopen the following September.

Two years later, St. Casimir's Church put part of its property up for sale when it ended its operation of the Polish National Home, the community center in which the parish had invested $100,000 two decades before.[36] The club's restaurant had already discontinued serving dinners, and several of its bowling leagues had moved to other locations earlier in the year when rumors spread that the facility might close. The building had become "a big financial headache," Father Walczak told a reporter, explaining that, as the cost of maintaining the structure had gone up, the parish had lost many of the volunteers who had run its programs. The Polish Young Men's Citizen Club, which rented the building from the parish, now had eighty members, less than half the number that it could call upon when the facility opened. "We're in a different generation," Walczak said, adding that the "changing nature of the neighborhood" had been a factor in the decision to close the center.

The sale of the Polish National Home was a preliminary step in the parish's decision to relocate to Irondequoit, a move announced in September 1975.[37] Having used the original church on Ernst Street as its base of activity for six decades, the congregation debated whether to remodel the structure or rebuild elsewhere, and decided after a difficult vote to invest in fifteen acres of suburban property a mile to the north. The new church on Simpson Road would be of modern design and built on one level to accommodate older parishioners, many of whom now lived in Irondequoit. Six months after announcement of the parish's decision to move, its property was sold to the Northside Church of Christ, a congregation that had had to vacate its church near the Upper Falls because of urban renewal. St. Casimir's parishioners left the Ernst Street property at the end of June, and worshipped at All Saints Episcopal Church until their new facility was ready the following year.

At the time that St. Casimir's Parish departed, the neighborhood known through all of its history as Polish Town was no longer distinguishable as an ethnic community. Reporters visited to record the changes, and spoke with residents who recalled earlier days: networks of extended families, the churches filled with worshippers on Sundays, activities each night of the week at neighborhood clubs, Polish spoken in homes and shops from Norton Street to Avenue D. "The street names are the same," one reporter commented.[38] "Pulaski and Sobieski and Kosciusko and Warsaw.... And on those little streets there is still pride.... They still brag about Warsaw Street being the cleanest in Rochester, about how they washed the sidewalks and cleaned the gutters so when the street sweepers rolled by there was nothing to pick up."

The day began uneventfully on Hudson Avenue, but ended with a flourish as members of the local media clambered up the steps of St. Stanislaus Church trailing spotlights and microphones.[39] That afternoon, the Vatican had announced the election of the Roman Catholic Church's new pope: Karol Wojtyla, a cardinal from Poland and the first pope chosen from outside Italy in 455 years. "A Polish pope. ... Did you hear?" buzzed quickly from one parishioner's home to the next. A few hours later, 1,000 people crowded the church for an unscheduled Mass of Thanksgiving, some beaming on camera afterward as reporters sought their reaction: "A pope of our own kind.... I called my father, my aunt, and everybody I could think of.... The Polish people have been down so long because of Polish jokes.... This is a proud moment for us."

Wojtyla's election to the papacy in October 1978 was without dispute the happiest news that Polonia had received in the decade. After years dominated by the decline of the community's institutions and change in the neighborhood that had previously signified its identity, here was reason to celebrate affiliation and heritage. Pope John Paul II was at once an international figure and a man whose background and experience evoked his homeland's history, a strapping man who prayed intensely, denounced oppression, sang folksongs, loved theater, and skied mountains. To convey their jubilation, Father Joseph Jankowiak and parishioners of St. Stanislaus dispatched a telegram to Wojtyla after he was named pope: "The Parish of St. Stanislaus Kostka of Rochester, New York, rejoices over your selection as our Holy Father. We pledge our prayers and fidelity, asking God to bless you always."

The attention drawn to Poland with Wojtyla's election heightened for local families as the eighties began and *Solidarnosc,* the first independent trade union in Soviet-controlled Eastern Europe, challenged the authority of Poland's Communist government. In the summer of 1980, many followed intently news of the strikes that began in the Gdansk shipyards and brought Solidarity to prominence. Interviewed that winter as Soviet troops gathered at Poland's border, Americans of Polish descent applauded Solidarity: "The people over there have suffered so much. . . . Everybody wants freedom. . . . We all have relatives there. We don't know if letters or Christmas presents get through. . . . The Polish people are going to lead this revolution."[40]

The following winter, when the imposition of martial law shattered the Solidarity movement's momentum, Polish societies and the three Polish churches acted quickly to organize a relief campaign. Five days after the government moved to suppress the union, thirty community representatives established a Committee to Aid Poland to channel local donations to Polish citizens.[41] Working in conjunction with the Diocese of Rochester, the committee agreed to forward funds raised for the purchase of food, clothing, and medical supplies to the National Council of Bishops in Poland. The campaign opened with a Mass for Peace at St. Stanislaus Church, and continued with a downtown rally at which the committee appealed for contributions and launched the sale of 30,000 buttons labeled "Solidarity: U.S. Chapter."

The appeal netted $42,000 and sold 13,000 buttons in its first thirty days, aided by support from many groups and individuals. Bishop Matthew H. Clark asked parishioners in the Rochester Diocese's 188 churches to contribute to the fund, the Hudson Avenue Area Association donated posters, and advertising executive John Hammond produced Christmas cards that could be purchased as a donation in another's name. During two weeks in January, Anthony Zamiara, president of Maplecrest Foods, Inc., contributed a percentage of the profit from the sale of his company's sausage in area supermarkets to the Rochester drive, and sponsored a similar campaign in Buffalo stores. Henry Bilinski, a self-employed carpet installer who had emigrated from Poland after the war, began an individual appeal by soliciting contributions of "just a dollar" from relatives, acquaintances, customers, business executives, and politicians. Bilinski raised $30,000 in one month, reasoning that "if everybody in America just takes the pennies out of their dresser drawers, it would help quite a bit."

Most impressive in the response it elicited was a benefit dinner sponsored by *Rozwoj Polek,* the local chapter of the Polish Women's Alliance.[42] On a blustery winter weekend, the fund-raiser drew 1,700 people from all parts of the county for platefuls of steaming Polish food and a chance to donate to Polish relief. Three hours before the event was scheduled to end, guests had consumed the last of the 4,500 *pierogi* that Gabriela Jaskot and her crew had made, and had to content themselves with what little remained of 340 pounds of Polish sausage, 120 pounds of *golabki,* 60 loaves of rye bread, and 41 gallons of *kapusta.* Surprised themselves at the size of the crowd, members of the alliance said that they had rolled and filled "all the *pierogi* they could imagine anyone eating." Proceeds from the benefit boosted the amount in the local relief fund, which surpassed $96,000 at the end of March.

That month, a second committee was formed to sponsor the resettlement of Poles who had fled their country since the declaration of martial law.[43] The Committee to Aid Newcomers from Poland worked in collaboration with the Interchurch Refugee Assistance Project to provide Polish refugees with housing, food, and clothing when they arrived from Europe, then assisted them in finding employment and settling permanently in the area. Many of those whom the committee sponsored were young men and women, couples who sought opportunities for themselves and their children in the United States.

In addition to a score of families who came to Rochester under the auspices of the Newcomers' Committee, others from Poland settled in the area in the eighties, many of them admitted to the United States with political asylum. They left a country where hopes for change engendered with the rise of Solidarity had been crushed by government repression and a failing economy. For the most part young and well educated, they had spent their lives in a socialist system, and crossed to the West with the expectation that they would gain greater control over their lives.

Tomasz Mokrzan left Poland in 1986, unexpectedly granted a passport after his application had been rejected several times.[44] Although neither knew when they would be reunited, he and his wife Jolanta agreed that he should take the opportunity to emigrate while she remained in Wroclaw with their two-year-old daughter Bogusia. Three weeks after Tomasz's papers were signed, he traveled to West Germany, hoping that he could arrange his family's resettlement in Canada.

Mokrzan had grown up in Wroclaw, an industrial center of 700,000 people in Lower Silesia. Both of his parents had been repatriated to the area when the Soviets appropriated eastern Poland after World War II, and both had spent the war years under Nazi domination—his father sent to a work camp at age fourteen when the war began, and his mother arrested in Wilno in 1943. Tomasz, the youngest of the couple's three sons, entered the Technical University of Wroclaw in 1979 to study electrical engineering and became active in NZS *(Niezalezne Zrzeszenie Studentow)*, a student organization allied with Solidarity.

During the months after the 1980 Gdansk accord, when Solidarity enjoyed government recognition, the mood in Poland was one of excitement and expectation, a time that Mokrzan describes as "spring for everyone. . . . People believed that they could change things for the better." Early in 1981, signs of trouble appeared as police harrassed union leaders during the provocation in Bydgoszcz and the government launched a propaganda campaign to discredit Solidarity. On December 13th, a blustery winter day, Tomasz was working on his car at home when a friend brought the news that General Wojciech Jaruzelski had imposed martial law, outlawing Solidarity and shutting down the country's communication and transportation systems. Intent to see what was happening in the city, Mokrzan pedaled through snow on his bicycle to the center of Wroclaw, where he found factories blockaded and the university closed. A group of students, among them one of his brothers, organized a strike on university grounds but were dispersed the following night when police smashed the college's gates, destroyed duplicating equipment, and beat those who resisted them.

During the next semesters, Tomasz worked part-time and lost a year in his studies, his plans disrupted in the unsettled months of martial law. When he enrolled again for full-time study in 1984, he helped NZS print and distribute publications in support of Solidarity, and took part in street demonstrations in which he and his friends suffered beatings. One semester, he was selected to infiltrate a Communist-controlled student organization, posing as a member in order to obtain the group's mailing list for NZS.

The same year, Tomasz married Jolanta Jedynak, a girl from his neighborhood who was studying psychology at the university. Approaching the end of his studies and ready to start a family, he began to think about leaving Poland where the optimism of 1980 had been subdued by government strictures and an economy in chaos. Like others who stood in tedious lines for rationed goods, Mokrzan began to feel that, in Poland, it would be impossible to determine the course of his future. If they were to leave, he and Jolanta agreed that it would not be simply to earn money and return, but rather to begin their lives again.

When his passport was granted in 1986, Tomasz departed for West Germany to join a friend who had emigrated earlier. He lived for fourteen months in Munich, where he found a position as a radio technician that allowed him to send money to his family. Although his first inclination had been to settle in Canada, he took advantage of the opportunity to enter the United States as a political refugee in 1987, under sponsorship of an uncle, Stanley Mokshan, who lived in the Rochester area.

Tomasz's first weeks in the United States were difficult, beginning with his initial view of the Rochester area, an unfavorable impression formed while riding with his uncle from the airport. He had found Munich clean and comfortable, a city with striking architecture and efficient public services. In Rochester, in contrast, he saw buildings of undistinguished design and roads in need of repair. More critically, he had made the transition to life in Munich easily since he spoke German and had been able to find work on his own. Now, because he spoke little English, Tomasz felt dependent on his uncle and quickly discovered to his frustration that, in the United States, a person has limited mobility without a car.

He also experienced setbacks in looking for work. In Europe, his credentials had been sufficient introduction for employers; the university at which he had earned his degree and his program of studies conveyed his abilities. In the United States, Mokrzan found that he needed a resume to present his case, a document with which he was unfamiliar and which he did not know how to prepare.

While searching for a job, Tomasz enrolled in English language classes at two school districts near his uncle's home in Greece, attending sessions in both the morning and the evening. In his spare time, he walked to nearby shopping malls where he practiced reading signs and using English vocabulary, or retreated to the basement of his uncle's house where he struggled to read materials on engineering in English. One of his teachers took an interest in his job search, and referred the young man to a career counselor who helped him develop a resume and prepare for interviews. In August, Tomasz received two offers of employment and accepted the position with higher pay, starting as a radio technician for $8 an hour with the L. J. Raymart company.

Shortly afterward, he bought a car and began to look for an apartment, hoping that Jolanta and Bogusia would be granted passports soon. On Sundays he attended Mass with his uncle's family at St. John the Evangelist Church, but despite his new knowledge of English felt out of place at the services. When his uncle suggested that he visit St. Stanislaus Parish, Tomasz drove to the church on Hudson Avenue a few times on free afternoons. On one of his visits he was befriended by Father Mieczyslaw Zygadlo, who encouraged him to attend the parish's Polish language Mass and introduced him to other young immigrants. Among the group of several hundred people who made up the congregation of the Polish Mass, Mokrzan met a number who had been born in Wroclaw and many who had had experiences similar to his own after making the decision to emigrate.

In February 1988, Mokrzan returned to the Rochester airport for a reunion with his wife and daughter, from whom he had been separated for two years. The family settled into a modest apartment on the city's west side, and Jolanta enrolled at the State University of New York at Brockport to continue her studies. During the next year, Tomasz found a new position, promoted to design engineer with Henrietta ENI, Inc., and the family grew to four when Jolanta gave birth to the couple's second child, a son named Zbyszek.

A new beginning: Jolanta and Tomasz Mokrzan stand beside Father Mieczyslaw Zygadlo at their son Zbyszek's baptism. (Courtesy of Mr. and Mrs. Tomasz Mokrzan)

Although there are aspects of life in Poland that they miss and aspects of life in the United States that they find unappealing, the Mokrzans are content with their new beginning. Tomasz speaks enthusiastically of his work designing radio frequency equipment that is marketed throughout the world, and notes with satisfaction that some of his designs are used in Poland. While busy caring for Bogusia and Zbyszek, Jolanta has continued college courses and will soon complete her degree. Both are active at St. Stanislaus Parish, where Tomasz is a lector at the Polish Mass and Jolanta has helped develop a summer program for children. Together, the couple have organized a troop of Polish Scouts, *Harcerstwo* whom they have taken on camping trips to Canada and Massachusetts. Bogusia, a lively child who converses easily in both Polish and English, has entered first grade, and her parents have saved enough money to purchase a home in Irondequoit. "Now, we are more independent here," Tomasz says of his family. "We know more people and we understand more about this country. Now, we are beginning to feel a sense of belonging."

A century separates families like the Mokrzans from the first Poles who arrived in Rochester in the 1880s. In many respects, their experiences are vastly different: one group's background formed in villages barely feeling the effects of industrialization, the other's shaped in an age of technology and Cold War politics. Despite the differences of 100 years, the newest immigrants represent continuity with the Poles who came to Rochester earliest, and with those who have come to the area each decade during the last century. Overall, they have been young and vigorous, and many have departed from a homeland under foreign rule or ravaged by war. Most have come with the hope of bettering their circumstances, and have experienced the difficulty of separation from their previous lives.

In Rochester, they formed and have maintained a Polonia that has welcomed each subsequent group of newcomers and that has experienced considerable change since its beginnings. A century ago, the Polish community was a small, self-contained settlement buttressed by open fields, centered around one Roman

Catholic parish and deliberately remote from the routines of the city. In the next decades, the community grew in size, added shops and organizations, fought a bitter quarrel about identity, sent its young men to Europe to fight on Poland's behalf, and gradually opened to the life of the rest of the city. During that time, Polonia evolved into a neighborhood, the Polish Town that at its height straddled a half-mile radius of homes, churches, businesses, and clubs. The years after World War II brought adjustment of a different type as Polish Town surrendered its identity and Rochesterians of Polish descent dispersed throughout the metropolitan area.

Today, a large proportion of the persons of Polish descent who live in Monroe County (30,000, by conservative estimate) trace their roots in Rochester to this community. Although many have no connection now with the Polish churches and organizations, some return sporadically to take part in holiday services and other traditions. Some who grew up in areas far removed from Hudson Avenue come to celebrate weddings and births, marking continuity in families who have seen three or more generations married and baptized in the Polish churches.

Others remain involved in a community that has retained a distinctive identity through the 1980s. Although in some respects the community is fragmented— divided, for instance, into parish groups, or into groups of Americans of Polish descent and new immigrants—it draws cohesiveness from the interest that its members have in their heritage. Some express this interest in activity at the parishes, institutions that have figured prominently in Polonia's history. Others support longstanding organizations like Centrala, the Falcons, the Polish American Citizens Club, veterans' posts, and the lodges of the Polish National Alliance. Occasionally, some begin a new enterprise like the Polish Federal Credit Union, a savings institution chartered in 1975 that holds approximately $4 million in assets.

Some enjoy celebrations like Centrala's annual Polish Fest, a three-day reunion for hundreds who gather from throughout the county to dance lively polkas and heap their plates with homemade Polish food. Some devote time to passing traditions on to children: in the Polish language school that offers instruction on Saturdays; in children's organizations like the Polish Scouts; and in folk dance groups like the *Wianki* that the members of *Rozwoj Polek* have sponsored since the forties. Families who have arrived in recent decades fill St. Stanislaus Church for its weekly Polish Mass, and have organized activities that form an identity for "new Polonia": a choir that sings traditional Polish hymns; a young musicians' group of flutists, guitarists, and violinists; religious traditions like the procession that marks the feast of Corpus Christi.

The Polonaise Dance Ensemble, sponsored by Council 27 of the PNA, was formed to teach children Polish culture, traditions, and heritage. (Courtesy of Helen Jasionowicz)

In a meeting hall in the basement of St. Stanislaus School, members of an older Polonia congregate in a Golden Age Club, the majority of whose members grew up half a century ago in the neighborhood formed by immigrants. Most in the group have been acquainted for decades and share memories of households where only Polish was spoken, of corner groceries that opened at dawn, of summers spent harvesting fruit on Kujawa's farm, of baseball games at Aljo Field and dances at the Falcon Club. Their experience represents a colorful portion of the community's history, recalled in snatches when they convene for conversation and hands of cards.

Sometimes, larger groups assemble to acknowledge the neighborhood's past, as several hundred did in 1981 when the Rochester Public Library rechristened its Hudson Avenue branch in honor of Kazimierz Pulaski.[45] The ceremony marked the library's fiftieth anniversary, and responded to a petition carrying 700 signatures that affirmed support for designating the building the "Pulaski Library," the name that Centrala had requested half a century earlier. Many returned in 1983 when a box of mementos, sealed for fifty years in the library wall behind the Pulaski plaque, was discovered and its contents displayed. Inside were items chronicling eight years of Pulaski Day celebrations: programs dating to 1929; a lapel button and streetcar pass bearing Pulaski's likeness; a sheaf of papers recording details of the parades, speeches, memorial ceremonies, and assemblies that distinguished observance of Pulaski Day in the thirties.

A broader interest in history draws some to events at St. John Fisher College, performances and lectures on topics of Polish studies underwritten by the family of Ludwik and Aniela Skalny. Others commemorate Poland's history in annual observances like the *akademia* of speeches and songs that honors the signing of the country's eighteenth century Constitution. Sometimes, there is special recognition of Poland's place in history, like the 1989 week of remembrance that marked the fiftieth anniversary of the country's invasion and the start of World War II.[46]

Many Rochesterians born in Poland or of Polish descent honor the "ties of blood" that have figured strongly in the community's history through the contact that they have with relatives in Europe. Some travel to their own or a parent's birthplace, or sponsor a brother's, aunt's, or cousin's visit to the United States. Many keep up a flow of correspondence with family members that includes gifts of money and supplies when times are troubled in Poland.

The community's new troop of Harcerstwo. (Courtesy of Mr. and Mrs. Tomasz Mokrzan)

In addition to these individual contacts, communication is formally promoted in the activities of the Krakow-Rochester Sister Cities Committee, formed in 1973.[47] The charter that representatives of the two cities signed that year made Rochester the first American community to have an affiliate for cultural exchange in Eastern Europe. Chaired since then by John T. Skalny, John B. Stenclik, and Wojciech and Maria Przezdziecki, the committee has organized a scholarship program that enables young people from Rochester to study at Krakow's Jagiellonian University, hosted visits to Rochester by government officials and educators from Krakow, and initiated the first exchange program in the United States for high school students from a Soviet bloc country. In collaboration with the Association for Teenage Diplomats, the committee places two teenagers from Krakow in local high schools each year, and follows that visit by a trip to Poland for two Rochester students the next summer. "[It] doesn't happen easily, but this is a real message of friendship that these youngsters are here," City Councilwoman Joan Hensler said when Sylwia Ploszaj and Stefania Zdunek, the first pair of exchange students, arrived in 1986.

The reemergence of Solidarity as a political force in Poland, powerfully represented in the 1989 elections that gave the country an independent, non-Communist government for the first time in fifty years, has provided the local community with new opportunities to initiate contacts and to aid Poland. Early in 1990, the Polonia Civic Centre, headed by Eugene Golomb, sponsored a three-day benefit dinner that garnered $8,000 for assistance to Poland. The Sister Cities Committee, working with Major Thomas P. Ryan, Jr., and other local officials, has sponsored visits by Solidarity members eager to expand their knowledge of the procedures of American government.[48] In 1990, three representatives of new Polish regional governments received an orientation to the organization of city services, and Zygmunt Ziobrowski, a city planner from Krakow, compared notes with Rochester planners on transportation, environmental protection, and historic preservation.

In conjunction with the University of Rochester's Strong Medical Center, the committee has also established a partnership with the Children's Hospital of Krakow.[49] Two physicians from Strong, Dr. Raymond Mayewski and Dr. Ralph Jozefowicz, visited Poland in November 1989 to launch the project, then organized a visit to the medical center the following May for Dr. Andrzej Mazurek, chief of staff of the Krakow hospital. The partnership yielded two initial donations for

At the dedication of the Pulaski Community Library, 1981. (Courtesy of Mr. and Mrs. John B. Stenclik)

Centrala and the Krakow—Rochester Sister Cities Committee collaborated to send Stephen Flor to study in Poland in 1975. Standing left to right are Lottie Rysztak, Councilman Urban Kress, Edmund Przysinda, Stephen Flor, Mayor Thomas P. Ryan, Jr., Gabriela Jaskot, John T. Skalny, and Charles Zurek. (Courtesy of the City of Rochester and John T. Skalny)

the Children's Hospital: $4,000 for medical journals and hospital equipment raised by St. Stanislaus Parish, and $3,000 in computer equipment donated by Centrala. In 1990, the committee initiated plans to sponsor training at Strong for junior physicians from Krakow, focusing in particular on health care procedures that the doctors would not have an opportunity to study in Poland.

In his capacity as president of the Rochester Teachers Association (RTA) and vice president of the American Federation of Teachers (AFT), Dr. Adam Urbanski, a postwar immigrant, has helped to build collaboration between the AFT and Teachers Solidarity in Poland.[50] Early in the eighties, when labor unions throughout the world expressed their interest in supporting the Polish workers' movement, AFT officials asked Urbanski to serve as their liaison with Solidarity. Initially, he helped establish communication between the two unions—for instance, by translating speeches given by Polish labor leaders, and by placing telephone calls on behalf of the AFT to Solidarity leader Lech Walesa. Later, as the AFT expanded its support for Solidarity, he took part in development of "Adopt a Family," a program through which chapters of the AFT provide assistance directly to the families of Solidarity members in Poland.

In August 1988, Urbanski traveled to Poland with AFT President Albert Shanker and Vice President Sandra Feldman to participate in the International Human Rights Conference in Nowa Huta, the first independent international conference held in a Soviet bloc nation. It was Adam's first visit to his homeland since his family fled using false papers in 1957, when he was ten years old, and he traveled with mixed feelings of exhilaration and apprehension. Granted visas on the pretext that they were traveling as tourists, the AFT group arrived at the Warsaw airport where Urbanski was singled out for interrogation and search by military officials, successfully concealing in his wallet a slip of paper with the names of Solidarity contacts. At the conference in Nowa Huta, the town where he had been born, Adam spoke about American education and participated in the last illegal protests in Poland before the round table talks that culminated in free elections in 1989.

Since his visit to Poland, Urbanski has continued to work with other AFT officials on behalf of Solidarity. In spring 1989, he hosted visits to Rochester for Wiktor Kulerski, deputy minister of education for Poland's new government, and Andrzej Janowski, a Warsaw professor and member of the new Polish parliament.

As members of the national board of directors of the AFT's Education for Democracy project, he and his brother Henry, a State University of New York professor, helped organize a stay in Poland in summer 1990 for ten New York State teachers who instructed their Polish peers in democratic procedures. In regard to the future of the AFT's support for Solidarity, Adam believes that individual contact such as teacher exchange and student exchange can help promote democracy in "a country that is yearning for it." For his part in fostering understanding of Poland, he will continue a practice initiated when he became president of the RTA in 1981: visiting local public school classrooms to share with students the experience of growing up in a Communist-controlled nation that now, after forty years of imposed government, is re-creating democracy.

Adam Urbanski spoke with Lech Walesa a number of times on the telephone on behalf of the AFT. The two met for the first time in Washington, D.C., in 1989. (Courtesy of Dr. Adam Urbanski)

Regarded in the context of change since the 1950s, Rochester's Polish community is less easily identifiable than it was during the decades when it claimed a neighborhood. Memberships in the parishes and organizations are significantly smaller than years ago, and in differing degrees each faces the dilemmas of declining numbers, proportionately few young members, and sufficient financial support.[51] In 1985, for instance, the stockholders of Polish People's Home reluctantly voted to sell their Hudson Avenue clubhouse, citing loss of members and escalating costs. The same year, members of St. Theresa's Parish feared that their church might be forced to close when, upon the retirement of Father Felix Bracikowski, neither the Franciscan Fathers who had staffed the parish since its founding nor the Rochester Diocese was able to provide the congregation with a priest. After deliberations that were at times high with emotion, parishioners and diocesan officials agreed that Father Andrew Grzela of St. Stanislaus Parish would serve as pastor of both churches, with St. Theresa's retaining a separate identity.

Regarded in a larger context, however—against the backdrop of its full history—Rochester's Polonia can be credited with longevity and with considerable success. Its contributions to the Rochester area, often taken for granted in the panorama of local history, are traced in one sense in the development of a northside neighborhood long distinguished by pride in home ownership, supported by a network of parishes, organizations, and businesses, and characterized by self-help among its residents. In another sense, its contributions are measured in the experience of thousands of individuals who, imparted values in Polonia's families and educated in its schools, have gone on to lives of service and accomplishment.

It was in the larger context of the community's history that 1,200 people gathered in November 1989 to celebrate the opening of St. Stanislaus Parish's centennial year, on the site where Bernard McQuaid blessed a modest church in the fields at the city's edge.[52] Drawn from throughout the Rochester area, those in attendance represented various affiliations with the first immigrants' church. Some had been parishioners through a lifetime, some had attended the parish school, others had joined the congregation after arriving in the area from Poland. A few had been born in the community's early years and recalled the original chapel on St. Stanislaus Street. Others, younger by several decades, marched with the Polish Scouts or studied the images of great-grandparents in photos displayed at

210

the back of the church.

As a group, those who crowded the pews and stood in the aisles at St. Stanislaus Church at its centennial observance represented both the history and the future possibilities of Polonia: the cumulative experience of senior members, raised in a community known as Polish Town . . . continuity and fraternity expressed by those who came as members of St. Theresa's and St. Casimir's Parishes, or as representatives of Polonia's societies . . . interest in heritage on the part of those who trace their roots to the community through three or more generations . . . vitality evident among immigrants who have arrived recently from Poland, young couples and their children who bring new interests, new points of view, and new energies.

"Stand shoulder to shoulder," Bernard McQuaid urged a small group of newcomers from Poland in 1890, believing that they could accomplish a great deal in their adopted land if they drew strength from their shared identity and worked together. At the close of its first century in Rochester, the Polish community is perhaps best judged by its response to that expectation, evidenced not only in formation of the parishes and schools that McQuaid anticipated, but also in the values that the community has often expressed: regard for religious faith and for family life, loyalty to both the United States and Poland, a sense of fraternity, a generous spirit, respect for heritage and tradition. Those values are worth noting in the stories that comprise the community's first hundred years, and worth replicating in the stories that will be written in the second.

Radoslaw Jurczuk portrayed Father Szadzinski and Margaret Cremaldi portrayed Sister Wojcieszka at St. Stanislaus Parish's centennial celebration. (Courtesy of the Rochester Catholic Courier)

SERVICE FROM THE HEART

Gabriela Jaskot

Spend fifteen minutes in Gabriela Jaskot's home, and you will be swept up in the whirlwind of activity to which this wife, mother, volunteer at two parishes, and mainstay of community organizations has devoted herself for sixty years. As a visitor arrives, Mrs. Jaskot is leaving on an errand for the Polish Women's Alliance, but dashes back to the house to pull from her closet the children's folk costume that the visitor has asked to borrow. As she smooths the skirt and arranges the ribbons on the headpiece, the telephone rings—not with one call, but with three in quick succession. The first caller needs information about a project of the Polonia Civic Centre. The second wants to know when raffle tickets for an upcoming event will be printed. The third caller is Gabriela's granddaughter, busy with plans for her wedding and drawing on the advice of a woman who has prepared dinners for more receptions than most people attend in a lifetime.

Gabriela Kramarczyk Jaskot's involvement with the Polish community began shortly after her arrival in Rochester.[53] Born in 1910 near Annopol in central Poland, she grew up on a small farm that her father worked until it was seized by German soldiers during World War I. Seeking stability for his family, Jan Kramarczyk immigrated to Rochester in 1918 and found employment as a mason, sending money from his earnings to his wife and four children. In April 1926, when her father's savings could pay for passage for three, Gabriela sailed for the United States with her older sister and brother. Six months later, Jan's wife and their youngest child followed, and the family moved into a home on Clifford Avenue.

Originally members of St. Stanislaus Parish, the Kramarczyks were among the families who established St. Theresa's Church in 1927. Gabriela's marriage to Stanley Jaskot in January 1929 was the first wedding celebrated in the church on

Mark Street which the couple has supported since that time. The mother of two daughters who graduated from St. Theresa's School, Mrs. Jaskot has volunteered for work with a number of parish groups including the Holy Rosary Society, Parish Council, Mothers Club, Bingo Committee, and the organizing committees for parish jubilee celebrations.

Equally visible on the grounds of St. Stanislaus Church, Mrs. Jaskot has spent thousands of hours in the parish kitchen preparing traditional Polish food for banquets and benefits. Scores of couples have begun married life at the receptions that she has catered in St. Stanislaus Hall during the past three decades. For many years, Gabriela also supervised preparation of Polish food for the parish festival, a three-day event during which guests consume several thousand *pierogi* and *golabki,* devour hundreds of Polish sausage links, and consume dozens of loaves of rye bread.

Her interest in promoting Polish heritage led Mrs. Jaskot to involvement with several community groups, memberships that in many cases she has held for decades: the Polish Women's Alliance, the Polonia Civic Centre, the Polish Arts Group, the Ladies Auxiliary of the Polish Army Veterans, the Krakow-Rochester Sister Cities Committee. As coordinator of *Wianki,* the folk dance group of the Polish Women's Alliance, she has helped to teach the *mazurka* and *krakowiak* to children for fifty years. Many organizations have benefited from her skills as a caterer, hosting under her supervision dinners for Polish relief and receptions at which local Polonia has welcomed many guests, including the members of Poland's Olympic soccer team, the performers of folk dance groups, and the crews of several "tall ships" that docked at Rochester harbor during the city's sesquicentennial celebration. In 1982, Mrs. Jaskot was elected the first woman president of Centrala, and during her tenure the organization initiated Polish Fest—a weekend of music, dancing, food, and celebration open to all in the Rochester community.

In 1989, the same year that she celebrated the sixtieth anniversary of her marriage, Mrs. Jaskot was recognized for her work on behalf of Polonia by the Women's Scholarship Committee of St. Bernard's Institute. The group honored her and seven other women from the Rochester area for outstanding contributions to the local Catholic community. Surprised but pleased to be selected for the award along with a physician, an educator, an advocate for the homeless, and the superior generals of two religious congregations, Mrs. Jaskot summed up her years of service: "At first, I made nothing of [the award]. I never worked to be recognized for what I've done. What I did, I did from my heart."

IN SEA BREEZE FOR HALF A CENTURY

Vic & Irv's Restaurant

On a blustery Saturday in February, during the slow season at Vic & Irv's Restaurant, customers step to the counter in a steady stream, loosening coats and mufflers as they place their orders for white hots, Texas hots, onion rings, and the specialty of the house, ground round steaks with hot sauce. Outside along Culver Road, the wind blows cold across Lake Ontario and the rides at Sea Breeze Park stand covered with icicles and snow. Inside, grounds sizzle on the grill, fries bubble in oil, and coffee perks as Victor Anuszkiewicz moves between the kitchen and the front counter, overseeing service in the restaurant that he has run for fifty years.[54]

Vic spends eighty hours a week at the restaurant, a light schedule compared to the 108-hour week he worked on his first full-time job in 1932, the year he managed Stanley Wagner's lakefront hot dog stand. In the thirties, Stanley's Place was one of a half dozen restaurants at the base of Culver Road, patronized by bathers and families on outings at Sea Breeze Park. Vic's schedule—sixteen hours a day for six days, twelve hours on the seventh—added $16 a week to the $23 that his father, Antoni, earned as a tailor at Fashion Park. Wagner was Antoni Anuszkiewicz's cousin, and his stand offered one of the few opportunities for employment to a young man just out of high school during the Great Depression.

Antoni Anuszkiewicz and his wife Joanna Krawiec, immigrants from Poland, were married in Rochester and raised a family of three children in homes on Thomas and Dayton Street. Victor, the oldest, graduated from Benjamin Franklin High School in 1931, when he signed on for full-time work at Stanley's Place. Vic had held a part-time job at the restaurant since he was a freshman, walking or riding the streetcar regularly to Sea Breeze to help Wagner sell hots, soft drinks, and ice cream.

Since the 1890s, Sea Breeze had been a bustling summer resort which drew hundreds of thousands of visitors annually to its thirty acres along the lake. In the 1920s, the park sported a carousel, other rides and concessions, acrobatic "thrillers" like the high wire and bicycle jump, picnic pavilions, open air stage shows, and a dance hall—amusements that attracted as many as 25,000 patrons on a pleasant summer Sunday, and drew as many as 400,000 fares on trolleys and trains each July and August. The road around the park, a steep incline dipping down to the lake, became a prime location for stands like Stanley's Place, all of which catered to the crowds enjoying picnics and outings.

After working three summer seasons at Wagner's stand, Anuszkiewicz decided that he had gained enough experience to open his own restaurant. With a bank loan of $300, he rented and remodeled a shack at the top of the hill across from the park, and opened "Vic's Stand" for business in March 1934. Trade was slow at first, as Vic competed for customers with restaurants that had built a reputation over several seasons. By the end of November, however, he had earned enough profit to repay the bank loan, and decided to open the stand again the following spring.

In 1937, Vic's brother Irv, who was working at Delco, joined Vic to help with the operation. In an effort to compete with other restaurants near the park that stayed open until past midnight, the brothers alternated shifts during sixteen-hour days. Vic, who had saved $50 to buy an automobile, drove to the lake to open the stand for lunch and worked until Irv arrived for the evening. While his brother took over the counter, Vic often slept a few hours in his car before returning to finish the day's work, from 11:00 p.m. until closing at 3:00 a.m.

From November through March, when the stand was closed for the winter, Vic operated the restaurant concession in St. Stanislaus Parish's bowling alleys, at the request of Father Joseph Balcerak. The thirties were exciting years at the parish hall, when the Filaret girls' basketball team, under the direction of Roy Van Graflan, played in the auditorium on double bills with the Rochester Seagrams with Les Harrison as captain. Both the Filarets and the Seagrams, who later became the Rochester Royals, went on to wide acclaim, and Vic would long recall the exhilarating games played during the seasons in which he ran the concession.

In 1942, Vic entered the service and Irv leased a stand below the park, two doors from Stanley's Place. The new location seemed promising, and when Vic returned the brothers looked for space that they could buy along the lake. They were able to purchase a popular location for $12,000 when Wagner closed his restaurant in 1945. On the site of Stanley's Place, Vic and Irv invested an additional $8,000 in the construction of a new stand—a low building with garage doors, designed to be converted into an automotive service station if their restaurant failed.

Forty years later, Vic & Irv's draws customers year round, as it has since its opening on Thanksgiving Day 1947. The menu has changed little during that time: red hots, pork hots, daisy ham and fish sandwiches, french fried potatoes, onion rings, frozen custard. Patrons still crowd the counter for large patties of ground round steak, laddled with a spicy sauce that Vic's parents concocted in their Dayton Street kitchen. The recipe is a family secret that none of the Anuszkiewiczes will reveal, not even to the editors of the gourmet foods magazine who offered to publish the formula.

After Irv died in 1973, Vic and his wife Frieda received help from their children—Robert, Susan, and Vic, Jr.—in operating the stand. Vic, Jr., left a position at Eastman Kodak Company to take Irv's place as co-manager, splitting shifts with his father on weekdays, when the restaurant is open thirteen hours a day, and on weekends, when customers can order grounds with hot sauce from lunch hour through 2:00 a.m. During the height of the summer season, the stand that the Anuszkiewicz brothers once managed on their own employs a crew of thirty: mostly high school and college students, some the children of employees who worked the counter two or three decades ago.

The stand has never advertised, beyond a few lines in church bulletins and a brief experiment with radio spots during the fifties. Customers have spread the word themselves and some have carried their enthusiasm far, like the business-man who routinely picked up a dozen white hots before leaving on out-of-town trips. For some who grew up in Rochester and now live elsewhere, no visit home would be complete without a drive to Sea Breeze for a ground round drenched in hot sauce, served with an order of onion rings at Vic & Irv's.

AN INTERNATIONAL FIRM
FOUNDED ON ERNST STREET
The L. Skalny Basket Company, Inc.

When Rochester's economy faltered in 1928, Ludwik Skalny lost his job as a weaver for a floral basket company. Skalny was an artisan skilled in weaving willow furniture and baskets, a craft he had learned as a boy in Poland. In a workshop set up in his Ernst Street home, he decided to go into business for himself—weaving sample baskets which he slung across one arm and carried to floral shops. Unlikely as his prospects for success must have seemed to those who saw him toting samples from florist to florist, Skalny never returned to another man's employment. Over the next thirty years, with the assistance of his family, he built his cottage industry into a prosperous firm, known in 1960 as the L. Skalny Basket Company, Inc., one of the largest importers of wickerware in the United States.[55]

Skalny was born in 1889 in Bieliny, in southeastern Poland where willow grows abundantly and residents have traditionally made their living weaving furniture and baskets. In 1907, he departed for the United States and settled first in Boston where he married Aniela Mierzwa, a young woman from Rudnik-nad-Sanem, a town not far from Bieliny. Shortly after their first child, John, was born in 1911, the couple moved to Rochester and lived in rented rooms while Ludwik worked as a furniture weaver for a willow manufacturing company. During World War I, the family moved to Detroit where Ludwik took a series of factory jobs.

In 1920, the Skalnys returned to Rochester and Ludwik found steady employment with the Bidlack Basket Company. Within a short time, he and Aniela were able to purchase a home on Ernst Street for their family of five children (John,

The Skalny Family in 1969. Standing behind Ludwik and Aniela are John, Bernard, Joseph, Anna, and Edward. (Courtesy of Mr. and Mrs. John T. Skalny)

Joseph, Anna, Edward, and Bernard). At the end of the decade, however, Skalny was again without work, and made the decision to go into business for himself.

Unwilling to borrow money from friends, he wove baskets at home and carried samples to local floral shops. Several florists, including George Boucher, H. E. Wilson, New York Florist, and J. B. Keller, became regular customers who ordered large quantities of Skalny's designs. Aniela, regarded by her children as "the power behind the scenes," transcribed the orders that her husband solicited on his rounds, and recorded the business' expenditures and receipts. Within a few years, Skalny was able to build an addition to his home where he increased production and enlisted the help of his teenage sons in painting and packaging completed baskets. In 1936, when he found that he could no longer meet the demand for baskets working at home, Skalny rented a loft at 113 North Water Street and hired other Poles trained in willow weaving—each an efficient craftsman with strong wrists who could turn out dozens of baskets a day.

The Second World War hurt Skalny's trade, principally because he could not procure raw materials for his product: willow imported from South America, rattancore shipped from the Orient, metal for basket linings, corrugated boxes for packing. The Water Street warehouse operated with a small crew as several of his weavers and four of his children entered military service. While he watched his domestic inventory dwindle, Skalny also received the disheartening news that he had lost a full shipment of baskets from Poland, destroyed when the freighter M/S *Pilsudski* went down in the Baltic Sea. With their capacity for production limited, Ludwik and Aniela specialized for several years in manufacturing floral and fruit baskets for Easter. As their son Joseph later recalled, "It was the Easter season that helped us through the war."

In the late forties, Skalny restructured his operation with the help of his children, each of whom assumed responsibility for one aspect of the business: John supervised finance; Edward handled shipping; Joseph coordinated production and sales; Anna, a University of Rochester graduate, managed the office; Bernard, the youngest son, worked at the plant while attending UR and stayed on in the family business after graduation. Additional weavers arrived from Poland, many of them displaced persons for whom Ludwik provided employment while Aniela helped with their resettlement.

While the company's craftsmen wove baskets in the loft, Skalny's children traveled to Europe and the Orient to establish contacts with overseas suppliers. John's trip to Poland in 1947, arranged with the assistance of an uncle who was mayor of Rudnik-nad-Sanem, became the first of several trips which would open new doors for the firm. In 1954, the Skalnys purchased a large building on Pullman Avenue to accommodate their expanding sales and inventory. The company served approximately 12,000 outlets across the United States, and imported wickerware from locations around the world, including Poland, Yugoslavia, Hungary, Rumania, Portugal, Spain, Madeira, Mexico, Japan, Hong Kong, China, Taiwan, and South Korea. Gradually, as domestic labor costs rose and their original crew of weavers retired, the Skalnys phased out manufacturing and concentrated on imports, purchasing approximately 700 varieties of wickerware from countries on three continents and shipping orders to every state, Canada, and Puerto Rico.

In 1958, the Skalnys reorganized their firm into a family corporation with

Ludwik as chairman of the board and his children as executive officers. Skalny maintained his interest in the company's routine, and visited the office daily until his health failed in 1969 when he was eighty years old. He died a few weeks later, the head of an international firm who was content to live in a home on Ernst Street near St. Casimir's Church, where he had long been an active member.

In 1978, the family sold their wholesale import business to a firm which continued operation in Rochester for two years before moving the company to Shelton, Connecticut. In 1983, Ludwik's grandson, Bernard S. Skalny, started a new basket import company in Rochester under the name "Willow Specialties." He was joined by his brother Gregory and his father, Bernard L. Skalny, who serves as chairman of the board.

Family members have remained in Rochester where they have established an educational and charitable foundation, the Louis Skalny Foundation Trust, through which they have made generous contributions to local hospitals, the Rotary Endowment Fund, Rochester Institute of Technology, the University of Rochester, the Kosciuszko Foundation, the Theological Seminary of the Polish National Catholic Church, the Children's Hospital of Krakow, and other causes. Joseph Skalny and his wife Irene have underwritten as many as eighteen scholarships a year for students majoring in management and communications at St. John Fisher College, and have established a meeting room in the Interfaith Chapel at RIT. John and his wife Leona have established scholarships at RIT and St. John Fisher College, and have helped the Krakow-Rochester Sister Cities Committee sponsor summer study in Poland for local students. Anna, influenced by the work of Mother Teresa, has established a scholarship to help needy students in India become physicians. She has also set up an endowment at RIT for the purchase of library books in the field of arts and crafts.

The Skalny Foundation's largest contribution to the community has been its support of St. John Fisher College's Institute for Polish Studies. The program has sponsored academic courses in Polish history, a sequence of Polish language instruction, and an annual Lecture and Artist Series that has brought Polish musicians and poets, folk ensembles, scholars of immigrant history, and members of Solidarity to the campus. The institute has also provided the college's Lavery Library with a collection of books and periodicals in the field of Eastern European studies, and publishes a research journal *(Polish American Studies)* in conjunction with the Polish American Historical Association. In 1989, in recognition of the contributions of the family, the college established a Skalny Room in the Lavery Library which will house a Polish history collection of documents and memorabilia. "We have always talked about doing something of significance to foster better understanding of Polish culture," Bernard and his wife Stasia told a reporter when the institute was founded. "It's our way of giving something back to the community."

The following list itemizes sources that were particularly valuable in the preparation of this study. The list is not meant to be comprehensive, but rather to present the archival collections, printed materials, and published documents to which I referred most frequently. In the case of parish archives, I have highlighted documents that represent the earliest available sources and, in some instances, the only written records on a particular aspect of parish history. Because I relied extensively on oral history—the recollections of many individuals whose experience reflects Rochester Polonia's story—I have also included a list of persons interviewed for the study, and a list of those who shared scrapbooks and other personal collections of materials.

Polish Community Records

Archives of St. Stanislaus Kostka Parish (Rochester)

"Day Book of St. Stanislaus Church," 1888-1890.

Deed of Purchase for Property in Town Lot 45, drawn up by the realty firm of Block and Blauw, Nov. 1, 1889.

Record of Parish Vote: Location of St. Stanislaus Kostka Church, Nov. 24, 1889.

"Liber Status Animarum" (Register of St. Stanislaus Kostka Parish), 1890-1906.

"Nowa Kolonja Polska w Rochester," *Echo,* Buffalo, NY, Feb. 27, 1890, p. 1.

Szadzinski, Teofil. "Chronica Ecclesiae Parochialis St. Stanislai Kostkae" (Chronicle of St. Stanislaus Kostka Parish), 1890-1909.

"Parafia Sw. Stanislawa Kostki, w Rochester, N. Y.," included in a directory of Polish parishes in the northeastern United States, ca. 1908, pp. 592-95.

"Roczny Wykaz" (Annual Statement and Report), St. Stanislaus Kostka Parish, 1930s-1970s.

Archives of St. Casimir's Polish National Catholic Parish (Rochester)

Kaczmarek, Wojciech. "Obchod 25 Letni Tow. Sw. Kazim.," account of the history of the Society of St. Casimir, written on the occasion of the society's 25th anniversary, May 1, 1912.

"Wydanie Jubileuszowe Na Pamiatke 20-to Letniej Rocznicy," 20th anniversary program booklet, St. Casimir's Parish, 1928.

"Pamietnik Srebrnego Jubileuszu 25 Lat Istnienia Parafji Polskiego Narodowego Katolickiego Kosciola Sw. Kazimierza w Rochester, N.Y.," 25th anniversary program booklet, St. Casimir's Parish, 1933.

"Pamietnik w Rocznice 30to Lecia Powstania Parafji Sw. Kazimierza," 30th anniversary program booklet, St. Casimir's Parish, 1938.

"Pamietnik Otwarcia Polskiego Domu Narodowego," program for the opening of the Polish National Home, Rochester, NY, Oct. 28, 1951.

"Zloty Jubileusz," 50th anniversary program booklet, St. Casimir's Parish, 1958.

Archives of the Parish of St. Theresa of the Child Jesus (Rochester)

Deed of Purchase for Property in the Henry S. Brown Resubdivision, Parish of St. Theresa of the Child Jesus, Feb. 20, 1928.

"Parish Journal," Parish of St. Theresa of the Child Jesus, Oct. 1927-Dec. 1938.

"Minutes of the Meetings of the Board of Trustees," Parish of St. Theresa of the Child Jesus, Jan. 6, 1928-May 11, 1976.

Financial Reports, Parish of St. Theresa of the Child Jesus, 1927-1952.

"Souvenir Album of the Silver Jubilee of St. Theresa Church," 1952.

"Golden Jubilee Souvenir Album, St. Theresa Church," 1977.

Organizations

Bartles, Stanley P. "Rochester Polish People's Home," handwritten document, Aug. 14, 1989.

Chlebowski-Laboski, Henry, and Roman Kwiatkowski. "History of the Rochester Echo Singing Association, Inc." 50th anniversary program booklet of the Echo Singing Association, Rochester, NY, Oct. 31, 1959.

Stenclik, John. "Historia Gniazda 52 w Rochester, N. Y.," Jan. 1953.

"Konstytucja: Prawa, Przepisy, i Regulamin" (Constitution of the Polonia Civic Centre, Rochester, NY), Nov. 14, 1938.

Untitled written account of Pulaski Day observances, 1929-1937. Records of the Polonia Civic Centre, Rochester, NY, Oct. 9, 1937.

"Polish Fest '84," program booklet distributed by the Polonia Civic Centre, Rochester, NY, 1984. (Contains brief histories of 15 local Polish community organizations.)

Polish Arts Group of Rochester, NY, 25th anniversary program booklet, Sept. 29, 1979.

Polish American Citizens Club of Rochester, NY, 75th anniversary program booklet, 1989.

Polish Young Men's Citizen Club, Inc., Rochester, NY, 50th anniversary program booklet, 1971.

Interviews

The author conducted each of the following interviews in Rochester, New York, unless otherwise noted. Interviews that took the form of correspondence between the author and an individual are specified.

Mr. and Mrs. Peter Anuszkiewicz (Jan. 15, 1989)

Victor Anuszkiewicz, Sr. (Feb. 6, 1988)

Sylvia Furlong Baglin and Gertrude Furlong Newberry (Feb. 17, 1985)

Edward Bartles (March 12, 1989)

Barbara Kwiatkowski Brodie (Dec. 3, 1988)

Marie Lorentz Fortuna, letters to the author (Aug. 1, 1982, and Feb. 1988)

Helena Kwiatkowski Grycz (Aug. 23, 1980, and Jan. 29, 1983)

Jozef Grzebieniak (Dec. 11, 1988)

Anna Jablonski Harvick (Sept. 26, 1987)

Leon Holowacz (Dec. 11, 1988, and Jan. 8, 1989)

Paul Iglinski (March 21, 1989)

Mr. and Mrs. Theodore Jablonski, Jr. (Sept. 20, 1987)

Wlodzimierz Jablonski (Dec. 11, 1988)

Mr. and Mrs. Stanley Jaskot (Sept. 13, 1986)

Mieczyslaw Jopek (March 12, 1989)

Alphonse Kolb (Nov. 15, 1977)

Harriet Tokarski Kowalski (June 1, 1982)

Mr. and Mrs. Henry J. Kowalski (Jan. 5, 1986)

Mr. and Mrs. Louis R. Kubiak (June 27, 1982, and Jan. 20, 1985)

Mr. and Mrs. Roman Kwiatkowski (Feb. 15, 1986)

Julia Leszczynski (July 20, 1980)

Olga Pulawski Lorentz (Nov. 16, 1988; Bristol, NY)

Mrs. Leon Lustyk (Dec. 15, 1985)

Mr. and Mrs. Edward Maslanka and Olga Maslanka Riegel (June 21, 1982)

Mr. and Mrs. Theodore Mietus (May 10, 1982)

Mr. and Mrs. Tomasz Mokrzan (June 26, 1990)

Mr. and Mrs. Walter Nowak (Aug. 11, 1980)

Lillian Okolowicz (July 26, 1980)

Sophie Cwalina Parks (June 3, 1982)

Agnes and Catherine Pawlik (Aug. 1982)

Wanda Pietrzak (Sept. 3, 1988)

John Pospula (Sept. 15, Oct. 21, Oct. 28, and Nov. 4, 1984)

Sophie Graczyk Presnal (July 20, 1980)

Josephine Anuszkiewicz Rafalak (June 16, 1982, and Aug. 27, 1986)

Mr. and Mrs. Mitchell Rakus (May 10, 1982)

Julian Ramotowski (Dec. 11, 1988, and Jan. 8, 1989)

Leo T. Sawyko, letter to the author (Nov. 2, 1987)

Aniela Mierzwa Skalny (June 27, 1982)

Mr. and Mrs. John T. Skalny (Aug. 12, 1982)

Mr. and Mrs. Anthony Stachura (June 27, 1982)

Lillian Szatkowski (July 20, 1980)

Dr. Adam Urbanski (Nov. 21, 1990)

Rev. Melvin Walczak (Feb. 1983)

Carl and Dean Wojtczak (May 15, 1988)

Zosia Jezowski Zablotski and Stasia Jezowski Skalny (Aug. 1990)

Anthony, Angela, Frank, and Barbara Zamiara (March 14, 1988)

Mr. and Mrs. Leonard Zlotnik (Dec. 8, 1985)

Members of St. Casimir's Polish National Catholic Parish: Mary Karpinski, Virginia Koscielny Kelly, Peter Zagurski, John Zelazny (Feb. 6, 1983)

Members of the Golden Age Club of St. Stanislaus Kostka Parish: Helen Eurack Kula, Josephine Sojka Modzel, Mr. and Mrs. Joseph Podgorski, Dorothy Wojciechowski Sobczak (Aug. 27, 1986); Rev. Valentine Jankowiak, Mr. and Mrs. Bernard Mysliwiec, Irene Wisniewski, Harriet Wisniewski Kelly, and Martha Zielinski (Jan. 10, 1990)

Scrapbooks and Personal Collections of Materials

Alexander J. Altavena (records of the Hudson Avenue Area Association)
Karol Anders
Walter Cieslinski (Nest 52 of the Polish Falcons of America)
Mr. and Mrs. Louis R. Kubiak (scrapbook of Ludwik Kubiak)
Mr. and Mrs. Roman Kwiatkowski (scrapbook of Anna Kwiatkowski Lawrence)
Olga Pulawski Lorentz (scrapbooks and memoirs of Leopold Lorentz)
Mr. and Mrs. Leon Lustyk (memoirs and mementos of Tadeusz Gedgowd and Marta Graczyk Gedgowd)
Wanda Pietrzak
Julian Ramotowski
John T. Skalny
Rev. Alexander J. Stec
Mr. and Mrs. John B. Stenclik (scrapbook of John Stenclik)
Zosia Jezowski Zablotski (issues of *Dziennik dla Wszystkich,* Buffalo, NY, 1930s-1950s)

Local History Collections

Archives of the Rochester Diocese
Particularly pertinent to this study is Bernard McQuaid's correspondence with Teofil Szadzinski and others regarding St. Stanislaus Kostka Parish, 1889-1906 (McQuaid Papers). The files for St. Stanislaus Parish and St. Theresa's Parish were also consulted.

St. Bernard's Institute (Rochester)
Catholic Journal (Rochester, 1889-1929)
Catholic Courier and Journal (Rochester, 1929-1932)
Catholic Courier (Rochester, 1932-1945 and 1989-present)
Catholic Courier Journal (Rochester, 1945-1989)

Archives of the Sisters of St. Joseph, Rochester
"A Few Sketches or Incidents of the Late Sister M. Adalbert's Life, Written by Her and Translated into English by Her Cousin, Sister M. Barbara."

Archives of the Association of Monroe American Baptist Churches (Rochester)
Information regarding Christ Polish Baptist Church is found in the "Minutes of the Monroe Baptist Association" (1916-1920), and in the "Annual Reports of the Baptist Union of Rochester and Monroe County" (1921-1945).

Rochester Public Library, Local History Division
The extensive resources of the Local History Division are invaluable in the study of any aspect of Rochester history. RPL also has a microfilm collection of local newspapers, which were consulted frequently for this study:
Democrat and Chronicle (Rochester, 1870-present)
Post Express (Rochester, 1882-1923)
Rochester Herald (Rochester, 1879-1926)
Times-Union (Rochester, 1918-present)
Union and Advertiser (Rochester, 1856-1918)
Also useful in this study were RPL's news clippings file on the Polish community, and the records of the General Pulaski Community Library (Hudson Avenue Branch).

Rochester's Polish Community

Hendrickson, Catherine Harding. "Continuity and Change in Two Rochester Neighborhoods: 1890-1958." Doctoral dissertation, State University of New York at Buffalo, 1975.

Lyon, Norman T. *History of the Polish People in Rochester.* Buffalo, NY: *Dziennik dla Wszystkich,* 1935.

History of Rochester

Buttino, Lou, and Mark Hare. *The Remaking of a City: Rochester, New York (1964-1984).* Dubuque: Kendall/Hunt Publishing Co., 1984.

McKelvey, Blake. *Rochester, The Flower City: 1855-1890.* Cambridge: Harvard University Press, 1949.

––––––––. *Rochester, The Quest for Quality: 1890-1925.* Cambridge: Harvard University Press, 1956.

––––––––. *Rochester, An Emerging Metropolis: 1925-1961.* Rochester: Christopher Press, Inc., 1961.

––––––––. *Rochester on the Genesee: The Growth of a City.* Syracuse: Syracuse University Press, 1973.

McNamara, Robert F. *The Diocese of Rochester: 1868-1968.* Rochester: The Diocese of Rochester, 1968.

Polish American History

Bodnar, John. *The Transplanted: A History of Immigrants in Urban America.* Bloomington: Indiana University Press, 1985.

Buczek, Daniel. *Immigrant Pastor: The Life of the Rt. Rev. Lucyan Bojnowski of New Britain, Connecticut.* Waterbury, CT: Heminway Corp., 1974.

Bukowczyk, John. *And My Children Did Not Know Me: A History of the Polish-Americans.* Bloomington: Indiana University Press, 1987.

Czyn Zbrojny Wychodztwa Polskiego w Ameryce. New York: The Polish Army Veterans Association of America, 1957.

Greene, Victor. *For God and Country: The Rise of Polish and Lithuanian Ethnic Consciousness in America.* Madison: The State Historical Society of Wisconsin, 1975.

Groniowski, Krzysztof. "The Socioeconomic Base of Polish Emigration to North America: 1854-1939." In *The Polish Presence in Canada and America,* ed. Frank Renkiewicz, 1-11. Toronto: The Multicultural History Society of Ontario, 1982.

Hapak, Joseph T. "The Polish Military Commission: 1917-1919." In *Polish American Studies,* 38 (Autumn 1981): 26-38.

Kruszka, Waclaw. *Historja Polska w Ameryce; Od Czasow Najdawniejszych as do Najnowszych,* 2 vols. Pittsburgh: *Sokol Polski,* 1978.

Kuzniewski, Anthony J. *Faith and Fatherland: The Polish Church War in Wisconsin, 1896-1918.* Notre Dame: University of Notre Dame Press, 1980.

Orton, Lawrence D. *Polish Detroit and the Kolasinski Affair.* Detroit: Wayne State University Press, 1981.

Parot, Joseph J. *Polish Catholics in Chicago: 1850-1920.* DeKalb: Northern Illinois University Press, 1981.

Pienkos, Donald E. *PNA: A Centennial History of the Polish National Alliance of the United States of North America.* New York: Columbia University Press, 1984.

Renkiewicz, Frank. "An Economy of Self-Help: Fraternal Capitalism and the Evolution of Polish America." In *Studies in Ethnicity: The East European Experience in America,* ed. Charles A. Ward, Philip Shasko, and Donald E. Pienkos, 71-91. Boulder, CO: East European Monographs, 1980.

––––––––. "Polish American Workers: 1880-1980." In *Pastor of the Poles: Polish American Essays Presented to Right Reverend Monsignor John P. Wodarski,* ed. Stanislaus A. Blejwas and Mieczyslaw B. Biskupski, 116-36. New Britain, CT: Polish Studies Program Monographs, 1982.

Szymczak, Robert. "An Act of Devotion: The Polish Grey Samaritans and the American Relief Effort in Poland, 1919-1921." In *Polish American Studies,* 43 (Spring 1986), 13-36.

Thomas, William I. and Florian Znaniecki. *The Polish Peasant in Europe and America,* 2 vols. New York: Alfred A. Knopf, 1927.

Waldo, Artur L. *Sokolstwo: Przednia Straz Narodu.* Pittsburgh: Nakladem Sokolstwa Polskiego w Ameryce, 1953.

Wlodarski, Stephen. *The Origin and Growth of the Polish National Catholic Church.* Scranton, PA: The Polish National Catholic Church, 1974.

Wytrwal, Joseph A. *Poles in American History and Tradition.* Detroit: Endurance Press, 1969.

The following journals provide valuable research on many aspects of Polish American history: *Polish American Studies: A Journal of Polish American History and Culture,* pub. by the Polish American Historical Association; *The Polish Review,* pub. by the Polish Institute of Arts and Sciences of America, Inc.; *PNCC Studies,* pub. by the Commission on History and Archives of the Polish National Catholic Church.

Polish History

Dziewanowski, M. K. *Joseph Pilsudski: A European Federalist, 1918-1922.* Stanford: Hoover Institution Press, 1969.

Halecki, Oscar. *A History of Poland.* New York: David McKay Co., Inc., 1976.

Korbonski, Stefan. *The Polish Underground State: A Guide to the Underground, 1939-1945.* New York: Colombia University Press, 1978.

Lukas, Richard C. *The Forgotten Holocaust: The Poles Under German Occupation, 1939-1944.* Lexington: The University of Kentucky Press, 1986.

Nowak, Jan. *Courier from Warsaw.* Detroit: Wayne State University Press, 1982.

Peszke, Michael A. "The Polish Armed Forces in Exile." In *The Polish Review,* 26 (1981), 67-113, and 32 (1987), 33-69 and 133-74.

Watt, Richard M. *Bitter Glory: Poland and Its Fate, 1918-1939.* New York: Simon and Schuster, 1982.

Zamoyski, Adam. *Paderewski.* New York: Atheneum, 1982.

Zamoyski, Adam. *The Polish Way: A Thousand-Year History of the Poles and Their Culture.* New York: Franklin Watts, Inc., 1988.

Notes

AMABC: Archives of the Association of Monroe American Baptist Churches, Rochester.
ARD: Archives, Rochester Diocese.
ASCP: Archives of St. Casimir's Polish National Catholic Parish, Rochester.
ASSP: Archives of St. Stanislaus Kostka Parish, Rochester.
ASTP: Archives of St. Theresa's Parish, Rochester.
CC: *Catholic Courier* (Rochester, 1932-1945 and 1989-present). See also *CC & J, CCJ,* and *CJ.*
CC & J: *Catholic Courier and Journal* (Rochester, 1929-1932). See also *CC, CCJ,* and *CJ.*
CCJ: *Catholic Courier Journal* (Rochester, 1945-1989). See also *CC, CC & J,* and *CJ.*
CJ: *Catholic Journal* (Rochester, 1889-1929). See also *CC, CC & J,* and *CCJ.*
DC: *Democrat and Chronicle* (Rochester, 1870-present).
HPPR: Norman Lyon, *History of the Polish People in Rochester* (Buffalo: *Dziennik dla Wszystkich,* 1935).
PE: *Post Express* (Rochester, 1882-1923).
RH: *Rochester Herald* (Rochester, 1879-1926).
RPL: Rochester Public Library.
TU: *Times-Union* (Rochester, 1918-present).
UA: *Union and Advertiser* (Rochester, 1856-1918).

Chapter 1
Nowe Zycie: New Life

1. John Bodnar, *The Transplanted: A History of Immigrants in Urban America* (Bloomington: Indiana University Press, 1985), pp. 1-56; John Bukowczyk, *And My Children Did Not Know Me: A History of the Polish-Americans* (Bloomington: Indiana University Press, 1987), pp. 1-15; Victor Greene, *For God and Country: The Rise of Polish and Lithuanian Ethnic Consciousness in America* (Madison: The State Historical Society of Wisconsin, 1975), pp. 18-20; Krzysztof Groniowski, "The Socioeconomic Base of Polish Emigration to North America: 1854-1939," *The Polish Presence in Canada and America,* ed. Frank Renkiewicz (Toronto: The Multicultural History Society of Ontario, 1982), pp. 1-11; James L. Stokesbury, *A Short History Of World War I* (New York: William Morrow & Co., Inc., 1981), pp. 11-12.

2. In addition to approximately 2.2 million Polish Catholics who immigrated to the United States before 1914, approximately two million Jews left Poland, Lithuania, and Russia for America between 1881 and 1924. See James Stuart Olson, *The Ethnic Dimension in American History* (New York: St. Martin's Press, 1979), p. 274. Polish Jews began arriving in Rochester in the mid-seventies, settling initially in the area around Chatham, Joiner, and Nassau Streets. In 1874, they organized a congregation, Temple Beth Israel, and held services for the next five years in an upper room in Jordan's Block on East Main Street. In 1879, the congregation dedicated a small synagogue on Chatham Street. Seven years later, Beth Israel moved into a larger, more elaborate "shul" seating 800 people on Leopold Street, a building the congregation occupied until 1973 that is now listed on the National Register of Historic Places. For a history of Rochester's Polish Jewish immigrants, see Blake McKelvey's "The Jews of Rochester," *American Jewish Historical Society,* no. 11, part 1 (Sept. 1950), and Stuart E. Rosenberg's *The Jewish Community in Rochester: 1843-1925* (New York: Columbia University Press, 1954).

3. Two advertisements for trans-Atlantic passage appeared on the front page of *Echo,* a Polish language newspaper published in Buffalo (February 27, 1890, ASSP). For a $22 fare, the Red Star Line promised each passenger his or her own mattress, pillow, plate, and eating utensils during the voyage from Antwerp to New York. The steamships of Inman Lines, which advertised spacious decks and three smokestacks apiece, were said to make the journey from Bremen to New York in seven days. Although ads for these lines suggested a comfortable voyage, many immigrants spent their crossing in steerage along with livestock. See Bukowczyk, pp. 16-18.

4. See Greene's discussion in the first chapter of *For God and Country,* pp. 14-27, and John Bodnar's "Immigration and Modernization: The Case of Slavic Peasants in Industrial America," *Journal of Social History* (1976), pp. 49-50. Bodnar writes: "Denied opportunities for significant occupational mobility, particularly since earlier arrivals such as the Irish and Germans already held skilled industrial jobs, Slavs turned intensely to home ownership as a means of solidifying their precarious economic status. . . . Slavs exceeded nearly every ethnic group in urban America in purchasing homes. While the market value of their residences was consistently below native-born whites and other immigrant groups such as Germans, Irish, and Jews, seldom did anyone exceed their propensity to become homeowners."

5. Greene, pp. 14-27; Olson, pp. 241-47; Joseph J. Parot, *Polish Catholics in Chicago: 1850-1920* (DeKalb: Northern Illinois University Press, 1981), pp. 20-22. A glimpse of the intensity and mysticism of Polish Catholicism may be seen in Adam Bujak and Marjorie B. Young's *Journeys to Glory* (New York: Harper & Row, 1976).

6. Wojciech Kaczmarek, "Obchod 25 Letni Tow. Sw. Kazim.," account of the history of St. Casimir's Society, written on the occasion of the group's 25th anniversary, May 1, 1912, p. 1 (ASCP).

7. Blake McKelvey, *Rochester, The Flower City: 1855-1890* (Cambridge: Harvard University Press, 1949), p. 373. According to McKelvey, one unofficial count showed that 3,702 immigrants passed through Rochester on the trains in 1885. In contrast, 380 immigrants remained in Rochester.

8. Blake McKelvey, *Rochester, The Quest for Quality: 1890-1925* (Cambridge: Harvard University Press, 1956), pp. 1-7. In 1890, Rochester was ranked the 22nd largest city in the country.

9. Statistics describing the ethnic groups represented in the city in 1890 are taken from McKelvey, *The Flower City,* pp. 375-89.

10. McKelvey, *The Flower City* (pp. 381-82) and *The Quest for Quality* (pp. 21-22); Robert F. McNamara, *The Diocese of Rochester: 1868-1968* (Rochester: The Diocese of Rochester, 1968), chapters 5, 6, and 7; Rosenberg, chapters 3-7.

11. In addition to three major synagogues organized by the 1870s (Berith Kodesh, Aitz Raanon, and Beth Israel), there were a number of smaller Jewish congregations in Rochester at the end of the century, including a half-dozen Orthodox groups and one small Hasidic group. For a fuller dicussion, see Rosenberg's study, chapters 4 and 7.

12. For a discussion of Rochester's growth as an industrial center between 1875 and 1890, see McKelvey, *The Flower City,* pp. 200-56.

13. McKelvey, *The Flower City,* pp. 223-28.

14. McKelvey, *The Flower City,* p. 210.

15. In his *History of the Polish People in Rochester* (Buffalo: *Dziennik dla Wszystkich,* 1935) (hereafter cited as HPPR), Norman T. Lyon reports that a few Poles from German Pomerania had also arrived in Rochester and settled in the neighborhood of St. Boniface Church, southeast of the Four Corners (p. 20).

16. In his account of the history of St. Casimir's Society, Wojciech Kaczmarek, one of the first Polish settlers in Rochester, shares his recollection that the Poles felt uncomfortable and dissatisfied in the German parishes. "As exiles," Kaczmarek writes, "we yearned for our dear homeland. We were as homeless wanderers among strangers."

17. Kaczmarek indicates that the Polish families invited Rev. Antoni Klawiter of Buffalo to advise them regarding the formation of a Polish parish (p. 1). Klawiter served as pastor of St. Hyacinth's Parish in Dunkirk, NY, from 1881 to 1884, as assistant at St. Stanislaus Parish of Buffalo from 1884 to 1886, and as pastor of St. Adalbert's Parish of Buffalo from 1886 to 1890. Kaczmarek writes that Klawiter referred them to Fridolin Pascalar of St. Michael's Parish for support in organizing a church in Rochester. Klawiter's career, which was both colorful and controversial, is discussed by Stanley L. Cuba in "Rev. Anthony Klawiter: Polish Roman and National Catholic Builder-Priest," *Polish American Studies,* vol. 40, no. 2 (Autumn 1983), pp. 59-92.

18. The Society of St. Casimir may have existed earlier at St. Joseph's Parish (Kaczmarek, p. 1, and *HPPR,* pp. 22-23). Its "open proclamation," however, and the beginning of its activities under Pascalar's guidance can be dated to the meeting on May 16, 1887. See also "History of St. Stanislaus Church of Rochester," 1890-1960, p. 2, and "Day Book of St. Stanislaus Church," 1888-1890 (ASSP).

19. Letter from Rt. Rev. Bernard McQuaid to Rev. Fridolin Pascalar, June 23, 1887 (ASSP). Kaczmarek writes that Rev. Ciszek came from Buffalo to hold serivces (p. 1), while *HPPR* mentions Rev. Zareczny (p. 22). Parish records provide the names of additional visiting priests: Grabowski, Kozlowski, Pitass, Szulak, and Szumanowski ("Day Book of St. Stanislaus Church," pp. 1 and 3; "St. Stanislaus Church, Rochester, N.Y., Historical Data," 1940, p. 1, ASSP).

20. A discussion of McQuaid's tenure as Bishop of Rochester is contained in McNamara's *The Diocese of Rochester,* chapters 5-8.

21. James Hennesey, *American Catholics: A History of the Roman Catholic Community in the United States* (New York: Oxford University Press, 1981), p 173; McNamara, *The Diocese of Rochester,* pp. 197-99.

22. McNamara, *The Diocese of Rochester,* pp. 198-99.

23. McNamara, *The Diocese of Rochester,* pp. 200-03.

24. "Polish Catholic Church: Organizing a New Congregation on St. Joseph Street, This City," *UA,* April 4, 1888, p. 3; "Day Book of St. Stanislaus Church," p. 1; "Church's 50-Year Record Cited," *CC,* vol. 12, no. 46 (Nov. 14, 1940), pp. 1, 11.

25. Waclaw Kruszka, *Historja Polska w Ameryce: Od Czasow Najdawniejszych az do Najnowszych,* vol. 2 (Pittsburgh: *Sokol Polski,* 1978), pp. 670-71.

26. "Polish Catholic Church: Organizing a New Congregation on St. Joseph Street, This City," *UA*.

27. St. Stanislaus Kostka Parish of Rochester is ranked by Kruszka the seventh Polish Catholic congregation founded in the state.

28. "Day Book of St. Stanislaus Church," pp. 1-2.

29. The reason for the Poles' change of heart regarding their parish's location is not entirely clear, but *HPPR* suggests that the St. Joseph Street lots were selected at the urging of St. Michael's parishioners, whose loan made the purchase possible, and that the Hudson Avenue land was chosen later by the Poles who were determined "to decide for themselves the location of the building" (p. 25). Kaczmarek states more directly that the lots on St. Joseph Street were too close to the German neighborhood for the Poles' liking (p. 1). The "History of St. Stanislaus Parish," 1890-1960, indicates that the land exchange had the support of Pascalar (p. 2).

30. The agreement drawn up by Block and Blauw (Nov. 1, 1889) is held in the archives of St. Stanislaus Kostka Parish.

31. The pages of notebook paper on which the Polish immigrants registered their votes, as well as Pascalar's record of the outcome, are held in the archives of St. Stanislaus Kostka Parish.

32. Kaczmarek, p. 1.

33. Untitled notice, *RH*, Feb. 12, 1890, p. 6; "Day Book of St. Stanislaus Church," p. 5.

34. "Nowa Kolonja Polska w Rochester," *Echo*, Buffalo, NY, Feb. 27, 1890, p. 1 (ASSP).

35. "St. Stanislaus Church: The Cornerstone Laid Yesterday by Bishop McQuaid," UA, Aug. 4, 1890, p. 7; "St. Stanislaus," *The Historical Pictorial Edition of the Catholic Journal: A Historical Summary*, pub. 1914 by the Catholic Journal Publishing Co., Rochester, NY, pp. 111-15.

36. "Day Book of St. Stanislaus Church," p. 5.

37. "History of St. Stanislaus Church of Rochester," 1890-1960, pp. 3-4; Robert F. McNamara, "The Catholic Church in the United States" (notes from a course in American Catholic Church history offered at St. Bernard's Seminary, Rochester, NY, 1979-1980 edition), p. 137.

38. Kruszka, pp. 670-71; John D. Sauter, *The American College of Louvain: 1857-1898* (Louvain: 1959), p. 238.

39. Letter from Teofil Szadzinski to Rt. Rev. Bernard McQuaid, Dec. 24, 1889 (ARD). Andrew Smelsz, the schoolmate to whom Szadzinski refers, was also a native of Prussian Poland, born in Zakrzewo in 1865. After completing studies at Louvain, he was ordained in June 1891, and worked from 1891 to 1902 in the Rochester Diocese (St. Patrick's Cathedral, St. Mary's Church, the Naples Mission). In 1902, Smelsz tranferred to the Diocese of Pittsburgh, and later served as pastor of the Polish Church of the Nativity of the BVM in Plymouth, PA (letter to the author from Robert F. McNamara, Jan. 3, 1990). "St. Stanislaus Church, Rochester, N.Y., Historical Data" indicates that, while in Rochester, he attended the cornerstone laying and the dedication of St. Stanislaus School.

40. "Day Book of St. Stanislaus Church," p. 5.

41. "Ordained a Priest: Impressive Services at St. Patrick's Cathedral This Morning," *UA*, Sept. 8, 1890, p. 5; Kaczmarek, p. 1.

42. "St. Stanislaus Church: Polish Catholic Edifice Dedicated by Bishop McQuaid," *UA*, Nov. 17, 1890, p. 7.

43. "Buried in the Ruins: The New Roof of St. Stanislaus Church Caves In," *UA*, Aug. 21, 1890, p. 5; "How the Roof Fell: Investigating the Fatal Accident at St. Stanislaus Church," *UA*, Aug. 22, 1890, p. 5.

44. *The Historical Pictorial Edition of the Catholic Journal*, pp. 111, 113.

45. "St. Stanislaus Church: Polish Catholic Edifice Dedicated by Bishop McQuaid," *UA*; "Liber Status Animarum," 1890-1906 (Parish Register, ASSP), p. 1.

46. "Buried in the Ruins," *UA*; "How the Roof Fell, *UA*.

47. "City Matters: Another Victim of Apoplexy," *UA*, July 11, 1857, p. 3; "Death of Francis S. Wolowski," *UA*, July 13, 1857, p. 3; *HPPR*, pp. 15-16; W. Henry Archacki, "A Brief History of Polish Freemasonry," Silver Anniversary Monograph, Kosciuszko Lodge No. 1085 of Free and Accepted Masons, New York, NY, pp. 33-38; John B. Mullan, "Early Masonic History in Rochester," *The Rochester Historical Society Publication Fund Series,* vol 7, ed. Edward R. Foreman (Rochester: The Rochester Historical Society, 1928), pp. 11-14. Additional assistance in compiling Wolowski's story was provided by John T. Skalny of Craftsman Lodge No. 969 of Free and Accepted Masons, Rochester, NY, and Jack McKinney of the Friends of Mt. Hope Cemetery.

Chapter 1
Pages 1-19

1. "Liber Status Animarum," 1890-1906, p. 1. See also Szadzinski's record of baptisms for the 1890s (ASSP).

2. "Little Poland: Its Buildings, Customs, Amusements, Societies and Scholars," *PE*, April 24, 1893, p. 7.

3. "Suburban Rochester: Among the Poles on Hudson Avenue," *UA*, Dec. 14, 1895, p. 39.

4. The term "Polonia" (Latin for "Poland") is used to describe individual Polish immigrant settlements, as well as the larger community of Poles living outside their homeland.

5. *HPPR*, p. 40. The City of Rochester spells the street named for Tadeusz Kosciuszko "Kosciusko" (dropping the "z"). The city's spelling is used in subsequent references to the street in this publication.

6. *HPPR*, pp. 38-39; "Little Poland," *PE*; "S. Zielinski," article included in a directory of Polish parishes in the northeastern United States, pub. ca. 1908, p. 595 (ASSP).

7. *HPPR*, pp. 42-48; "Przewodnik Adresowy w Rochester, N. Y.," in the directory of Polish parishes in the northeastern United States, p. 593.

8. Kruszka, pp. 670-71.

9. Descriptions of the occupations of Polish immigrant men and the responsibilities of Polish housewives are based upon information in "Little Poland," *PE*; "Suburban Rochester," *UA*; *HPPR*, p. 31; and interviews with Lillian Okolowicz (July 26, 1980), Helena Grycz (Aug. 23, 1980), Harriet Kowalski (June 1, 1982), Josephine Rafalak (June 16, 1982), Mr. and Mrs. Edward Maslanka and Olga Maslanka Riegel (June 21, 1982), Aniela Skalny and Mr. and Mrs. Anthony Stachura (June 27, 1982), and Mary Karpinski, Virginia Koscielny Kelly, Peter Zagurski, and John Zelazny (Feb. 6, 1983). (All interviews conducted in Rochester, NY.)

10. "Suburban Rochester," *UA*.

11. "Little Poland," *PE*.

12. The description of wedding celebrations is based upon interviews with Julia Leszczynski, Sophie Presnal, and Lillian Szatkowski (July 20, 1980); Mr. and Mrs. Walter Nowak (Aug. 11, 1980); Sophie Parks (June 3, 1982); Lillian Okolowicz; Helena Grycz; Harriet Kowalski; Mary Karpinski, Virginia Koscielny Kelly, Peter Zagurski, and John Zelazny. (All interviews conducted in Rochester, NY.)

13. "Little Poland," *PE*.

14. "Suburban Rochester," *UA*; "Trouble in Polish Town: Three Boys Fined for Tearing Down a House," *PE*, Jan. 8, 1896, p. 8; "Poles in Court: St. Stanislaus Church Matters Aired in Public," *RH*, Sept. 21, 1905, p. 6; "Pole Acquitted," *RH*, Sept. 22, 1905, p. 6. Americans' stereotypical view of Polish immigrants is discussed in two articles in the Autumn 1985 issue of *Polish American Studies:* "The Eastern European Immigrant in American Literature: The View of the Host Culture, 1900-1930," by Robin G. Elliott (pp. 25-45), and "Puritans and Poles: The New England Literary Image of the Polish Peasant Immigrant," by Stanislaus A. Blejwas (pp. 46-88).

15. "Trouble in Polish Town," *PE*.

16. "Serious Stabbing: Another Cutting Affray in the Polish Settlement," *UA*, Jan. 3, 1896, p. 6; "The Death of Dorschel," *UA*, July 22, 1890, p. 6; "Suburban Rochester," *UA*. Regarding Rochester's temperance movement, see McKelvey, *The Quest for Quality*, pp. 120-23.

17. "Suburban Rochester," *UA*.

18. "Little Poland," *PE*.

19. "In Honor of Mitkiewics [sic]: Hundredth Anniversary of Birth of Poland's Greatest Poet, Celebrated Yesterday at Zoller's Hall," *RH*, May 9, 1898, p. 6.

20. "To Make Merry: Poles Will Observe Christmas with Quaint Customs," *RH*, Dec. 22, 1903, p. 6.

21. "Day Book of St. Stanislaus Church," pp. 7, 9; Teofil Szadzinski, "Chronica Ecclesiae Parochialis St. Stanislai Kostkae," 1890-1909 (Chronicle of St. Stanislaus Kostka Parish), entries for April 4 and Nov. 22, 1891 (ASSP). Father John Fitzgerald, rector of Holy Cross Parish, purchased the statue of St. Stanislaus for the Poles, requesting in return that those who saw it in the church would remember and pray for him.

22. *HPPR*, pp. 35-36; Szadzinski, "Chronica"; "A Church Row Revived: St. Stanislaus and the National Polish Alliance," *RH*, Sept. 19, 1896, p. 6.

23. Resolution passed by the Board of Trustees of St. Stanislaus Kostka Parish, authorizing a loan of $2,000 from St. Bernard's Seminary (ASSP); Szadzinski, "Chronica," entry for June 30, 1891; "History of St. Stanislaus Church of Rochester," 1890-1960, pp. 3-4; interviews with Helena Grycz and Mr. and Mrs. Walter Nowak. Szadzinski's rectory still stands, but not on its original site. In 1917 his successor, Father Ignacy Klejna, held an auction and sold the rectory to the highest bidder—the Sewilo family, who moved the house to Norton Street. The new rectory completed during Klejna's pastorate

228

continues to be used as the residence for parish priests. For an interesting profile of a Polish pastor's life, see Daniel Buczek's *Immigrant Pastor: The Life of Rt. Rev. Msgr. Lucyan Bojnowski of New Britain, Connecticut* (Waterbury, CT: Heminway Corp, 1974).

24. Szadzinski, "Chronica," entries for Sept. 11, 1892; June 11, 1893; Aug. 15, 1898; Nov. 5, 1899; Nov. 16, 1900.

25. John Bodnar has observed: "Slavic immigrants to America and their children never denied the value of education itself. They did, however, conceive of education as having specific functions which were unrelated to social advancement. Above all else, education for immigrant children was for the purpose of retaining the cultural, linguistic, and religious values of the ethnic group. . . . Language preservation acquired a sense of importance before 1918 because of the European heritage of foreign domination. . . . Since Polish culture was threatened not only by Americanization but, in Europe, by Germany and Russia, its preservation in America seemed essential." ("Materialism and Morality: Slavic-American Immigrants and Education, 1890-1940," *The Journal of Ethnic Studies,* vol. 3, no. 4, pp. 1-2.) Thomas and Znaniecki point out that the parish school served other important functions in a Polish immigrant settlement: it brought a sense of unity and stability to a developing community, and helped ensure the settlement's continuity through future generations. See *The Polish Peasant in Europe and America,* vol. 2 (New York: Alfred A. Knopf, 1927), pp. 1531-33.

26. Szadzinski, "Chronica," entry for Nov. 9, 1891; "History of St. Stanislaus Church of Rochester," 1890-1960, pp. 4, 17-18; interviews with Sophie Presnal, Lillian Szatkowski, and Helena Grycz.

27. McNamara, *The Diocese of Rochester,* pp. 162-78, 188-92.

28. McNamara, *The Diocese of Rochester,* p. 189. It should be pointed out that, before his appointment as bishop of Rochester, McQuaid served as assistant to Bishop James Roosevelt Bayley of Newark, NJ. Under Bayley's direction, McQuaid helped establish the system of parochial schools that would give Newark the second highest proportion of parish schools in the country. (McNamara, pp. 118-21.)

29. Letter from Teofil Szadzinski to Rt. Rev. Bernard McQuaid, Dec. 24, 1889.

30. "A Few Sketches or Incidents of the Late Sister M. Adalbert's Life, Written by Her and Translated into English by Her Cousin, Sister M. Barbara," pp. 1-2 (Archives of the Sisters of St. Joseph, Rochester, NY). The name "Wojcieszka" is the feminine form of "Wojciech" (Adalbert). Sr. Adalbert was known as Sr. Wojcieszka at St. Stanislaus Parish.

31. Szadzinski, "Chronica," entries for Aug. 26 and Oct. 4, 1896; "History of St. Stanislaus Parish," 1890-1960, p. 18. The school was designed by architect W. Foster Kelly.

32. Szadzinski, "Chronica," entry for Oct. 29, 1896; "Celebrated a Glorious Defeat: 66th Anniversary of the Polish 'November Insurrection,'" *DC,* Nov. 29, 1896, p. 13; "Celebration by Polish Residents: Patriotic Programme," *DC,* Nov. 30, 1896, p. 10.

33. Szadzinski, "Chronica," entry for March 28, 1897 (pp. 16-17).

34. Szadzinski, "Chronica," entry for May 9, 1897; "History of St. Stanislaus Church of Rochester," 1890-1960, p. 18; interviews with Julia Leszczynski, Sophie Presnal, Lillian Szatkowski, Mr. and Mrs. Walter Nowak, Harriet Kowalski, and Josephine Rafalak.

35. "Liber Status Animarum," 1890-1906, p. 1; "History of St. Stanislaus Church of Rochester," 1890-1960, p. 18. St. Stanislaus School's first five teachers were Srs. Wojcieszka, Wladyslawa, Ludmila, Barbara, and Catherine.

36. "A Few Sketches or Incidents of the Late Sister M. Adalbert's Life," pp. 1-3; obituary of Sister M. Adalbert, *TU,* March 20, 1961, p. 31.

37. The story of Szadzinski's visit with Leon Czolgosz is found in local newspaper reports: "Czolgosz Asks for Polish Priest," *RH,* Oct. 23, 1901, p. 1; "Czolgosz Receives a Rochester Priest," *DC,* Oct. 23, 1901, p. 9; "Czolgosz is on Probation: Must Renounce Anarchy Before Church Can Receive Him," *PE,* Oct. 23, 1901, p. 3; "Change Over Czolgosz: Father Fudzinski, Who Visited Assassin, Says He is a Christian," *DC,* Oct. 26, 1901, p. 1; "Czolgosz Will Die Repentant," *PE,* Oct. 26, 1901, p. 1; "Czolgosz Awaiting the Summons to the Electric Chair," *RH,* Oct. 29, 1901, p. 1; "State Disposes of Remains of Czolgosz," *RH,* Oct. 30, 1901, p. 1. A profile of Czolgosz is presented in A. Wesley Johns' *The Man Who Shot McKinley* (South Brunswick, NJ: A. S. Barnes, 1970). The anecdote regarding Szadzinski and his altar boy was related to Robert F. McNamara by Rev. Daniel O'Rourke, former pastor of Our Mother of Sorrows Church in Greece, New York. The curious altar boy was Patrick J. Byrne, a native of Auburn who became a Maryknoll missionary and served in the Far East. He was appointed a bishop and apostolic delegate to Korea in 1949, and was taken prisoner by Korean Communists the following year. Bishop Byrne died following a death march in North Korea in November 1950. (McNamara, "Auburn Honors Planned for Bishop Byrne," *CCJ,* Oct. 11, 1968, pp. 1-2.)

1. "St. Stanislaus Church: Polish Catholic Edifice Dedicated by Bishop McQuaid," *UA*.

2. For discussions of Polish immigrants' conflict between faith and fatherland, see Bukowczyk, pp. 39-51; Greene, chapters 4-6; Parot, chapters 1-3; and Donald E. Pienkos, *PNA: A Centennial History of the Polish National Alliance of the United States of North America* (New York: Columbia University Press, 1984), part 1, chapters 2 and 3.

3. Pienkos, pp. 50-98.

4. Approximately 12 percent of Polish immigrants' income was given to the American Catholic Church. The extent of the immigrants' donations to the Church caused the PNA to call for lay supervision of parish treasuries in 1892. (Greene, pp. 96-97.)

5. Robert F. McNamara, "The Catholic Church in the United States" (notes from a course in American Catholic Church history offered at St. Bernard's Seminary, Rochester, 1979-80 edition), pp. 187-217; Parot, pp. 97-99.

6. Hennesey, pp. ix, 173.

7. For a discussion of the trusteeist movement among American Catholics, see Robert F. McNamara's studies: "Trusteeism in the Atlantic States, 1785-1863," *The Catholic Historical Review,* vol. 30, no. 2 (July 1944), pp. 135-154; "Trusteeism: Flood Tide of the Epidemic," chapter 8 in "The Catholic Church in the United States" (pp. 109-24); "Trusteeism," *The New Catholic Encyclopedia* (Washington, D. C.: Catholic University of America, 1967), vol. 14, pp. 323-25. Also, Patrick W. Carey's "Arguments for Lay Participation in Philadelphia Catholicism, 1820-1829," *Records of the American Catholic Historical Society of Philadelphia,* vol. 92, nos. 1-4 (March - Dec. 1981), pp. 43-58, and *People, Priests, and Prelates: Ecclesiastical Democracy and the Tensions of Trusteeism* (Notre Dame: University of Notre Dame Press, 1987).

8. The alternatives open to Polish priests in America are represented in the careers of Lucyan Bojnowski of Connecticut, Waclaw Kruszka of Wisconsin, and Franciszek Hodur of Pennsylvania. Bojnowski insisted on loyalty to the Church, Kruszka campaigned for the appointment of Polish American bishops, and Hodur led Polish immigrants in formation of an independent church. See Buczek, *Immigrant Pastor: The Life of the Rt. Rev. Msgr. Lucyan Bojnowski of New Britain, Connecticut;* Anthony J. Kuzniewski, *Faith and Fatherland: The Polish Church War in Wisconsin, 1896-1918* (Notre Dame: University of Notre Dame Press, 1980); Stephen Wlodarski, *The Origin and Growth of the Polish National Catholic Church* (Scranton: The Polish National Catholic Church, 1974).

9. Bukowczyk, pp. 42-45; Greene, pp. 100-21; Parot, pp. 95-132; Lawrence D. Orton, *Polish Detroit and the Kolasinski Affair* (Detroit: Wayne State University Press, 1981).

10. See Wlodarski's study; also, Theodore Andrews, *The Polish National Catholic Church in America and Poland* (London: SPCK, 1953). The PNCC continued to grow, extending its missionary efforts in the 1920s to Canada and Poland. In 1971, the PNCC counted 160 parishes in the United States and Canada, and 80 in Poland under separate administration. (Wlodarski, pp. 142-43, 155.)

11. Kaczmarek, p. 1; *HPPR*, pp. 49-55.

12. Kaczmarek, p. 1; Rev. Teofil Szadzinski to Rt. Rev. Bernard McQuaid, Dec. 26, 1893 (ARD); "A Church Row Revived: St. Stanislaus and the National Polish Alliance," *RH*.

13. Rev. Teofil Szadzinski to Rt. Rev. Bernard McQuaid, Dec. 26 and 30, 1893 (ARD).

14. Kaczmarek, p. 1; "A Church Row Revived: St. Stanislaus and the National Polish Alliance," *RH*. Kaczmarek's account indicates that members of Group 216 were not readily admitted to neighboring parishes, but had to search the diocese for a pastor who would accept them.

15. "A Church Row Revived: St. Stanislaus and the National Polish Alliance," *RH;* "Antonio Was Expelled: Now Sues His Old Society for Damages," *UA*, Oct. 7, 1896, p. 6.

16. "Church Factions Fight: St. Stanislaus Church Members Use Pistols and Stones," *RH*, Jan. 2, 1896, p. 6; "Polish Church Trouble: It is the Old Question Regarding the National Alliance," *UA*, Jan. 3, 1896, p. 6.

17. *HPPR*, pp. 61-62; McNamara, *The Diocese of Rochester,* pp. 203-04. As McNamara points out, the rule forbidding the display in church of the insignia of societies not strictly religious was diocesanwide. The disagreement over the PNA was cited as a major cause of the formation of St. Casimir's Church in the parish's 25th anniversary program booklet ("Pamietnik Srebrnego Jubileuszu, Sw. Kazimierza w Rochester, N. Y.," 1933), p. 22 (ASCP).

18. Rev. Teofil Szadzinski to Rt. Rev. Bernard McQuaid, June 5, 1899 (ARD).

19. Szadzinski, "Chronica," entry for 1899; "History of St. Stanislaus Church," 1890-1960, p. 5. McQuaid may have recalled Szadzinski to Rochester because the priest from Buffalo assigned to St. Stanislaus Parish in his absence had left unexpectedly. Various reasons have been given for the priest's departure. (Kaczmarek, p. 2; interview with Helena Grycz, Jan. 29, 1983.)

20. Rev. Teofil Szadzinski to Rt. Rev. Bernard McQuaid, Oct. 12, 1899 (ARD); Tomasz Maraszinski, Jozef Ciechanowski, and Wojciech Maciejewski to Rt. Rev. Bernard McQuaid, Dec. 11, 1899 (ARD).

21. Committee from St. Stanislaus Congregation to Rt. Rev. Bernard McQuaid, March 30, 1900 (ARD).

22. Rev. Teofil Szadzinski to Rt. Rev. Bernard McQuaid, Oct. 12, 1899; McNamara, *The Diocese of Rochester,* p. 205.

23. Kaczmarek, p. 2; interview with Helena Grycz, Jan 29, 1983; "New Church for Poles Planned," *DC,* Aug, 23, 1905, p. 9. There were two trustees for the parish, appointed by the pastor. Part of their responsibility was to review financial records.

24. Kaczmarek, p. 2; "Rochester, New York," *Straz (The Guard),* Scranton, PA, May 6, 1920, p. 1.

25. Kaczmarek, p. 3; Cardinal James Gibbons to Rt. Rev. Bernard McQuaid, Sept. 1, 1905 (ARD); McNamara, *The Diocese of Rochester,* p. 205. The Rochester Poles were probably not aware that Gibbons favored rapid assimilation of immigrants and was not a supporter of ethnic parishes.

26. Kaczmarek, p. 3; Rev. Josaphat Bok to Rt. Rev. Bernard McQuaid, Sept. 13, 1905 (ARD); McNamara, *The Diocese of Rochester,* p. 205.

27. "Polish Catholic Church Row Breaks Out Again," *RH,* Aug. 21, 1905, p. 6; "Church Factions in Another Row," *DC,* Aug. 21, 1905, p. 11; "New Church For Poles Planned," *DC;* interview with Helena Grycz, Jan 29, 1983; *HPPR,* p. 77. The *DC* suggests that Szadzinski's supporters wanted to form the new society in his defense, a tactic of which the pastor reportedly did not approve.

28. "Church Factions in Another Row," *DC.*

29. "The Polish Church Trouble," *UA,* Aug. 28, 1905, p. 4. McQuaid's letter was reprinted in full in the *UA* and in the *CJ* on Sept. 2, 1905. A Polish translation of the letter, presumably the version that Szadzinski read to parishioners, is held in the archives of St. Stanislaus Parish.

30. "New Church for Poles Planned," *DC;* "Poles Will Build," *RH,* Aug. 24, 1905, p. 8; "Poles Vote to Establish an Independent Church," *DC,* Aug. 24, 1905, p. 9; "Meeting of Women of St. Stanislaus Church," *DC,* Aug. 26, 1905, p. 10.

31. Apostolic Delegate Diomede Falconio to Rt. Rev. Bernard McQuaid, March 29 and April 9, 1906 (ARD).

32. "Poles Start on Warpath Again," *RH,* Feb. 12, 1906, p. 6.

33. Kaczmarek, p. 4; 20th anniversary program booklet, St. Casimir's Polish National Catholic Church ("Wydanie Jubileuszowe Na Pamiatke 20-to Letniej Rocznicy," 1928), pp. 5-9 (ASCP).

34. Kaczmarek, p. 4; "History of St. Stanislaus Church," 1890-1960, p. 8; McNamara, *The Diocese of Rochester,* p. 206.

35. Kaczmarek, p. 4; 20th anniversary program booklet, St. Casimir's Polish National Catholic Church (1928), pp. 5-9.

36. "History of St. Stanislaus Church," 1890-1960, p. 5.

37. "Few Words as to Polish Seceders," *DC,* July 6, 1908, p. 9; McNamara, *The Diocese of Rochester,* p. 206.

38. "New Polish Church to be Consecrated," *The Rochester Evening Times,* Aug. 15, 1908, p. 3; "Church and Cemetery to be Consecrated," *DC,* Aug. 15, 1908, p. 8; "Polish National Catholic Church: Cornerstone of New Edifice to be Consecrated by Bishop," RH, Aug. 15, 1908, p. 6; "Gala Day for Polish People: Cornerstone of St. Casimir's Church is Blessed," *RH,* Aug. 17, 1908, p. 8.

39. McNamara, *The Diocese of Rochester,* p. 207.

40. "Polish Priest Dies After Long Illness," *DC,* Aug. 27, 1909, p. 15; "Priest Dies After Lingering Illness," *PE,* Aug. 27, 1909, p. 7; "Father Szadzinski, Polish Priest, Passes Away," *RH,* Aug. 27, 1909, p. 11; "Funeral of Rev. Father Szadzinski," *PE,* Aug. 30, 1909, p. 8; "Funeral of Rector Held from Church," *DC,* Aug. 31, 1909, p. 10; "Polish Rector Laid at Rest," *RH,* Aug. 31, 1909, p. 11.

41. "Church Factions in Another Row," *DC;* "Bunch of Warrants Out for Combative Poles," *DC,* Aug. 22, 1905, p. 11; "Many Poles in Police Court," *DC,* Aug. 23, 1905, p. 10; "Lawyers Sarcastic: Bechtold and Forsyth Indulge in Saucy Remarks," *PE,* Sept. 8, 1905, p. 7; "Jury Trials for Polish Church Cases," *UA,* Sept. 8, 1905, p. 9; "Polish Church Troubles: Skirmish Preliminary to the Trials of the Defendants in Police Court," *RH,* Sept. 9, 1905, p. 11; "St. Stanislaus Trouble," *PE,* Sept. 20, 1905, p. 6; "Poles in Court: St. Stanislaus' Church Matters Aired in Public," *RH,* Sept. 21, 1905, p. 6; "Polish Case is Long Drawn Out," *DC,* Sept. 21, 1905, p. 13; "Hearing Continued Today," *PE,* Sept. 21, 1905, p. 6; "Acquittal: Jury in Pole's Trial was Out Twenty Minutes," *DC,* Sept. 22, 1905, p. 12; "Pole Acquitted," *RH,* Sept. 22, 1905, p. 6; "Acquitted by Jury," *PE,* Sept. 22, 1905, p. 7; "Polish Case Dismissed: Ten Prisoners Discharged and Some Held for Grand Jury," *RH,* Sept. 30, 1905, p. 6; "Session Ends in Many True Bills: Grand Jury Makes Final Presentment," *DC,* Oct. 18, 1905, p. 12.

1. H. Hylas Wheaton, "A Survey of Rochester's Polish-Town," *The Common Good of Civic and Social Rochester,* vol. 5, no. 4 (Jan. 1912), pp. 26-29, and no. 11 (Aug. 1912), pp. 11-15.

2. Discussions of the importance of societies in Polish immigrant communities were written early in the twentieth century. See "The Organized Life of Slavs in America" in Emily Balch's *Our Slavic Fellow Citizens* (New York: Charities Publications Committee, 1910), pp. 378-95, and William I. Thomas and Florian Znaniecki's *The Polish Peasant in Europe and America,* vol. 2 (New York: Alfred A. Knopf, 1927), pp. 1511-1644. For recent studies, see Bukowczyk, pp. 38-39, and Frank Renkiewicz, "An Economy of Self-Help: Fraternal Capitalism and the Evolution of Polish America," *Studies in Ethnicity: The East European Experience in America,* ed. Charles A. Ward, Philip Shasko, and Donald E. Pienkos (Boulder, CO: East European Monographs, 1980), pp. 71-91.

3. *HPPR,* pp. 35-36; "St. Stanislaus Church, Rochester, N. Y., Historical Data," 1940, p. 2; descriptions of the Knights of Kosciuszko, Knights of St. Stanislaus, Society of St. Joseph, and Society of St. John the Baptist, in the 20th anniversary program booklet of St. Casimir's Parish, 1928.

4. Certificate of Incorporation of the St. Casimir Society of Rochester, NY, recorded July 7, 1908, by the City of Rochester, County of Monroe, and State of New York (copy filed in the office of the Clerk of Monroe County).

5. "Konstytucya Towarzystwa Sw. Stanislawa K., przy Kosciele Sw. Stanislawa K. w Rochester, N. Y.," 1924 (ASSP).

6. The practice of selecting many officers was common in the organizations, a guarantee that "every active and fairly intelligent individual, of whatever sex and age, is sure of becoming sometime a public dignitary; and even if the existing organization does not give him enough opportunities, he can always initiate a new institution and gain recognition as organizer and charter member." (Thomas and Znaniecki, p. 1539.)

7. *HPPR,* pp. 142-43; interview with Josephine Anuszkiewicz Rafalak.

8. *HPPR,* pp. 89-91; "Lodge 1020, PNA," brief history of the organization, p. 1 (property of Eugene Golomb, Rochester, NY). *HPPR* indicates that Group 1020 was chartered in 1909, while the lodge history indicates that the group was chartered in 1910.

9. John Stenclik, "Historia Gniazda 52 w Rochester, N. Y.," Jan. 1953, pp. 1-2 (archives of Nest 52 of the Polish Falcons of America); "Zloty Jubileusz Gn. 52 w Rochester, N. Y.," *Sokol Polski,* March 3, 1955, pp. 1, 3; *HPPR,* pp. 73-74. According to *HPPR,* members of Nest 52 voted to affiliate themselves with the PNA in 1906, and until 1923 were chartered as Group 783. That year, Group 783 dissolved as a separate lodge and merged with Group 216, Rochester's original PNA chapter. The national Falcons organization had formally separated itself from the PNA several years earlier. See Pienkos, *PNA Centennial History,* pp. 85-88 and 227-28.

10. Artur L. Waldo, *Sokolstwo: Przednia Straz Narodu* (Pittsburgh: Nakladem Sokolstwa Polskiego w Ameryce, 1953), pp. 87-89, 319, 321.

11. Stenclik, pp. 2-3; *HPPR,* pp. 74-76, 103-05; interviews with John Pospula, Sept. 15, Oct. 21, Oct. 28, and Nov. 4, 1984 (Rochester, NY).

12. *HPPR,* pp. 69-71.

13. Regarding *Proletariat,* see Lucjan Blit, *The Origins of Polish Socialism* (Cambridge, England: the University Press, 1971). Regarding PPS and Jozef Pilsudski's membership in the organization, see M. K. Dziewanowski, *Joseph Pilsudski: A European Federalist, 1918-1922* (Stanford: Hoover Institution Press, 1969), pp. 31-35; Rom Landau, *Pilsudski and Poland* (New York: the Dial Press, 1929), pp. 34-39; and Richard M. Watt, *Bitter Glory: Poland and Its Fate, 1918-1939* (New York: Simon and Schuster, 1982), pp. 25-26.

14. Renkiewicz, "An Economy of Self-Help," pp. 77-78, and "Polish American Workers, 1880-1980," *Pastor of the Poles: Polish American Essays Presented to Right Reverend Monsignor John P. Wodarski,* ed. Stanislaus A. Blejwas and Mieczyslaw B. Biskupski (New Britain, CT: 1982), pp. 6-8.

15. Joseph W. Wieczerzak, "Bishop Francis Hodur and the Socialists: Associations and Disassociations," *Polish American Studies,* vol. 40, no. 2 (Autumn 1983), pp. 5-35.

16. *HPPR,* p. 71; Stanley P. Bartles, "Rochester Polish People's Home," handwritten history, Aug. 14, 1989, p. 1.

17. *HPPR,* pp. 71-72, 83, 87.

18. *HPPR,* pp. 80, 82; description of the Moniuszko Singing Circle, 20th anniversary program booklet, St. Casimir's Parish, 1928.

19. Henry Chlebowski-Laboski and Roman Kwiatkowski, "History of the Rochester Echo Singing Association, Inc.," 50th anniversary program booklet of the Echo Singing Association, Rochester, NY,

Oct. 31, 1959 (archives of the Echo Singing Association); *HPPR,* pp. 80-82.

20. The eight additional members, considered charter members of the Echo society, were Stanislaw Binkowski, Antoni Glatz, Walenty Jablonski, Walenty Kotwas, Jozef Kowalski, Boleslaw Naglik, Antoni Paprocki, and Jozef Paprocki. (See Chlebowski-Laboski and Kwiatkowski, summary of activities for 1909.)

21. *HPPR,* pp. 84-85; James Neil Paprocki, "Paprocki Families and Those Descendants Who Came to the United States of America," 1988, p. 5.

22. Interview with Mr. and Mrs. Edward Maslanka and Olga Maslanka Riegel, June 21, 1982 (Rochester, NY); letter from Susan M. Eltscher, archival/reference assistant of the American Baptist Historical Society, to the author, June 16, 1982; *HPPR,* pp. 91-93.

23. Lawrence B. Davis, *Immigrants, Baptists, and the Protestant Mind in America* (Chicago: University of Illinois Press, 1973), pp. 97-130.

24. Davis, pp. 101-02.

25. Davis, pp. 105, 112, 113.

26. There were 28,000 Polish National Catholics in 1923 (Andrews, p. 36), compared to 1,400 Polish Baptists in 1921 (Davis, p. 112).

27. Interview with Mr. and Mrs. Edward Maslanka and Olga Maslanka Riegel; *HPPR,* p. 92. Antoni Maslanka, who was born in Poland in 1880 and became one of Adamus' first followers in Rochester, traveled an adventurous route from Europe to the United States. Fleeing induction in the Russian Army during the Russo-Japanese War, Maslanka made his way to Italy where he found work as a crew member on a Barnum and Bailey cargo ship. He sailed to the United States by way of Africa and South America, where the ship stopped to pick up camels, lions, tigers, and reptiles for the circus. After debarking in New York, Maslanka worked in coal mines in Pennsylvania, then tried his luck briefly in Chicago and Detroit before settling in Rochester in 1909. Adamus was one of the first persons to befriend him in Rochester.

28. "Minutes of the Monroe Baptist Association," Rochester, NY, 1916, p. 30 (AMABC).

29. Interview with Mr. and Mrs. Edward Maslanka and Olga Maslanka Riegel.

30. "Minutes of the Monroe Baptist Association," October 1917, p. 23 (AMABC). See also Treasurer's Reports for 1927, 1934, and 1935 in the "Annual Reports of the Baptist Union of Rochester and Monroe County" (AMABC). The Baptist Union provided similar support to its Italian mission at Bay and Niagara Streets.

31. Letter from Susan Eltscher to the author. Adamus later served as pastor of the First Polish Baptist Church in Buffalo, and as instructor at the International Baptist Seminary in East Orange, NJ. Pastors of Christ Polish Baptist Church after Ryszard Lesik were John E. Adams (1923-25), John Czajkowski (1925-32), John Gilewicz (1932-35), Carl O. Hedeen (1935-37), Florian L. Lewno (1937-43), and William Cileski (1943-45).

32. "Second Annual Report of the Baptist Union of Rochester and Monroe County," 1922, p. 10; "Minutes of the Monroe Baptist Association," 1919, p. 28 (AMABC).

33. Wheaton, Aug. 1912, p. 12.

34. Celia Viggo, "Rochester's Voice of the People," *TU,* Sept. 15, 1984, pp. 1, 4-7.

35. Wheaton, Jan. 1912 and Aug. 1912.

36. Editorial note preceding Wheaton's article, Aug. 1912, p. 11.

37. Edwin A. Rumball, "Populus Rocestriensis [sic]: An Introduction to the Demography of Rochester, N. Y.," pub. ca. 1912 by The Common Good Publishing Co., Rochester, NY, pp. 17-18.

38. "Fifteen-Acre Block Burns: $150,000 Loss," *DC,* May 3, 1913, p. 19; "Varying Estimates on Hudson Avenue Fire," *PE,* May 3, 1913, p. 6; "Fire Destroys Lumber Yard and Many Houses," *RH,* May 3, 1913, p. 9; "Polish Town in State of Panic When Fifteen-Acre Lumber Yard and Houses Owned by Stephen Zielinski Are Destroyed," *UA,* May 3, 1913, p. 9. It is interesting to note that, sometime after the lumberyard burned, neighborhood residents rushed to the vicinity of Hudson Avenue and Norton Street again, thinking that Zielinski's property was on fire a second time. In this case, the original church of St. Stanislaus was ablaze, its front section destroyed before fire crews stopped the flames. One newspaper repeated a rumor that spread among parishioners: that an arsonist from St. Casimir's Church had ignited the fire. This accusation, which was not confirmed, illustrates the depth of ill feeling that lingered in the community among members of the two parishes. ("Fire Damage of $10,000 to St. Stanislaus's Hall; Incendiary, Says Priest," undated newspaper article, property of Eugene Antczak, Rochester, NY). The fire occurred during the pastorate of Ignacy Klejna, at some time between 1913 and 1918.

Chapter 4
Pages 47–61

1. *HPPR,* pp. 103-04; Jan Lorys, "Before the 'Blue Army'," *Polish Heritage,* vol. 34, no. 1 (Spring 1983), p. 6.

2. See, for instance, Adam Zamoyski's *The Polish Way: A Thousand-Year History of the Poles and Their Culture* (New York: Franklin Watts, Inc., 1988), chapters 16-18.

3. Parot, pp. 33-34; Pienkos, pp. 52-57.

4. Pienkos, p. 98.

5. Lorys, p. 6.

6. Louis J. Zake, "The National Department and the Polish American Community: 1916-1923," *Polish American Studies,* vol. 38, no. 2 (Autumn 1981), pp. 16-17.

7. Watt, pp. 44-45. The Polish Legion, which included Pilsudski's First Brigade, numbered 12,000 men in 1916.

8. Watt, pp. 44-51. Polish men were conscripted by each of the countries that ruled their homeland (Prussia, Russia, and Austria) and, tragically, sometimes found themselves fighting against other Poles.

9. Nevin O. Winter, *The New Poland* (Boston: L. C. Page and Co., Inc., 1923), p. 95.

10. Watt, p. 49.

11. Lorys, p. 7.

12. Zake, pp. 17-25.

13. See descriptions of Paderewski's campaign for Poland in Adam Zamoyski's *Paderewski* (New York: Atheneum, 1982), pp. 147-79; Joseph A. Wytrwal's *Poles in American History and Tradition* (Detroit: Endurance Press, 1969), pp. 325-37; and Watt's *Bitter Glory,* pp. 52-54.

14. Wytrwal, p. 328.

15. Paderewski called Edward House "the noblest man I have ever had the honour to know." (Zamoyski, *Paderewski,* p. 157.)

16. Zamoyski, *Paderewski,* pp. 157-58.

17. Joseph T. Hapak, "The Polish Military Commission: 1917-1919," *Polish American Studies,* vol. 38, no. 2 (Autumn 1981), pp. 26-38.

18. Hapak, pp. 36-38; Adam Urbanski, "Americanism and the Polish-American Press" (doctoral dissertation, the University of Rochester, NY, 1974), p. 47; Wytrwal, p. 334.

19. The statistics cited are from Wytrwal, pp. 339 and 347; Urbanski, p. 47; and Parot, p. 170.

20. Interviews with John Pospula, Sept. 15, Oct. 21, Oct. 28, and Nov. 4, 1984 (Rochester, NY); *HPPR,* p. 103; "Historia Gniazda 52," history of Nest 52 of the Polish Falcons of America, Rochester, NY, 40th anniversary program booklet, 1945, pp. 1-3 (archives of Nest 52).

21. HPPR, pp. 112-13.

22. "For Polish Sufferers: Local Committee Makes Appeal for Funds for Relief Work as Result of European War," *UA,* June 8, 1915, p. 9. The letter of appeal was signed by Franciszek Mietus, Andrzej Nawrocki, and Jozef Koscielny.

23. *HPPR,* pp. 112-13. The KON lost its influence locally, as nationally, after the withdrawal of the Polish Falcons in September 1914.

24. *HPPR,* pp. 113-15; "Local Poles Hand Paderewski Purse for Relief of Sufferers," *UA,* Nov. 17, 1916, p. 13; "Music and the Drama: Convention Hall," *PE,* Nov. 17, 1916, p. 5. According to *HPPR,* it was in Rochester on November 16th that Paderewski learned by cablegram of the death of Henryk Sienkiewicz, news that added an element of "poignant tragedy" to the day's events.

25. The story of John Pospula's journey to America and enlistment in the Polish Army is based upon the author's interviews with him. Much of the information that he provided about his enlistment and training is verified in "Those Who Went Forth to Serve," vol. 2 of *The World War Service Record of Rochester and Monroe County,* ed. Edward R. Foreman, pub. by the City of Rochester, 1928, pp. 1763-66. The only major discrepancy relates to Pospula's departure for France. While he recalled sailing from New York City with other soldiers in March 1918, the *Service Record* indicates that he sailed for France in December 1917. Additional information about recruitment and training for the "army of Kosciuszko" is contained in Hapak's "The Polish Military Commission," and in *Czyn Zbrojny Wychodztwa Polskiego w Ameryce* (New York: The Polish Army Veterans Association of America, 1957).

26. *HPPR,* pp. 117-18.

27. *HPPR,* p. 116; "Poles Leave To-Day for Camp," *PE,* Oct. 15, 1917, p. 7; "Men Going from this City to Join Polish Recruits," *DC,* Oct. 15, 1917, p. 15; "Polish Anniversary: Societies to Turn Out To-Night as Escort to Volunteers for Polish Army," *UA,* Oct. 15, 1917, p. 8; "Recruiting Station for Poles Opened in City," *PE,* Oct. 17, 1917, p. 6; "To Fight for Free Poland," *RH,* Oct. 17, 1917, p. 9; "Rochester Will Be Well Represented in Army of Poles Fighting with Allies," *DC,* Oct. 19, 1917, p. 21; obituary of S. K. Kowalski

in *Gazeta Tygodniowa* (Schenectady, NY), Nov. 27, 1941, p. 13. Kowalski was placed in charge of Rochester's recruiting station temporarily, until an officer of the Polish Army was assigned to the Rochester unit.

28. "Recruiting Station for Poles Opened in City," *PE;* "To Fight for Free Poland," *RH.* After the Armistice was signed in November 1918, the Falcons continued to recruit American Poles for Haller's army, which early in 1919 joined Polish forces battling with Ukrainians for control of territory in Galicia and with Bolsheviks for control of territory on the Russian border. (See Watt, pp. 72-77 and 89-103).

29. "Will Fight to Deliver Poland," *RH,* July 8, 1918, p. 11.

30. *HPPR,* pp. 116 and 119-20; "Those Who Went Forth to Serve," p. 1763. One newspaper report maintained that the number of local Poles in the US forces was much higher: 2,000 men. ("Poles Declare Agitation Bears German Stamp," *DC,* July 6, 1919, p. 44.)

31. *HPPR,* p. 116; "Commission of Poles to Visit this City Soon," *DC,* Dec. 16, 1917, p. 5.

32. *HPPR,* p. 128; "Enter Training for Service in Mother Country," *DC,* July 11, 1918, p. 19; "German Officers . . . Without Feeling: Charge of Polish Countess in Address Here," undated newspaper article in the scrapbook of Ludwik Kubiak (property of Mr. and Mrs. Louis R. Kubiak, Rochester, NY). Turczynowicz's account of the invasion of Suwalki is presented in her book *When the Prussians Came to Poland* (New York: G. P. Putnam's Sons, 1916).

33. *HPPR,* p. 128; "Enter Training for Service in Mother Country," *DC. HPPR* lists eight names and the newspaper account lists nine; taken together, the two lists include the names of ten local women.

34. "Enter Training for Service in Mother Country," *DC.*

35. Robert Szymczak, "An Act of Devotion: The Polish Grey Samaritans and the American Relief Effort in Poland, 1919-1921," *Polish American Studies,* vol. 43, no. 1 (Spring 1986), pp. 16-18.

36. Szymczak, p. 18; written memoirs of Marta Graczyk Gedgowd (documents in the possession of Mr. and Mrs. Leon Lustyk, Rochester, NY), and "Samaritans Going Overseas," undated newspaper article in the scrapbook of Ludwik Kubiak.

37. *HPPR,* p. 128; Szymczak, p. 22.

38. Szymczak, pp. 22-26.

39. "Young Woman Relief Worker from Rochester Arrested as Spy in Capital of Lithuania," *DC,* Dec. 1, 1920, p. 24.

40. Szymczak, pp. 27-28.

41. Szymczak, p. 36.

42. "Polish Mass Meeting Addressed by Member of French Commission," *RH,* Jan. 7, 1918, p. 11.

43. As a superintendent with New York State Railways, Kubiak supervised the maintenance and repair of city streetcars. Following World War I, he served as president of the local Polish Falcon Nest, and aided in the resettlement of new immigrants from Poland. He died at age 55 in 1933. (Interview with Louis R. Kubiak, Jan. 20, 1985, Rochester, NY.)

44. "Polish Mass Meeting Addressed by Member of French Commission," *RH;* "Poles in Mass Meeting Protest Bitterly Against Charges that Jews are Massacred in Poland," *RH,* Dec. 16, 1918, p. 8; "Poles of Rochester Cheer News that Young Woman is to be Freed by Lithuanians," *DC,* Dec. 6, 1920, p. 26; "Poland's Share in War for Democracy: One of Topics for Chamber Luncheon Today," *DC,* Jan. 29, 1919, p. 17; "Polish Military Band in Two Concerts To-Day," *RH,* May 10, 1918, p. 16.

45. *HPPR,* pp. 123-27.

46. "Ignace Paderewski and Lieutenant P. Perigord to Speak Here Tomorrow," *TU,* June 11, 1918, p. 13; "Many Eager to Hear Talk by Paderewski," *DC,* June 11, 1918, p. 12; "Very Existence at Stake, Says Great Musician," *DC,* June 13, 1918, p. 19; "Victory of Allies Sure, They Assert: Paderewski and Perigord Give Message to Rochester," *RH,* June 13, 1918, p. 9; "No Doubt of Victory for Allies, Says Lieutenant Perigord, of France," *TU,* June 12, 1918, p. 8; "Huge Crowd Honors Priest and Musician: Chamber of Commerce Jammed at Luncheon," *PE,* June 12, 1918, p. 9. *HPPR* reports that, on the afternoon following Paderewski's address, Madame Paderewska was honored at a tea given at the home of Mrs. Maksymilian Sosnowska, 1399 Norton Street (p. 127).

47. *HPPR,* pp. 126-27.

48. "Citizens Give Themselves Up to Unrestrained Celebration of the Most Glorious News of History," *PE,* Nov. 11, 1918, p. 6; "Announcement of Peace Rouses Entire Rochester to Delirium of Delight," *TU,* Nov. 11, 1918, p. 9; "City Lets Go in Wild Way as War Ends," *DC,* Nov. 12, 1918, p. 17; "From Daybreak to Daybreak Rochester Celebrates Most Glorious Event in History," *RH,* Nov. 12, 1918, p. 9.

49. The matter of re-establishing Poland's borders proved to be one of the most troublesome issues of the Paris Peace Conference. See Watt, pp. 62-78.

50. Hapak, p. 36; Urbanski, p. 47; Wytrwal, pp. 339 and 344.

51. Parot, pp. 171-72; Urbanski, p. 37; Wytrwal, pp. 345-46; Zake, p. 24.

52. Wytrwal, pp. 345-46.

53. Paderewski's message was delivered to Rochesterians by Jan Smulski in an appearance at the Chamber of Commerce in January 1919. "Poland's Share in War for Democracy: One of Topics for Chamber Luncheon Today," *DC*; "Warns that Hun Peril Still Exists," *RH*, Jan. 30, 1919, p. 8.

54. Parot presents an interesting discussion of the emergence of Polish Americans' dual patriotism in *Polish Catholics in Chicago*, pp. 161-78.

55. *HPPR*, pp. 118-19. Budyenny's Cavalry was a Red Army unit under the command of Semyon Mikhailovich Budyenny, whose horsemen were infamous and feared in the Polish countryside. See Watt, pp. 120-24.

56. Interview with Virginia Koscielny Kelly, Feb. 6, 1983 (Rochester, NY); *HPPR*, p. 118; "Those Who Died for Us," vol. 1 of *The World War Service Record*, pub. by the City of Rochester, 1924, p. 232.

57. *HPPR*, p. 119; "Those Who Died for Us," pp. 405-06.

58. *HPPR*, p. 127.

59. Undated article in the scrapbook of Ludwik Kubiak; *HPPR*, pp. 143 and 162-64. Fathers Szupa and Wysoczynski came to Rochester in 1925. It is not clear whether they were recognized for work in the communities in which they lived during the war, or for contributions to postwar efforts in Rochester.

60. Parot, p. 177. Wytrwal cites statistics compiled in 1924 that indicate that 96,200 Polish immigrants returned to Poland to live between 1919 and 1923, along with 32,500 persons of Polish descent born in the United States.

61. Obituary of S. K. Kowalski in *Gazeta Tygodniowa*; "S. K. Kowalski Dies at 80 of Long Illness," *DC*, Nov. 22, 1941, p. 12; "S. K. Kowalski Rites Arranged for Monday," *TU*, Nov. 22, 1941, p. 2A.

62. Interviews with Sylvia Furlong Baglin and Gertrude Furlong Newberry, Feb. 17, 1985 (Rochester, NY); undated news release from Antonia Sawyer, Inc., Aeolian Hall, New York, NY (property of Sylvia Furlong Baglin).

63. The profile of Marta Graczyk Gedgowd is based upon her memoirs and undated newspaper articles in the possession of Mr. and Mrs. Leon Lustyk, and upon an interview with Mrs. Lustyk, Dec. 15, 1985 (Rochester, NY). See also "Young Woman Relief Worker from Rochester Arrested as Spy in Capital of Lithuania," *DC*; "Poles of Rochester Cheer News that Young Woman is to be Freed by Lithuanians," *DC*; "Those Who Supported the Service," vol. 3 of *The World War Service Record*, pub. by the City of Rochester, 1930, pp. 138-39.

Chapter 6
New Ventures

1. Lubomirski's visit received detailed coverage in the local press. See "Princes Will Arrive Monday: Polish Ambassador and Party Coming Here," *RH*, Jan. 17, 1920, p. 15; "Mayor Will Officially Welcome Prince Lubomirski, Ambassador of Poland, to Rochester To-day," *RH*, Jan. 19, 1920, p. 10; "Polish Prince Visits Kodak Park Plant," *TU*, Jan. 20, 1920, p. 8; "Temporary Aid Only Request Poland Makes," *RH*, Jan. 20, 1920, p. 9; "Poland's Ambassador Addresses Factory Hands in Native Tongue," *DC*, Jan. 21, 1920, p. 21; "Polish Prince Attends Mass This Morning," *TU*, Jan. 21, 1920, p. 9; "Polish Ambassador and Party Spend Busy Day Sight-Seeing and Being Entertained," *RH*, Jan. 21, 1920, p. 9; "Big Gathering of Poles at Convention Hall," *TU*, Jan. 22, 1920, p. 16; "Old Custom is Observed in Greeting When Ambassador Visits Polish Organization," *DC*, Jan. 22, 1920, p. 28; "Prince Calls for Genuine Americanism," *RH*, Jan. 22, 1920, p. 11.

2. The brief existence of the Polish Clothing Manufacturing Company is described in *HPPR*, pp. 138-39. Rochester Auto and Tool Company is listed under automobile supply companies in *The Rochester Directory*, 1920-21, p. 877, and 1921-22, p. 904 (Rochester: Sampson and Murdoch Co., Inc.). The 1920-21 *Directory* names Konstanty Wassill of Norton Street as president of the company; the 1921-22 *Directory* lists Peter Wadelski of Pulaski Street as president. For a description of the Polish Mechanics Corporation, see "Old Custom is Observed in Greeting When Ambassador Visits Polish Organization," *DC*.

3. "Prince Calls for Genuine Americanism," *RH*; "Old Custom is Observed in Greeting When Ambassador Visits Polish Organization," *DC*.

4. McKelvey, *The Quest for Quality*, chapters 11 and 12.

5. McKelvey, *The Quest for Quality*, pp. 326-29.

6. See McKelvey's statistics on Rochester's immigrant population in *The Quest for Quality*, pp. 327-28, and in *Rochester: An Emerging Metropolis, 1925-1961* (Rochester: Christopher Press, 1961), pp. 6-8.

7. The local press covered the Homelands Exhibition lavishly. See "Homelands Exhibition Opens at Exposition Park Tomorrow Night," *TU*, April 9, 1920, p. 9; "Homelands Exhibit to Open To-night," *RH*, April 10, 1920, pp. 9 and 11; "Crowds See First Show at Homelands," *RH*, April 11, 1920, p. 13; "Folk

Dances by Various Groups Attract Attention at the Homelands Exhibition," *TU,* April 15, 1920, p. 9; "Drenching Downpour Fails to Keep Multitude Away from Big Homelands Exhibition and Evening Performance," *RH,* April 16, 1920, p. 11; "Children's Special Program at Homelands Exhibition Today," *TU,* April 17, 1920, p. 8.

8. "Why You Should See the Homelands Exhibition," *TU,* April 10, 1920, p. 12.

9. "Crowds See First Show at Homelands," *RH;* "Children's Special Program at Homelands Exhibition Today," *TU;* "Poles and Italians at Homelands," *RH,* April 18, 1920, p. 13.

10. "Polish Potter Interesting Figure at the Homelands," *RH,* April 16, 1920, p. 11.

11. See editions of *The Rochester Directory* for the 1920s.

12. See advertisements placed by Trzeciak in *HPPR* and in the program booklet of "The Nit Wit Minstrels," presented by the St. Stanislaus Parish Athletic Club, Feb. 5 and 6, 1933 (ASSP). See Kwapich's advertisements in the 20th and 30th anniversary booklets of St. Casimir's Parish, 1928 and 1938 (ASCP). In the program booklet for the community's 1937 Pulaski Day observance, Kaleta's pharmacy claimed exclusive sale of Kwapich's liniment, advertised as the cure for "that lame feeling, sprains, bruises."

13. *HPPR,* pp. 138-39; Catherine Harding Hendrickson, "Continuity and Change in Two Rochester Neighborhoods: 1890-1958" (doctoral dissertation, State University of New York at Buffalo, 1975), pp. 133, 137.

14. Stock certificate of the Polish Clothing Manufacturing Co., Inc., given to the author by Mr. William Auchter of Rochester, NY.

15. *HPPR,* p. 139; McKelvey, *The Quest for Quality,* p. 343.

16. Interview with Mr. and Mrs. Leonard Zlotnik, Dec. 8, 1985 (Rochester, NY); *HPPR,* p. 139.

17. Lelesh and Openchowski are listed in the 1924 *Rochester Directory,* both at the business address 1119 Hudson Avenue (office of the *Rochester Rekord*). Casimir Mrzywka is also listed that year as treasurer of the *Rochester Rekord,* Inc.

18. Although no attempt was made to resurrect the *Rochester Rekord,* a Syracuse resident named J. Lindner began publication of a Polish language weekly, *Tygodnik Polski,* in 1928. The newspaper, billed as "the only American newspaper published in the Polish language in Rochester, New York," featured several pages of international and national news, and one page of notes from the Polish neighborhood. The 1929 *Rochester Directory* lists Lindner's local business address as 934 Hudson Avenue. One issue of *Tygodnik Polski* (year 2, no. 2; Jan. 11, 1929) is held in the Local History collection of RPL.

19. *HPPR,* pp. 139-40; "History of Pulaski Post No. 782," program booklet from Polish Fest '84, distributed by the Polonia Civic Centre, Aug. 1984, pp. 36-37.

20. *HPPR,* pp. 140-41; "Polish Army Veterans Association of America and Ladies Auxiliary," program booklet for Polish Fest '84, pp. 20-21.

21. *HPPR,* pp. 141; golden anniversary program booklet, Polish Young Men's Citizen Club, Inc., 1971, pp. 3-4 (ASCP).

22. *HPPR,* p. 89; "Polish American Citizens Club," program booklet for Polish Fest '84, p. 33; 75th anniversary program booklet, Polish American Citizens Club of Rochester, 1989, p. 1.

23. *HPPR,* pp. 148-49; "Polonja Musi Zrozumiec Wlasny Interes," *Tygodnik Polski* (Rochester, NY), Jan. 11, 1929, p. 8; "John Felerski Dies at Age 56," *DC,* Dec. 26, 1948, p. 1B; "Funeral Rites Arranged for John Felerski," *TU,* Dec. 27, 1948, p. 2B.

24. *HPPR,* p. 149.

25. Obituary of John Kaleta, *DC,* June 21, 1990, p. 4C.

26. *HPPR,* p. 148.

27. *HPPR,* pp. 145-47; Bartles, "Rochester Polish People's Home," pp. 1-2. The petition for incorporation was filed by Franciszek Kryszewski, Waleryn Dziekonski, Stanley Klodzinski, Joseph Majewski, Karl Bauer, Anthony Zaczek, Edward Kosalka, and Andrew Strzeciwilk.

28. Andrzej Brozek, *Polonia Amerykanska: 1854-1939* (Warsaw, 1977), p. 119; John Fitzpatrick, Papers (Archives of the Chicago Historical Society, box 10, filedrawer 72).

29. *The Amalgamated in Rochester: 1915-1939,* pub. Feb. 1939 by the Rochester Joint Board of the Amalgamated Clothing Workers of America, pp. 28-29; *Report of the General Executive Board of the Amalgamated Clothing Workers of America to the Sixth Biennial Convention,* May 12-17, 1924 (New York: Allied Printing Trades Council, 1924), pp. 70-75. The other three Polish locals were in Chicago, Baltimore, and New York City. (See Frank Renkiewicz's "Polish American Workers: 1880-1980," p. 127.)

30. *The Amalgamated in Rochester,* pp. 10-20; 1924 *Report of the General Executive Board of the ACWA,* p. 72; Hendrickson, pp. 99-104 and 135-41.

31. "Political Action Urged in Speech Before Workers," *DC,* May 2, 1924, p. 31.

32. *HPPR,* p. 150.

33. Chlebowski-Laboski and Kwiatkowski, summary of activities for 1920-1934.

34. *HPPR,* pp. 152-53; "Rochester, NY: Polscy studenci zorganizowali Kolko Filaretow," undated newspaper article; "Program: Akademja Ku Czci Henryka Sienkiewicza," Towarzystwo Filaretow i Filaretek, program booklet, Nov. 28, 1926; "Rochester, NY: Filareci Swieca Wielki Tryumf," *Telegram,* Dec. 3, 1926 (all in the scrapbook of Anna Kwiatkowski Lawrence, property of Mr. and Mrs. Roman Kwiatkowski, Rochester, NY). The name "Filaret" is taken from the Greek *philoe aretes,* meaning "lovers of virtue."

35. *HPPR,* pp. 154-55.

36. *HPPR,* pp. 156-57.

37. Interview with Mr. and Mrs. Henry Kowalski, Jan. 5, 1986 (Rochester, NY); interview with Mr. and Mrs. Bernard Mysliwiec, Jan. 10, 1990 (Rochester, NY).

38. See advertisements in the *DC,* July 2, 1920, p. 4, and July 5, 1920, p. 8.

39. "Polish Drive Gains $3,500 Through Rally," *RH,* July 5, 1920, p. 11; "Polish District Headquarters in Rochester Now," *DC,* July 6, 1920, p. 22; "Polish Bond Sales Aggregate $110,000," *TU,* July 7, 1920, p. 15.

40. In July 1919, local Jews, Ukrainians, and Lithuanians held rallies to protest alleged mistreatment of their nationalities by the Polish government. The Polish Citizens Committee responded that the reports of Polish cruelty were unjustified and reflected a German scheme to undermine the new Polish Republic, and that the Polish Army had entered territory claimed by Lithuanians and Ukrainians in an effort to halt the spread of Bolshevism. See "Protest Against Alleged Cruelty of Polish Army: Lithuanians and Ukrainians Parade and Have Meeting," *DC,* July 6, 1919, p. 36; "Poles Declare Agitation Bears German Stamp," *DC,* July 6, 1919, p. 44; "Denies Helping Hun Cause and Accuses Poles: Ruthenian Pastor Answers Article in This Paper," *DC,* July 7, 1919, p. 17; "See Annexation as Purpose of Polish Invasion: Lithuanians Say Claim of 'Protection' is Pretext," *DC,* July 9, 1919, p. 23. See also descriptions of the local Ukrainian community's protests in *Historical Documentary of the Ukrainian Community of Rochester, New York,* by James D. Bratush (Rochester: Christopher Press, Inc., 1973), pp. 13-14, 77, 87-88, 92-96, 393.

41. Watt, pp. 62-78 and 153-74.

42. Watt, p. 75.

43. The commission included Henry Morgenthau, Brigadier General Edwin Jadwin, and Homer H. Johnson. Its report, released in January 1920, concluded that acts of violence against Jews in Poland, which had claimed 280 lives, were sporadic incidents and not premeditated by the government: "Just as the Jews would resent being condemned for the action of a few of their undesirable coreligionists, so it would be correspondingly unfair to condemn the Polish nation as a whole for the violence committed by uncontrolled troops or mobs." ("Polanders Vindicated by Committee," *TU,* Jan. 19, 1920, p. 20.)

44. "Polish General Sharply Scored in Protest Here," *DC,* Nov. 26, 1923, p. 20.

45. "Polish Army Commander to be City's Guest To-day at Many Affairs in His Honor," *DC,* Nov. 28, 1923, p. 23.

46. "Mayor Not Affected by Haller Protest: To Be Out of City," *TU,* Nov. 26, 1923, p. 8.

47. "Polish General Departs After Strenuous Day in City," *DC,* Nov. 29, 1923, p. 22.

48. "George Eastman Receives Polish Cross of Honor," *DC,* Dec. 11, 1927, p. 1; "Eastman's War Relief Work Recognized by Republic of Poland," *TU,* Dec. 12, 1927, p. 28.

49. "George Eastman Receives Cross of Honor," *DC.* The *TU* expressed interest in Eastman's expedition, describing in detail his plans to hunt for African game. ("Eastman Will Leave Tonight on Africa Trip," Dec. 12, 1927, p. 9.)

50. "History of St. Stanislaus Church of Rochester," 1890-1960, pp. 11 and 18-19.

51. Enrollment Statistics, St. Stanislaus Kostka School, 1928-29 through 1931-32 (ASSP).

52. "History of St. Stanislaus Church of Rochester," 1890-1960, pp. 11 and 18-19; McNamara, *The Diocese of Rochester,* p. 375.

53. McNamara, *The Diocese of Rochester,* p. 375.

54. "History of Church," souvenir album of the silver jubilee of St. Theresa's Church, Rochester, NY, Oct. 26, 1952, p. 8, and "History of Our Church," souvenir album of the golden jubilee of St. Theresa's Church, Rochester, NY, 1977, p. 5 (ASTP); interview with Mr. and Mrs. Stanley Jaskot, Sept. 13, 1986 (Rochester, NY).

55. The men listed are identified as founders of the parish in the 1952 and 1977 souvenir albums. Polanowski and Leon Szarlacki are named as the parish's first two trustees.

56. "Decretum Erectionis Novae Paroeciae Pro Fidelibus Linguae Polonicae in Civitate Roffensi," issued by Rt. Rev. Thomas F. Hickey, Sept. 10, 1927 (copy in the scrapbook of Rev. Alexander J. Stec, Rochester, NY); "Parish Journal," Oct. 1927-Dec. 1938 (ASTP).

57. "New Catholic Parish," *CJ,* Sept. 30, 1927, p. 5; "History of Our Church," p. 5.

58. "Parish Journal," Oct. 1927-Dec. 1938; interview with Mr. and Mrs. Stanley Jaskot.

59. Deed of purchase for property in the Henry S. Brown Resubdivision, Feb. 20, 1928 (ASTP); "Parish Journal," Oct. 1927-Dec. 1938; "Minutes of the Meetings of the Board of Trustees, Parish of St. Theresa of the Child Jesus," Jan. 6, 1928-May 11, 1976 (ASTP).

60. "Church Lays Cornerstone of New Home," *DC,* July 5, 1928, p. 16; "Bishop Hickey Officiates at Stone Laying," *TU,* July 5, 1928, p. 8; "Bishop Hickey Officiates at Stone Laying, *CJ,* July 6, 1928, p. 5.

61. "Parish Journal," Oct. 1927-Dec. 1938; "History of Our Church," p. 6; planting list for the grounds of St. Theresa's Parish (ASTP).

62. "New Church Dedicated by Archbishop," *DC,* Dec. 10, 1928, p. 18; "New Church Dedicated by Archbishop," *TU,* Dec. 10, 1928, p. 9; *HPPR,* p. 151; Financial Reports: 1927-1952, St. Theresa's Parish (ASTP).

63. McKelvey, *An Emerging Metropolis,* p. 6; Ward S. Miller, "The Sinews of a City: Part 1, The Poles," *DC,* July 24, 1933, p. 3.

64. Emily's story is still recounted by members of St. Stanislaus Parish. It is also described in the local press: "Girl Plays Before Prince," *DC,* Jan. 23, 1920, p. 28; "Miss Emily Dukat Dead of Pneumonia," *DC,* Jan. 30, 1920, p. 19; "Influenza Claims Young Violinist of Great Promise" and "Flowers Sent by Prince to Funeral of Girl Violinist," undated newspaper articles in the scrapbook of Ludwik Kubiak.

65. Interview with Henry Kowalski and Arlene Felerski Kowalski; "Adam Felerski, Polish Leader, Dies at Home," *DC,* Jan. 29, 1946, p. 15.

66. Interview with Carl and Dean Wojtczak, May 15, 1988 (Rochester, NY); interviews with Sophie Parks and Mr. and Mrs. Leonard Zlotnik; advertisements for Wojtczak's bakery in the 20th and 30th anniversary program booklets of St. Casimir's Parish (1928 and 1938); "Nine Rochesterians Receive Distinguished Papal Honors" and "Five Laymen Receive High Papal Honors," *DC,* March 10, 1931, pp. 1 and 14; obituaries of Walter Wojtczak (*DC,* Aug. 8, 1975, p. 4B) and Madeline Wojtczak (*DC,* Feb. 20, 1980, p. 3B).

Chapter 7
Unity, Guidance, Commonweal

1. Interviews with Helen Eurack Kula, Josephine Sojka Modzel, and Dorothy Wojciechowski Sobczak, Aug. 27, 1986 (Rochester, NY).

2. McKelvey, *An Emerging Metropolis,* p. 55; McKelvey, *Rochester on the Genesee* (Syracuse: Syracuse University Press, 1973), pp. 190-91.

3. McKelvey, *An Emerging Metropolis,* pp. 55-59; Edwin Sayers, "The Great Depression," *Upstate Magazine, DC,* Feb. 24, 1980, pp. 7-8.

4. "Communications from the City Manager, Nov. 1, 1930," *Proceedings of the Council of the City of Rochester: 1930* (Rochester: Alliance Press, 1930), pp. 708-10; "Report of the Coordination Committee on Unemployment as of January 16, 1931," *Proceedings of the Council of the City of Rochester: 1931,* p. 25.

5. McKelvey, *An Emerging Metropolis,* pp. 62-65, 70; McKelvey, *Rochester on the Genesee,* p. 192; Sayers, pp. 8, 10.

6. McKelvey, *An Emerging Metropolis,* pp. 74-76.

7. McKelvey, *An Emerging Metropolis,* pp. 72-73; Sayers, p. 12; "City's NRA Parade to Move at 7 Tonight," *DC,* Sept. 26, 1933, pp. 1 and 5; "Entire City Waits Start of NRA Parade," *TU,* Sept. 26, 1933, pp. 1 and 8; "175,000 Cheer NRA Parade," *DC,* Sept. 27, 1933, pp. 1 and 14; "175,000 Watch Huge NRA Celebration," *TU,* Sept. 27, 1933, pp. 1 and 8.

8. "Radical Groups Will Parade Next Monday," *DC,* April 28, 1933, p. 19; "Radicals to March in May Day Parades," *DC,* May 1, 1933, p. 13.

9. Interviews with Josephine Rafalak and Dorothy Sobczak; Hendrickson, pp. 162-63.

10. Interviews with Mr. and Mrs. Roman Kwiatkowski, Feb. 15, 1986 (Rochester, NY), Agnes and Catherine Pawlik, Aug. 1982 (Rochester, NY); members of St. Stanislaus Parish's Golden Age Club, Aug. 27, 1986 (Rochester, NY), and Mr. and Mrs. Stanley Jaskot.

11. Interviews with members of St. Stanislaus Parish's Golden Age Club; "Poprawka Do Konstytucji, Tow. Sw. Stanislawa Kostki, Artykul 18" (1935), Amendment to the 1924 Constitution of the Society of St. Stanislaus, St. Stanislaus Kostka Parish; interview with Aniela Skalny and Mr. and Mrs. Anthony Stachura, June 27, 1982 (Rochester, NY).

12. Almost without exception, the Polish Americans interviewed about the Great Depression for this study referred to the shame associated with welfare, and mentioned their families' determination not to accept public assistance. Hendrickson cites statistics that show a disproportionately low percentage of Polish families on public relief from 1933 through 1938 (p. 164).

13. Hendrickson, p. 159.

14. "Outline of Parish Historical Reports," St. Theresa's Parish, 1961 (ARD); "History of Our Church," golden jubilee program booklet, St. Theresa's Parish, 1977; Parish Financial Reports: 1927-1952, St. Theresa's Parish (ASTP).

15. "History of St. Casimir's Polish National Catholic Church, Rochester, N. Y.," silver jubilee program booklet (1933); "St. Casimir's Church Plans Celebration: Will Observe Silver Jubilee at Sunday Morning Service," undated newspaper article in the scrapbook of John T. Skalny (Rochester, NY).

16. "History of St. Stanislaus Church of Rochester," 1890-1960, pp. 13-15.

17. Miller, "The Sinews of a City."

18. "Minutes of the 12th Annual Meeting, Baptist Union of Rochester and Monroe County," June 9, 1932, p. 9; "Fifteenth Annual Report, Baptist Union of Rochester and Monroe County," 1935, pp. 3-4.

19. See advertisements in the 25th and 30th anniversary program booklets of St. Casimir's Parish (1933 and 1938), and in the program of "The Nit Wit Minstrels," Feb. 5 and 6, 1933.

20. Interview with Zosia Jezowski Zablotski, Aug. 17, 1990 (Rochester, NY); summary of Stanislaw Jezowski's career, written by Stasia Jezowski Skalny, Aug. 1990 (Rochester, NY); "Stanley Jezowski Dies; Ex-Polish Daily Newsman," July 1, 1969 (newspaper clipping, property of Zosia Zablotski). Jezowski was Rochester editor of *Dziennik dla Wszystkich* until the newspaper ended its operations in 1956. Until 1963, he served as local news representative for *Nowy Swiat,* based in New York City.

21. See Bukowczyk's discussion of American Polonia during the Great Depression in *And My Children Did Not Know Me,* pp. 75-78. It should be noted that local Polish Americans' mobility was also limited by real estate restrictions that prohibited sale of property to Poles in some Rochester suburbs before World War II. (Michael Ziegler, "Ethnic Restrictions May Be Hiding in Area Deeds," *DC,* Aug. 17, 1986, pp. 1B and 4B.)

22. Interviews with members of St. Stanislaus Parish's Golden Age Club, Aug. 27, 1986 (Helen Kula, Josephine Modzel, Mr. and Mrs. Joseph Podgorski, Josephine Rafalak, Dorothy Sobczak), and Jan. 10, 1990 (Rev. Valentine Jankowiak, Mr. and Mrs. Bernard Mysliwiec, Irene Wisniewski, Harriet Wisniewski Kelly, and Martha Zielinski); interview with Agnes and Catherine Pawlik.

23. "Filaret Girls, Champions of Western N. Y.," Nov. 25, 1933 (newspaper clipping in the scrapbook of Karol Anders (Rochester, NY); "The Powerful Filarets: Rochester Girls Make New Basketball Record," *Life,* April 3, 1944, pp. 43-46; Jim Myers, "Filarets Were 'All-Winning'," *DC,* Dec. 20, 1980, p. 7A. The 1933 article lists Leona Dronzewski, Helen Duncan, Irene Grzywinski, Florence Holliday, Agnes Jankowiak, Florence Kowalewski, Helen Kozcki, Virginia Malinowski, Elva Payne, Pauline Osinski, and Gertrude Renczys as members of the Filarets that season. Other records name Florence and Sally Czarniak as members of the team in 1932-33.

24. *HPPR,* pp. 160-65.

25. *HPPR,* p. 166; Hendrickson, p. 176.

26. Letter from Marie Lorentz Fortuna to the author, Aug. 1, 1982; "Edmund Lorentz Dies: Ex-Interpreter for Court," *TU,* June 17, 1959, p. 44; "Edmund F. Lorentz, Interpreter for FBI, Passes in Capital," *DC,* June 17, 1959, p. 22.

27. Constitution of the Polonia Civic Centre, Rochester, NY *(Konstytucja: Prawa, Przepisy i Regulamin "Centrali"),* approved Nov. 14, 1938, pp. 22-24.

28. Articles describing the Charity Ball of 1935 are found in the scrapbook of John T. Skalny ("Plan Charity Ball for Polish Group," and "Centrala Will Entertain at Charity Ball").

29. *HPPR,* pp. 176-77; "Centennial Fete for Poles Sunday," *TU,* Aug. 18, 1934, p. 9; "Centennial Polish Day Draws 10,000," *DC,* Aug. 20, 1934, pp. 11 and 13.

30. "Centrala Field Day to Open with Polish Parade at Noon," *TU,* July 14, 1935, p. 4B; "Polish Community Marks 50th Anniversary of Colony," *DC,* July 15, 1935, p. 15; "Polish People Mark Date of Settling Here," *TU,* July 15, 1935, p. 8; "Poles to Dine Old Settlers," *DC,* April 11, 1937, p. 2B.

31. Resolution to welcome General Jozef Haller, *Proceedings of the Council of the City of Rochester: 1934,* April 10, 1934, pp. 124-26.

32. "Polish Chief in Great War to Visit Here," *TU,* May 9, 1934, p. 8; "Rochester is Host to General Haller, Hero of World War," *TU,* May 11, 1934, pp. 1 and 9; "General Jozef Haller Honored at Parade by Rochester Poles," *TU,* May 12, 1934, p. 8; "Practical Steps to Preserve World Peace Told by Gannett," *TU,* May 12, 1934, p. 13. Local press accounts name John Bernacki, Adam Felerski, John Felerski, and Wladyslaw Jarus as among those who welcomed Haller to Rochester on behalf of the Polish community. The general was accompanied by his son, Lieutenant Erik Haller; Franciszek Dziob, national commander of the Polish World War Veterans; and Captain Stanislaw Palaszewski, a personal aide.

33. "Protest Flying Flag of Poles," *TU,* May 10, 1934, p. 23.

34. Written account of Pulaski Day observances, from the records of the Polonia Civic Centre, Oct. 9, 1937, p. 1.

35. Written account of Pulaski Day observances, from the records of the Polonia Civic Centre, pp.

2-4; "Church Service and Parade Mark Pulaski Observance," *TU,* Oct. 19, 1929, p. 9; "Rochester Unites with its Polish People in Tribute to General Casimir Pulaski," *DC,* Oct. 20, 1929, pp. 25-26; program booklet for the observance of "Brigadier-General Casimir Pulaski Memorial Day," Oct. 19, 1929 (records of the General Pulaski Community Library, Rochester, NY).

36. *Proceedings of the Council of the City of Rochester: 1930,* March 3 (p. 164), March 17 (p. 183), and June 9 (p. 469). The dedication of Pulaski Park did not take place until ten years later, in October 1940.

37. Letter from the Polonia Republican League to the City Council, City of Rochester, NY, received and filed March 31, 1930 *(Proceedings of the Council of the City of Rochester: 1930,* p. 212).

38. "Joint Resolution and Petition to the Common Council of City of Rochester, N. Y.," from the Polish American Citizens' Central Committee, March 30, 1931.

39. Written account of Pulaski Day observances, from the records of the Polonia Civic Centre, pp. 4-5; "Librarian's Report," July 17, 1931, *Minutes of Meetings of the Board of Trustees, RPL;* Records of the Board of Trustees, May 26, 1932, RPL.

40. Minutes of Meetings of the Pulaski Tablet Committee, Oct. 5, 1931, and March 10, 1932, *Minutes of Meetings of the Board of Trustees, RPL;* written account of Pulaski Day observances, from the records of the Polonia Civic Centre, pp. 4-5; interview with Alphonse Kolb, Nov. 15, 1977 (Rochester, NY). Henry Bielski, the Reverend John Czajkowski, S. K. Kowalski, Frank Mietus, Joseph Paprocki, and Joseph Zielinski represented Centrala on the Tablet Committee.

41. Written account of Pulaski Day observances, from the records of the Polonia Civic Centre, p. 6; "Poles to Mark Pulaski Day in Special Rites," *DC,* Oct. 8, 1933, p. 2B; "Rochester Poles to Honor Pulaski, Kosciuszko Today," *DC,* Oct. 11, 1933, p. 15; "Polish Heroes Given Tribute in Ceremonies," *TU,* Oct. 12, 1933, p. 8; "Bronze Pulaski Plaque Unveiled in Hudson Branch Library," *DC,* Oct. 12, 1933, p. 16; John A. Lowe, "Annual Report of the Director for 1933," *Minutes of Meetings of the Board of Trustees, RPL*

42. Written account of Pulaski Day observances, from the records of the Polonia Civic Centre, pp. 7-11; "Polish Honor to Dr. Rhees Opens Exhibit in Art Gallery," *DC,* Oct. 12, 1934, p. 20; "Rites Honor Memory of Pulaski," *TU,* Oct. 11, 1937, p. 19; program booklets for Pulaski Day observances, Oct. 11, 1936, and Oct. 10 and 11, 1937 (records of the General Pulaski Community Library).

43. McKelvey, *An Emerging Metropolis,* pp. 114-15.

44. "Communications from the City Manager," Oct. 14, 1938, *Proceedings of the Council of the City of Rochester: 1938,* pp. 315-17.

45. "Communications from the City Manager," Oct. 14, 1939, *Proceedings of the Council of the City of Rochester: 1939,* p. 278.

46. McKelvey, *Rochester on the Genesee,* p. 194.

47. Hendrickson, pp. 122, 165.

48. Norman Nairn, "Throng Pays Great Tribute as Paderewski's Magic Moves Eastman Audience," *DC,* May 22, 1939, p. 9; A. J. Warner, "Audience Pays Tribute to Paderewski," *TU,* May 22, 1939, p. 6.

49. "Poles of City Pay Homage to Paderewski," *DC,* May 22, 1939, p. 12; "Paderewski Honored by City's Poles," *TU,* May 22, 1939, p. 3A.

50. "Paderewski Feared Done with Stage: Pianist Stricken as New Yorkers Wait," *TU,* May 26, 1939, p. 1; "Paderewski Career Feared Ended with Concert in Rochester: Illness Forces Tour's Close," *TU,* May 26, 1939, p. 16; "Heart Attack Cancels Paderewski Concert," *DC,* May 26, 1939, p. 1. See also Zamoyski's *Paderewski,* pp. 230-31.

51. Letter from Marie Lorentz Fortuna to the author; interview with John T. Skalny, Aug. 12, 1982 (Rochester, NY); "Among the Local Great and Near-Great," *Rochester Sunday American,* May 3, 1936, p. 2L; "Edmund F. Lorentz, Interpreter for FBI, Passes in Capital," *DC;* "Edmund Lorentz Dies: Ex-Interpreter for Court," *TU.*

52. Interview with Anthony, Angela, Frank, and Barbara Zamiara, March 14, 1988 (Rochester, NY).

53. Interview with Mr. and Mrs. Theodore Jablonski, Jr., Sept. 20, 1987 (Rochester, NY); interview with Anna Jablonski Harvick, Sept. 26, 1987 (Rochester, NY); advertisement for Jablonski's grocery in the 30th anniversary program booklet of St. Casimir's Parish (1938), p. 40; letter from Leo T. Sawyko to the author, Nov. 2, 1987; "A History of the Browncroft Area," prepared by the Browncroft Neighborhood Association History Committee, City of Rochester Sesquicentennial History Project, 1984, pp. 8-18. Jozef Jablonski, one of Teofil's brothers, graduated from Harvard University and taught art at Harvard and at Marshall College. Another brother, Jan, studied at the Eastman School of Music and played first violin with the Rochester Philharmonic and Cleveland Symphony Orchestras.

1. "Foreignborn Stand Loyal to America," *DC,* Sept. 4, 1939, p. 15.

2. "Heavy Exodus Heralds Holiday," *TU,* Sept. 2, 1939, p. 1A. Similarly, the *DC* made light of international events in a commentary on the end of the season: "Fall refused neutrality pleas last night, and today will open its major offensive against declining summer. . . . Kindly all season, the weatherman was in a fighting mood last night and threatened to becloud the closing day." ("School Near, Vacations End, Autumn's Here," Sept. 4, 1939, p. 15.)

3. "10,000 Poles in Rochester Asked to Help Homeland," *DC,* Sept. 3, 1939, p. 1C. Estimates of the number of Rochesterians of Polish descent varied substantially at this time. In contrast to the figure of 10,000 Polish Americans cited in the Sept. 3rd article, William Brodie stated that the city had 35,000 residents of Polish descent in an April 4, 1939, report. ("Poles Rally in Support of Homeland Against Nazis," *TU,* p. 2A.) Adam Felerski referred to 22,000 Rochesterians of Polish descent in a June 3, 1940, article. ("Italy Moves Feared Ban on Polish Aid," *TU,* p. 2A.)

4. "Poles Rally in Support of Homeland Against Nazis," *TU.*

5. "City Poles Aid Defense Fund," *DC,* April 28, 1939, p. 11.

6. John Dougherty, "Poland Won't Budge, Declare Ex-Countrymen," *TU,* Aug. 29, 1939, p. 1A; "30-Second Interview," *DC,* Aug. 27, 1939, p. 1A.

7. See M. K. Dziewanowski's analysis of the Polish campaign in *War At Any Price* (Englewood Cliffs, NJ: Prentice-Hall, Inc., 1987), pp. 61-72. Although Poles looked to the support of Britain and France, both of whom declared war against Germany on September 3rd, Poland's allies provided virtually no military assistance during the weeks when Poles fought to repel superior armies on two fronts.

8. "Polish Group Alters Plans on War Relief," *DC,* Sept. 7, 1939, p. 16.

9. "Polish Group Alters Plans on War Relief," *DC;* "War Relief Committee Formed by City's Poles," *TU,* Sept. 7, 1939, p. 3A; "Women Here Start Knitting in Aid of Polish Soldiers," *DC,* Sept. 8, 1939, p. 20; "Polish Unit Here Expects Swift OK on Relief Efforts," *DC,* Sept. 12, 1939, p. 13.

10. "Polish Unit Here Expects Swift OK on Relief Efforts," *DC;* "Red Cross Will Distribute Funds Collected Here for Polish Needy," *DC,* Sept, 19, 1939, p. 13.

11. McKelvey, *An Emerging Metropolis,* pp. 120-22.

12. Laurence Thompson, *1940* (New York: William Morrow and Company, Inc., 1966), p. 180. A year after the US entered World War II, Assistant City Historian Blake McKelvey commented on Rochester's initial isolationism: "The German invasion of Poland early in September, 1939, stimulated a fervent desire among practically all Rochesterians that America should stay out of this struggle. . . . During the long months of the so-called 'phoney war' following the collapse of Poland, the chief concern in Rochester was lest America's sympathies lead her to intervene where her interests were not involved. . . . Not until France fell in June, 1940, did the community begin to shake off its lethargy." ("Rochester's First Year in the War for Survival," *Rochester History,* vol. 5, no. 1, Jan. 1943, p. 2.)

13. Cabell Phillips, *The 1940's: Decade of Triumph and Trouble* (New York: MacMillan Publishing Co., Inc., 1975), pp. 5-7.

14. See editorials in the *DC:* "Will He Save Himself?" Aug. 25, 1939, p. 14; "Realism Their Only Hope," Aug. 28, 1939, p. 8; "Congress Must Control Policy," Aug. 31, 1939, p. 12; "Let's Keep Our Perspective," Sept. 1, 1939, p. 14.

15. "Why We Should Stay Out," *DC,* Sept. 3, 1939, p. 12.

16. See, for example, "Hails Russia's German Pact as Peace Stroke," letter from Ralph Testa to the editor of the *DC,* Aug. 25, 1939, p. 14; "A Polish View of 'Lebensraum,'" letter from Wladyslaw (Walter) Jarus to the editor of the *DC,* Aug. 28, 1939, p. 8; "Would End German Threat," letter from an "observer" to the editor of the *DC,* Aug. 28, 1939, p. 8; "Sees Hitler at End of His Expansion," letter from George H. Backhouse to the editor of the *DC,* Aug. 31, 1939, p. 12.

17. See, for example, "Send Europe Food, No Arms, Writer Urges," letter from S. C. Romano to the editor of the *DC,* Sept. 7, 1939, p. 12; "Keep America Out," letter from Ralph Malta to the editor of the *TU,* Sept. 21, 1939, p. 22.

18. "Foreignborn Stand Loyal to America," *DC;* McKelvey, *An Emerging Metropolis,* pp. 121, 123.

19. McKelvey, *An Emerging Metropolis,* pp. 122-23.

20. McKelvey, *An Emerging Metropolis,* pp. 123 and 126-27.

21. McKelvey, *An Emerging Metropolis,* pp. 121 and 125-26.

22. "Polish Falcons Compete in Mass Athletic Drills," *DC,* July 7, 1940, p. 1C; "3,000 Falcons Parade, Drill, Chant Anthem," *DC,* July 8, 1940, p. 11.

23. "Balk Mars with Needle and Thread," *TU,* Oct. 4, 1939, p. 3A; "Busy Fingers Enlisted," *TU,* Oct. 13, 1939, p. 2A; "$1,000 Raised Here for Polish Relief," *DC,* Nov. 8, 1939, p. 32; "Poles Raise $1,000 for Overseas Aid," *TU,* Nov. 7, 1939, p. 1A.

24. "Priest to Describe Siege of Warsaw," *DC,* Nov. 5, 1939, p. 4C; "Poland Sure to Rise Again, Priest Holds," *DC,* Nov. 6, 1939, p. 14.

25. "Lecturer Offers Warsaw Photos," *DC,* Nov. 6, 1939, p. 14; "Films Show Nazi Bombings," *TU,* Nov. 13, 1939, p. 2A; "Prize War Pictures Due Here Today," *DC,* Nov. 12, 1939, p. 8C; "World Fellowship Sought by Pacifist Group Here," *DC,* Nov. 12, 1939, p. 2C.

26. "Rochester Poles Start Series of Benefits for War Victims," *DC,* Oct. 1, 1939, p. 1C.

27. "Charity Ball Aids Poles," *TU,* Jan. 19, 1940, p. 16; "Polish Chefs Set for Ball," *DC,* Jan. 19, 1940, p. 22.

28. "$12,000 Sought in Rochester to Aid Poles," *DC,* June 3, 1940, p. 13; "Italy Moves Feared Ban on Polish Aid," *TU.*

29. "Allies Sure to Win, Avers Polish Leader; Homeland Will 'Rise Again,' He Declares," *DC,* April 4, 1940, p. 18; "Polish Hero Predicts Reich Defeat," *TU,* April 4, 1940, p. 2A; "Poles Told Nation Sure to Rise Again," *TU,* Sept. 23, 1940, p. 3A; "Poles Honor Dead in War in Rites Here," *DC,* Sept. 23, 1940, p. 13.

30. "Rochesterians Baffled in Trying to Send Aid to Kin in Poland," *DC,* March 10, 1940, p. 9C.

31. The Rochester press covered the Falcon convention extensively: "Vanguard to Arrive Today for Convention of Falcons," *DC,* July 3, 1940, p. 13; "3,000 Polish Falcons Parade Here Today; Allied-bound Ambulance in Line of March," *DC,* July 4, 1940, p. 18; "Falcons See War Aid Unit," and "Falcons Ready to Serve, Says '18 Army Organizer," *DC,* July 5, 1940, p. 17; "Athletic Circus Launched for U.S., Canadian Poles," *DC,* July 5, 1940, p. 15; "Falcons Pledge Support for Defense Program," *TU,* July 5, 1940, p. 3A; "Falcon Rally Drawing 1,000 More to City," *DC,* July 6, 1940, p. 12; "Polish Falcons Poised for Athletic Festival," *TU,* July 6, 1940, p. 1A; "Polish Falcons Compete in Mass Athletic Drills," *DC;* "Polish Falcons Launch 22d National Convention," *TU,* July 8, 1940, p. 3A; "3,000 Falcons Parade, Drill, Chant Anthem," *DC;* "Back U. S. Defense, Polish Falcons Urged," *DC,* July 9, 1940, p. 13; "Falcons Pledged to Defend America," *TU,* July 9, 1940, p. 1A; "Falcons Pledge Aid to America," *TU,* July 10, 1940, p. 3A; "Falcons Re-Elect Leader to Fifth 4-Year Term," *DC,* July 10, 1940, p. 15. See also the special section devoted to the Falcon convention in the July 3, 1940, edition of *Dziennik dla Wszystkich,* pp. 15-18.

32. Dziewanowski, *War At Any Price,* pp. 93-113.

33. "1,000 Poles Said to Face Death Daily," *TU,* Oct. 7, 1940, p. 1A; "Polish 'Y' Head Slates Talks in 3-Day Visit," *DC,* Oct. 7, 1940, p. 14; "Rebirth of Poland Forecast by Refugee Aid Chief Here," *DC,* Oct. 8, 1940, p. 13.

34. "Polish Americans Rally for Pulaski Park Dedication," *TU,* Oct. 14, 1940, p. 2A; "Polish Residents Dedicate Pulaski Park, Honor Hero," *DC,* Oct. 14, 1940, p. 14. Residents of the northeast side had originally proposed the renaming of the park ten years earlier. See *Proceedings of the Council of the City of Rochester: 1930,* March 3 (p. 164), March 17 (p. 183), and June 9 (p. 469).

35. "Poles' 'Spirit' Wins Praise" and "Poles Seek Intervention for Imprisoned Countrymen," *DC,* Feb. 10, 1941, p. 13; "Poland Day Speaker Asks Aid for Captives Sent to Siberia," *TU,* Feb. 10, 1941, p. 3A.

36. Phillips, pp. 38-41 and 66-69.

37. Interview with Mr. and Mrs. Peter Anuszkiewicz, Jan. 15, 1989 (Rochester, NY). The position of the *Castor* at the time of the Pearl Harbor attack is identified in *Pearl Harbor: Why, How, Fleet Salvage and Final Appraisal,* by Vice Admiral Homer N. Wallin, USN (section forwarded to Frank Anders by Bernard F. Cavalcante, Head of Operational Archives Branch, US Naval Historical Center, in correspondence on July 7, 1988).

38. McKelvey, "Rochester's First Year in the War for Survival," p. 27; *An Emerging Metropolis,* pp. 130-31; *Rochester on the Genesee,* pp. 202-03. McKelvey identifies a "score" of local servicemen stationed in Hawaii and the Philippines on December 7, 1941.

39. Interview with Mr. and Mrs. Peter Anuszkiewicz.

40. "Kin in City Seek Tidings from Hawaii," *DC,* Dec. 8, 1941, pp. 15, 16, and 25; "60 Vicinity Men Serve in Isles," *DC,* Dec. 8, 1941, p. 16; "Families Here Seek News of Kin in Pacific War Zone," *DC,* Dec. 9, 1941, pp. 18, 22; McKelvey, "Rochester's First Year in the War for Survival," p. 5; "Heavy Guard Placed Over Arms Plants," *DC,* Dec. 8, 1941, p. 15; "Flyers' Wings Clipped; Airport Under Guard," and "Flags Wave, Citizens Offer Aid," *TU,* Dec. 9, 1941, p. 3A.

41. Frank Gannett, "War with Japan Means War with Germany . . . The Die is Cast . . . We Must Conquer," *DC,* Dec. 8, 1941, p. 1, and *TU,* Dec. 8, 1941, p. 1A.

42. Statistics on the number of local residents in service are taken from McKelvey ("Rochester's First Year in the War for Survival," pp. 27-28; *An Emerging Metropolis,* pp. 131-32; *Rochester on the Genesee,* p. 205), and the reference files of the Local History Collection, RPL.

43. A total 697 men and 11 women from St. Stanislaus Parish entered American military service, along with 126 men and 3 women from St. Theresa's Parish (roster of servicemen and women, compiled by the Rochester Catholic Diocese, 1945, ARD). See also the typed roster of approximately

600 names of St. Stanislaus parishioners in service (ca. 1942 or 1943, ASSP). The number of St. Casimir's parishioners in service is cited in "Church Burns Old Mortgage, Opens Campaign" (newspaper article in the scrapbook of John T. Skalny), on the occasion of the parish's mortgage burning celebration in November 1944. These numbers, based upon parish records, do not reflect men and women of Polish descent who were not affiliated with the Polish parishes.

44. Interview with Wanda Pietrzak, Sept. 3, 1988 (Rochester, NY); "9 Nurses Off to Help Army," *DC,* Aug. 20, 1942, and "Furloughed Nurse Reports on Life in Louisiana Camp," *DC,* Jan. 3, 1943 (articles in the World War II news clippings file, RPL); McKelvey, "Rochester's First Year in the War for Survival," p. 29.

45. "Poles Honor War Dead in Rites Here," *DC;* "Poles Told Nation Sure to Rise Again," *TU.*

46. "Poles Urged to Volunteer," *DC,* Jan. 17, 1942, p. 12.

47. "Rochester Poles Plan Unit to Aid Enlistment Drive," *DC,* Sept. 23, 1941, p. 16. The Polish military mission in Canada is described by Aloysius Balawyder in *The Maple Leaf and The White Eagle: Canadian-Polish Relations, 1918-1978* (New York: Columbia University Press, 1980), pp. 111-21, and in "Polish Nation Shapes an Army, Navy and Air Force Across the River from Detroit," *Detroit Free Press,* Sept. 9, 1941 (article in the scrapbook of Leopold Lorentz, property of Olga Lorentz of Bristol, NY). The campaign fell far below expectations, drawing fewer than 500 recruits from the US and Canada to the Polish forces. See Michael A. Peszke's "The Polish Armed Forces in Exile: Sept. 1939-July 1941" (Part 1), *The Polish Review,* vol. 26, no. 1 (1981), p. 103. Service in the US forces held greater appeal for Polonia's young men—most of whom were second or third generation Polish Americans—particularly after the US entered the war. Wytrwal has estimated that 900,000 Polish Americans served in the US armed forces during the war. According to the Sept. 9, 1941, article in the *Detroit Free Press,* 200,000 Americans of Polish descent were estimated to have enlisted in the US Army by summer 1941, when the Polish Army opened its induction center at Windsor.

48. "Youth Seeks Place in War," *DC,* Sept. 16, 1941, p. 13; "Polish Army Enlistments Pushed Here," *TU,* Sept. 16, 1941, p. 3A; "Youth Takes Test for Polish Army," *DC,* Sept. 24, 1941, p. 14; "Youth Joins Polish Air Corps to Drop Bombs on Germany," *DC,* Sept. 27, 1941, p. 12; "Wedding Bells," undated newspaper article regarding Mercer's engagement to Maxine White, in the scrapbook of Leopold Lorentz. Mercer completed training in Canada and became a flyer with the Polish Air Corps in England. He was honorably discharged in June 1941 after suffering injuries in battle.

49. "Poles Here Fete New Volunteer," newspaper article in the scrapbook of Leopold Lorentz, Oct. 4, 1941; "Ex-Sailor Drives for Polish Army," *TU,* Dec. 11, 1941, p. 4A.

50. Lorentz's story is based upon the letters, notes, and newspaper articles in his three scrapbooks, upon an interview with his widow, Olga Lorentz (Nov. 16, 1988, in Bristol, NY), and upon correspondence with his sister, Mildred Lorentz Fortuna of Williamsville, NY (Feb. 1988). See in particular letters to his family (Oct. 1941-July 1942), samples of his writing for the Polish Army recruitment campaign, newspaper articles and notes about his recruitment tour in New York State and New England, and his newspaper series "With the Polish Armed Forces in Canada" (Oct. 1941-July 1942).

51. Lorentz's scrapbooks contain newspaper articles that describe his appearances as a recruiter, and correspondence with national Falcon President Teofil Starzynski. In his letters to Lorentz, Starzynski expresses disappointment at the low number of recruits Lorentz is able to enlist. In response, Lorentz describes the difficulty of convincing young men to join the Polish forces, and outlines in detail his recruitment activities in the cities at which he stopped.

52. "Polish Dance Helps in War," *DC,* Jan. 17, 1943, p. 10B.

53. McKelvey, "Rochester's First Year in the War for Survival," p. 11. That year, the Polish Relief Committee received a matching grant of $15,000 from the Community Chest.

54. "Ksiega Dochodow i Rozchodow, Parafji Sw. Stanislawa Kostki, Rochester, NY," 1939-1949, pp. 472-73.

55. Chlebowski-Laboski and Kwiatkowski, summary of activities for 1939-1945.

56. "Clothing Drive Set for Poles," *DC,* Feb. 8, 1945, p. 12; "Drive for Poland Starts Feb. 25," *TU,* Feb. 9, 1945, p. 11A; "Clothing Drive Set for Poles," *DC,* Feb. 14, 1945, p. 14; "Pupils Help Relief Drive for Poland," *DC,* Feb. 21, 1945, p. 17; "Polish Pickup Help Needed," *DC,* Feb. 24, 1945, p. 10; "Citywide Drive for Poles Nets 100 Tons of Clothing," *DC,* Feb. 26, 1945, p. 17; "Clothing Drive Nets 100 Tons for Poland," *TU,* Feb. 26, 1945, p. 1A.

57. "Silence at Noon Today to Honor Poles," *DC,* July 30, 1942, p. 16; "City Pauses to Pay Tribute to Polish Woman Martyrs," *DC,* July 31, 1942, p. 15; "Poland Hailed on Its Holiday," *DC,* May 3, 1943, p. 14; "Poland Day Rites Bring Refugee from Homeland," *TU,* May 3, 1943, p. 1A; "Consul Talks to Poles Here," *DC,* May 4, 1943, p. 15; "Polish Exhibit Tells of Fight," *TU,* July 20, 1943, p. 3A; "'Poland Fights On' Exhibit Depicts Struggle to Combat Tyranny," *DC,* July 21, 1943, p. 24; "Poles Plan Masses for Gen. Sikorski," *DC,* July 6, 1943, p. 15; "Poles of City Pay Tribute to Gen. Sikorski," *DC,* July 12, 1943, p. 13; "Poles Pay Tribute to Dead Hero," *TU,* July 12, 1943, p. 3A.

58. "City Groups Set Tribute for Poland," *DC,* Sept. 15, 1943, p. 16; "Fight for Post-War Independence, Poles Told," *TU,* Sept. 30, 1943, p. 3A; "Tribute to Poland," *TU* editorial, Sept. 30, 1943, p. 22; "Tribute to Poland," program of the public meeting held Sept. 29, 1943, at Benjamin Franklin High School, Rochester, NY.

59. "Polish Americans Eye Eastern Front Moves," *TU,* Jan. 3, 1944, p. 1A.

60. "Polish Groups at Conclave to Stress Restored Nation," *DC,* May 28, 1944, p. 5A; "Russia Seeks Poland Grab, Session Told," *DC,* May 29, 1944, p. 10; "U.S. Poles List Seven Aims in New Congress," *DC,* May 30, 1944, p. 3; "Polish Party Asks for Aid on Territory," *DC,* May 31, 1944, p. 3; "Polish-American Group Eyes Nation After War," *TU,* May 29, 1944, p. 2; "Poles Ask FDR to Aid Homeland," *TU,* May 30, 1944, p. 2; "Polish Unity at Congress Held Victory," *DC,* June 2, 1944, p. 26. For additional information, see Richard C. Lukas' "The Polish American Congress and the Polish Question, 1944-1947," *Polish American Studies,* vol. 38, no. 2 (Autumn 1981), pp. 39-53.

61. "Poles Slate Rally for Dewey Votes," *TU,* Aug. 15, 1944, p. 3A; "Polish GOP Parley Calls Delegates," *TU,* Aug. 24, 1944, p. 3A.

62. There are numerous accounts of the Warsaw Uprising, including descriptions in Richard C. Lukas' *The Forgotten Holocaust: The Poles Under German Occupation, 1939-1944* (Lexington: The University Press of Kentucky, 1986), Jan Nowak's *Courier from Warsaw* (Detroit: Wayne State University Press, 1982), and Stewart Steven's *The Poles* (New York: Macmillan, 1982).

63. "City's Poles Pay Tribute to Defenders of Warsaw," *DC,* Aug. 28, 1944, p. 15; "Memorial to Warsaw's Heroes," *TU,* Aug. 28, 1944, p. 3A.

64. "Poles to Note Fifth Year of War's Ordeal," *DC,* Sept. 3, 1944, p. 3B; "Poles Slate Rally Today," *DC,* Sept. 10, 1944, p. 2B; "Russ-Pole Status Involves Justice, Avers Ex-Official," *DC,* Sept. 11, 1944, p. 14; "Uphold Poles, Ex-Aide Urges," *TU,* Sept. 11, 1944, p. 3A.

65. "'Safe Return' Leads Wishes at Polish Rite," *DC,* Jan. 10, 1944, p. 15; "Poles Observe Old Ceremony," *TU,* Jan. 10, 1944, p. 2A.

66. For descriptions of the role of the First Polish Armoured Division in the 1944-45 European campaign, see Dziewanowski, *War At Any Price,* pp. 302-04; Zygmunt Nagorski, *Falaise: Gap Has Been Closed* (London: C. Tinling and Co., Ltd., 1944); and Leopold Lorentz, *Caen to Wilhelmshaven: Album of the First Polish Armoured Division* (Edinburgh: Erroll Publishing Co., Ltd., 1947). Regarding formation and service record of the Polish forces in exile, see Peszke's series in *The Polish Review:* vol. 26, no. 1 (1981), pp. 67-113; vol. 32, no. 1 (1987), pp. 33-69; and vol. 32, no. 2 (1987), pp. 133-174.

67. Lorentz's experiences with the Polish Army in Britain are described in the letters, notes, and newspaper articles in his scrapbooks. See in particular letters to his family (1942 and 1943); Mrs. Turbyne's letters to the Lorentz family (Nov. 14 and 27, 1943); and "Diary of a Polish Soldier (Somewhere in Scotland)" and "Diary of a Polish Soldier (Somewhere in England)," 1943-45.

68. See Lorentz's letters to his family and "Diary of a Polish Soldier (Somewhere in Scotland)," 1943-44. Peszke writes that the soldiers of the First Polish Armoured Division experienced frustration during their long wait to be called to combat: "There was an initial period of despondency, accentuated by the dismal Scottish climate, the quality of life in unheated tents and barracks, lack of money, different food, and worry about loved ones back in Poland." (*The Polish Review,* 1981, p. 98.)

69. See in particular articles in *Sokol Polski* (Jan. 17 and 31, 1946); notes dated Aug. 26, 1944; and "A Letter from Leopold Lorentz (Royal Hospital, England), Nov. 16, 1944," all in Lorentz's scrapbooks.

70. "Polish Leaders Score 'Partition,'" *TU,* Feb. 14, 1945, p. 1A.

71. "Lawmaker Asks Overthrow of Yalta Polish Decision," *DC,* April 19, 1945, p. 16; "O'Konski Asks Free Election, 1939 Boundaries for Poland," *TU,* April 19, 1945, p. 2A; "District Poles Convene Here," *DC,* June 11, 1945, p. 14; "Polish Parley Asks Justice," *TU,* June 11, 1945, p. 2A; "Poles Urge U.S. Uphold Policy for Freedom," *DC,* Jan. 7, 1946, p. 15; "U.S. Policy Shift Urged," *TU,* Jan. 7, 1946, p. 2A; "Polish Group Hits Wallace, Byrnes Ideas," *DC,* Oct. 7, 1946, p. 17; "Poles Back Truman Plan," *DC,* March 31, 1947, p. 15; "Speakers Ask Aid to Poland," *DC,* Oct. 13, 1947, p. 17; "Aid Polish Liberty, Resolution Urges," *DC,* Oct. 16, 1950, p. 14.

72. Names of those who died in the war are recorded on a plaque mounted in St. Stanislaus Kostka Church, Rochester, NY.

73. "Polish Club Honors Memory of Member Killed in War," *DC,* April 1, 1946, p. 17; "Plaque Honors Song Group War Hero," *TU,* April 1, 1946, p. 12.

74. Interview with Olga Lorentz; "Soldier Returns Home After 6-Year Absence," *TU,* Dec. 24, 1947, p. 1A; "Veteran Returns With War Bride; Served Long in Polish Army," undated newspaper article in the scrapbook of John T. Skalny.

75. Text of "Citizen of the Day" award given to William C. Brodie, March 26, 1952 (from the news clippings file, RPL); "Ex-DPs to Present Polish Play to Aid Friends Still Homeless," *DC,* March 19, 1950, p. 3B; "Displaced Children Get Baskets," *TU,* April 8, 1950, p. 11; "Reunion of Polish DP Family Awaits GI's Return from Korea," *DC,* June 28, 1951, p. 23; interview with Olga Lorentz; interview with Barbara

Kwiatkowski Brodie, Dec. 3, 1988 (Rochester, NY). Polish Jews resettled in Rochester with the help of the local Jewish community. For the stories of two of these refugees, see George Pfeffer, "I Lived to Tell of the Nazi Horrors," *DC,* March 26, 1989, p. 15A, and Del Ray, "Most of Kin Killed in War, Refugee Finds Hope Here," *TU,* in the news clippings file of the RPL.

76. Interview with Mieczyslaw Jopek, March 12, 1989 (Rochester, NY); interviews with Leon Holowacz, Dec. 11, 1988, and Jan. 8, 1989 (Rochester, NY). Leopold Lorentz shared his anger and sadness at the fate of Polish soldiers unable to return to their homes after the war in *Caen to Wilhelmshaven,* pp. 29-31.

77. Interview with Jozef Grzebieniak, Dec. 11, 1988 (Rochester, NY).

78. Interview with Paul Iglinski, March 21, 1989 (Rochester, NY); Jean Walrath, "Pole from Siberia Awaits Citizenship," *DC,* April 10, 1949, p. 1B.

79. Interview with Wlodzimierz Jablonski, Dec. 11, 1988 (Rochester, NY); Del Ray, "Heroic Warsaw Stand Relived by City's Poles," *TU,* July 29, 1954, p. 25; Eugene Marino, "Polish World War II Survivors Witnessed Era of Loss, Hate," *DC,* Aug. 27, 1989, pp. 1A, 7A.

80. Interview with Olga Lorentz; Bill Beeney, "Housewife Recalls Days in Polish Underground," *DC,* June 20, 1950, p. 19; "Veteran Returns with Bride; Served Long in Polish Army" (newspaper article in the scrapbook of John T. Skalny); "Heroic Stand Relived by City's Poles," *TU.*

81. Interviews with Julian Ramotowski, Dec. 11, 1988, and Jan. 8, 1989 (Rochester, NY); "Daring Sea Voyagers from Poland Periled in Barge Canal," *DC,* Aug. 22, 1939, p. 11; "Polish Sailors Tour City," *TU,* Aug. 22, 1939, p. 3A; "Polish Folk Get Homeland News from Voyagers," *DC,* Aug. 23, 1939, p. 18; "Nazi Grab Means War, Polish Guests Declare," *TU,* Aug. 23, 1939, p. 3A; additional newspaper articles and memorabilia in the possession of Julian Ramotowski.

82. Interview with Edward Bartles, March 12, 1989 (Rochester, NY); letter from Edward Bartles to Frank Anders (Jan. 19, 1989). McKelvey refers to the organization of the "Genesees" in "Rochester's First Year in the War for Survival," p. 28. The attack on the Kure naval base is described in Wilbur H. Morrison's *Above and Beyond: 1941-1945* (New York: St. Martin's Press, 1983), pp. 285-87, and in John Winton's *War in the Pacific: Pearl Harbor to Tokyo Bay* (New York: Mayflower Books, Inc., 1978), pp. 186-87.

83. Interview with Barbara Kwiatkowski Brodie; 1938 Constitution of the Polonia Civic Centre; series of articles in the *DC* and the *TU* on Centrala's clothing drive, Feb. 8-26, 1945; text of the "Citizen of the Day" award given to William C. Brodie; "Polonia Civic Center to Fete its President at Testimonial," *DC,* Oct. 14, 1956, p. 5B; Ruth B. Chamberlain, "Around the Town: Festivities Launch Holiday Season," *TU,* Nov. 23, 1973, p. 2C; obituary of William C. Brodie, *DC,* Feb. 24, 1974, p. 3B.

Chapter 9
If You Don't Have Your History. . . .

1. "City Launches Housing Plan for Low-Income Families," *TU,* May 18, 1949, pp. 1 and 27; "State Agrees to Loan City Up to 3 Million for Housing Project," *DC,* May 19, 1949, p. 21; "Neighbors' Protests on Housing Plan 'Swamp' Councilman," *DC,* May 21, 1949, p. 15; "Rally Snags Low-Cost Homes Plan," *TU,* May 24, 1949, p. 1; Andrew Wolfe, "Mr. Homeowner Speaks Mind on Housing Plan," *TU,* May 24, 1949, p. 17.

2. McKelvey writes that "a crime wave . . . erupted in the Baden-Ormond district in 1946. The occurrence of three murders on Kelly Street within a week focused attention on that severely blighted neighborhood." (*An Emerging Metropolis,* p. 250.)

3. "Council Agrees to Pass Up Action on Housing Plan," *DC,* May 25, 1949, p. 21; "22nd Ward Gives Lesson: Human Right to Property," *TU,* May 25, 1949, p. 24. The editors of the *DC* were less sympathetic than those of the *TU* toward the stance taken by neighborhood residents. See "Objectors Should Help Constructively," *DC,* May 25, 1949, p. 18. The housing project was eventually built in the Baden-Ormond neighborhood, completed and named Hanover Houses in 1952.

4. "Bernstein Hits Color Bias of Many in U. S.," *DC,* June 17, 1949, p. 27; "Housing Bias Deplored by Bernstein," *TU,* June 17, 1949, p. 29. In 1949, when speaking about the problem of juvenile delinquency in poor neighborhoods, Bernstein reiterated the accusation that Polish Americans' prejudice had overturned the city's housing plan. In a strongly worded radio address, he charged that "a group of bigoted people, most of them also members of a minority group who had suffered persecution, said that if colored people were placed in their neighborhood in a housing project, blood would flow." ("'Get Tough' Policy on Teen-age Gangs Assailed by Rabbi," *DC,* April 30, 1956, p. 13; "Get-Tough-with-Kids Policy Hit by Rabbi," *TU,* April 30, 1956, p. 25.) City Councilman Leonard Tomczak took issue with Bernstein's remarks in a public statement in which he called the charge of bigotry "nonsense" and maintained that residents of the northeast side believed strongly in "private home

ownership." ("Tomczak Criticizes Rabbi Bernstein's Delinquency Stand," *DC,* May 1, 1956, p. 19.) The debate in the press continued, in Bernstein's retort that Tomczak had misinterpreted his remarks ("Misrepresented by Councilman, Says Bernstein," *DC,* May 2, 1956, p. 20) and in a letter to the editor of the *DC* in which Tomczak described at length his views on delinquency, which were in marked contrast to Bernstein's. ("Delinquency Starts in Homes," *DC,* May 2, 1956, p. 14.)

5. For a discussion of Rochester during the postwar years, see McKelvey, *An Emerging Metropolis,* chapters 15, 16, and 17.

6. McKelvey, *An Emerging Metropolis,* chapters 16, 17, and 23.

7. "Clean Sweep," article printed in the Gannett Rochester press, undated copy in the author's possession.

8. Statistics on the Polish parishes are taken from the following: "Roczny Wykaz, 1946" (Annual Statement and Report), St. Stanislaus Kostka Parish, p. 2, and "Roczny Wykaz, 1954," p. 4 (ASSP); "Burning of Mortgage, 60th Anniversary Celebration Slated at St. Stanislaus," *CCJ,* Dec. 8, 1950, p. 1A; 30th anniversary booklet, St. Casimir's Polish National Catholic Church, 1938, p. 25; "Outline of Parish Historical Reports," St. Theresa's Parish, 1961.

9. "Zloty Jubileusz Gn. 52 w Rochester, N. Y.," *Sokol Polski,* March 3, 1955, pp. 1 and 3; "Polish Falcons Try Their Wings for National Gym Instructor," *DC,* Jan. 19, 1951 (RPL, "Polish Community" news clippings file).

10. Chlebowski-Laboski and Kwiatkowski, summary of activities for 1947 and 1948.

11. The longevity of Polish-owned businesses can be traced in advertisements that appeared in program booklets for events in the Polish neighborhood over several decades. See, for example, the 1928, 1933, and 1938 anniversary booklets of St. Casimir's Parish; "Pamietnik Otwarcia Polskiego Domu Narodowego," the program for the opening of the Polish National Home, Rochester, NY, Oct. 28, 1951 (ASCP); and the silver jubilee booklet of St. Theresa's Parish, 1952.

12. "History of St. Stanislaus Church," 1890-1960, pp. 16 and 19.

13. "St. Casimir's Church Maps $100,000 Center," *TU,* June 3, 1949, p. 27; articles in the scrapbook of John T. Skalny ("Pastor Burns Mortgage at St. Casimir's" and "Church Burns Old Mortgage, Opens Campaign," Nov. 1944; "Polish Home Rites Slated Tomorrow," "Polish Home Ceremony Set," "Soil Breaking Starts New Polish Center," and "Ground Broken for Polish Recreation Hall," April 1950).

14. Wojciech Kolacki, "On the Dedication of the Polish National Home, Rochester, N. Y.," in the program booklet for the opening of the Polish National Home (Oct. 28, 1951).

15. "Polish Falcons Will Dedicate Remodeled Clubhouse Today," *DC,* May 1, 1949, p. 9B; "Zloty Jubileusz Gn. 52 w Rochester, N. Y.," *Sokol Polski;* John Stenclik, "Historia Gniazda 52 w Rochester, N.Y.," Jan. 1953, p. 5; 75th anniversary program, Nest 52 of the Polish Falcons of America, Oct. 4, 1980 (archives of Nest 52); "Joseph Paprocki Dies; Headed Polish Falcons," *DC,* June 8, 1949, p. 21. For Paprocki, a retired Hudson Avenue grocer whose parents had been among the first Polish immigrants in Rochester, dedication of the clubhouse culminated almost four decades of service with Nest 52, nine as its president. A month after the remodeled building opened, Paprocki collapsed and died of a heart attack outside St. Stanislaus Hall, where he had been attending a meeting of the Polish Relief Committee.

16. Chlebowski-Laboski and Kwiatkowski, summary of activities for 1951, 1952, and 1955; "Polish American Citizens Club," program for Polish Fest '84, p. 33.

17. "City Poles to Petition U. N. for Release of Clergymen," *DC,* Nov. 9, 1953 (RPL, "Polish Community" news clippings file); "Petition to U. N., Pope Received," *DC,* March 1, 1954, p. 15; "Polish Veterans of World War II," program for Polish Fest '84, p. 49; "Exhibit on Poland Opens at Museum," *DC,* Sept. 11, 1954, p. 13. The exhibit at the museum included photographs of tapestries, armor, jewelry, and other treasures from the Polish Royal Castle at Wawel, smuggled for safekeeping from Poland to Canada at the start of World War II. For the story of the odyssey of these art treasures, retained in Canada until 1961, see Balawyder's *The Maple Leaf and the White Eagle: Canadian-Polish Relations, 1918-1978,* pp. 187-218.

18. Constitution of the Polish Arts Group of Rochester, NY, adopted Dec. 3, 1954, and 25th anniversary program of the Polish Arts Group of Rochester, NY (Sept. 29, 1979) (property of the PAG); "'Barriers into Bridges,' Polish Culture Clubs Stress 'Understanding,'" *TU,* Aug. 14, 1958, p. 23; "Recently Discovered Music Feature of Polish Conclave," *DC,* Aug. 17, 1958, and "Polish Cultural Clubs to Hold National Convention at UR," *DC,* Aug. 9, 1958 (RPL, "Polish Community" news clippings file). Dr. Richard Brzustowicz, Dr. Mitchel Nowak, Stanley Gordon, Bernard Skalny, Wanda Pietrzak, and Leopold Lorentz served as presidents of the PAG during its first ten years.

19. See, for example, "Speakers Ask Aid to Poland," *DC,* Oct. 13, 1947, p. 17; "Aid Polish Liberty, Resolution Urges," *DC,* Oct. 16, 1950, p. 14; Ruth B. Chamberlain, "Polish Arts Dinner Dance to Aid 2 Schools," *TU,* Oct. 15, 1959, p. 36; "$2,000 Collected for Polish Help," *DC,* May 26, 1958, p. 16.

20. "Local Dinner to Honor Leader of Free Poles," *DC,* May 21, 1956, p. 14; "Red Aims Same, Says

Pole General," *DC,* May 22, 1956, p. 23; Vince Spezzano, "Co-Existence? It's Impossible," *TU,* May 22, 1956, p. 17.

21. "Polish Americans Plan Testimonial," *DC,* Sept. 21, 1946, p. 9. Felerski was appointed field representative of the New York State Office of Civilian Mobilization by Governor Dewey in 1944.

22. "New Chief," and "Woman Heads Pulaski Post" (1949 newspaper clippings, property of Wanda Pietrzak, Rochester, NY); "7 Named to Commission to Operate War Memorial," Jan. 9, 1954 (newspaper clipping in the scrapbook of Rev. Alexander J. Stec); Calvin Mayne, "City Beat: Politicos Taking Notice of Her," *TU,* April 13, 1954, p. 17; 25th anniversary program of the Polish Arts Group.

23. "Councilman-Elect Honored by St. Stanislaus Group" and "Tomczak Takes Oath of Councilman in Rite" (1953 newspaper articles in the scrapbook of Rev. Alexander J. Stec); obituaries for Leonard V. Tomczak in *TU* (Feb. 3, 1983, p. 3B) and *DC* (Feb. 5, 1983, p. 3B).

24. Literature from Charlotte King's 1963 City Council campaign, "King, Ex-GOP Ward Leader, Takes Oath as U. S. Marshal," "New U. S. Marshal," and "News from Rochester, N. Y." (in the scrapbook of John T. Skalny).

25. "Parade Precedes Fete Honoring Pulaski," *DC,* Oct. 11, 1948, p. 17; "Parade, Daylong Celebration Honor Memory of Pulaski," *DC,* Oct. 10, 1949, p. 19; "Parade Marks Tributes to Memory of Pulaski," *DC,* Oct. 16, 1950, p. 14.

26. "Lights On in Hudson Avenue," *DC,* Oct. 1, 1962, p. 18; records of the Hudson Avenue Area Association (property of Alexander J. Altavena, Rochester, NY). At the time of the "Parade of Light," hardware store owner Edmund Przysinda was treasurer of the association. Former City Councilman Leonard Tomczak was program chairman for the event, and funeral home director Walter Kroll was parade director.

27. McKelvey, *Rochester on the Genesee,* pp. 247-66; Lou Buttino and Mark Hare, *The Remaking of a City: Rochester, New York, 1964-1984* (Dubuque: Kendall/Hunt Publishing Co., 1984), pp. 1-12.

28. Statistics cited are from McKelvey, *Rochester on the Genesee,* p. 241, and "Community Profiles: Community Analysis Model, Rochester Region," prepared by the Center for Governmental Research, Inc., Rochester, NY, Feb. 1983, pp. 14 and 90.

29. Information about ethnicity, employment, population stability, and poverty is taken from Buttino and Hare, pp. 3-4; McKelvey, *Rochester on the Genesee,* pp. 241-43; and "Community Profiles, Community Analysis Model," pp. 14 and 90.

30. "History of Our Church," golden jubilee program booklet, St. Theresa's Parish; notes for a history of St. Theresa's Parish, handwritten document, 1960s (ASTP); "St. Stanislaus Parish Marks 75th Anniversary," *CCJ,* Nov. 5, 1965, p. 5; Saralee Orton Tiede, "St. Stanislaus' 75 Years," *TU,* Nov. 6, 1965, p. 7A; "Annual Statement and Report for Year 1961," St. Stanislaus Parish (ASSP).

31. See, for example, advertisements in the golden jubilee program booklet of St. Casimir's Polish National Catholic Parish (1958, ASCP); program of the 51st Annual Concert and Ball of the Rochester Echo Singing Association, Inc. (1960, ASSP); list of members of the Hudson Avenue Area Association, Feb. 27, 1964 (property of Alexander J. Altavena).

32. For statistics on the parishes' membership, see "Annual Report, 1973-74," St. Stanislaus Parish (ASSP); Dan Lovely, "Fear Walks the Streets of Polish Town," *DC,* Dec. 2, 1974, pp. 1B and 6B; Nancy Kreisler, "Century-Old 'Polish Town' Disappearing," *TU,* Aug. 8, 1974, pp. 1B and 2B; "St. Theresa's Marks 50th Anniversary," *CCJ,* Sept. 21, 1977 (article in the scrapbook of Rev. Alexander J. Stec).

33. Del Ray, "'Polish Town' Losing Identity," *TU* (undated article in the scrapbook of Rev. Alexander J. Stec).

34. Dan Lovely, "Fear Walks the Streets of Polish Town," *DC;* Stuart Elliott, "Wilson Makes a Hit with Poles," *TU,* Sept. 30, 1974, p. 3B; Dan Lovely, "Wilson Out to Meet the People: The Face Behind the Narrow Tie," *DC,* Sept. 30, 1974, p. 6B.

35. "St. Theresa," *Northeast Rochester Tribune,* June 1972, p. 7; notes for a history of St. Theresa's Parish, 1960s.

36. "Hudson Avenue to Lose Bit of Its Polish Flavor," *TU,* Dec. 14, 1974, p. 3A.

37. Stuart Elliott, "Polish Church Follows Members to the Suburbs," *TU,* Sept. 29, 1975, pp. 1A and 10A; Stuart Elliott, "St. Casimir's Church Sold to Northside Church of Christ," *TU,* June 17, 1976, p. 6B.

38. Dan Lovely, "Fear Walks the Streets of Polish Town," *DC.*

39. "Polish Cardinal Elected Pope in Bold Break with Tradition," *DC,* Oct. 17, 1978, pp. 1A and 3A; Michael Ziegler, "Their Heritage Shines," *DC,* Oct. 17, 1978, pp. 1A and 3A; Sherry Jacobson, "St. Stanislaus Bells Peal the Joy," *TU,* Oct. 17, 1978, p. 20A; telegram sent to Pope John Paul II from St. Stanislaus Kostka Parish, Rochester, NY (copy in the scrapbook of Rev. Alexander J. Stec).

40. Bill O'Brien, "Polka or Fight—It's Up to the Russians," *DC,* Dec. 17, 1980, pp. 1B and 8B; Linda Hansen, "Poles Here Feel Tension, Pray Soviets Won't Invade," *TU,* March 30, 1981, pp. 1A and 8A.

41. John Gallagher, "Funds Sought to Help Ease Poland's Pain," *DC,* Dec. 18, 1981, pp. 1B and 2B; Dick Mitchell, "Local Donations for Polish Relief Reach $6,000," *DC,* Dec. 23, 1981, p. 4B; Jim Myers, "Two

Food Chains, Packer Join Aid-to-Poland Drive," *DC,* Jan. 20, 1982, p. 8B; "Fund Hits $41,796," *CCJ,* Jan. 20, 1982, p. 1; "Maplecrest, Star Team to Aid Polish Fund," *CCJ,* Jan. 20, 1982, p. 3; "Local Food Market Promotes Tribute to Poland Fund Drive," *Irondequoit Press* (Irondequoit, NY), Jan. 21, 1982, p. 7; Jack Jones, "One-Man Relief Fund," *DC,* Jan. 30, 1982, pp. 1B and 2B. For local Polish American families' reactions to the imposition of martial law, see Gary Gerew, "Prayers for Poland," *DC,* Dec. 14, 1981, p. 1B; Laura Abbott and Sue Smith, "Waiting and Worrying," *TU,* Dec. 14, 1981, p. 1B; John Gallagher, "Mail from Poland Arriving Censored," *DC,* Dec. 31, 1981, pp. 1B and 2B.

42. Bob Mnzesheimer, "Benefit, Ever So Briefly, Reunites a Neighborhood," *DC,* Feb. 1, 1982, p. 1C; Sue Smith, "Polish Weekend Feast a Huge Success," *TU,* Feb. 1, 1982, p. 6B; "Polish Fund Hits $96,000," *CCJ,* March 31, 1982 (article in the scrapbook of Rev. Alexander J. Stec). At the end of 1982, to mark the first anniversary of the imposition of martial law, the Polonia Civic Centre sponsored the collection of 8,000 pairs of shoes for shipment to Poland, 500 of which were donated by shoe wholesaler Haskell Rosenberg. ("Local Donors Sending Shoes to Poland," *DC,* Dec. 11, 1982, p. 1B.)

43. Minutes of the meetings of the Committee to Aid Newcomers from Poland, March 9 and 31, 1982 (records of the committee). See also Jolie N. Griffin, "Solidarity Member Leaves Prison, Regrets Behind," *DC,* Dec. 6, 1982, pp. 1B and 6B. The committee, convened by Rev. Andrew Grzela, was co-chaired by Sister Eileen Conheady, SSJ, and Wojciech Przezdziecki.

44. Interview with Tomasz and Jolanta Mokrzan, June 26, 1990 (Rochester, NY).

45. "Renaming the Library at Hudson Avenue and Norton Street," petition presented to the RPL's Board of Trustees, May 1981, and "Renaming the Hudson Branch Library," memo from Stephen Lesnak, Branch Administrator, to the RPL Board of Trustees, June 18, 1981; program for the Rededication and 50th Anniversary Celebration, General Pulaski Community Library, Rochester, NY, Oct. 11, 1981 (records of the Pulaski Community Library); "An Overdue Honor," *DC,* Oct. 10, 1981, p. 8A; Kathleen Urbanic, "The Missing Cache," *Upstate Magazine, DC,* March 11, 1979; pp. 24-31; Peter B. Taub, "Polish Community Recovers Buried Treasure," *TU,* Oct. 8, 1983, p. 23; Kathleen Urbanic, "The Secret of Pulaski's Plaque: A Short History of Events Spanning 50 Years at the Pulaski Community Library," Oct. 1983 (records of the Pulaski Community Library). William Krutenat of Eirtech Instruments, Inc., Rochester, NY, conducted the probe of the library wall with metal detectors and supervised the excavation that uncovered the box of mementos.

46. Eugene Marino, "Polish World War II Survivors Witnessed Era of Loss, Hate," *DC;* Alan Morrell, "Bells, March Part of War's Remembrance," *DC,* Sept. 1, 1989, p. 1B. Dr. M. B. Biskupski, Eugene Golomb, Adolph Jeff, and Frederic Skalny were members of the coordinating committee for the week of remembrance.

47. The proposal for a sister city exchange was initiated in 1969 when Mayor Frank Lamb and a delegation of Rochesterians visited Krakow. Rochester Mayor Stephen May and Krakow President Jerzy Pekala signed the charter in 1973. See "Krakow-Rochester Sister Cities Committee," in *People-to-People: Rochester, New York's, Sister Cities Program,* prepared for the City of Rochester by Daniel Karin, pp. 11-12; program booklet for the Krakow-Rochester Sister Cities Committee's banquet, Sept. 22, 1984 (records of the committee); Andy Pollack, "Two Polish High Schoolers Taking Classes in Area," *DC,* Sept. 4, 1986, pp. 1A and 3A.

48. "SCI Launches Poland Project," *Memo to Members, Sister Cities International,* May 1990, pp. 1 and 3 (records of the Krakow-Rochester Sister Cities Committee); Sherrie Negrea, "City Planners' Concerns Same in Any Language," *DC,* July 6, 1990, pp. 1B and 2B.

49. Timothy Kirn, "Sister City Seeks Cure for 'Fatal Air'," *TU,* May 23, 1990, pp. 1B and 8B; minutes of the meetings of the Krakow-Rochester Sister Cities Committee, Feb. 12 and April 9, 1990 (records of the committee).

50. Interview with Dr. Adam Urbanski, Nov. 21, 1990 (Rochester, NY); Vincent Taylor, "Teachers' Union Official Finds Tension at Polish Conference," *DC,* Sept. 5, 1988, pp. 1B and 2B; Sandy Feldman, "Poland and Czechoslovakia: A Report to the UFT Executive Board and AFT Executive Committee" (property of Dr. Adam Urbanski); Vincent Taylor, "Polish Law Needs Overhaul, Solidarity Visitor Here Says," *DC,* June 16, 1989, pp. 1B and 2B; Linda K. Wertheimer, "Democracy in Teacher's Lesson Plan," *DC,* July 17, 1990, p. 3B. For the story of the Urbanski family's emigration from Poland after World War II, a journey that took them through nine countries in four years, see Marie McCullough, "Escape from Poland," *TU,* Jan. 23, 1982, pp. 4 and 5.

51. Bartles, "Rochester Polish People's Home," p. 2; Teresa A. Parsons, "Mergers, Clusters and Closings: Parishes Grow Through Crisis to Community," *CCJ,* April 10, 1986, pp. 1 and 5; interview with Mr. and Mrs. Stanley Jaskot.

52. "St. Stanislaus Kostka Church, Opening Centennial Service (1890-1990)," Nov. 12, 1989 (ASSP); "A Hundred Year Heritage: The Opening Ceremonies of St. Stanislaus Kostka Parish's Centennial Year," Nov. 12, 1989 (videotape produced by Pearl Video, Rochester, NY, ASSP).

53. Interview with Mr. and Mrs. Stanley Jaskot; Jody McPhillips, "Polonia is Up to the Times," *DC,*

April 18, 1982, p. 8B; Lee Strong, "Trio Reveals Range of Women's Gifts to Church," *CC,* June 15, 1989, pp. 1 and 8.

54. Interview with Victor Anuszkiewicz, Sr., Feb. 6, 1988 (Rochester, NY); advertisement for Stanley's Place in the 20th anniversary program booklet of St. Casimir's Polish National Catholic Church, 1928; RPL, "Sea Breeze" news clippings file (Charles M. Walker, "An Amusement Park that Pays," March 29, 1924; "Sea Breeze Sold in $85,000 Deal," *DC,* April 2, 1946; Bill Beeney, "Amusement Park Reaches the Century Mark," *DC,* Aug. 12, 1979); Dave Stearns, "The People are into Enjoying Life," *TU,* Aug. 4, 1982, pp. 1C, 3C, and 4C; Barbara Vancheri, "Look Twice, It Really is Vic & Irv's in Sea Breeze," *DC,* Feb. 22, 1983, p. 1A.

55. Interviews with Aniela Skalny and John T. Skalny; Andrew Wolfe, "Basketmaking in a 'Hidden Plant,'" *TU,* Feb. 13, 1950, p. 32; Don Record, "Baskets Weave Success Story," *DC,* May 8, 1960, p. 18D; "Louis Skalny Dies at 80; Started Basket Company," *TU,* May 19, 1969, p. 3B; "Basket Company Hit Hard by Import Charge," *TU,* Aug. 18, 1971, p. 4B; Jim Memmott, "Rediscovering Poland: Fisher Program Focuses on Language, History, Immigrants," *TU,* Feb. 1, 1982, pp. 1B and 6B; "Fisher Banquet Features Brzezinski," *CCJ,* Sept. 4, 1985, p. 4; program from the Endowment Banquet of the Institute for Polish Studies, St. John Fisher College of Rochester, Sept. 9, 1985 (records of the institute); "The Skalnys: A Polish American Odyssey," *The Polish American,* vol. 5, no. 6 (June 1986), pp. 20-23, no. 7 (July 1986), pp. 13-15, and no. 8 (August 1986), pp. 24-26; "Fisher Dedicates Library Room to Skalny Family," *Irondequoit Press,* Aug. 8, 1989, p. 6; articles in the scrapbook of John T. Skalny ("City Man Finds Poland Shopping Expensive," and "John T. Skalny Returns from European Buying Trip," 1947; "Polish American Family Makes Thoughtful Investment in Tomorrow's America," May 15, 1985).

—Q—

—R—

KATHLEEN URBANIC has written articles about Rochester's Polish community for research journals, local history publications, and local newspapers. She prepared a history of St. Stanislaus Kostka Parish for the congregation's 90th anniversary, organized a slide/tape history and displays of memorabilia for the parish's centennial year, and has conducted tours of St. Stanislaus Church for groups interested in the building's architecture and religious symbolism.

FRANK ANDERS (Anuszkiewicz) has written and illustrated three children's books for Whitman Publishing Company, including *Grandmother and Machek,* a tale recounted by his mother. He has designed covers for the *New York Herald Tribune,* and has exhibited his photography at the Rundel Memorial Library and the Albright-Knox Gallery in Buffalo. His work has been recognized with awards for watercolors, photography, and television advertising.